Carl Paul Caspari, William Wright, William Robertson Smith, Michael
Jan de Goeje

A Grammar of the Arabic Language

Vol. 1

Carl Paul Caspari, William Wright, William Robertson Smith, Michael Jan de Goeje

A Grammar of the Arabic Language
Vol. 1

ISBN/EAN: 9783744762229

Printed in Europe, USA, Canada, Australia, Japan

Cover: Foto ©Thomas Meinert / pixelio.de

More available books at **www.hansebooks.com**

A GRAMMAR

OF THE

ARABIC LANGUAGE,

TRANSLATED

FROM THE GERMAN OF CASPARI,

AND EDITED

WITH NUMEROUS ADDITIONS AND CORRECTIONS

BY

W. WRIGHT, LL.D.,

LATE PROFESSOR OF ARABIC IN THE UNIVERSITY OF CAMBRIDGE.

THIRD EDITION

REVISED BY

W. ROBERTSON SMITH,

LATE PROFESSOR OF ARABIC IN THE UNIVERSITY OF CAMBRIDGE

AND

M. J. DE GOEJE,

PROFESSOR OF ARABIC IN THE UNIVERSITY OF LEYDEN.

VOLUME I.

CAMBRIDGE:
AT THE UNIVERSITY PRESS.

1896

PREFACE TO THE THIRD EDITION.

THE Second Edition of Wright's Grammar of the Arabic language had been out of print long before the death of its author, but he was never able to find the leisure necessary for preparing a New Edition. The demand for it having become more and more pressing, Prof. W. Robertson Smith, who well deserved the honour of succeeding to Wright's chair, resolved to undertake this task. He began it with his usual ardour, but the illness which cut short his invaluable life soon interrupted the work. At his death 56 pages had been printed, whilst the revision had extended over 30 pages more. Robertson Smith had made use of some notes of mine, which he had marked with my initials, and it was for this reason among others that the Syndics of the Cambridge University Press invited me, through Prof. Bevan, to continue the revision. After earnest deliberation I consented, influenced chiefly by my respect for the excellent work of one of my dearest friends and by a desire to complete that which another dear friend had begun. Moreover Prof. Bevan promised his assistance in correcting the English style and in seeing the book through the press.

I have of course adhered to the method followed by Robertson Smith in that part of the Grammar which he revised. Trifling corrections and additions and such suggestions as had already been made by A. Müller, Fleischer and other scholars, are given in square brackets. Only in those cases where it seemed necessary to take all the responsibility upon myself, have I added my initials. Besides the printed list of additions and corrections at the end of the Second Volume, Wright had noted here and there on the margin of his own copy some new examples (chiefly from the *Naḳāïḍ*) which have been inserted, unless they seemed quite superfluous, without any distinctive sign. I have found but very few notes by Robertson Smith on the portion which he had not definitely revised; almost all of these have been marked with his initials. Wright's own text has been altered in a comparatively small number of passages (for instance § 252, § 353), where I felt sure that he would have done it himself. Once or twice Wright has noted on the margin "wants revision."

The notes bearing upon the Comparative Grammar of the Semitic languages have for the most part been replaced by references to Wright's Comparative Grammar, published after his death by Robertson Smith (1890).

I have to acknowledge my obligations to Mr Du Pré Thornton, who drew my attention to several omissions. But my warmest thanks must be given to my dear friend and colleague Prof. Bevan, who has not only taken upon himself all the trouble of seeing this revised edition through the press, but by many judicious remarks has contributed much to the improving of it.

The Second Volume is now in the printers' hands.

M. J. DE GOEJE.

LEYDEN,
February, 1896.

PREFACE TO THE SECOND EDITION.

A SECOND Edition of my revised and enlarged translation of Caspari's Arabic Grammar having been called for, I have thought it my duty not simply to reprint the book, but to subject it again to a thorough revision. In fact, the present is almost a new work; for there is hardly a section which has not undergone alteration, and much additional matter has been given, as the very size of this volume (351 pages instead of 257) shows.

In revising the book I have availed myself of the labours of Arab Grammarians, both ancient and modern. Of the former I may mention in particular the *'Alfīya* (اَلْأَلْفِيَّة) of 'Ibn Mālik, with the Commentary of 'Ibn 'Aḳīl (ed. Dieterici, 1851, and the Beirūt edition of 1872); the *Mufaṣṣal* (اَلْمُفَصَّل) of 'el-Zamahšarī (ed. Broch, 1859); and the *Lāmīyatu 'l-'Af'āl* (لَامِيَّة ٱلْأَفْعَال) of 'Ibn Mālik, with the Commentary of his son Badru 'd-dīn (ed. Volck, 1866). Of recent native works I have diligently used the *Miṣbāḥu 'l-Ṭālib fī Baḥti 'l-Maṭālib* (مِصْبَاحُ ٱلطَّالِب فِى بَحْثِ ٱلْمَطَالِب), that is, the *Baḥtu 'l-Maṭālib* of the Maronite Gabriel Farḥāt, with the notes of Buṭrus 'el-Bistānī (Beirūt, 1854); 'el-Bistānī's smaller Grammar, founded upon the above, entitled *Miftāḥu 'l-Miṣbāḥ* (مِفْتَاحُ ٱلْمِصْبَاح), second edition, Beirūt, 1867); and Nāṣif 'el-Yāziǧī's *Faṣlu 'l-Ḥiṭāb* (فَصْلُ ٱلْخِطَاب), second edition, Beirūt, 1866).

Among European Grammarians I have made constant use of the works of S. de Sacy (Grammaire Arabe, 2de éd., 1831), Ewald (Grammatica Critica Linguæ Arabicæ, 1831–33), and Lumsden (A Grammar of the Arabic Language, vol. i., 1813); which last, however, is based on the system of the Arab Grammarians, and therefore but ill-adapted, apart from its bulk and rarity, for the use of beginners. I have also consulted with advantage the grammar of Professor Lagus of Helsingfors (Lärokurs i Arabiska Språket, 1869). But I am indebted above all to the labours of Professor Fleischer of Leipzig, whose notes on the first volume of De Sacy's Grammar (as far as p. 359) have appeared from time to time in the *Berichte der Königl. Sächsischen Gesellschaft der Wissenschaften* (1863–64–66–70), in which periodical the student will also find the treatises of the same scholar *Ueber einige Arten der Nominalapposition im Arabischen* (1862) and *Ueber das Verhältniss und die Construction der Sach- und Stoffwörter im Arabischen* (1856).

In the notes which touch upon the comparative grammar of the Semitic languages, I have not found much to alter, except in matters of detail. I have read, I believe, nearly everything that has been published of late years upon this subject—the fanciful lucubrations of Von Raumer and Raabe, as well as the learned and scholarly treatises of Nöldeke, Philippi, and Tegnér. My standpoint remains, however, nearly the same as it formerly was. The ancient Semitic languages—Arabic and Æthiopic, Assyrian, Canaanitic (Phœnician and Hebrew), and Aramaic (so-called Chaldee and Syriac)—are as closely connected with each other as the Romance languages—Italian, Spanish, Portuguese, Provençal, and French: they are all daughters of a deceased mother, standing to them in the relation of Latin to the other European languages just specified. In some points the north Semitic tongues, particularly the Hebrew, may bear the greatest resemblance to this parent speech; but, on the whole, the south Semitic dialects, Arabic and Æthiopic,—but especially the former, —have, I still think, preserved a higher degree of likeness to the original Semitic language. The Hebrew of the Pentateuch, and the Assyrian*, as it appears in even the oldest inscriptions, seem

---

* As regards Assyrian, I rely chiefly upon the well-known works of Oppert, Sayce, and Schrader.

to me to have already attained nearly the same stage of grammatical development (or decay) as the post-classical Arabic, the spoken language of mediæval and modern times.

I have to thank the Home Government of India for contributing the sum of fifty pounds towards defraying the expenses of printing this work; and some of the local Governments for subscribing for a certain number of copies; namely, the Government of Bengal, twenty, and the Home Department (Fort William), twenty-five; the Government of Bombay, ten; of Madras, ten; and of the Punjab, sixty copies. My friend and former schoolfellow, Mr D. Murray (of Adelaide, S. Australia), has also given pecuniary aid to the same extent as the India Office, and thereby laid me, and I hope I may say other Orientalists, under a fresh obligation.

Professor Fleischer of Leipzig will, I trust, look upon the dedication as a mark of respect for the Oriental scholarship of Germany, whereof he is one of the worthiest representatives; and as a slight acknowledgment of much kindness and help, extending over a period of more than twenty years, from the publication of my first work in 1852 down to the present year, in which, amid the congratulations of numerous pupils and friends, he has celebrated the fiftieth anniversary of his doctorate.

W. WRIGHT.

CAMBRIDGE,
1st July, 1874.

The Syndics of the Press are indebted to the liberality of Mr F. Du Pré Thornton for the copyright of this Grammar, which he purchased after the death of the author and presented to them with a view to the publication of a New Edition.

They desire to take this opportunity of expressing their gratitude to Prof. de Goeje for the courtesy with which he acceded to their request that he would complete the revision and for the great labour which he has expended upon the task in the midst of many important literary engagements.

CONTENTS.

PART FIRST.

ORTHOGRAPHY AND ORTHOËPY.

PART SECOND.

ETYMOLOGY OR THE PARTS OF SPEECH.

I. THE VERB.

A. GENERAL VIEW.

II. THE NOUN.

A. THE NOUNS SUBSTANTIVE AND ADJECTIVE.

PART FIRST.
ORTHOGRAPHY AND ORTHOËPY.

I. THE LETTERS AS CONSONANTS.

1. Arabic, like Hebrew and Syriac, is written and read from
right to left. The letters of the alphabet (حُرُوفُ ٱلْهِجَآءِ, حُرُوفُ
ٱلتَّهَجِّى, ٱلْحُرُوفُ ٱلْهِجَائِيَّةُ, or حُرُوفُ ٱلْمُعْجَمِ) are twenty-eight in
number, and are all consonants, though three of them are also used
as vowels (see § 3). They vary in form, according as they are connected with a preceding or following letter, and, for the most part,
terminate in a bold stroke, when they stand alone or at the end of
a word. The following Table gives the letters in their usual order,
along with their names and numerical values.

NAME.	FIGURE.				NUMERICAL VALUE.
	Unconnected.	Connected.			
		With a preceding letter.	With a following letter.	With both.	
أَلِفٌ Elif.	ا	ا	. . .		1
بَآءٌ Bā.	ب	ب	ﺑ	ﺒ	2
تَآءٌ Tā.	ت	ت	ﺗ	ﺘ	400
ثَآءٌ Ṯā.	ث	ث	ﺛ	ﺜ	500
جِيمٌ Ǧīm.	ج	ﺞ [ﺝ]	ﺟ	ﺠ [ﺝ]	3
حَآءٌ Ḥā.	ح	ﺢ [ﺡ]	ﺣ	ﺤ [ﺡ]	8
خَآءٌ Ḫā.	خ	ﺦ [ﺥ]	ﺧ	ﺨ [ﺥ]	600
دَالٌ Dāl.	د	ﺪ			4
ذَالٌ Ḏāl.	ذ	ﺬ	. . .	. . .	700

	NAME.	FIGURE.				NUMERICAL VALUE.
		Unconnected.	Connected.			
			With a preceding letter.	With a following letter.	With both.	
A	رَآء Ra.	ر	ر ر			200
	زَاى (زَآء) Zay.	ز	ز ز			7
	سِين Sīn.	س	س	ﺳ	ﺴ	60
	شِين Śīn.	ش	ش	ﺷ	ﺸ	300
	صَاد Ṣād.	ص	ﺺ	ﺻ	ﺼ	90
B	ضَاد Ḍād.	ض	ﺾ	ﺿ	ﻀ	800
	طَآء Ṭā.	ط	ﻂ ﻃ	ط	ﻄ	9
	ظَآء Ẓā.	ظ	ﻆ ﻇ	ظ	ﻈ	900
	عَيْن 'Ain.	ع	ﻊ	ﻋ	ﻌ	70
	غَيْن Ġain.	غ	ﻎ	ﻏ	ﻐ	1000
	فَآء Fā.	ف	ﻒ	ﻓ	ﻔ	80
C	قَاف Ḳāf.	ق	ﻖ	ﻓ	ﻗ	100
	كَاف Kāf.	ك ک	ﻚ	ﻛ ک	ﻜ ﻛ	20
	لَام Lām.	ل	ﻞ	ﻟ	ﻠ	30
	مِيم Mīm.	م م	ﻢ م	ﻣ م	ﻤ	40
	نُون Nūn.	ن	ﻦ	ﻧ	ﻨ	50
	هَآء Hā.	ه ة	ﻪ ه	ﻬ ه	ﻫ	5
	وَاو Wāw.	و و	و			6
	يَآء Yā.	ي ى	ﻲ ى ﻳ	ﻳ	ﻴ	10

REM. *a.* ا in connection with a preceding ل forms the figures A ﻻ, ﻵ, ﻶ. This combination is called *lām-ĕlif*, and is generally reckoned a twenty-ninth letter of the alphabet, and inserted before ى. The object of it is merely to distinguish ĕlif as the long vowel *ā*, § 3, from ĕlif as the spiritus lenis (ĕlif with hĕmza, ﺃ, § 15).

REM. *b.* The order of the letters ه and و is sometimes inverted. The Arabs of Northern Africa arrange the letters in a different sequence; viz.

غ ع ض ص ن م د ل ك ظ ط ز ر ذ د خ ح ج ث ت ب ا   B
ى لا و ه ش س ق ف

They distinguish ف from ق by giving the former a single point below, and the latter one above, thus : ڢ ڢ *f*, but ڧ ڧ *k**. At the end of a word these points are usually omitted, ﻬ, ﻴ.

REM. *c.* In manuscripts and elegantly printed books many of the letters are interwoven with one another, and form ligatures, of which the following are examples.

ﻜﺒ *bh.*	ﺴﺶ *sh.*	ﻗﻰ *fy.*
ﻜﺘ *th.*	ﺿﻤ *dh.*	ﻟﻎ *lg.*
ﻐﺢ *gh.*	ﻌﻊ *'g.*	ﻤﻠ *lmh.*
ﺤﺠ *hgg.*	ﻔﺦ *fh*	ﻜﻲ *yh.*	C

[These ligatures, in which one letter stands above another, are very inconvenient to printers, especially when, as in this book, English and Arabic are intermingled ; and most founts have some device to bring the letters into line. Thus ﺤﺞ appears as ﺣﺎﻛﺠ, or, in the fount used for this grammar, as ﺣﺠﻤ. The latter method is a recent innovation, first introduced by Lane in his D Arabic Lexicon, and its extreme simplicity and convenience have caused it to be largely adopted in modern founts, not only in Europe but in the East. But in writing Arabic the student ought to use the old ligatures as they are shewn in Mss. or in the more elegant Eastern founts.]

---

* This is not confined, in the earliest times, to African Mss. In some old Mss., on the other hand, *k* has the point below, ڢ, ﻤ, or even ﻗ, ﻗ.

A

Rem. *d.* Those letters which are identical in form, and distinguished from one another in writing only by the aid of the small dots usually called *diacritical points* (نُقْطَةٌ, plur. نُقَطٌ), are divided by the grammarians into اَلْحُرُوفُ ٱلْمُهْمَلَةُ, *the loose* or *free*, i.e. *unpointed, letters*, and اَلْحُرُوفُ ٱلْمُعْجَمَةُ, *the bolted* or *fastened*, i.e. *pointed, letters*. To the former class belong ح, د, ر, س, ص, ط, and ع; to the latter خ, ذ, ز, ش, ض, ظ and غ. The letters ب, ت, ث and ى are generally distinguished as follows:

B

ب is called اَلْبَآءُ ٱلْمُوَحَّدَةُ, *the ﺏ with one point* (ﺏ);

ت   „   اَلتَّآءُ ٱلْمُثَنَّاةُ مِنْ فَوْقِهَا, *the ﺕ with two points above* (ﺕ);

ى   „   اَلْيَآءُ ٱلْمُثَنَّاةُ مِنْ تَحْتِهَا, *the ﻯ with two points below* (ﻯ)*;

ث   „   اَلثَّآءُ ٱلْمُثَلَّثَةُ, *the ﺙ with three points* (ﺙ).

The unpointed letters are sometimes still further distinguished from the pointed by various contrivances, such as writing the letter in a smaller size below the line, placing a point below, or an angular mark above, and the like; so that we find in carefully written

C

manuscripts ط ط; ص ص ض ض; تﺧ ﺧ س س بﺱ; ر ر ز; د د ذ; ح ح
ع ع; etc. Also ﻫ or ﺓ by way of distinction from ﺓ. In some old Mss. ش has only one point above, and then س takes a point below.

Rem. *e.* The letters are also divided into the following classes, which take their names from the particular part of the vocal organs that is chiefly instrumental in producing their sounds.

و م ف ب اَلْحُرُوفُ ٱلشَّفَوِيَّةُ or اَلشَّفَهِيَّةُ, *the labials* (شَفَةٌ *a lip*).

اَلْحُرُوفُ ٱللِّثْوِيَّةُ, *the gingivals*, ظ ذ ث, in uttering which the

D

tongue is pressed against the gum (اَللِّثَةُ).

اَلْحُرُوفُ ٱلْأَسَلِيَّةُ, *the sibilants*, ص س ز, which are pronounced with the tip of the tongue (اَلْأَسَلَةُ).

---

* [With final ى the use of the two points below is optional. Some modern prints, especially those issued at Bairût, always insert them except when the ى represents *ĕlif maḳṣūra* (§ 7, rem. *b*): thus كَيْ, لِي, but رَمَى.]

اَلْحُرُوفُ ٱلذَّلْقِيَّةُ or اَلذَّوْلَقِيَّةُ, the liquids ن, ل, ر, which are pro- A
nounced with the extremity of the tongue (اَلذَّلْقُ or اَلذَّوْلَقُ).

اَلْحُرُوفُ ٱلشَّجْرِيَّةُ, the letters ج, ش, ض, which are uttered
through the open orifice of the lips (اَلشَّجْرُ).

اَلْحُرُوفُ or اَلنِّطَعِيَّةُ ٱلنِّطَعِيَّةُ, the letters ط, د, ت, which are uttered
by pressing the tongue against the rough or corrugated portion of
the palate (اَلنِّطَعُ or اَلنِّطَعُ).

اَلْحَرْفَانِ ٱللَّهَوِيَّتَانِ, the letters ق and ك, in uttering which the B
uvula (اَللَّهَاةُ) is brought into play.

٥. اَلْحُرُوفُ ٱلْحَلْقِيَّةُ or حُرُوفُ ٱلْحَلْقِ, the gutturals, أ ح خ ع غ.
The letters ا و ى are called اَلْحُرُوفُ ٱللَّيِّنَةُ or حُرُوفُ ٱللِّينِ, *the
soft letters*, and حُرُوفُ ٱلْعِلَّةِ, *the weak letters*.

2. The correct pronunciation of some of these letters, for example ح and ع, it is scarcely possible for a European to acquire,
except by long intercourse with natives. The following hints will, C
however, enable the learner to approximate to their sounds.

ا with *hèmza* (أ, إ, see § 15) is the *spiritus lenis* of the Greeks,
the א of the Hebrews (as in תִּאְלַף, זְאֵב, אָמַר). It may be compared with the *h* in the French word *homme* or English *hour*.

ب is our *b*.

ت is the Italian dental, softer than our *t*.

ث is pronounced like the Greek θ, or *th* in *thing*. The Turks
and Persians usually convert it into the surd *s*, as in *sing*. [In Egypt
it is commonly confounded with ت, less often with س.]   D

ج corresponds to our *g* in *gem*. In Egypt and some parts of
Arabia, however, it has the sound of the Heb. ג, or our *g* in *get*.

ح, the Heb. ח, is a very sharp but smooth guttural aspirate,
stronger than ه, but not rough like خ. Europeans, as well as Turks
and Persians, rarely attain the correct pronunciation of it.

خ has the sound of *ch* in the Scotch word *loch*, or the German *Rache*.

د is the Italian dental, softer than our *d*.

ذ bears the same relation to د that ث does to ت. It is sounded

A like the δ of the modern Greeks, or *th* in *that, with.* The Turks and Persians usually convert it into *z.* [In Egypt it is sometimes *z* but oftener *d.*]

ر is in all positions a distinctly articulated lingual *r*, as in *run.*

ز is the English *z.*

س is the surd *s* in *sit, mist;* ش, *sh* in *shut.*

ص, the Heb. צ, is a strongly articulated *s*, somewhat like *ss* in *hiss.*

B ض is an aspirated *d*, strongly articulated between the front part of the side of the tongue and the molar teeth (somewhat like *th* in *this*). The Turks and Persians usually pronounce it like *z.* [In Egypt it is an emphatic *d*, without aspiration, more difficult to an English tongue than the true Bedouin ض.]

ط, the Heb. ט, is a strongly articulated palatal *t.*

ظ bears, strictly speaking, the same relation to ط that ث and ذ do to ت and د. It is usually pronounced like a strongly articulated palatal *z*, though many of the Arabs give it the same sound as ض C [with which it is often confounded in Mss.]. The Turks and Persians change it into a common *z.* To distinguish it from ض, ظ is sometimes spoken of as أَلْظَّا ٱلْمُشَالَة.

ع, the Heb. ע, is a strong (but to [most] Europeans, as well as Turks and Persians, unpronounceable) guttural, related in its nature to ح, with which it is sometimes confounded. It is described as produced by a smart compression of the upper part of the windpipe and forcible emission of the breath. It is wrong to treat it, in any of the Semitic languages, as a mere vowel-letter, or (worse still) as D a nasal *n* or *ng.*

غ is a guttural *g*, accompanied by a grating or rattling sound, as in gargling, of which we have no example in English. The γ of the modern Greeks, the Northumbrian *r*, and the French *r grasséyé*, are approximations to it*.

ف is our *f.*

ق, the Heb. ק, is a strongly articulated guttural *k*; but in parts of Arabia, and throughout Northern Africa, it is pronounced as a

---

* [Hence غ is sometimes replaced by ر as in the Yemenite مُضَّار for مُضَّاغ, Hamdānī ed. Müller 193, 17 etc., and often in Mss.—De G.]

hard *g*; whilst in [Cairo and some parts of] Syria it is vulgarly con- A
founded with êlif hĕmzatum, as *'ultu, ya'ûlu,* for *ḳultu, yaḳûlu.*

ك, ل, م, and ن, are exactly our *k, l, m, n.* When immediately
followed by the letter ب, without any vowel coming between them,
ن takes the sound of *m* : as جَنْب *g̈ĕmb,* عَنْبَر *'ambar,* شَنْبَآءُ *s̈ĕmbâ'u,*
not *g̈ĕnb, 'anbar, s̈ĕnbâ'u.*

ه is our *h.* It is distinctly aspirated at the end, as well as at
the beginning, of a syllable ; e. g. هُمْ *hum,* أَهْلَكَ *'ahlaka.* In the
grammatical termination ة ـَ, the dotted ة [called هَاءُ ٱلتَّأْنِيثِ] is pronounced like ت, *t)*.* B

و and ى are precisely our *w* and *y.* The Turks and Persians
usually give و the sound of *v.*

II. THE VOWELS AND DIPHTHONGS.

3. The Arabs had originally no signs for the short vowels. To
indicate the long vowels and diphthongs they made use of the three
consonants that come nearest to them in sound: viz. ا (without *hĕmza,*
see § 1, rem. *a,* and § 15) for *â,* ى for *î* and *ai,* و for *û* and *au.* E. g., C
لا *lâ,* فى *fî,* كى *kai,* ذو *d̲û,* لو *lau.*

4. At a later period the following signs were invented to express
the short vowels.

(*a*) ـَ *fĕth* (فَتْحٌ) or *fĕtha* (فَتْحَةٌ), *a, ĕ* (as in *pet*), *e* (nearly the
French *e muet*); e.g. خَلَقَ *halaḳa,* شَمْسٌ *s̈ĕmsun,* كَرِيمٌ *kerîmun.*

(*b*) ـِ *kĕsr* (كَسْرٌ) or *kĕsra* (كَسْرَةٌ), *i* (as in *pin*), *ĭ* (a dull, obscure *i,*
resembling the Welsh *y,* or the *i* in *bird*); e.g. بِه *bihi,* أَقِطٌ *aḳĭtun.* D

(*c*) ـُ *ḍamm* (ضَمٌّ) or *ḍamma* (ضَمَّةٌ), *u* (as in *bull*), *o, ö* (nearly as
the German *ö* in *Mörtel,* or the French *eu* in *jeune*) ; e.g. لَهُ *lahu,*
حُجَّةٌ *ḧög̈g̈ĕtun,* عُمْرٌ *'ömrun.*

---

* In point of fact, this figure ة is merely a compromise between
the ancient ت ـَ (Heb. ת ָ, ת ַ), the old pausal ه ـَ (*ah*), and the
modern ه ـَ (Heb. ה ָ), in which last the ه is silent.

A   Rem. *a.* The distinction between the names *fĕth, kĕsr, ḍamm,* and *fĕtha, kĕsra, ḍamma,* is that the former denote the *sounds a, i, u,* the latter the *marks* $\stackrel{\prime}{-}$, $\_\,$, $\stackrel{\prime}{-}$. Compare the Hebrew פַּתַח, שְׁבָר, and קִבּוּץ. The terms نَصْب and رَفْع, commonly used of the case-endings *a, u,* are sometimes applied to $\stackrel{\prime}{-}$, $\stackrel{\prime}{-}$ in other positions; e.g. اَلْحَرُورِيَّة بِنَصْب اَلْحَاء. [Another name for *ḍamm* is *ḳabw,* قَبْو.— De G.]

Rem. *b.* A vowel is called حَرَكَة, *a motion,* plur. حَرَكَات; its B   mark is termed شَكْل, *form* or *figure,* plur. أَشْكَال or شُكُول.

Rem. *c.* In the oldest Mss. of the Ḳor'ān, the vowels are expressed by dots (usually red), one above for fetḥa, one below for kĕsra, and one in the middle, or on the line, for ḍamma. As regards the signs $\stackrel{\prime}{-}$, $\_\,$, $\stackrel{\prime}{-}$ the third is a small و and the other two are probably derived from ا and ى or ـ respectively.

5. Rules for the cases in which these vowel-marks retain their original sounds, *a, i, u,* and for those in which they are modified, through the influence of the stronger or weaker consonants, into *è, e,* C   *ì, o,* or *ö,* can scarcely be laid down with certainty; for the various dialects of the spoken Arabic differ from one another in these points; and besides, owing to the emphasis with which the consonants are uttered, the vowels are in general somewhat indistinctly enunciated. The following rules may, however, be given for the guidance of the learner*.

(*a*) When preceded or followed by the strong gutturals ح خ ع غ ء or the emphatic consonants ص ض ط ظ ق, fetḥa is pronounced as *a,* though with the emphatic consonants its sound becomes rather obscure, D   approaching to that of the Swedish *å*; e.g. خَمْر *ḫamrun,* لَعْب *la'bun,* بَقِى *bāḳiya,* صَدْر *ṣadrun.* Under the same circumstances kĕsra is

---

* [Learners whose ears and vocal organs are good, and who have an opportunity of hearing and practising the correct pronunciation of the consonants, will find that the proper shades of sound in the three vowels come without effort when the consonants are spoken rightly and naturally. The approximate rules for pronunciation here given are mainly useful as a guide towards the right way of holding the mouth in pronouncing the consonants as well as the vowels.]

pronounced as *i̊*, e.g. عِلْمٌ *'ilmun*, سِحْرٌ *siḥrun*, قِشْرٌ *ḳišrun* ; whilst A dạmma assumes the sound of an obscure *o*, inclining with the gutturals (especially ح and ع) to *ö* ; e.g. لَطَفَ *laṭafa*, لُطْفٌ *loṭfun*, حُسْنٌ *hosnun* or *ḥösnun*, رُعْبٌ *roʻbun*, عُمْرٌ *ʻömrun*.

(*b*) In shut syllables in which there are neither guttural nor emphatic consonants,—and in open syllables which neither commence with, nor immediately precede, one of those letters,—fètḥa either has a weaker, less clear sound, approaching to that of *a* in the English words *hat*, *cap*, e.g. كَتَبْتَ *katabta*, أَكْبَرُ *'akbaru* ; or it becomes a B simple *ĕ* or *e* (the latter especially in a short open syllable followed by a long one), e.g. بَلْ *bĕl*, مَرْكَبٌ *mèrkĕbun*, سَمَكٌ *sèmĕkun*, سَمِينٌ *semīnun*, مَدِينَةٌ *medīnètun*. It retains, however, its pure sound of *a* before and after *r* (which partakes of the nature of the emphatics), when that letter is doubled or follows a long *ā* or *ū*, e.g. جَرَّةٌ *ǧarratun*, مَرَّةٌ *marratun*, غَارَةٌ *ǧāratun*, صُورَةٌ *sūratun* ; and also in general at the end of a word.

6. The long vowels *ā*, *ī*, *ū*, are indicated by placing the marks C of the short vowels before the letters ١, ى, and و, respectively, e.g. قَالَ *ḳāla*, بِيعَ *bī'a*, سُوقٌ *sūḳun* ; in which case these letters are called حُرُوفُ ٱلْمَدّ, *literae productionis*, "letters of prolongation." The combinations ى ِ and و ُ must always be pronounced *ī* and *ū*, not *ē* and *ō* ; though after the emphatic consonants و ُ inclines to the sound of *ō*, and *ī* to that of the French *u* or German *ü*, e.g. طُورٌ, طِينٌ, nearly *ṭōrun*, *ṭūnun*.

REM. *a*. *ā* was at first more rarely marked than the other D long vowels, and hence it happens that, at a later period, after the invention of the vowel-points, it was indicated in some very common words merely by a fètḥa ; e.g. هَرُونُ, إِسْحَقُ, إِبْرَهِيمُ, ٱلرَّحْمَنُ, ٱللَّهُ, هَكَذَا, هَهُنَا, هَذَا, ذَلِكَ, لَكِنْ or لَكِنَّ, ٱلْقِيَمَةُ, ٱلسَّمَوَاتُ, ٱلْمَلَئِكَةُ. More exactly, however, the fètḥa should be written perpendicularly in this case, so as to resemble a small ĕlif ; e.g. ٱلْمَلَئِكَةُ, ٱلرَّحْمَنُ, ٱللَّهُ, ٱلْقِيَمَةُ (*the resurrection*, to be carefully distinguished from ٱلسَّمَوَاتُ

A   اَلْقِيمَة *ẻl-ḳīmètu*, price, value), هٰهُنَا, ذٰلِكَ. The words ثَلَاثَة, ثَلَاثٌ,

and ثَلَاثُونَ, are also frequently written defectively ثَلَثَة, ثَلَثٌ,

ثَلَثُونَ; and occasionally some other vocables, such as ثَمَنِيَة and

ثَمَنُونَ; تَبْرَكَ and تَعَلَى; رَمَضَنُ, سُلَيْمٰنُ, and other proper names

ending in ـانُ; اَلشَّيْطٰنُ; مُعْوِيَة; خُلْدُ, مٰلِكُ, اَلْحٰرِثُ, اَلْقٰسِمُ, and

other proper names of the forms فَاعِلٌ and اَلْفَاعِلُ; دِينُرٌ; etc. This

is more common in Maġribī Mss. than in others.—The long vowel

ī is in a very few instances written defectively at the end of a word,

B   e.g. اَلْحَافِ, *ẻl-Ḥāfī*, اَلْعَاصِ, *ẻl-'Aṣī*, حُذَيْفَةُ بْنُ اليَمَانِ, *Ḥoḏeifètu 'bnu*

'l-Yèmānī, for اَلْمُهْتَدِ; اَلْيَمَانِى, اَلْعَاصِى, اَلْحَافِى, for *اَلْمُهْتَدِى.

REM. *b.* The letter *o*, preceded by ḍamma, is used by the Arabs
of North Africa and Spain to indicate a final *o* in foreign words; e.g.
قَارْلُه, *Carlo;* دُونْ بِطْرُه, *Don Pedro;* وَادِى آرُه, *the river Guadiaro.*

REM. *c.* The sound of ـا inclines, in later times and in certain
localities, from *ā* to *ē*, just as that of fètha does from *a* to *è* (see

C   § 4, *a*, and § 5, *b*). This change is called اَلْإِمَالَة, *ẻl-'imāla*, the
" deflection " of the sound of *a* and *ā* towards that of *i* and *ī*. The
Maġribī Arabs actually pronounce *ā* in many cases as *ī*. Hence
رِكَابٌ *rikāb*, لٰكِنْ *lākin,* بَابٌ *bāb,* لِسَانٌ *lisān,* are sounded *rikēb,*
lēkin, bīb, lisīn; and, conversely, the Spanish names *Beja, Jaen,*
Caniles, Lebrilla, are written بَاجَه, جَيَّان, قَنَالَش, لَبْرَالَه.

7.   ا corresponds to fètha, ى to kèsra, and و to ḍamma; whence

D   ا is called أُخْتُ الْفَتْحَة, *the sister of fètha,* ى أُخْتُ الْكَسْرَة, *the sister of*
kèsra, and و, أُخْتُ الضَّمَّة, *the sister of ḍamma.* Fètha before ى and
و forms the diphthongs *ai* and *au*, which retain their original clear
sound after the harder gutturals and the emphatics, e.g. صَيْفٌ *saifun,*

---

* [The omission of final ى in these cases is hardly a mere orthographical irregularity, but expresses a variant pronunciation in which
the final *ī* was shortened or dropped. See Nöldeke, *Gesch. d. Qorān's,*
p. 251.]

خَوُفٌ *ḥaufun*; but after the other letters become nearly *ē* (Hcb. 'ֵ=) A and *ō* (Hcb. 'ֹ–), e. g. سَيْفٌ *sêfun*, مَوْتٌ *môtun* (almost *sāfun*, *môtun*).

Rem. *a.* After و at the end of a word, both when preceded by damma and by fètḥa, ا is often written, particularly in the plural of verbs; e. g. نَصَرُوا, رَمَوْا, يَغْزُوا. This ا, in itself quite superfluous (èlif otiosum), is intended to guard against the possibility of the preceding و being separated from the body of the word to which it belongs, and so being mistaken for the conjunction وَ *and*. It is called أَلِفُ ٱلْوِقَايَة, *the guarding èlif*, or ٱلْأَلِفُ ٱلْفَاصِلَةُ, *the separating èlif*.

Rem. *b.* ى at the end of a word after a fètḥa is pronounced B like ا, e. g. فَتَى *fatā*, رَمَى *ramā*, إِلَى *'ilā**, and is called, like ا itself in the same position (e. g. بَهْنَسَا *Bèhnesā*, غَزَا *gazā*), ٱلْأَلِفُ ٱلْمَقْصُورَةُ, *the èlif that can be abbreviated*, in contradistinction to *the lengthened èlif*, ٱلْأَلِفُ ٱلْمَمْدُودَةُ (see § 22 and § 23, rem. *a*), which is protected by hèmza. It receives this name because, when it comes in contact with a *hèmza conjunctionis* (see § 19, rem. *f*), it is shortened in pronunciation before the following consonant, as are the و and ى in أَبُو and أَبِى before ٱلْوَزِيرِ (see § 20, *b*)†.

Rem. *c.* If a pronominal suffix be added to a word ending C in ى–, the ى is sometimes retained according to old custom, as in رَمَاهُ or رَمَيهُ, but it is commonly changed into ا, as رَمَاهُ.

---

* [But ى–, with the mark *gèzma* (see § 10), as in كَى, يَدَى is the diphthong *ai*.] The diphthong *ai*, when final, is often marked in old Mss. by the letters اى suprascript; e. g. يَدَى, يَدَى مُعْطَآءٍ كُلِّ, i. e. *yèdai*, not *yèdā*.

† [It would seem that the early scribes who fixed the orthographical usage made a distinction of sound between ى– and ا–, pronouncing D the former nearly as *ē*; cf. rem. *d*. On the other hand many Mss., even very ancient ones, write ا– where the received rules require ى–. According to the grammarians *èlif maksūra* is always written ى– in words of more than three letters unless the penultimate letter is Yā (as يَحْيَا *he will live*, دُنْيَا *world*). In words of three letters, the origin of the final *ā* must be considered; a "converted Yā" gives ى–, a "converted Wāw" gives ا–. See the details below §§ 167, 169, 213 etc.]

A   REM. *d.* In some words ending in ــاة we often find ـوة instead of ـاة, as غَدْوَةٌ, نَجْوَةٌ, زَكْوَةٌ or زَكَوةٌ, صَلْوَةٌ or صَلَوةٌ, حَيْوَةٌ or حَيَوةٌ, مَنْوَةٌ, مِشْكَوةٌ, and so also الرِّبَوا, رِبَوا for رِبًا, الرِّبَا; further ـية for ـاة in the loan-word تَوْرَيةٌ or تَوْرِيَةٌ; according to which older mode of writing we ought to pronounce the ـاة nearly as *ā̊* or *ē* respectively*.

8. The marks of the short vowels when doubled are pronounced with the addition of the sound *n*, ـً *an*, ـٍ *in*, ـٌ or ـٌ *un*. This is called

B   التَّنْوِينُ, the *tènwīn* or "nunation" (from the name of the letter ن *nūn*), and takes place only at the end of a word; e.g. مَدِينَةً *medīnètan*, بِنْتٍ *bintin*, مَالٌ *mālun*. See § 308.

REM. *a.* ـً takes an ا after all the consonants except ة; as بَابًا, رِيحًا, but خَلِيفَةً. However, when it precedes a ى, no ا is written, as in هُدًى; nor, according to the older orthography, when it accompanies a hèmza, as in شَيْءٍ, for which we more usually find شَيْئًا. This èlif in no way affects the quantity of the vowel, which is always short: *bāban*, *rīḥan*.

C   REM. *b.* To one word و is added, without in any way affecting the sound of the tènwīn, viz. to the proper name عَمْرُو *'Amr* (not *'Amrū*), genit. عَمْرُو, accus. عَمْرًا, rarely عَمْرُوا, [or, when the tènwīn falls away (§ 315, *a*, rem. *b*) عَمْرُو in all three cases], so written to distinguish it from another proper name that has the same radical letters, viz. عُمَرُ *'Omar*, genit. and accus. عُمَرَ. The و of عَمْرُو and عَمْرُو is, however, often neglected in old manuscripts. [Cf. the use of ا to represent tènwīn in proper names in the

D   Nabataean inscriptions.]

REM. *c.* In old Mss. of the Ḳor'ān, the tènwīn is expressed by doubling the dots which represent the vowels; ـ٬ = ـً, ـ٬ = ـٍ, ٬ـ = ـٌ .

---

* [The prophet said أَفْعُو for أَفْعَى, حَذُو for حَذَا. Zamaḫšarī, *Fāïḳ* i. 114.--De G.]

III. OTHER ORTHOGRAPHIC SIGNS. A

A. *Gĕzma or Sukūn.*

9. *Gĕzma,* جَزْمٌ or جَزْمَةٌ (*amputation*), ْ, is written over the final consonant of all shut syllables, and serves, when another syllable follows, to separate the two; e. g. بَلْ *bĕl,* هُمْ *hum,* كَتَبْتُمْ *katabtum,* سَفْسَفَ *sĕfsĕfa,* قُرْآنٌ *ḳor-'ānun* (not *ḳo-rānun*). It corresponds therefore to the *Shĕvā quiescens* of the Hebrew, with which its other name سُكُونٌ, *rest,* coincides.

Rem. *a.* A letter which has no following vowel is called حَرْفٌ B سَاكِنٌ, *a quiescent letter,* as opposed to حَرْفٌ مُتَحَرِّكٌ, *a movent letter.* See § 4, rem. *b.*

Rem. *b.* Letters that are assimilated to a following letter, which receives in consequence the *tĕsdīd* or mark of doubling (see § 11 and § 14), are retained in writing, but not marked with a gĕzma; e.g. أَرَدْتَ, مِنْ رَبِّهِ, ٱلرَّحْمٰنُ, not أَرَدْتَ, مِن رَّبِّهِ, ٱلرَّحْمٰنُ.

Rem. *c.* The same distinction exists between the words *gĕzm* and *gĕzma,* as between *fĕth* and *fĕtha,* etc. (see § 4, rem. *a*).

Rem. *d.* Older forms of the gĕzma are ـٔ and ـٚ, whence the C later ـٚ, instead of the common ـْ or ـٚ. In some old Mss. of the Ḳorān a small horizontal (red) stroke is used, ـٜ.

10. ى and و, when they form a diphthong with fĕtha, are marked with a gĕzma, as لَيْلٌ, يَوْمٌ, كَىْ, يَدَىْ; but when they stand for *ĕlif productionis* they do not take this sign (see § 7, rem. *b, c, d*).

Rem. In many manuscripts a gĕzma is placed even over the letters of prolongation, e. g. قَالَ, صَبُورٌ, سِيْمَ; and over the ĕlif maksūra, e. g. عَلَىْ, هُدَىْ for عَلَى, هُدَى.

B. *Tĕsdīd or Shĕdda.* D

11. A consonant that is to be doubled, or, as the Arabs say, strengthened (مُشَدَّد), without the interposition of a vowel (see rem. *a*), is written only once, but marked with the sign ّ, which is called

A اَلتَّشْدِيدُ, the *tèšdīd* (*strengthening*)*; e.g. اَلْكُلَّ *èl-kulla*, كُلَّ *kullan*,

اَلسَّمِّ *ès-sèmmi*, سَمٍّ *sèmmin*, اَلْمُرُّ *èl-murru*, مُرٌّ *murrun*. It corresponds
therefore to the *Daghesh forte* of the Hebrew.

REM. *a*. The solitary exception to this rule, in the verbal forms
قُوِولَ *ḳūwila* and تُقُوولَ *tuḳūwila*, instead of قُوِّلَ and تُقُوِّلَ, admits
of an easy explanation (see § 159).—When a consonant is repeated
in such a manner that a vowel is interposed between its first and
second occurrence, no doubling, properly so called, takes place, and

B consequently the tèšdīd is not required; e.g. فَرَرْتَ, 2d pers. sing.
masc. Perf. of فَرَّ; تَفَتَّتَتْ, 3d pers. sing. fem. Perf. of the fifth form
of فَتَّ.

REM. *b*. A consonant can be doubled, and receive tèšdīd, only
when a vowel precedes and follows it. The cases treated of in § 14
form no exception to this rule.

REM. *c*. All consonants whatsoever, not even êlif hèmzatum
excepted, admit of being doubled and take tèšdīd. Hence we speak
and write رَأَّسٌ *ra"âsun*, سَأَّلَ *sa"âlun*, نَأَّجٌ *na"âǧun*.

C REM. *d*. ّ is an abbreviated شّ, the first radical of the name
تَشْدِيدٌ, or the first letter of the name شَدَّةُ, which the African Arabs
use instead of the other. Or it may stand for شد (from مُشَدَّدٌ), since
in the oldest and most carefully written manuscripts its form is ـ.
Its opposite is ـ, i.e. خف (from مُخَفَّفٌ *lightened*, *single*); e.g.
سِرًّا وَعَلَانِيَةً *secretly and openly*.

REM. *e*. Tèšdīd, in combination with ـٌ, ـٌ, ـٌ, ـٌ, is placed between the consonants and these vowel-marks, as may be seen from
D the above examples. In combination with ـ the Egyptians write
ـ instead of ـ; but elsewhere, at least in old manuscripts, ـ may
stand for ـ as well as ـ. The African Arabs constantly write
ـ, ـ, ـ, for ـ, ـ, ـ. In the oldest Mss. of the Ḳor'ân, tèšdīd is
expressed by ⌒ or ᴗ, which, when accompanied by kèsra, is sometimes written, as in African Mss., below the line. In African
Mss. the vowel is not always written with the sèdda; ـ alone may
be = ـ, &c.

---

* [The *nomen unitatis* is تَشْدِيدة.—De G.]

12. Těšdīd is either *necessary* or *euphonic.*

A

13. The *necessary těšdīd*, which always follows a vowel, whether short (as in عَلَّقَ) or long (as in مَادٌ), indicates a doubling upon which the signification of the word depends. Thus أَمَرَ (*ámara*) means *he commanded*, but أَمَّرَ (*ámmara*), *he appointed some one commander;* مُرٌّ (*murrun*) is *bitter*, but a word مُرٌ (*murun*) does not exist in the language.

REM. The Arabs do not readily tolerate a syllable containing a long vowel and terminating in a consonant. Consequently *těšdīd* B *necessarium* scarcely ever follows the long vowels و and ى, as in تَوُدُّ ٱلثَّوْبُ, though it is sometimes found after ا, as in مَادَّةٌ, مَارٌّ, يَكْتُبَانِّ (see § 25). Nor does it occur after the diphthongs ـَوْ and ـَىْ, save in rare instances, like خُوَيْصَّةٌ and دُوَيْبَّةٌ [see § 277].

14. The *euphonic těšdīd* always follows a vowelless consonant, which, though expressed in writing, is, to avoid harshness of sound, passed over in pronunciation and assimilated to a following consonant. It is used :—

(*a*) With the letters ت, ث, د, ذ, ر, ز, س, ش, ص, ض, ط, ظ, C ل, ن, (dentals, sibilants, and liquids,) after the article اَلْ; e.g. اَلتَّمْرُ *ĕt-těmru;* اَلرَّحْمَانُ *'ar-raḥmānu;* اَلشَّمْسُ *ĕš-šèmsu;* اَلظُّلْمُ *'az-ẓolmu;* اَللَّيْلُ *ĕl-lèilu*, or, in African and Spanish manuscripts, اَلَّيْلُ.

REM. *a.* These letters are called اَلْحُرُوفُ ٱلشَّمْسِيَّةُ, *the solar letters*, because the word شَمْسُ, *sun*, happens to begin with one of them ; and the other letters of the alphabet اَلْحُرُوفُ ٱلْقَمَرِيَّةُ, *the lunar letters*, because the word قَمَرُ, *moon*, commences with one of D them.

REM. *b.* This assimilation is extended by some to the ل of هَلْ and بَلْ, especially before ر, as هَلْ رَأَيْتَ.

(*b*) With the letters ر, ل, م, و, ى, after *n* with gĕzm, e.g. مِن رَّبِّهِ *mir rabbihi,* مِن لَّيْلٍ, أَن يَّقْتُلَ; and after the nunation, e.g. كِتَابٌ مُّبِينٌ *kitābum mubīnun*, for *kitābun mubīnun.* The *n* of the

A words من, عَن, أَن, is often not written when they are combined with

أَن for أَلَّ, عَن مَّا for عَمَّا, مِن مَّن or مِمَّن for مِمَّن. e.g. ; لَا ,مَن, مَا.

REM. *a.* If to the above letters we add ن itself, as أَن تَكْتُبَ, the mnemonic word is يَرْمُلُونَ.

REM. *b.* أَن for أَلَّ is equally common with أَلَّا, but مِمَّا, عَمَّن, مِمَّن, عَمَّا, are hardly ever written separately; مَن, لَّ, on the contrary, always. Similarly we find إِنْ لَّ for إِلَّا (*if not*), إِمَّا for إِنْ مَّا (*if,* with

B redundant مَا) and occasionally أَمَّا for أَنْ مَّا (*that,* with redundant مَا).

(*c*) With the letter ت after ث, د, ذ, ض, ط, ظ (dentals), in certain parts of the verb ; e.g. لَبِثْتُ *lĕbittu* for لَبِثْتُ *lĕbiṭtu;* أَرَدْتُّ *'aratta* for أَرَدْتُ *'aradtu ;* اتَّخَذْتُّمْ *'attaḥattum* for اتَّخَذْتُمْ *'attaḥadtum;* بَسَطْتُّمْ *basattum* for بَسَطْتُمْ *basaṭtum.* Many grammarians, however, reject this kind of assimilation altogether, and rightly, because the absorption of a strong radical consonant, such as د, ض or ط, by a

C weaker servile letter, like ت, is an unnatural mutilation of an essential part of the word.

REM. *a.* Still more to be condemned are such assimilations as عُدُّ for عُدْتُ, خَبَّطَ for خَبَطْتَ.

REM. *b.* If the verb ends in ت, it naturally unites with the second ت in the above cases, so that only one ت is written, but the union of the two is indicated by the tĕšdīd ; as بَتَّ for بَتَتُّ.

C. *Hĕmza or Nĕbra.*

D **15.** Élif, when it is not a mere letter of prolongation, but a consonant, pronounced like the *spiritus lenis,* is distinguished by the mark ٔ *hĕmza* (هَمْز or هَمْزَة, *compression,* viz. of the upper part of the windpipe, see § 4, rem. *a*), which is also sometimes called *nĕbra* (نَبْرَة, *elevation*); e.g. خَطَأً, أَمَرَ, خَطَأٌ, إِقْلِيدٌ, اقْرَأ, رَأْس, قَرَأَ, سَأَلَ, أَسَدَ.

REM. *a.* In cases where an *ĕlif conjunctionis* (see § 19, *a, b, c,* and rem. *d, e*) at the beginning of a word receives its own vowel, the grammarians omit the hĕmza and write merely the vowel ; e.g. اقْتُلْ, ابْنٌ, اقْرَأ *praise belongs to God,* الْحَمْدُ لِلّٰه.

REM. *b.* ‸ is probably a small ع, and indicates that the *èlif* is to A be pronounced almost as *'ain.* In African (and certain other) Mss. it is sometimes actually written ع ; e. g. اِذْ, أَخْلُقُ. In the oldest Mss. of the Kor'ân, hèmza is indicated by doubling the vowel-points; e. g., القرْان = اَلْقُرْءَانُ, المـ.و.منون اَلْمُؤْمِنُونَ. It is also marked in such Mss. by a large yellow or green dot, varying in position according to the accompanying vowel (see above, § 4, rem. *c*).

REM. *c.* Hèmza is written between the ا and the vowel that accompanies it, or the gèzma (see the examples given above) ; but B we often find خَاسِئِينَ for خَاسِئِينَ, سَئِرَ for سَئِرَ (see § 16), and occasionally خَطَاءً or خَطَاءً for خَطَاءً, أَنَّ or أَنَّ for إِنَّ, سُئِلَ for سُئِلَ or سُئِلَ, and the like.

REM. *d.* The effect of the hèmza is most sensible to a European ear at the commencement of a syllable in the middle of a word, preceded by a shut syllable; e. g. مَسْأَلَةٌ, *mas-'alatun* (not *ma-salatun*) اَلْقُرْءَانُ, *èl-ḳor-'ânu* (not *èl-ḳo-rânu*).

16. ى and و take hèmza, when they stand in place of an *èlif* C *hèmzatum** (in which case the two points of the letter ى are commonly omitted); e. g. جِئْتُ for جِئْتُ, جَاءَتْ for جَاءَتْ, خَاسِئِينَ for خَاسِئِينَ, بُؤْسٌ for بُؤْسٌ, رَأْسٌ, بَأْسٌ رُؤُوسٌ for رَأْوُسٌ.

17. Hèmza alone (ء) is written instead of أ, ا, ى, ؤ, in the following cases.

(*a*) Always at the end of a word, after a letter of prolongation or a consonant with gèzma, e. g. جَاءَ, *ǵâ'a*, رِدَاءً, رِدَاءً; جِىءَ, *ǵî'a,* D رَدِيءٌ, سُوءٌ *sû'un* ; ضَوْءٌ, قَىْءٌ, ظَمْءٌ, or more commonly ظَمْأً (see § 8, rem. *a*); and in the middle of a word, after an *èlif productionis*, provided the hèmza has the vowel fètha, as أَعْدَاءَكُمْ, يَتَسَاءَلُونَ (but for أَعْدَاوُكُمْ and أَعْدَاءَكُمْ the Arabs usually write أَعْدَآئِكُمْ and أَعْدَآءَكُمْ).

REM. Accusatives like شَيْئًا and ظَمْأً are often written, though

---

A   contrary to rule, ظِمْأً, شَيْأً ; and in old Mss. we find such instances
as رِدَآءَ for رِدَآءٍ.

(*b*) Frequently in the middle of words, after the letters of prolongation و and ى, or after a consonant with *ğezma*, e.g. مَقْرُوءَةٌ
for مَقْرُوءَةٌ, مُوئِبَاتٌ for مُوئِبَاتٌ, تَوْءَمُ for تَوْأَمُ, يَسْئَلُ for يَسْأَلُ ; and also
after kèsra and ḍamma before the ى and و of prolongation, e.g.

B   رُؤُوسٌ for رُؤُوسٌ, خَاطِئِينَ for خَاطِئِينَ. Hèmza between *īa, ūa, āi, īi,*
āū, and *ūū,* is, however, more frequently, though improperly, placed
over the letter of prolongation itself; e.g. مَقْرُوءَةٌ for مَقْرُوءَةٌ, خَطِيَّةٌ for
خَطِيئَةٌ or خَطِيئَةٌ, رُوؤُسٌ for رُؤُوسٌ or رُؤُوسٌ, which words must always be
pronounced *makrū'atun, ḫaṭī'atun, ru'ūsun.*

REM. *a.* After a consonant with *ğezma*, which is connected with
a following letter, hèmza and its vowel may be placed above the
C   connecting line; as أَسْئَلُ, for أَسْأَلُ.

REM. *b.* A hèmza preceded by *u* or *i*, and followed by *a* or *ā,*
may be changed into pure و or ى; as جُوَنٌ for جُؤَنٌ, سُوَالٌ for
سُؤَالٌ; مِئَةٌ for مِئَةٌ, لِيَامُ for لِئَامُ.—If preceded by *ū* or *ī,* or the
diphthong *ai,* the hèmza may likewise be changed into و or ى,
whatever be the following vowel; as مَقْرُوءَةٌ for مَقْرُوءَةٌ, from مَقْرُوءَةٌ;
فَيٌّ for فَيْءٌ, نَبِيٌّ from نَبِيءٌ; بَرِيَّةٌ for بَرِيئَةٌ, from بَرِيئَةٌ; نَبِيٌّ for نَبِيءٌ

D   شَيَّا for شَيْئًا.—If the hèmza has *ğezma,* it may [lose its consonantal
power and] be changed into the letter of prolongation that is homogeneous with the preceding vowel, as رَأْسُ for رَأْسُ, لُومُ for لُؤْمُ,
بِيرُ for بِئْرُ; necessarily so, if the preceding consonant be an èlif with
hèmza, as أَمَنَ or آمَنَ, أُومِنُ, إِيمَانٌ for أَأْمَنَ, أُؤْمِنُ, إِئْمَانٌ. [This
is called تَخْفِيفُ ٱلْهَمْزَة.]

REM. *c.* The name دَاوُودُ or دَاوُدُ, *David,* is often written دَاوُدُ,
but must always be pronounced *Dā'ūdu.*

D. *Waṣla.*

18. When the vowels with hèmza (ﺍ ﺇ ﺃ), at the commencement of A a word, are absorbed by the final vowel of the preceding word, the elision of the spiritus lenis is marked by the sign ‍ﺻ, written over the èlif, and called وَصْل, or وَصْلَة, or صِلَة (see § 4, rem. *a*), i.e. *union;* e.g. رَأَيْتُ ٱبْنَكَ عَبْدُ ٱلْمَلِكِ 'abdu 'l-mèliki for عَبْدُ ٱلْمَلِكِ 'abdu èl-mèliki; raèitu 'bnaka for رَأَيْتُ إِبْنَكَ raèitu 'ibnaka.

REM. *a.* ‍ﺻ seems to be an abbreviation of ص in وَصْل or صِلَة; or rather, it is the word صِلَة itself. In the oldest Mss. of the B Ḳorʾān the waṣl is indicated by a stroke (usually red), which sometimes varies in position, according to the preceding vowel. In ancient Maġribī Mss. the stroke is used, with a point to indicate the original vowel of the elided èlif; e.g., عَرَضَ; فِ , سَبِيلِ لٰٱللّٰه , i.e. ٱللّٰه; اَلْحَيْوَة i.e. اَلْحَيْوَة. Hence even in modern African Mss. we find Ꞁ Ꞁ Ꞁ ˙ꓳ ꓳ instead of the usual ٰٱ.

REM. *b.* Though we have written in the above examples ٱلْمَلِك and إِبْنَكَ, yet the student must not forget that the more correct C orthography is اَلْمَلِك and ٱبْنَكَ. See § 15, rem. *a*, and § 19, rem. *d*.

19. This elision takes place in the following cases.

(*a*) With the ٱ of the article اَل; as أَبُو ٱلْوَزِيرِ for أَبُو ٱلْوَزِيرِ, *the father of the wèzīr.*

(*b*) With the ٳ and ٱ of the Imperatives of the first form of the regular verb; as قَالَ اسْمَعْ for قَالَ ٱسْمَعْ, *he said, listen;* قَالَ ٱقْتُلْ for D قَالَ ٱقْتُلْ, *he said, kill.*

(*c*) With the ٳ of the Perfect Active, Imperative, and Nomen actionis of the seventh and all the following forms of the verb (see § 35), and the ٱ of the Perfect Passive in the same forms; e.g. هُوَ ٱنْهَزَمَ for هُوَ ٱنْهَزَمَ, *he was put to flight;* وَٱسْتُعْمِلَ for وَٱسْتُعْمِلَ, *and he was appointed governor;* اَلْٱقْتِدَارُ *the being able* (to do something); اِلَ ٱلْٱنْقِرَاضِ . *till the downfall* or *extinction.*

A   (*d*) With the إ of the following eight nouns:

اِبْنٌ, and اِبْنُمٌ or اِبْنَمٌ, *a son.*   اِبْنَةٌ, *a daughter.*

اِثْنَانِ, *two* (masc.).   اِثْنَتَانِ, *two* (fem.).

اِمْرُؤٌ, or اِمْرُؤٌ, *a man.*   اِمْرَأَةٌ, *a woman.*

اِسْتٌ, *the anus.*   اِسْمٌ (rarely اُسْمٌ), *a name.*

REM. *a.* With the article اِمْرُؤٌ and اِمْرَأَةٌ take, in classical
B   Arabic, the form اَلْمَرُءُ and اَلْمَرْأَةُ.

REM. *b.* The hèmza of أَيْمُنٌ, *oaths*, is also elided after the
asseverative particle لَ, and occasionally after the prepositions مَعَ
and مِنْ (which then takes fètḥa instead of ġèzma); as لَأَيْمُنُ ٱللّٰهِ
by God (lit. *by the oaths of God*), for which we may also write
لَيْمُنُ ٱللّٰهِ, omitting the ا altogether, or, in a contracted form,
لَيْمُ ٱللّٰهِ.

C   REM. *c.* In the above words and forms, the vowel with hèmza
is in part original, but has been weakened through constant use (as
in the article, and in أَيْمُنٌ after لَ); in part merely prosthetic, that
is to say, prefixed for the sake of euphony to words beginning with
a vowelless consonant, and consequently it vanishes as soon as a
vowel precedes it, because it is then no longer necessary.

REM. *d.* It is naturally an absurd error to write آ at the beginning of a sentence instead of èlif with hèmza, as ٱلْحَمْدُ للّٰهِ instead
of ٱلْحَمْدُ للّٰهِ. The Arabs themselves never do so, but, to indicate
D   that the èlif is an *èlif conjunctionis* (see rem. *f*), they omit the hèmza
and express only its accompanying vowel, as ٱلْحَمْدُ للّٰهِ. See § 15,
rem. *a*, and § 18, rem. *b*.

REM. *e.* In more modern Arabic the elision of the *èlif conjunctionis* (see rem. *f*) is neglected, especially after the article, as
بَعْدَ إِنْقِرَاضِهِمْ, بِئْسَ ٱلْإِسْمُ, إِلَى ٱلْإِنْقِرَاضِ, اَلْإِقْتِدَارُ; but the grammarians brand this as خُرُوجٌ عَنْ كَلَامِ ٱلْعَرَبِ وَلَحْنٌ فَاحِشٌ.

Rem. *f.* The ĕlif which takes waṣla is called أَلِفُ ٱلْوَصْلِ or هَمْزَةُ A

ٱلْوَصْلِ, *ĕlif* or *hĕmza conjunctionis*, the connective ĕlif; the opposite

being أَلِفُ ٱلْقَطْعِ, *ĕlif sejunctionis* or *separationis*, the disjunctive ĕlif.

20. The ĕlif conjunctionis may be preceded either by a short
vowel, a long vowel, a diphthong, or a consonant with gĕzma. To
these different cases the following rules apply.

(*a*) A short vowel simply absorbs the ĕlif conjunctionis with its
vowel; see § 19, *b* and *c*.   B

(*b*) A long vowel is shortened in pronunciation, according to
the rule laid down in § 25; e.g. فِى ٱلنَّاسِ *fī 'n-nāsi, among men;*

أَبُو ٱلْوَزِيرِ *'abŭ 'l-wĕzīri, the father of the wĕzīr,* for *fī* and *'abŭ.*
This abbreviation of the naturally long vowel is retained even when
the *lām* of the article no longer closes the syllable containing that
vowel, but begins the next syllable, in consequence of the elision
of a following ĕlif (either according to § 19 or by poetic license).
Hence فِى ٱلْٱبْتِدَآءِ, *in the beginning,* is pronounced as if written C

ذُو ٱلْٱعْلَالِ ;فَلِٱبْتِدَآءِ (for ٱلْأَرْضِ), *upon the earth,* as فَلِٱرْضِ ; فِى . ٱلْأَرْضِ
(for ٱلْأَعْلَالِ), *subject to change (a weak letter),* as ذُلِٱعْلَالٍ.   In the first
of these examples the ١ is an ĕlif conjunctionis; in the other two
it is an ĕlif separationis, but has been changed for the sake of the
metre into an ĕlif conjunctionis. The suffixes of the 1st pers. sing.,

ـِى and نِى, may assume before the article the older forms ـِىَ and

نِىَ; e.g. نَعْمَتِىَ ٱلَّتِى *my grace which,* ٱهْدِنِىَ ٱلصَّرَاطَ *guide me on the* D
way, instead of نَعْمَتِى ٱلَّتِى and ٱهْدِنِى ٱلصَّرَاطَ, which latter forms are
equally admissible.

(*c*) A diphthong is resolved into two simple vowels, according to the law stated in § 25, viz. *ai* into *ăĭ*, and *au* into *ăŭ*; as

فِى عَيْنَىِ ٱلْمَلِكِ *fī 'ainăĭ 'l-mĕliki, in the eyes of the king,* for

ٱخْشَىِ ٱلْقَوْمَ ; فِى عَيْنَىْ ٱلْمَلِكِ *iḫšăĭ 'l-ḳauma, fear the people;*

مُصْطَفَىِ ٱللَّهِ *muṣṭafăŭ 'llāhi, the elect of God,* for مُصْطَفَىْ ٱللَّهِ.   The
silent ĕlif (§ 7, rem. *a*) does not prevent the resolution of the diph-

A thong, as رَمَوُا ٱلْحِجَارَةَ *ramāŭ 'l-ḥiǧārata, they threw the stones;* فَلَمَّا رَأَوُا ٱلنَّجْمَ *fa-lammā ra'aŭ 'n-nĕǧma, and after they saw the star.* But أَوْ and لَوْ take *kèsra*, as أَوِ ٱسْمُهُ *or his name;* لَوِ ٱسْتُقْبَلَ *if he went to meet.*

(*d*) A consonant with ǧèzma either takes its original vowel, if it had one; or assumes that which belongs to the èlif conjunctionis; or adopts the lightest of the three vowels, which in its nature approaches nearest to the ǧèzma, viz. kèsra. Hence the pronouns of the 2d and 3d pers. plur. masc., أَنْتُمْ *you,* and هُمْ *they,* the pronominal suffixes of the same pronouns, كُمْ *your, you* (accus.), and هُمْ *their, them,* and the verbal termination of the 2d pers. plur. masc. Perf. تُمْ, take *ḍamma* (in which they originally ended); as أَنْتُمُ ٱلْكَاذِبُونَ *ye are the liars;* لَعَنَهُمُ ٱللّٰهُ *may God curse them!* رَأَيْتُمُ ٱلرَّجُلَ *ye have seen the man.* The same is the case with مُذْ, *since, from which time forth,* because it is contracted for مُنْذُ. The preposition مِنْ, *from,* takes *fètḥa* before the article, but in other cases *kèsra;* as مِنَ ٱلرَّجُلِ, مِنِ أَيْنِهِ. All other words ending in a consonant with ǧèzma take *kèsra;* viz. nouns having the tènwīn, as مُحَمَّدٌ ٱلنَّبِىِّ *Moḥammèduni 'n-nèbīyu;* the pronoun مَنْ, as مَنِ ٱلْكَذَّابُ *mani 'l-kaḏḏābu;* verbal forms like قَتَلَتِ ٱلرُّومُ, ٱجْلِسْ, تَكْتُبْ, قَتَلَتْ as *katalati 'r-Rūmu;* and particles, such as عَنْ, إِنْ, بَلْ, قَدْ, هَلْ, لٰكِنْ, etc.

Rem. *a.* In certain cases where هُمْ becomes هِمْ (see § 185, rem. *b*) the waṣl may be made either with ḍamma or kèsra, هُمُ or هِمِ.

Rem. *b.* If the vowel of a prosthetic èlif be ḍamma, the waṣl is sometimes effected by throwing it back upon the preceding vowelless consonant or tènwīn; as قُلِ ٱنْظُرُوا, for قُلِ ٱنْظُرُوا, instead of سَلَامٌ ٱدْخُلُوا; وَقَالَتِ ٱخْرُجْ; قُلِ ٱنْظُرُوا *selāmunu 'dḫulū.*

Rem. *c.* The final ن of the second Energetic of verbs (see § 97) is rejected, so that the waṣl is effected by the preceding fètḥa; as

لَا تَضْرِبْ اَبْنَكَ *lā taḍriba 'bnaka,* and not لَا تَضْرِبَنَّ اَبْنَكَ *lā taḍribani* A *'bnaka.*

21. ا is altogether omitted in the following cases.

(*a*) In the solemn introductory formula بِاسْمِ اللَّه, for بِاِسْمِ اللَّه, *in the name of God,* בשם האלהים. As a compensation for the omission of the ا, the copyists of Mss. are accustomed to prolong the upward stroke of the letter ب, thus: بِسْمِ.

(*b*) In the word اِبْنُ, *son,* in a genealogical series, that is to say, B when the name of the son precedes, and that of his father follows in the genitive; provided always that the said series, as a whole, forms part either of the subject or the predicate of a sentence. For example,

ضَرَبَ زَيْدُ بْنُ خَٰلِدٍ سَعْدَ بْنَ عَوْفِ بْنِ عَبْدِ اللَّه *Zeid, the son of Ḫālid, struck Sa'd, the son of 'Auf, the son of 'Abdu 'llāh.* [Cf. § 315, rem. *b.*]
But if the second noun be not in apposition to the first, but form part of the predicate, so that the two together make a complete sentence, then the ا is retained; as زَيْدٌ اَبْنُ عَمْرٍو *Zeid (is) the son of* C *'Amr;* عُمَرُ اَبْنُ الْخَطَّاب *'Omar (is) the son of el-Ḫaṭṭāb.*

REM. *a.* Even in the first case the ا of اِبْنُ is retained, if that word happens to stand at the beginning of a line.

REM. *b.* If the name following اِبْنُ be that of the mother or grandfather, the ا is retained; as عِيسَى اَبْنُ مَرْيَمَ, *Jesus the son of Mary;* عَمَّارُ اَبْنُ مَنْصُورٍ, *'Ammār the (grand)son of Manṣūr.* Likewise, if the following name be not the real name of the father, but a D surname or nickname; as مِقْدَادُ اَبْنُ الْأَسْوَدِ, *Miḳdād the son of el-'Aswad* (the real name of *el-'Aswad,* "the black," being *'Amr,* عَمْرُو). Or if the series be interrupted in any way, as by the interposition of an adjective; e.g. يَحْيَى الْكَرِيمُ اَبْنُ مَيْمُونٍ, *Yaḥyā the noble, the son of Meimūn;* رِدْبَى كَظِرْبَى اَبْنُ مُوسَى, *Ridbā (pronounced like the word ẓirbā) the son of Mūsā.*

(*c*) In the article اَل, when it is preceded:

(*α*) by the preposition لِ *to,* as لِلرَّجُلِ *to the man,* for لِالرَّجُلِ.

A If the first letter of the noun be ل, then the ل of the article is also omitted, as لِلَّيْلَة *to the night*, for لِلْلَيْلَة, and that for لِلَّيْلَة.

    (β) by the affirmative particle لَ *truly, verily*, as لَلْحَقّ, for لَلْحَقّ*.

    (d) In nouns, verbs, and the article أَل, when preceded by the interrogative particle أَ; as أَأَبْنُكَ, for أَابْنُكَ, *is thy son—*? أَنْكَسَرَتْ, for أَأَنْكَسَرَتْ, *is it* (fem.) *broken?* أَتَّخَذْتُمْ, for أَأَتَّخَذْتُمْ, *have ye received?*

B أَلْمَآءُ, for أَأَلْمَآءُ, *is the water—?* The ĕlif of the article may however be retained, so that أَلْمَآءُ with the interrogative أَ is often written أَآلْمَآءُ.

    REM. *a.* In this last case, according to some, when the second ĕlif has fĕtḥa, the two ĕlifs may blend into one with mĕdda (see below); as أَلْحَسَنُ عِنْدَكَ, *is ĕl-Ḥasan in thy house?* for أَأَلْحَسَنُ; آيْمُنُ ٱللَّهِ الْقُرَشِىٌّ أَمْ ٱلثَّقَفِى, *he of Ḳorĕis or he of Ṯaḳif?* يَمِينُكَ, *is thy oath 'by God'?* (see § 19, rem. *b*) for أَأَيْمُنُ ٱللَّهِ.

C   REM. *b.* The prosthetic ĕlif of the Imperative of سَأَلَ, *to ask*, is frequently omitted, in Mss. of the Ḳorʾān, after the conjunction فَ; as فَسْأَلْ, for فَاسْأَلْ. [Cf. § 140, rem. *a.*]

E. *Mĕdda or Maṭṭa.*

22. When ĕlif with hĕmza and a simple vowel or tĕnwīn (أ, اً, etc.) is preceded by an ĕlif of prolongation (ـَا), then a mere hĕmza is written instead of the former, and the sign of prolongation, ٓ mĕdda or maṭṭa

D (مَدّ, مَدّة or مَطّة, i.e. *lengthening, extension*), is placed over the latter; e.g. سَمَآءٌ *semā'un*, جَآءَ *ḡā'a*, يَتَسَآءَلُونَ *yatasā'alūna*, for سَمَأٌ, جَأَ, يَتَسَأَلُونَ.

    REM. *a.* As mentioned above (§ 17, *a*, rem.), we find in old Mss. such forms as جَأَآ, رِدَأَآ, for جَآءَ, رِدَآءَ.

    REM. *b.* In the oldest and best Mss., the form of the mĕdda is مــد (i.e. مد). Its opposite is قصر (i.e. قَصْرٌ, *shortening*), though

---

   * [Note also the cases, in poetry, cited in § 358, rem. *c*; further the contracted tribal names بَلْعَنْبَرِ, بَنُو ٱلْعَنْبَرِ for بَلْحَرِث, بَنُو ٱلْحَرِثِ.—De G.]

this is but rarely written. In some old Mss. of the Ḳor'ān mèdda A is expressed by a horizontal yellow line $\sim$.

23. When, at the beginning of a syllable, an ĕlif with hèmza and fètḥa (آ) is followed by an ĕlif of prolongation or an ĕlif with hèmza and gèzma (أ), then the two are commonly represented in writing by a single ĕlif with mèdda; e.g. اَكلُونَ for اَأْكلُونَ, إِسْأَادٌ for إِسْآدٌ, اٰمَنَّا for اَأُمَنَّا (see § 17, rem. *b*). In this case it is not usual to write either the hèmza, or the vowel, along with the mèdda. [But we some- B times find آ, see § 174.]

REM. *a.* آ is called اَلْأَلِفُ ٱلْمَمْدُودَةُ, *the lengthened* or *long ĕlif,* in opposition to اَلْأَلِفُ ٱلْمَقْصُورَةُ, *the ĕlif that can be abbreviated* or *shortened* (§ 7, rem. *b*).

REM. *b.* Occasionally a long ĕlif at the beginning of a word is written with hèmza and a perpendicular fètḥa, instead of with mèdda (see § 6, rem. *a*); e.g. أَمَنَّا instead of اٰمَنَّا or اَأُمَنَّا.

REM. *c.* Mèdda is sometimes placed over the other letters of C prolongation, و and ی, when followed by an ĕlif hèmzatum, only the hèmza being written (§ 17, *a*); as يَسْوَا, يَجِیَا. Also over the final vowels of the pronominal forms أَنْتُمُ, كُمُ, ه or هُمُ.هِمِ, or هِمِ, and the verbal termination تُمُ, when they are used as long in poetry; e.g. هُمُ, أَنْتُمُ.

REM. *d.* The mark $\sim$, often written over abbreviations of words, has nothing in common with mèdda but the form. So تَع for تَعَالَی, *He (God) is exalted above all*; عَمِ for السَّلَامُ عَلَيْهِ, *peace be* D *upon him!* صَلَعَمِ for صَلَّی ٱللَّهُ عَلَيْهِ وَسَلَّمَ, *God bless him and grant him peace!* رضَه for رَضِیَ ٱللَّهُ عَنْهُ, *may God be well pleased with,* or *gracious to, him!* رَح or رحَه for رَحِمَهُ ٱللَّهُ, *may God have mercy upon him!* الَخ for آخِرِه or إِلَی آخِرِهَا, *to the end of it,* i.e. *etc.;* ثنَا for حَدَّثَنَا, *he narrated to us;* انَا or نَا for أَخْبَرَنَا, *he informed us;* حَ for حِينَئِذٍ, *then.*—The letters م مر are written over words or verses that have been erroneously transposed in a manuscript, for

A   مُوَخَّر, *to be placed last,* and مُقَدَّم, *to be placed first.*—On the margin of Mss. we often find words with the letters خ, ن, and صح over them. The first of these indicates a variant, and stands for نُسْخَة, *a copy, another manuscript;* the second means that a word has been indistinctly written in the text, and is repeated more clearly on the margin, بَيَان, *explanation;* the third implies that the marginal reading, and not that of the text, is, in the writer's opinion, the correct one صَح, *it is correct,* or تَصْحِيح, *correction, emendation.*

B   Written over a word in the text, صح stands for صَح, and denotes that the word is correct, though there may be something peculiar in its form or vocalization.—Again مَعا (i.e. مَعًا, *together*) is written over a word with double vocalization to indicate that both vowels are correct. لعل over a word on the margin implies a conjectural emendation لَعَلَّه, *perhaps it is.*

IV. THE SYLLABLE.

C   **24.** The vowel of a syllable that terminates in a vowel, which we call an open or simple syllable, may be either long or short; as قَال *kā-lă.*

25. The vowel of a syllable that terminates in a consonant, which we call a shut or compound syllable, is almost always short; as قُل *kŭl,* not قُول (Heb. קוּל). Generally speaking, it is only in pause, where the final short vowels are suppressed, that the ancient Arabic admits of such syllables as *īn, ūn, ān,* etc.

D   REM. Before a double consonant *ā* is however not infrequent (see § 13, rem.). [Such a long *ā* preceding a consonant with *ǵèzma* sometimes receives a *mèdda,* as ضَالُّون.]

26. A syllable cannot begin with two consonants, the first of which is destitute of a vowel, as *sf* or *fr.* Foreign words, which commence with a syllable of this sort, on passing into the Arabic language, take an additional vowel, usually before the first consonant; as إِسْفَنْج, σπόγγος; أَفْلَاطُون, Πλάτων; اَلْإِفْرَنْج, *the Franks (Europeans);* إِكْسِير, *an elixir,* τὸ ξηρόν (medicamentum siccum).

27. A syllable cannot end in two consonants, which are not either separated or followed by a vowel (except in pause).

V. THE ACCENT. A

28. The last syllable of a word consisting of two or more syllables does not take the accent. Exceptions are:

(*a*) The pausal forms of § 29 and § 30, in which the accent remains unaltered; as *ya-kát, ká-nún, mu'-mi-nín, ká-ti-bát, fi-rínd, 'a-kál, ma-fár, ku-béil, bil-láur, bu-néi.*

Rem. But words ending in ـىُّ, ـوُّ, ـَآءُ or ـآءُ, ـوُّءٌ, and ـىُّءٌ, throw back the accent as far as possible in their pausal forms; قُرَشِىٌّ *Ko-ra-śí-yun* becomes *Kó-ra-śí,* نَبِىٌّ *ne-bí-yun, né-bí;* عَدُوٌّ *'a-dú-wun, 'á-dú;* اِقْتِنَآءٌ *'ik-ti-ná-'un, 'ík-ti-ná;* حَمْرَآءُ *ham-rá-'u, hám-ra;* B مَقْرُوءٌ *mak-rú-'un, mák-rú;* بَطِىءٌ *ba-tí-un, bá-tí.*

(*b*) Monosyllables in combination with أَ, بِ, كَ, لَ, وَ, and فَ, which retain their original accent; as أَلَا *'a-lá,* أَفَلَا *'a-fa-lá,* بِمَا *bi-má,* بِهِ *bi-hí,* كَذَا *ka-dá,* لِمَنْ *li-mán,* لَنَا *la-ná,* وَلَمْ *wa-lám,* فَقَطْ *fa-kát,* وَقُلْ *wa-kúl.*

Rem. The only exception to this rule in old Arabic is the interrogative enclitic مَ; as بِمَ *bí-ma,* لِمَ *lí-ma,* in contrast with C بِمَا *bi-má,* لِمَا *li-má.* See § 351, rem.

29. The penult takes the accent when it is long by nature, i.e. is an open syllable containing a long vowel; as قَالَ *ká-la,* يَقُولُ *ya-kú-lu,* قَانُونٌ *ká-nú-nun,* مُؤْمِنِينَ *mu'-mi-ní-na,* كَاتِبَاتٌ *ká-ti-bá-tun.*

30. The penult has likewise the accent when it is a shut syllable and consequently long by position; as قَلْبٌ *kál-bun,* ذِئْبٌ *dí'-bun,* بُرْءٌ *búr-'un,* اِجْلِسْ *íg-lis,* فِرِنْدٌ *fi-rín-dun,* أَقَلُّ *'a-kál-lu,* مَغَرٌّ *ma-fár-* D *run,* يَقُولَنَّ *ya-kú-lán-na,* قُبَيْلَ *ku-béi-la,* بِلَّوْرٌ *bil-láu-run,* بُنَّىٌّ *bu-néi-yun.*

31. When the penult is short, the accent falls upon the antepenult, provided that the word has not more than three syllables, or, if it has four or more syllables, that the antepenult is long by nature or position; as كَتَبَ *ká-ta-ba,* كَتَبَتْ *ká-ta-bat,* كَتَبُوا *ká-ta-bú,* كَاتِبٌ *ká-ti-bun,* طَلَبٌ *tá-la-bun,* أَيْنَمَا *'éi-na-má;* تَرَاسَلُوا *ta-rá-*

A *sa-lū,* قَالُونَهُمْ *ḳa-nū-nu-hum,* كَتَبْتُمَا *ka-táb-tu-mā.* In other cases the accent is thrown as far back as possible; as كَتَبَتَا *ḱa-ta-ba-tā,* مَسْئَلَة *más-'a-la-tun,* مَسْئَلَتُهَا *más-'a-la-tu-hā,* قَصَبْتُهُمَا *ḱa-ṣa-ba-tu-hu-mā.*

REM. On deviations from these principles of accentuation, in Egypt and among the Bĕdawīn, see Lane in the Journal of the German Oriental Society, vol. iv., pp. 183–6, and Wallin in the same journal, vol. xii., pp. 670–3, [also Spitta, *Gram. des arab. Vulgärdialectes von Aegypten* (1880), p. 59 *sqq.*]

B
VI. THE NUMBERS.

32. To express numbers the Arabs use sometimes the letters of the alphabet, at other times peculiar signs. In the former case, the numerical value of the letters accords with the more ancient order of the Hebrew and Aramaic alphabets (see § 1). They are written from right to left, and usually distinguished from the surrounding words by a stroke placed over them, as غَضَعِ, 1874. This arrangement of the alphabet is called the *'Abuǵèd* or *'Abǵèd,* and is con-
C tained in the barbarous words:

أَبْجَدٍ هَوَزٍ حُطِيَ كَلَمْنَ سَعْفَصْ قُرِشَتْ ثَخُذْ ضَظَغْ

(otherwise pronounced:

(أَبْجَدْ هَوَّزْ حُطِّى كَلَمْنَ سَعْفَصْ قُرِشَتْ ثَخُذْ ضَظَغْ

or, as usual in North Africa:

أَبْجَدٍ هَوَزٍ حُطِيَ كَلَمْنَ صَعْفَضْ قُرِسَتْ ثَخُذْ ظَغُشْ

` The special numerical figures, ten in number, have been adopted
D by the Arabs from the Indians, and are therefore called اَلرَّقْمُ ٱلْهِنْدِيُّ, *the Indian notation.* They are the same that we Europeans make use of, calling them *Arabian,* because we took them from the Arabs. Their form, however, differs considerably from that which our ciphers have gradually assumed, as the following table shows.

Indian:	۱	۲	۳	۴	۵	۶	۷	۸	۹	۰
Arabic:	١	٢	٣	٤	٥	٦	٧	٨	٩	٠
Europ.:	1	2	3	4	5	6	7	8	9	0

They are compounded in exactly the same way as our numerals; e.g. ١٨٧٤, 1874.

PART SECOND.

ETYMOLOGY OR THE PARTS OF SPEECH.

I. THE VERB, اَلْفِعْلُ.   A

A. General View.

1. *The Forms of the Triliteral Verb.*

33. The great majority of the Arabic verbs are triliteral (ثُلَاثِيٌّ), that is to say, contain three radical letters, though quadriliteral (رُبَاعِيٌّ) verbs are by no means rare.

34. From the first or ground-form of the triliteral and quadri- B literal verbs are derived in different ways several other forms, which express various modifications of the idea conveyed by the first.

35. The derived forms of the triliteral verb are usually reckoned fifteen in number, but the learner may pass over the last four, because (with the exception of the twelfth) they are of very rare occurrence.

اِفْعَالَّ XI.	تَفَاعَلَ VI.	فَعَلَ I.
اِفْعَوْعَلَ XII.	اِنْفَعَلَ VII.	فَعَّلَ II.
اِفْعَوَّلَ XIII.	اِفْتَعَلَ VIII.	فَاعَلَ III. C
اِفْعَنْلَلَ XIV.	اِفْعَلَّ IX.	أَفْعَلَ IV.
اِفْعَنْلَى XV.	اِسْتَفْعَلَ X.	تَفَعَّلَ V.

REM. *a.* The 3d pers. sing. masc. Perf., being the simplest form of the verb, is commonly used as paradigm, but for shortness' sake we always render it into English by the infinitive; قَتَلَ *to kill*, instead of *he has killed*.

A   REM. *b.* The Arab grammarians use the verb فَعَلَ (פָּעַל) as paradigm, whence the first radical of the triliteral verb is called by them اَلْفَاۤ *the fā*, the second اَلْعَيْنُ *the 'ain*, and the third اَللَّامُ *the lām.*

    REM. *c.* As the above order and numbering of the conjugations are those adopted in all the European Lexicons, the learner should note them carefully.

    36. The *first* or ground-form is generally transitive (مُتَعَدٍّ) or intransitive (لَازِمٌ غَيْرُ مُتَعَدٍّ) in signification, according to the vowel which accompanies its second radical.

B   **37.** The vowel of the second radical is *a* in most of the transitive, and not a few of the intransitive verbs; e.g. ضَرَبَ *to beat,* كَتَبَ *to write,* قَتَلَ *to kill,* وَهَبَ *to give;* ذَهَبَ *to go away,* رَشَدَ *to go the right way,* جَلَسَ *to sit.*

    38. The vowel *i* in the same position has generally an intransitive signification, *u* invariably so. The distinction between them is, that *i* indicates a temporary state or condition, or a merely accidental quality in persons or things; whilst *u* indicates a permanent state, or a

C naturally inherent quality. E.g. فَرِحَ or جَذِلَ *to be glad,* حَزِنَ *to be sorry,* أَشِرَ or بَطِرَ *to be proud and insolent,* أَدِمَ *to become whitish,* شَهِبَ *to become gray,* سَلِمَ *to be safe and sound,* مَرِضَ *to be sick,* كَبِرَ *to become old,* عَمِىَ *to be blind;* but حَسُنَ *to be beautiful,* قَبُحَ *to be ugly,* ثَقُلَ *to be heavy,* شَرُفَ *to be high* or *noble*,* سَفُلَ *to be low or mean,* كَبُرَ *to be large,* صَغُرَ *to be small.*

D   REM. *a.* Many verbs of the form فَعِلَ are transitive according to our way of thinking, and therefore govern the accusative, e.g. عَلِمَ *to know* (scire), حَسِبَ *to think,* رَحِمَ *to pity* or *have mercy upon,* سَمِعَ *to hear.*

---

* [Or, *to become noble,* for the form with *u* of the second radical often means *to become what one was not before,* Kāmil, p. 415.—De G.]

Rem. *b.* The same three forms occur in Hebrew and Aramaic, A though the distinction is in these languages no longer so clearly marked. [See *Comp. Gr.* p. 165 *seq.*]

39. The *second* form (فَعَّلَ) is formed from the first (فَعَلَ) by doubling the second radical.

40. The signification agrees with the form in respect of being intensive (لِلْمُبَالَغَةِ) or extensive (لِلتَّكْثِيرِ). Originally it implies that an act is done with *great violence* (intensive), or during a *long time* (temporally extensive), or to or by a *number* of individuals (numerically extensive), or *repeatedly* (iterative or frequentative). E.g. ضَرَبَ *to* B *beat,* ضَرَّبَ *to beat violently ;* كَسَرَ *to break,* كَسَّرَ *to break in pieces ;* قَطَعَ *to cut,* قَطَّعَ *to cut in pieces ;* فَرَقَ *to separate,* فَرَّقَ *to disperse ;* قَتَلَ *to kill,* قَتَّلَ *to massacre ;* جَالَ *or* طَافَ *to go round,* جَوَّلَ *or* طَوَّفَ *to go round much* or *often ;* بَكَى *to weep,* بَكَّى *to weep much ;* مَوَّتَ ٱلْمَالُ *the cattle died off rapidly* or *in great numbers* (مَاتَ *to die*) ; بَرَكَ *the camel kneeled down,* بَرَّكَ ٱلنَّعَمُ *the (whole drove of) camels kneeled down.*

41. From this original intensive meaning arises the more usual C causative or *factitive* signification. Verbs that are *intransitive* in the first form become *transitive* in the second ; as فَرِحَ *to be glad,* فَرَّحَ *to gladden ;* ضَعُفَ *to be weak,* ضَعَّفَ *to weaken.* Those that are *transitive* in the first become *doubly transitive* or *causative* in the second ; as عَلِمَ *to know,* عَلَّمَ *to teach ;* كَتَبَ *to write,* كَتَّبَ *to teach to write ;* حَمَلَ *to carry,* حَمَّلَ *to make carry.*

Rem. *a.* The causative or factitive signification is common to D the second and fourth forms, the apparent difference being that it is original in the latter, but derived in the former.

Rem. *b.* The second form is often rather *declarative* or *estimative* than factitive in the strict sense of the term ; as كَذَبَ *to lie,* كَذَّبَ *to think* or *call one a liar ;* صَدَقَ *to tell the truth,* صَدَّقَ *to think that one tells the truth, to believe him.*

A   REM. *c.* The second form is frequently *denominative,* and expresses with various modifications the *making* or *doing of,* or *being occupied with,* the thing expressed by the noun from which it is derived ; e.g. خَيَّمَ *to pitch a tent* (خَيْمَةٌ), *to dwell* in a place, جَيَّشَ *to collect an army* (جَيْشٌ), رَخَّمَ *to pave with marble* (رُخَامٌ), قَوَّسَ *to become bent like a bow* (قَوْس), مَرَّضَ *to nurse the sick* (مَرِيض), جَلَّدَ *to skin* an animal, *to bind* a book (جِلْدٌ *the skin,* compare our " to stone fruit " and " to stone a person "), قَرَّدَ *to clean an animal of ticks* (قُرَادٌ), قَذَّى *to take a mote* (قَذًى) *out of the eye.* Compare in

B   Hebrew רִשֵּׁן, זִנֵּב, יִלֵּד, סִקֵּל, etc. Similarly, جَدَّعَهُ *he said to him* جَدْعًا لَكَ (*may thy nose,* or the like, *be cut off*), حَيَّاهُ *he said to him* حَيَّاكَ ٱللّٰه (*may God prolong thy life*), سَلَّمَ عَلَيْهِ *he said to him* سَلَامٌ عَلَيْكَ (*peace be upon thee*), كَبَّرَ *he shouted the Moslem war-cry,* مَنْ دَخَلَ ظَفَارِ حَمَّرَ (ٱللّٰه أَكْبَرُ), *he who enters* (the city of) *Ẓafār, must speak Ḥimyaritic* (the language of Ḥimyar, حِمْيَرُ). Sometimes, like the fourth form, it expresses movement towards a place ; as وَجَّهَ *to set out in any direction* (وَجْهُ), شَرَّقَ *to go to the east* (ٱلشَّرْقُ), غَرَّبَ *to go to the west* (ٱلْغَرْبُ).

C   REM. *d.* فَعَّلَ corresponds in form, as well as in signification, to the Heb. קִטֵּל and Aram. קַטֵּל, ܩܰܛܶܠ.—[See *Comp. Gr.* p. 198 *seq.*]

42. The *third* form (فَاعَلَ) is formed from the first (فَعَلَ) by lengthening the vowel-sound *ă* after the first radical, as is indicated by the *ĕlif productionis.*

43. It modifies the signification of the ground-form in the following ways.

D   (*a*) When فَعَلَ denotes an act that immediately affects an object (direct object or accusative), فَاعَلَ expresses *the effort* or *attempt to perform that act upon the object,* in which case the idea of *reciprocity* (ٱلْمُشَارَكَةُ) is added when the effort is necessarily or accidentally a mutual one. E. g. قَتَلَهُ *he killed him,* قَاتَلَهُ *he* (*tried to kill him* or) *fought with him* ; جَلَدَهُ *he beat him,* جَالَدَهُ *he fought with him* ; صَرَعَهُ

he threw him down, صَارَعَهُ he wrestled with him ; غَلَبَهُ he overcame him, A غَالَبَهُ he tried to overcome him ; سَبَقَهُ he outran him, سَابَقَهُ he ran a race with him ; شَرَفَهُ he surpassed him in rank, شَارَفَهُ he strove to do so ; فَخَرَهُ he surpassed him in glory, فَاخَرَهُ he strove to do so, he vied with him in rank and glory ; شَعَرَهُ he excelled him in composing poetry, شَاعَرَهُ he competed with him in doing so ; خَصَمَهُ he got the better of him in a lawsuit, خَاصَمَهُ he went to law with him.

(*b*) When the first or fourth form denotes an act, the relation B of which to an object is expressed by means of a preposition (indirect object), the third form *converts that indirect object into the immediate* or *direct object of the act* (accusative). The idea of *reciprocity* is here, as in the former case, more or less distinctly implied. E. g. كَتَبَ إِلَى ٱلْمَلِكِ he wrote (a letter) to the king, كَاتَبَ ٱلْمَلِكَ he wrote to the king, corresponded with him ; قَالَ لَهُ he said to him (something), قَاوَلَهُ he conversed with him ; أَرْسَلَ إِلَى ٱلسُّلْطَانِ he sent (a message) to the sultan, C رَاسَلَ ٱلسُّلْطَانَ do.; جَلَسَ عِنْدَ أَمِيرِ ٱلْمُؤْمِنِينَ he sat beside the Commander of the Faithful, جَالَسَ أَمِيرَ ٱلْمُؤْمِنِينَ do.; وَقَعَ بِهِ he fell upon him, attacked him, وَاقَعَهُ do.; أَشَارَ عَلَيْهِ he advised him, شَاوَرَهُ he consulted with him.

(*c*) When فَعَلَ denotes a quality or state, فَاعَلَ indicates *that one person makes use of that quality towards another and affects him thereby*, or *brings him into that state*. E. g. خَشُنَ to be rough or D harsh, خَاشَنَهُ he treated him harshly ; حَسُنَ to be good or kind, حَاسَنَهُ he treated him kindly ; لَانَ to be soft or gentle, لَايَنَهُ he treated him gently ; قَسَا to be hard, قَاسَاهُ he hardened himself against him or it ; نَعَمَ or نَعِمَ to lead a comfortable life, نَاعَمَهُ he procured him the means of doing so.

REM. *a.* The third form is sometimes *denominative*, but the ideas of effort and reciprocity are always more or less clearly implied. E.g. ضَاعَفَ to double, from ضِعْفٌ the like or equal ; طَارَقَ

A   *to double,* fold (طَرَقَ) *on* fold; عَافَاكَ ٱللّٰه *may God keep thee safe and well,* from عَافِيَة *robust health;* سَافَرَ *to go on a journey* (سَفَر).

REM. *b.* فَاعَلَ corresponds in form and signification to the Heb. קוֹטֵל (Arab. *ā* = Heb. *ō*); see *Comp. Gr.* p. 202 *seq.*

[REM. *c.* In a few verbs the third form is used in the sense of the fourth. Thus داخل, ساقط (*Gl. Geog.* s.v. دخل). Zamahšarī, *Fāik,* i. 197 cites باعده, جانأه, عالاه for أبعده *etc.* Also أبلغ = بالغ,

B   *Aghānī* xiii. 52.—De G.]

44. The *fourth* form (أَفْعَلَ) is formed by prefixing to the root the syllable اِ, in consequence of which the first radical loses its vowel.

45. Its signification is *factitive* or *causative* (لِلتَّعْدِيَة). If the verb is intransitive in the first form, it becomes transitive in the fourth; if transitive in the first, it becomes doubly transitive in the fourth. E.g. جَرَى *to run,* أَجْرَى *to make run;* جَلَسَ *to sit down,*

C   أَجْلَسَ *to bid one sit down;* أَكَلَ ٱلْخُبْزَ *he ate bread,* آكَلَهُ ٱلْخُبْزَ *he gave him bread to eat;* رَأَى ٱلشَّىْءَ *he saw the thing,* أَرَاهُ ٱلشَّىْءَ *he shewed him the thing.*

REM. *a.* When both the second and fourth forms of a verb are causative (§ 41, rem. *a*), they have in some cases different significations, in others the same. E.g. عَلِمَ *to know,* عَلَّمَ *to teach,* أَعْلَمَ *to inform one of a thing;* نَجَا *to escape,* نَجَّى *and* أَنْجَى *to set at liberty, to let go.*

D   REM. *b.* The fourth form is sometimes *declarative* or *estimative,* like the second; as أَبْخَلَهُ *he thought him,* or *found him to be, niggardly;* أَجْبَنَهُ *he thought him,* or *found him to be, cowardly;* أَحْمَدَهُ *he found him,* or *it, to be praiseworthy* or *commendable;* أَحْيَى ٱلْأَرْضَ *he found the district abounding in fresh herbage.*

REM. *c.* The fourth form comprises a great number of *denominatives,* many of which are apparently intransitive, because the Arabs often regard as an *act* what we view as a *state.* Such verbs combine with the idea of the noun, from which they are derived, that of a transitive verb, of which it is the direct object. E.g. أَبْقَلَ

to produce herbage (بَقْلَ), أَوْرَقَ *to put out leaves* (وَرَقَ), أَثْمَرَ *to bear* A
fruit (ثَمَر), أَمْطَرَ *to give or yield rain* (مَطَر); أَنْجَبَ *to beget a noble
son,* أَذْكَرَتْ, آنَثَتْ, *she bore a male or a female child,* أَتْأَمَتْ *she
bore twins* (compare "to flower," "to seed," "to calve," "to lamb");
أَبْلَغَ *to speak eloquently,* أَفْصَحَ *to speak with purity and correctness,*
أَبْلَى *to give a proof* (بَلَاءٌ) *of his prowess in battle;* أَسَاءَ, أَحْسَنَ,
to act well or ill, أَذْنَبَ *to commit a sin,* أَخْطَأَ *to commit a blunder,
fault or error,* أَصَابَ *to do or say what is right;* أَبْطَأَ *to be slow or* B
tardy; أَسْرَعَ *to make haste;* أَعْنَقَ *to run with outstretched neck;*
أَسَنَّ *to become fullgrown* (from سِنٌّ *a tooth*); أَقَامَ *to dwell or remain
in a place.*—Another class of these denominatives indicates movement towards a place (compare "to make for a place"), the entering
upon a period of time (being, doing, or suffering something therein),
getting into a state or condition, acquiring a quality, obtaining or
having something, or becoming something, of a certain kind*.
E. g. أَقْبَلَ *to advance,* أَدْبَرَ *to retire* ("reculer"), أَقْدَمَ *to go on boldly* C
(compare, in Hebrew, הֵימִין, *to go to the right,* and הִשְׂמְאִיל, *to
go to the left);* أَشْأَمَ *to go to Syria* (الشَّأْمُ), أَيْمَنَ *to go to êl-Yêmèn*
(الْيَمَنُ), أَنْجَدَ *to go to êl-Nêǧd* (النَّجْدُ), أَتْهَمَ *to go to Tihāma* (تِهَامَةُ),
أَعْرَقَ *to go to êl-'Irāk* (الْعِرَاقُ), أَحْرَمَ *to enter the ḥaram or sacred
territory;* أَمْسَى, أَظْهَرَ, أَصْبَحَ, *to enter upon the time of morning*
(الصَّبَاحُ), *mid-day* (الظُّهْرُ), *or evening* (الْمَسَاءُ); أَشْتَى, أَصَافَ, *to enter
upon the summer* (الصَّيْفُ) *or winter* (الشِّتَاءُ); أَجْمَلَ *to have many* D
camels, أَسْبَعَ *to abound in beasts of prey or to have one's flocks
devoured by them,* أَضَبَّ *to abound in lizards* (ضَبٌّ) *or to be foggy*
(ضَبَابٌ); أَقْفَرَ *to become desert,* أَجْدَبَ *to suffer from drought* (of
people) *or to be dry* (of a season), أَفْلَسَ *to become penniless* (to be

---

* [Hence in a few cases IV. serves (instead of VII. or VIII.)
as the مُطَاوِع of I. Thus كَبَّهُ *he threw him on his face,* أَكَبَّ *he fell on
his face,* حَجَمَهُ *he held him back,* أَحْجَمَ *he drew back, he retired.*]

A   *reduced to the last farthing*, (فَلِسَ),أَعْدَمَ،أَعْوَزَ, *to be reduced to utter want ;* أَغْيَمَ *to become cloudy*, أَخْلَقَ *to become worn out* (of a garment) ; أَشْكَلَ *to become dubious* or *confused ;* أَبَانَ *to become plain or clear ;* أَمْكَنَ *to become possible.*—Another shade of meaning (اَلسَّلْبُ, *deprivation*) may be exemplified by such words as أَخْفَرَ, *to break one's compact with a person ;* أَشْكَى *to remove one's cause of complaint ;* أَعْجَمَ ٱلْكِتَابَ *he pointed* (*the text of*) *the book*, literally,

B   *took away its* عُجْمَة, *obscurity* or *want of clearness.*

REM. *d.* أَفْعَلَ corresponds in form and signification to the Heb. הִקְטִיל, Phœn. יקטל (*iḳṭil*), Aram. אַקְטֵל, أَصْهَلَا. See *Comp. Gr.* p. 204 *seq.* The Hebrew, it will be observed, has ה as the prefix, instead of the feebler Arabic and Aramaic א. Some traces of the *h* are still discoverable in Arabic ; as هَرَاحَ for أَرَاحَ *to give rest to, to let rest ;* هَرَادَ for أَرَادَ *to wish ;* هَرَاقَ for أَرَاقَ *to pour out*

C   (הֵרִיק) : هَنَارَ for أَنَارَ *to mark a cloth ;* هَاتِ *give*, for آتِ (rad. أَتَى, אָתָה, *to come*) ; هَيْمَنَ = הֶאֱמִין *to believe.* Forms like هَرَاقَ are treated in Arabic as quadriliterals (see §§ 67, 69, and 118), e.g. imperf. يُهَرِيقُ or يُهَرِّيقُ،يُهَيْمِنُ, nom. patient. مُهَرَاقٌ or مُهَيْمِنٌ.

46. The *fifth* form (تَفَعَّلَ) is formed from the second (فَعَّلَ) by prefixing the syllable تَ.

D   **47.** This form annexes to the significations of the second the *reflexive* force of the syllable تَ ; it is the مُطَاوِعٌ of the second form, that is to say, it expresses the state into which the object of the action denoted by the second form is brought by that action, as its effect or result. In English it must often be rendered by the *passive.* E.g. تَكَسَّرَ *to be broken in pieces*, تَفَرَّقَ *to be dispersed*, تَقَطَّعَ *to be cut in pieces*, تَضَرَّبَ *to be moved* or *agitated ;* تَخَوَّفَ *to be afraid* (خَوَّفَ *to terrify*), تَقَلَّدَ سَيْفًا *he girt on his sword* (قَلَّدَهُ سَيْفًا *he girt a sword upon him*—another person) ; تَكَبَّرَ،تَعَظَّمَ, *to be proud ;* تَقَيَّسَ،تَنَزَّرَ, *to side*

with *Ḳais* or *Nizār*, تَزَرَّقَ, تَشَيَّعَ, to *adopt the tenets of the* '*Azārika* A
(اَلْأَزَارِقَةُ) or *of the* Šī'a (اَلشِّيعَةُ), تَعَرَّبَ to *call oneself an Arab*,
تَهَوَّدَ to *become a Jew* (يَهُودِيُّ), تَمَجَّسَ to *become a fire-worshipper*
(مَجُوسِيُّ), تَنَصَّرَ to *become a Christian* (نَصْرَانِيُّ), تَنَبَّأَ to *give oneself out*
as a prophet (نَبِيٌّ), تَأَسَّدَ to *become as bold* or *fierce as a lion* (أَسَدٌ),
تَنَمَّرَ to *become as savage as a leopard* (نَمِرٌ); تَحَلَّمَ to *try to acquire*,
or to *affect, clemency*, تَشَجَّعَ, تَمَرَّأَ, to *affect courage* or *manliness*, B
تَصَبَّرَ to *constrain oneself to endure with patience;* تَأَثَّمَ, تَحَرَّجَ, تَحَوَّبَ,
تَحَنَّثَ, to *abstain from*, or *avoid*, *sin* or *crime*, تَذَمَّمَ to *avoid blame*.

Rem. *a*. The idea of intensiveness may be traced even in cases
where it seems, at first sight, to have wholly disappeared, leaving
the fifth form apparently identical in meaning with the eighth.
Thus إِفْتَرَقَ ٱلنَّاسُ and تَفَرَّقَ ٱلنَّاسُ are both translated *the people*
dispersed, but إِفْتَرَقَ expresses the mere separation, تَفَرَّقَ the separa- C
tion into a great many groups or in various directions.

Rem. *b*. The idea of reflexiveness is often not very prominent,
especially in such verbs as govern an accusative; e. g. تَتَبَّعَ *to*
pursue step by step (literally, *to make oneself*, or *turn oneself into*, *a*
pursuer of something), تَطَلَّبَ to *seek earnestly*, تَعَرَّفَ to *try to*
understand, تَبَيَّنَ to *examine* or *study* a thing *carefully*, so that it
may be quite clear, تَيَقَّنَ, تَحَقَّقَ, to *ascertain* a thing *for certain*,
تَقَصَّى to *investigate thoroughly*, تَشَمَّمَ to *smell leisurely and carefully*,
تَبَصَّرَ to *look at long* or *repeatedly*, to *examine* or *study*, تَسَمَّعَ to *hear* D
or *listen to*, تَكَلَّمَ to *speak*, تَوَلَّى to *have charge of*, to *discharge the*
duties of, تَجَرَّعَ to *swallow by mouthfuls*, تَحَسَّى to *sip* or *sup*,
تَفَوَّقَ to *milk* or *suck at intervals*, تَعَرَّقَ to *gnaw*, تَأَبَّطَ to *put* or
take under one's arm, تَوَسَّدَ to *put under one's head as a pillow*,
تَدَيَّرَ to *take as an abode*, تَبَنَّى to *adopt as a son**.

---

* [In some cases the difference between II. and V. entirely disappears.
Thus for وَجَّهَ, قَوَّسَ (§ 41, rem. *c*) we may substitute تَوَجَّهَ, تَقَوَّسَ
without change of sense.]

A   REM. *c.* The above examples show that the subject of the fifth form is sometimes the direct object of the act (accusative), sometimes the indirect object (dative).

48. Out of the original reflexive signification arises a second, which is even more common, namely the *effective.* It differs from the passive in this—that the *passive* indicates that a person is the object of, or experiences the effect of, the action of *another;* whereas the *effective* implies that an act is done to a person, or a state produced in him, whether it be caused by *another* or by *himself.* E. g.

B عَلِمَ *to know,* عَلَّمَ *to teach,* تَعَلَّمَ *to become learned, to learn,* quite different from عُلِّمَ (passive of عَلَّمَ) *to be taught.* We can say عُلِّمَ وَلَمْ يَتَعَلَّمْ, *he was taught (received instruction), but did not learn (become learned)*.* Again, بَانَ *to be separate, distinct, clear,* بَيَّنَ *to make clear, explain,* تَبَيَّنَ *to appear clear* or *certain;* تَحَقَّقَ *to become, or prove to be, the reality* or *fact.*

REM. *a.* Such of these verbs as govern an accusative admit not C only of an impersonal, but also of a personal passive; e. g. تَعَلَّمَ الطِّبَّ *he learned the art of medicine,* تُعُلِّمَ الطِّبُّ *the art of medicine was learned.*

REM. *b.* تَفَعَّلَ sometimes assumes the form اِتَّفَعَّلَ (§ 111), whence we see its identity with the Heb. הִתְקַטֵּל or הִתְקַטַּל and the Aram. אִתְקְטֵל, إِصْطَ (see § 41, rem. *d*).

D ʻ**49.** The *sixth* form (تَفَاعَلَ) is formed from the third (فَاعَلَ), likewise by prefixing the syllable تَ.

50. It is the مُطَاوِعٌ (see § 47) of the third form, as بَاعَدْتُهُ فَتَبَاعَدَ, *I kept him aloof and he kept (or staid) aloof.*—The idea of effort and attempt, which is transitive in the third form, becomes *reflexive* in the sixth ; e. g. تَرَامَى *to throw oneself down* at full length, تَغَافَلَ *to be off one's guard, to neglect* a thing, تَبَارَكَ بِالشَّيْءِ *to draw a good omen from*

---

* Using a Scoticism, we might say, *he was learned* (= *taught*), but *did not learn.*

the thing, تَمَاوَتَ to pretend to be dead, تَعَامَى to pretend to be blind, A تَخَازَرَ to pretend to squint, تَبَاكَى to pretend to cry, تَمَارَضَ to feign sickness, تَجَاهَلَ to feign ignorance, تَخَادَعَ to pretend to be deceived.

Further, the possible reciprocity (اَلْمُشَارَكَةُ) of the third form becomes a *necessary reciprocity*, inasmuch as the sixth form includes the object of the third among the subjects that exercise an influence upon one another; e.g. قَاتَلَهُ *he fought with him,* تَقَاتَلَا *the two fought with one another;* كَالَمَهُ *the two spoke to him,* تَكَالَمُوا *they* (the three) B *conversed together;* جَاذَبَهُ ٱلثَّوْبَ *he tried to pull away the garment from him,* تَجَاذَبَا ٱلثَّوْبَ *the two pulled the garment to and fro between them;* نَازَعَهُمُ ٱلْحَدِيثَ *he conversed or argued with them,* تَنَازَعُوا ٱلْحَدِيثَ *they conversed together or argued with one another;* نَاسَاهُ ٱلْبَغْضَآءَ *he tried to make him forget the hatred between them,* تَنَاسَيَا ٱلْبَغْضَآءَ *the two forgot their mutual hatred;* whence in the passive, تُجُوذِبَ ٱلثَّوْبُ, تُنُوسِيَتِ ٱلْبَغْضَآءُ, and تُنُوزِعَ ٱلْحَدِيثُ.   C

REM. *a.* When used in speaking of God, the assertory (not optative) perfects تَبَارَكَ and تَعَالَى are examples of the reflexive signification of this form: تَبَارَكَ ٱللّٰهُ *God has made Himself (is become of and through Himself) blessed, or perfect, above all;* تَعَالَى ٱللّٰهُ *God has made Himself uplifted, or exalted, above all;* قَالَ ٱللّٰهُ تَبَارَكَ وَتَعَالَى *God (blessed and exalted is He above all) has said* [cf. vol. ii. § 1 f. rem.]. Somewhat similarly, تَعَاظَمَهُ ٱلْأَمْرُ D *the thing made itself (became or was) too great, or difficult, for him;* هُوَ أَمْرٌ لَا يَتَعَاظَمُهُ شَىْءٌ *it is a matter than which nothing makes itself greater (or more important), with which nothing can vie in importance.*

REM. *b.* As the reciprocal signification requires at least two subjects, the singular of the sixth form is in this case always collective; e.g. تَسَامَعَ بِه ٱلنَّاسُ *the people heard of it from one another,* تَتَابَعَتِ ٱلْأَمْطَارُ *the rains followed one another closely,* تَدَارَكَتِ ٱلْأَخْبَارُ *the tidings followed one another rapidly,* تَتَامَّتْ إِلَيْهِ

A   قُرَيْش (*the tribe of*) *Ḳoreïs came to him, all of them, following one another.*

> REM. *c.* The idea of reciprocity may be confined to the parts of one and the same thing; e.g. تَمَاسَكَ "partes habuit inter se cohaerentes," *to be of compact and firm build;* تَعَاوَنَتِ ٱلْمَرْأَةُ *the woman became middle-aged and corpulent* (each part of her body, as it were, supporting, and so strengthening, the others); تَدَاعَى ٱلْبِنَآءُ *the building cracked and threatened to fall* (as if its parts

B   called on one another to do so; compare تَدَاعَى عَلَيْهِ ٱلْعَدُوُّ *the enemy advanced against him from every side,* تَدَاعَتِ ٱلسَّحَابَةُ بِٱلْبَرْقِ وَٱلرَّعْدِ *the cloud lightened and thundered from every quarter).* [Hence this form is appropriate to actions that take place bit by bit, or by successive (and painful) efforts, as تَسَاقَطَ *to fall piece by piece,* تَحَامَلَ *to carry oneself with difficulty* (فِى ٱلْمَشْيِ, *in walking*).]

C   REM. *d.* تَفَاعَلَ sometimes assumes the form ٱتْفَاعَلَ (§ 111), and is consequently identical with the Heb. הִתְקוֹטֵל (see § 43, rem. *b*).

51. The *seventh* form (ٱنْفَعَلَ) is formed from the first (فَعَلَ) by prefixing a ن, before which is added a prosthetic ا to facilitate the pronunciation (see § 26).

> REM. For the cases in which this ا becomes آ, and why, see §§ 18 and 19, *c*, with rem. *c*; and as to the orthography ا instead of إ, § 19, rem. *d*.

D   **52.** The seventh form has also originally, as مُطَاوِع of the first, a *middle* or *reflexive* signification. It must be remarked, however, (*a*) that the reflexive pronoun contained in it is never the indirect object (dative), to which may be added another direct object (accusative), but always the direct object itself; and (*b*) that it never assumes the reciprocal signification. By these two points the seventh form is distinguished from the eighth, and approaches more nearly

---

* [See *Gl. Geog. s.v.* حمل, *Ḥamāsa* p. 20 first vs. and comm.— De G.]

to a passive. At the same time, the *effective* signification is often A developed in it out of the reflexive. E. g. اِنْشَقَّ *to open* (of a flower), lit. *to split itself;* اِنْكَسَرَ *to break* (intrans.), *to be broken;* اِنْقَطَعَ *to be cut off, to be ended, to end;* اِنْكَشَفَ *to be uncovered, to be made manifest, to appear;* اِنْحَطَمَ *to become broken, to break into pieces;* اِنْقَالَ *to be uttered* or *spoken.*

53. Sometimes the seventh form implies that a person allows B an act to be done in reference to him, or an effect to be produced upon him; e.g. اِنْهَزَمَ *to let oneself be put to flight, to flee;* اِنْقَادَ *to let oneself be led, to be docile* or *submissive;* اِنْخَدَعَ *to let oneself be deceived;* اِنْجَرَّ *to let oneself be drawn* or *dragged.*

REM. *a.* Hence it is clear that such words as اِنْحَمَقَ, from حَمُقَ, *to be stupid* or *foolish;* اِنْعَدَمَ *to be non-existent* or *missing, not to be found,* from عَدِمَ *not to have;* اِنْهَوَى, from هَوَى *to sink* C *down, to fall;* اِنْعَادَ *to be repeated,* from عَادَ *to return;* اِنْضَاقَ *to be in straits* or *distress,* from ضَاقَ *to be narrow;* are incorrectly formed, though in actual use, especially in more recent times.

REM. *b.* Sometimes, particularly in modern Arabic, the seventh form serves as the مُطَاوِعٌ of the fourth; e.g. اِنْغَلَقَ *to be bolted,* from أَغْلَقَ *to bolt;* اِنْطَفَأَ *to be extinguished,* from أَطْفَأَ *to extinguish;* اِنْصَلَحَ *to be put to rights,* from أَصْلَحَ *to put to rights.* [Similarly D اِنْزَعَحَ, اِنْطَلَقَ, اِنْضَجَعَ, the last in a tradition, and so ancient, *Faik* i. 63.—De G.]

REM. *c.* اِنْفَعَلَ corresponds to the Heb. נִקְטַל; see *Comp. Gr.* p. 215 *seq.*

54. The eighth form (اِفْتَعَلَ) is formed from the first (فَعَلَ) by inserting the syllable تَ between the first and second radicals. The first radical in consequence loses its vowel, and it becomes necessary to prefix the prosthetic ! (§ 51, rem.).

A   Rem. One would expect تـ to be placed *before* the first radical, as in the fifth and sixth forms, and in the Aramaic reflexive اֶצְטֲבַּע. [For a possible explanation of the actual form see *Comp. Gr.* p. 208.]

55. The eighth form is properly the *reflexive* or *middle voice* (مُطَاوِعٌ) of the first. The reflex object is either (*a*) the direct object or accusative, as فَرَقَ *to divide*, اِفْتَرَقَ *to go asunder, to part;* عَرَضَ *to place (something) before one,* اِعْتَرَضَ *to put oneself in the way, to oppose;*

B ضَرَبَ *to beat,* اِضْطَرَبَ *to move oneself to and fro, to be agitated* (compare the French *battre* and *se débattre*); or (*b*) the indirect object or dative, implying *for oneself, for one's own advantage,* as فَرَسَ *to tear a prey in pieces,* اِفْتَرَسَ *do.;* لَمَسَ *to touch,* اِلْتَمَسَ *to feel about for a thing, to seek for it;* كَسَبَ and اِكْتَسَبَ *to earn one's living;* حَطَبَ and اِحْتَطَبَ *to collect firewood;* كَالَ and اِكْتَالَ *to measure corn;* شَوَى and اِشْتَوَى *to roast* meat.

C   **56.** Out of the reflexive arises the *reciprocal* signification, which is common to this form with the sixth; as اِقْتَتَلَ ٱلنَّاسُ *the people fought with one another,* = تَقَاتَلَ ٱلنَّاسُ ; اِخْتَصَمَا *the two disputed with one another,* = تَخَاصَمَا ; اِسْتَبَقَا *the two tried to outrun one another,* = تَسَابَقَا ; اِجْتَوَرُوا *they were neighbours,* = تَجَاوَرُوا ; اِلْتَقَوْا *they met one another,* = تَلَاقَوْا.

D   **57.** Occasionally the original reflexive meaning passes into the *passive*, especially in verbs which have not got the seventh form (see § 113); as اِيتَفَكَ *to be overturned* (from أَفَكَ), اِرْتَدَعَ *to be turned back,* اِنْتَصَرَ *to be helped* (by God), *to be victorious;* اِمْتَلَأَ *to be full.*

     Rem. In not a few verbs the first and eighth forms agree, like the Greek active and middle voices, so closely in their signification, that they may be translated by the same word; e.g. قَصَّ and اِقْتَصَّ, *to follow one's track, to relate;* قَفَا and اِقْتَفَى, *to follow;* خَطَفَ and اِخْتَطَفَ, *to snatch away, to carry off by force.*

58. The *ninth* form (اِفْعَلَّ) is formed from the first (فَعَلَ) by A doubling the third radical; the eleventh (اِفْعَالَّ) from the ninth by lengthening the fètḥa of the second syllable.

Rem. As the third radical, when doubled, draws the accent upon the penult, the first radical, being more rapidly pronounced, loses its vowel, and therefore requires the prosthetic ا (see § 51, rem.).

59. Neither of these forms is very common, and the eleventh is the rarer of the two. They serve chiefly to express *colours* and B *defects*, these being qualities that cling very firmly to persons and things; and hence the doubling of the third radical, to show that the proper signification of both is *intensiveness* (اَلْمُبَالَغَةُ). E. g. اِصْفَرَّ and اِصْفَارَّ *to be yellow;* اِسْوَدَّ and اِسْوَادَّ *to be black;* اِبْيَضَّ and اِبْيَاضَّ *to be white;* اِيرَاقَّ (from وَرَقَ) *to become purple* (of a grape); اِعْوَجَّ and اِعْوَاجَّ *to be crooked;* اِضْجَمَّ and اِضْجَامَّ *to be wrymouthed* or *wry-necked;* اِحْوَلَّ *to squint,* اِحْوَالَّ *to become verdant;* اِزْوَرَّ and اِزْوَارَّ *to turn away* or *retire from;* اِرْبَدَّ *to be ash-coloured, to be stern* or *gloomy;* C اِرْبَتَّ or اِرْبَاتَّ *to be scattered* or *disordered;* اِرْغَادَّ *to become commingled, confused,* or *languid;* اِرْفَضَّ *to be dispersed, to drop* or *flow* (of tears), اِرْقَدَّ *to run quickly, to hasten;* اِشْعَانَّ *to be dishevelled* (of hair); اِبْهَارَّ ٱللَّيْلُ, *the night reached its middle point.*

Rem. *a.* If the third radical of the root is و or ى, the ninth and eleventh forms take the shape اِفْعَلَلَّ and اِفْعَالَلَّ; as اِجْذَوَى (for اِجْذَوَّى, see § 167, 2, *a*) *to stand* or *rest on the tips of the toes,* D اِرْعَوَى and اِحْوَاوَى *to be blackish brown* or *blackish green,* اِحْوَوَى *to refrain* or *abstain.*

Rem. *b.* According to some grammarians, the distinction between the ninth and eleventh forms is, that the ninth indicates permanent colours or qualities, the eleventh those that are transitory or mutable; as جَعَلَ يَحْمَارُّ تَارَةً وَيَصْفَارُّ أُخْرَى, *it began to become red at one time and yellow at another.* [Others hold that XI. indicates a

A higher degree of the quality than IX. : so most European grammarians, and the former editions of this work ; but this view was
ultimately abandoned by the author.   The better view seems to be
that the two forms are indistinguishable in sense : see Ḥafāġī's
comm. on the *Durrat al-ġawwāṣ* (Const. A. H. 1299) p. 50 *seq.*]

60. The *tenth* form (اِسْتَفْعَلَ) is formed by prefixing the letters
سْت to the first (فَعَلَ).   The prosthetic ا is necessary, according to
§ 26 (compare § 51, rem.), and the fetḥa of the first radical is thrown
B back upon the ت of اِسْت.

61. The tenth form converts the factitive signification of the
fourth into the *reflexive* or *middle*.   E. g. أَسْلَمَ to *give up, deliver over*,
اِسْتَسْلَمَ to *give oneself up* ; أَوْحَشَ to *grieve* or *distress*, اِسْتَوْحَشَ to
be grieved or *sorry* ; أَعَدَّ to *make ready, prepare, equip*, اِسْتَعَدَّ to *get
oneself ready, to be ready* ; أَخْلَصَ to *yield up* (*something*) *wholly*,
اِسْتَخْلَصَ to *claim* (*something*) *for oneself, to take entire possession*
(*of it*) ; أَحْيَا to *bring to life, to preserve alive*, اِسْتَحْيَا to *preserve alive*
C *for one's own advantage* ; اِسْتَجَابَ دُعَاءَهُ *He* (God) *answered*, or
accepted, his prayer, اِسْتَجَابَ لَهُ *he complied with his desire*, or *obeyed
him*, in doing something.

62. The tenth form often indicates that a person thinks that
a certain thing possesses, in reference to himself or for his benefit,
the quality expressed by the first form.   E. g. حَلَّ to *be lawful*,
اِسْتَحَلَّ *he thought that it was lawful* (for himself to do) ; وَجَبَ
to *be necessary*, اِسْتَوْجَبَ *he thought it was necessary* (for him) ;
D اِسْتَحْسَنَ to *think him*, or *it, good* or *beautiful* ; اِسْتَجَادَ to *think
it good* or *excellent* ; اِسْتَخَفَّ to *think it light, to think lightly of*,
or *despise, one* ; اِسْتَثْقَلَ to *find it heavy, oppressive* or *troublesome,
to think one a bore*.

REM.   In this case the factitive is combined with the middle
sense ; for as the fourth form (like the second) is frequently not

strictly factitive, but estimative or declarative (§ 45, rem. *b*), so A also the tenth. Hence اِسْتَوْجَبَ literally means *to make something necessary for oneself, to think it so* or *say it is so ;* but أَوْجَبَ *to make it necessary for others, to think* or *say that it is so.*

63. The tenth form likewise often expresses the *taking, seeking, asking for,* or *demanding,* what is meant by the *first.* E. g. غَفَرَ *to pardon,* اِسْتَغْفَرَ *to ask pardon ;* سَقَى *to give one to drink,* اِسْتَسْقَى *to ask for something to drink, to pray for rain ;* أَذِنَ *to permit,* اِسْتَأْذَنَ *to ask permission ;* غَاثَ *to help,* اِسْتَغَاثَ *to call for help ;* B حَضَرَ *to be present,* اِسْتَحْضَرَ *to require one's presence, to desire that he should be fetched.*

REM. This signification is also a combination of the factitive and middle : *to procure a drink, permission, &c., for oneself.*

64. In many verbs the tenth form has apparently a *neuter* sense, but in such cases a more minute examination shows that it was, at least originally, reflexive. E. g. اِسْتَقَامَ *to stand upright,* lit. *to hold oneself upright ;* اِسْتَكَانَ *to be humble,* lit. *to make oneself* C *humble, to conduct oneself humbly ;* اِسْتَحَقَّ *to be worthy of, to deserve,* lit. *to cause something to be due to oneself as a right* or *desert* (حَقَّ) ; اِسْتَحْيَا *to be ashamed,* lit. *to make oneself ashamed* (حَيِيَ *to be ashamed).*

65. The tenth form is frequently *denominative,* in which case it unites the factitive and reflexive or middle senses. E. g. اِسْتَوْلَى *to make oneself master* (وَلِيٌّ) *of a thing, to take possession of it ;* D اِسْتَخْلَفَ *to appoint one as deputy, successor,* or *caliph* (خَلِيفَةٌ) ; اِسْتَوْزَرَ, *to appoint one as wezīr* (وَزِيرٌ), *governor* (عَامِلٌ), اِسْتَقْضَى, اِسْتَعْمَلَ or *judge* (قَاضٍ).—Further, اِسْتَحْجَرَ *to become like* (lit. *to make itself like*) *stone* (حَجَرٌ) ; اِسْتَتْيَسَتِ ٱلْعَنْزُ *the she-goat became like a he-goat* (تَيْسٌ) ; اِسْتَنْوَقَ ٱلْجَمَلُ *the he-camel became like a she-camel* (نَاقَةٌ) ;

A اِنَّ ٱلْبُغَاثَ بِأَرْضِنَا يَسْتَنْسِرُ the kite in our country becomes a vulture (نَسْرٌ, our geese are all swans).

REM. The tenth form is probably the reflexive of a form سَفْعَلَ, which is not in use, corresponding to the Aram. ܡܣܰܚܠܶܠ, שִׁחְרֵר‎, and its passive אִשְׁתַּחְרֵר‎, ܐܶܣܬܰܚܠܰܠ, which stand in exactly the same relation to one another as the Arabic first and eighth. Perhaps سَلْقَى to throw down flat on the back, سَقْلَبَ to dash to the ground, and سَلْعَفَ to swallow, with one or two more, may be

B regarded as traces of the form سَفْعَلَ, since they are nearly identical in meaning with أَلْقَى, أَقْلَبَ, and أَلْعَفَ (IV. of لَقَى, قَلَبَ, and لعف). If so, سَلَقَ, which has the same signification as سَلْقَى, must be a later triliteral formation.

66. Of the remaining forms of the triliteral verb it may be sufficient to give a few examples, so as to exhibit their mode of formation.—XII. اِجْذَوْذَى to bear oneself erect (جَذَا do.); اِحْدَوْدَبَ to be arched, curved, or humpbacked (حَدِبَ do.); اِحْلَوْلَكَ to be jet

C black (حَلَكَ do.); اِحْلَوْلَى to be sweet (حَلُوَ do.); اِخْشَوْشَنَ to become very rough (خَشُنَ to be rough); اِخْضَوْضَرَ to become blackish brown or blackish green (=اِخْضَرَّ), to become soft or tender (خَضِرَ do.); اِخْضَوْضَلَ to become moist (=اِخْضَلَّ); اِعْرَوْرَى to ride on a horse without a saddle (عَرِىَ to be naked); اِعْشَوْشَبَ to be covered with luxuriant herbage (عَشِبَ); اِعْضَوْضَبَ to be gathered together (عَضَبَ

D to bind); اِغْدَوْدَنَ to be green and rank (of a plant), to be long and thick (of the hair).—XIII. اِخْرَوَّطَ to be long or last long, to go quickly (rad. خرط); اِجْلَوَّذَ to last long (rad. جلذ); اِعْلَوَّذَ to be heavy (عَلِذَ to be hard); اِعْلَوَّطَ to cling or adhere to firmly, to mount a camel (rad. علط).—XIV. اِجْحَنْشَشَ to be big (rad. جحش); اِسْحَنْكَكَ to be dark, to be obscure (rad. سحك); اِحْلَنْكَكَ to be jet black (حَلَكَ do.);

اِعْلَنْتَكَ *to be long and thick* (of the hair, rad. علك) ; اِعْفَنْجَجَ *to go* A *quickly* (rad. عفج) ; اِقْعَنْسَسَ *to have a hump in front* (the reverse of قَعِسَ, اِحْدَوْدَبَ *do.*).—XV. اِعْلَنْدَى *to be stout and strong* (عَلِدَ *to be hard*) ; اِحْبَنْطَى *to be swollen* or *inflated, to be filled with rage* (حَبِطَ *do.*).

Rem. All these forms are habitually intransitive, but there are a few exceptions, as XII. اِعْرَوْرَى ٱلْفَرَسَ *he mounted the horse;* B اِحْلَوْلَاهُ *he found it sweet* (but also اِحْلَوْلَى, *it was sweet*).—XV. عَلْوَتُّهُ = اِسْرَنْدَيْتُهُ Ibn Doraid, *Kit. al-Iṣṭiḳāḳ,* p. 227.

2. *The Quadriliteral Verb and its Forms.*

67. Quadriliteral (رُبَاعِىّ) verbs are formed in the following ways.

(*a*) A biliteral root, expressing a sound or movement, is repeated, to indicate the repetition of that sound or movement. E.g. بَأْبَأَ *to* C *say baba* (*papa*), غَرْغَرَ *to gargle,* وَسْوَسَ *to whisper,* زَلْزَلَ *to shake,* حَمْحَمَ *to neigh,* غَمْغَمَ *to bellow, to shout,* خَشْخَشَ *to make rustle* or *rattle.*

(*b*) A fourth letter, generally a liquid or sibilant, is prefixed or affixed to, or inserted in the middle of, a triliteral verbal form. E.g. شَمْخَرَ *to be proud* (شَمَخَ *to be high*) ; شَمْعَلَ *to be scattered* = شَمَعَ ; جَمْهَرَ *to collect* (compare جَمَّ and جَمَعَ) ; زَحْلَفَ *to roll along* D (زَحَفَ *to advance slowly*), *to drive back* (زَحَلَ *to withdraw, to retire*) ; سَنْبَسَ *to hasten* (perhaps connected with نَبَسَ) ; خَلْبَسَ *to deceive with soft words* = خَلَبَ ; جَلْمَطَ *to shave* the head = جَلَطَ ; زَحْوَلَ *to make retire* (زَحَلَ *to retire*).

(*c*) They are denominatives from nouns of more than three letters, some of them foreign words. E.g. جَوْرَبَ *to put stockings* (جَوْرَبٌ, Pers. كُورَبْ) *on one ;* جَلْبَبَ *to put on one the garment called a* جِلْبَابٌ ; قَلْنَسَ and قَلْسَى *to put on one the cap called a* قَلْنُسْوَةٌ ;

A قَطْرَنَ *to pitch,* from قَطْرَانٌ *pitch ;* تَمَنْطَقَ *to put on a girdle* (مِنْطَقَةٌ);
تَسَرْوَلَ *to put on trousers or drawers* (سَرَاوِيلُ, Pers. شَلْوَارٌ); تَمَدْرَعَ
to wear a مِدْرَعَةٌ *or tunic ;* تَمَنْدَلَ *to wipe one's fingers with a napkin*
(مَنْدِيلٌ *mantile*); تَمَسْكَنَ *to affect lowliness or humility, to abase*
oneself (مِسْكِينٌ *lowly, humble, poor*); تَمَذْهَبَ *to follow a sect* (مَذْهَبٌ);
تَمَعْدَدَ *to assimilate oneself* (in dress, etc.) *to the tribe of Ma'add*
B (مَعَدٌّ; تَلْمَذَ *to become a pupil or disciple* (تِلْمِيذٌ, Heb. תַּלְמִיד);
تَفَلْسَفَ *to philosophize* (from فَيْلَسُوفٌ, φιλόσοφος); بَيْطَرَ *to practise*
the veterinary art or farriery (بَيْطَارٌ *a farrier,* ἱππίατρος).

(*d*) They are combinations of the most prominent syllables or
letters in certain very common formulas. E.g. بَسْمَلَ *to say* بِسْمِ اللّٰه
(*in the name of God*); حَمْدَلَ *to say* اَلْحَمْدُ لِلّٰه (*praise belongs to*
God); حَوْقَلَ and حَوْلَقَ *to say* لَا حَوْلَ وَلَا قُوَّةَ إِلَّا بِاَللّٰه (*there is no*
C *power and no strength save in God*); فَذْلَكَ *to cast up an account,*
saying فَذٰلِكَ كَذَا وَكَذَا *this then is so and so much.*

68. The derived forms of the quadriliteral verb are three in
number.

فَعْلَلَ I.

افْعَلَلَّ IV.   افْعَنْلَلَ III.   تَفَعْلَلَ II.

69. The *first* form of the quadriliterals corresponds in formation
and conjugation to the *second* form of the triliterals, and is both
D transitive and intransitive in signification. E.g. شَمْلَلَ *to gather*
ripe dates, also *to be active or nimble ;* شَمْرَخَ *to pluck unripe dates ;*
دَحْرَجَ *to roll ;* زَهْزَقَ *to laugh much ;* هَرْوَلَ *to run quickly.*

70. The *second* form agrees in formation and signification with
the *fifth* of the triliteral verb. E.g. تَجَلْبَبَ *to put on or wear a*
جِلْبَابٌ; تَدَحْرَجَ *to roll along ;* تَسَلْطَنَ *to make oneself sultan* (سُلْطَانٌ),
to act as if one were sultan, to lord it over another ; تَشَيْطَنَ *to act*
like a devil (شَيْطَانٌ, שָׂטָן).

71. The *third* form of the quadriliteral verb corresponds to A the *seventh* of the triliteral, with this difference, that the characteristic ن is not prefixed, but inserted between the second and third radicals. E.g. اِبْرَنْشَقَ *to open* (of a flower), *to bloom* or *flourish;* اِحْرَنْجَمَ *to be gathered together in a mass* or *crowd;* اِحْوَنْصَلَ *to puff out its crop* (حَوْصَلَة, of a bird); اِسْلَنْطَحَ *to lie on one's face, stretched on the ground;* . اِسْلَنْقَى *to lie on one's back;* اِتْعَنْجَرَ *to flow.*

72. The *fourth* form of the quadriliterals, which answers to B the *ninth* of the triliterals, is intransitive, and expresses an extensively or intensively high degree of an intransitive act, state, or quality. E.g. اِدْلَهَمَّ *to be very dark;* اِشْمَخَرَّ *to be very high* or *proud;* اِضْمَحَلَّ *to vanish away;* اِسْبَطَرَّ *to lie stretched out on one's side;* اِشْمَعَلَّ *to make haste, to be scattered* or *dispersed;* اِبْذَعَرَّ *to be scattered* or *dispersed;* اِقْشَعَرَّ and اِشْمَأَزَّ *to shudder with horror;* اِطْمَأَنَّ *to be at* C *rest* (from طَمْأَنَ *to lean back*); اِحْزَأَلَّ *to rise high;* اِشْرَأَبَّ *to raise the head and stretch out the neck;* اِصْمَأَلَّ *to be very hard.*

3. The Voices.

73. All the verbal forms, both primitive and derivative, have two voices, the *active* and the *passive* ; with the exception of intransitive verbs of the form فَعُلَ (§ 38) and of the 9th, 11th, 12th, 13th, D 14th, and 15th forms (cf. § 66, rem.) as well as of those verbs of the forms فَعِلَ and فَعَلَ, which designate not an act (transitive or intransitive) but a state or condition (being or becoming), as خَضَرَ *to become green,* nearly =اِخْضَرَّ or اِخْضَوْضَرَ; صَلَحَ *to be good, right, in order,* = صَلُحَ; فَسَدَ *to be bad, wrong, in disorder,* = فَسُدَ. The subject of the active voice is always an agent (person or thing), whose act may affect an object, or not ; the subject of the passive voice is either the object of the former (personal passive), or the abstract idea of the act (impersonal passive).

w.   7

A   **74.** The passive is especially used in four cases; namely (*a*) when God, or some higher being, is indicated as the author of the act; (*b*) when the author is unknown, or at least not known for certain; (*c*) when the speaker or writer does not wish to name him; (*d*) when the attention of the hearer or reader is directed more to the person affected by the act (patiens, the patient), than to the doer of it (agens, the agent).

REM.   The active voice is called by the Arab grammarians

B   صِيغَةُ ٱلْفَاعِلِ *the mould* or *form of the agent,* بِنَاءُ ٱلْفَاعِلِ *the build of the agent,* بَابُ ٱلْفَاعِلِ *the category of the agent,* فِعْلُ ٱلْفَاعِلِ *the action of the agent,* and ٱلْفِعْلُ ٱلْمَبْنِىُّ (ٱلْمَصُوغُ) لِلْفَاعِلِ, or عَلَى ٱلْفَاعِلِ, *the action* (or *verb*) *put into that form of which the agent is the subject.* The passive voice is in like manner called صِيغَةُ

C   فِعْلُ مَا لَمْ يُسَمَّ ٱلْمَفْعُولِ *the mould* or *form of the patient,* etc.; also فَاعِلُهُ *the doing,* or *being done, of that, whereof the agent has not been named,* or, more shortly, مَا لَمْ يُسَمَّ فَاعِلُهُ, though this latter is, strictly speaking, equivalent to ٱلْمَفْعُولُ ٱلَّذِى لَمْ يُسَمَّ فَاعِلُهُ, *the patient whereof the agent has not been named,* i. e. the passive subject. The active voice is also shortly called ٱلْمَعْرُوفُ or ٱلْمَعْلُومُ, and the passive ٱلْمَجْهُولُ, elliptical forms of expression for ٱلْفِعْلُ

D   ٱلْمَعْرُوفُ (ٱلْمَعْلُومُ) فَاعِلُهُ, *the action of which the agent is known,* and ٱلْفِعْلُ ٱلْمَجْهُولُ فَاعِلُهُ, *the action of which the agent is unknown.* These terms, ٱلْمَعْرُوفُ or ٱلْمَعْلُومُ and ٱلْمَجْهُولُ, are also used to designate the subjects of the active and passive voices.

75. Verbs that express a state or condition, or signify an act which is, by its very nature, confined to the person of the subject, and cannot pass to another individual as its object (as مَرِضَ *to be sick,* نَامَ *to sleep*), are aptly called *neuter* verbs, since they are neither really active nor really passive, but something between the two. The Arab grammarians cannot class them otherwise than among the active verbs, and they therefore distinguish اَلْأَفْعَالُ ٱلْمُتَعَدِّيَةُ, *transitive verbs*, from A اَلْأَفْعَالُ غَيْرُ ٱلْمُتَعَدِّيَةِ, *intransitive verbs*, or اَلْأَفْعَالُ ٱللَّازِمَةُ, *verbs that are confined to the subject.*

76. The idea of the passive voice must not be thought to be absolutely identical with that of the fifth, seventh, and eighth forms. These are, strictly speaking, *effective* (see § 48), whilst the other is *purely passive.*

4. *The States (Tenses) of the Verb.*

77. The temporal forms of the Arabic verb are but *two* in B number, the one expressing a *finished* act, one that is done and completed in relation to other acts (the *Perfect*); the other an *unfinished* act, one that is just commencing or in progress (the *Imperfect*).

REM. *a.* The names *Preterite* and *Future*, by which these forms were often designated in older grammars do not accurately correspond to the ideas inherent in them. A Semitic Perfect or Imperfect has, in and of itself, no reference to the temporal C relations of the speaker (thinker or writer) and of other actions which are brought into juxtaposition with it. It is precisely these relations which determine in what sphere of time (past, present, or future) a Semitic Perfect or Imperfect lies, and by which of our tenses it is to be expressed—whether by our Past, Perfect, Pluperfect, or Future-perfect; by our Present, Imperfect, or Future. The Arabian Grammarians themselves have not, however, succeeded in keeping this important point distinctly in view, but have given an undue importance to the idea of time, in connection with the verbal forms, by their division of it into the past (اَلْمَاضِى), the present (اَلْحَاضِرُ or اَلْحَالُ), and the future (اَلْمُسْتَقْبَلُ), the first of D which they assign to the Perfect and the other two to the Imperfect.

REM. *b.* On the forms of these tenses see § 91 etc. The Syntax will give more precise information as to their meaning and use.

5. *The Moods.*

78. The Arabic verb has *five* moods; namely, the Indicative, Subjunctive, Jussive or Conditional, Imperative, and Energetic.

A   **79.** Of these moods the first is common to the perfect and imperfect states; the second and third are restricted to the imperfect; the fourth, or imperative, is expressed by a special form; and the fifth can be derived not only from the imperfect, but also from the imperative.

REM. On the forms of the moods see § 91 etc. The Syntax treats of their significations and use.

80. Instead of the Infinitive, the Arabs use *nouns expressing the*
B *action or quality* (nomina actionis or verbi). In place of participles, they have two *verbal adjectives*, the one denoting the *agent* (nomen agentis, active participle), and the other the *patient* (nomen patientis, passive participle). [Cf. § 192.]

6. *The Numbers, Persons, and Genders.*

81. There are three numbers, the *Singular* (اَلْمُفْرَدُ, اَلْفَرْدُ, or اَلْوَاحِدُ), the *Dual* (اَلتَّثْنِيَةُ or اَلْمُثَنَّى), and the *Plural* (اَلْجَمْعُ, اَلْجِمَاعُ,
C اَلْجَمِيعُ, اَلْمَجْمُوعُ, or اَلْمُكَثَّرُ); and likewise three persons, the *speaker* (first person), اَلْمُتَكَلِّمُ, the individual *spoken to* (second person), اَلْمُخَاطَبُ, and the individual *spoken of* (third person), اَلْغَائِبُ (*the absent*). The genders are two, namely the *masculine* (اَلْمُذَكَّرُ) and the *feminine* (اَلْمُؤَنَّثُ); but they are not distinguished from one another in some of the persons (1st pers. sing., 2d pers. dual, and 1st pers. plur.).

D   ### B. THE STRONG VERB (VERBUM FIRMUM).

82. Verbs are divided into *strong* (verba firma) and *weak* (verba infirma). We include the verba mediæ radicalis geminatæ ($y''y$) in the former class; the verbs which have ‍ا for one of their radicals, in the second (see § 128).

83. Strong verbs are those of which all the radical letters are *strong*, and consequently neither undergo any change, nor are rejected in any of the inflexions, but are retained throughout.

Rem. A verb which contains one of the two letters و or ي is A called فِعْلٌ مُعْتَلٌّ, *a weak verb,* as opposed to فِعْلٌ سَالِمٌ, *a verb that is free from defect, a sound verb.* A verb which has أ for one of its radicals, or which belongs to the class med. rad. gemin. (ع"ع), is designated by the special term فِعْلٌ صَحِيحٌ; but some grammarians treat صَحِيحٌ and سَالِمٌ as synonyms.

1. *The Active Voice of the First Form in the Strong Verb.—Table I.**   B

a. THE INFLEXION BY PERSONS.

84. The numbers, persons, and genders of the verb are expressed by means of personal pronouns, annexed to the various moods and tenses.

85. The personal pronoun [ضَمِيرٌ, مُضْمَرٌ: see § 190, *f.*] is either *separate* [مُنْفَصِلٌ], standing by itself, or *connected* [مُتَّصِلٌ], that is C *prefixed* or *suffixed.* The separate pronouns have longer, the connected shorter forms.

86. The *suffixed* pronouns are partly *verbal,* partly *nominal* suffixes.

87. The *verbal* suffixes express partly the *nominative,* partly the *accusative.* The former are much more closely united with the verb than the latter.

88. The connected pronouns which express the *nominative* to D the verb are also in part *prefixes.*

Rem. On the verbal suffixes which express the *accusative* see § 185; and on the nominal suffixes, § 317.

89. The following tables give a general view of the *separate* personal pronouns, and of those pronominal prefixes and suffixes which express the *nominative* to the verb.

---

* The *nomina verbi, agentis,* and *patientis,* are given along with the strictly verbal forms in all the Tables.

A   1. *Separate Pronouns.*

                                   Singular.

            Masc.   Common   Fem.

      3 p. هُوَ *he.*   هِىَ *she.*

      2 p. أَنْتَ *thou.*   . . .   أَنْتِ *thou.*

      1 p.   أَنَا *I.*

B   *Dual.*

      3 p.   هُمَا *they two.*

      2 p.   أَنْتُمَا *ye two.*

      1 p.   . . .

                                   Plural.

      3 p. هُمْ *they.*   هُنَّ *they.*

      2 p. أَنْتُمْ *ye.*   . . .   أَنْتُنَّ *ye.*

C   1 p. . . .   نَحْنُ *we.*

REM. *a.* When هُوَ and هِىَ are preceded by the conjunctions

وَ and فَ, *and*, the affirmative لَ, *certainly*, *surely*, or the interro-

gative أَ, the vowel of the ه may either be dropped or retained; as

فَهُوَ or وَهُوَ, فَهِىَ or فَهْىَ, لَهُوَ or لَهْوَ, أَهُوَ ۫ or أَهْىَ.

REM. *b.* The second syllable of أَنَا is regarded as short by the

D   old poets (⌣⌣), except in pause, where we find both أَنَا (⌣–) and

أَنَهْ*. Compare the Æthiopic *ănă*, which, in combination with the

enclitic particle *să*, becomes *ănsă*. أَنَا is, therefore, an example of

scriptio plena, to distinguish the pronoun from the particles أَنْ,

أَنَّ, إِنْ, إِنَّ. The *scriptio defectiva* is found, for example, in the

interjectional هَأَنَذَا or هَآأَنَذَا *here I am* (הִנֵּנִי, *eccome*), for هَا أَنَا ذَا.

The form أَنْ is said also to occur.

---

* But أَنَا, out of pause, is occasionally scanned as an iambus even in
old poetry. See Nöldeke in *ZDMG.* xxxviii. 418, note 3.

Rem. *c*.   Older forms of هُمْ and أَنْتُمْ are هُمُ and أَنْتُمُ, used in   A
poetry, and also in the *waṣl* (§ 20, *d*, and § 23, rem. *c*). [Though
written defectively this terminal *n* is commonly scanned as a long
vowel.]

Rem. *d*.   For a comparison of the pronominal forms of the
Arabic with those of the other Semitic languages see *Comp. Gr.*
p. 95 *seq.*

2. *Suffixed Pronouns, expressing the Nominative.*   B

Singular.

Masc.	Common	Fem.
3 p. . . .		ـَتْ *she.*
2 p. ـتَ *thou.*	. . .	ت (ـِى, ـِين) *thou.*
1 p. . . .	ـتُ *I.*	

Dual.

3 p. ـَا (ـَان, ـَا) *they two.*	. . .	ـَتَا (ـَان, ـَا) *they two.*
2 p. . . .	تُمَا (ـَان, ـَا) *ye two.*	. . . C
1 p.	. . .	

Plural.

3 p. ـُوا (ـُونَ, ـُوا) *they.*		نَ *they.*
2 p. تُمْ (ـُونَ, ـُوا) *ye.*	. . .	تُنَّ (نَ) *ye.*
1 p. . . .	نَا *we.*	. . .

Rem. *a*.   The forms within brackets are those of the Imperfect
and Imperative; the others those of the Perfect.

Rem. *b*.   The suffix of the 1st pers. plur. is sometimes shortened   D
in poetry (*nă*) and written defectively, نْ.

3. *Prefixed Pronouns, expressing the Nominative.*

Singular.

Masc.	Common.	Fem.
3 p. ى *he.*	. . .	ت *she.*
2 p.	ت *thou.*	
1 p.	أ *I.*	

A
Dual.

	Masc.	Common.	Fem.
3 p.	ى *they two.*	...	ت *they two.*
2 p.	...	ت *ye two.*	...
1 p.		...	...

Plural.

3 p.	ى *they.*
2 p.	ت *ye.*
1 p. ...	ن *we.* ...

B   REM. *a.* These forms are restricted to the Imperfect. They are called by the grammarians حُرُوفُ ٱلْمُضَارَعَة, and are comprised in the mnemonic word أَنَيْتُ or نَأْتِى.

REM. *b.* The prefix of the third person plural of the Imperfect is ى for both genders. But the grammarians cite some rare cases where, in the fem., ى is replaced by ت, so that the distinction between 3 pl. fem. and 2 pl. fem. is lost. Thus in the Ḳor'ān, Sūra xlii. 3, a reading تَتَفَطَّرْنَ for يَتَفَطَّرْنَ is recorded. This must be
C   explained as due to false analogy from the sing. In the Heb. תִּקְטֹלְנָה the false form has become the rule.

90. Of the two fèthas with which the first and third radicals of a verb are always pronounced (حَسُنَ ,فَرِحَ ,قَتَلَ), the former is rejected after prefixed pronouns, as تَقْتُلُ ,يَقْتُلُ; the latter before suffixed pronouns beginning with a consonant, as قَتَلَتْ ,قَتَلْنَا. When the suffix begins with a vowel, that vowel takes the place of the fètha,
D as قَتَلَتْ ,قَتَلُوا.

REM. *a.* When the third radical is ت, it unites in pronunciation with the ت in some of the suffixes. In such cases only one ت is written, and the union of the two is denoted by the tèsdīd. Thus from ثَبَتَ, *to stand firm*, we get ثَبَتَّ ,ثَبَتِّ ,ثَبَتُّمْ, for ثَبَتَّتَ, ثَبَتُّمْ ,ثَبَتِّ. See § 14, *c*, rem. *b.*

REM. *b.* When the third radical is one of the letters ث, د, ذ, ض, ط, ظ, it may unite in pronunciation with the ت of the suffixes, so as to form a double ت, but it is nevertheless retained in writing.

To indicate the assimilation, the ت takes tèśdîd, and the ġèzma, with which the third radical ought properly to be marked, is omitted. Thus, عَبَّدتُ for عَبَدْتُ, *I have served*; رَبَّطتَّ for رَبَطْتَ, *thou hast bound*; أَخَّذتُّمْ for أَخَذْتُمْ, *ye have taken.* On this assimilation see § 14, *c*.

REM. *c.* When the third radical is ن, it unites with the ن of the suffixes into a single ن with tèśdîd; as أَمَنَّ *they* (women) *believed*, أَمَنَّا *we believed*, for أَمَنَّ and أَمَنَّا.

REM. *d.* For a view of the Inflexion of the Perfect and Imperfect Indicative in Hebrew and Aramaic as compared with Arabic see *Comp. Gr.* p. 165 *seq.*

b. FORMS OF THE TENSES AND MOODS.

91. When the second radical of the Perfect has *fètḥa*, it may take either *ḍamma* or *kèsra* in the Imperfect; as قَتَلَ *to kill*, يَقْتُلُ; كَتَبَ *to write*, يَكْتُبُ; ضَرَبَ *to strike*, يَضْرِبُ; جَلَسَ *to sit down*, يَجْلِسُ. Many verbs admit of both forms; as عَطَسَ *to sneeze*, يَعْطُسُ and يَعْطِسُ; سَمَطَ *to remove the hair by scalding*, يَسْمُطُ or يَسْمِطُ; رَكَزَ *to stick upright into the ground*, يَرْكُزُ.

REM. *a.* Verbs, of which the second or third radical is a guttural letter, are an exception to the rule, for they commonly retain in the Imperfect the *fètḥa* of the Perfect; as فَعَلَ *to do*, يَفْعَلُ; قَطَعَ *to cut*, يَقْطَعُ; مَنَعَ *to hinder*, يَمْنَعُ; بَرَأَ *to create*, يَبْرَأُ; سَأَلَ *to ask*, يَسْأَلُ; ذَهَبَ *to go away*, يَذْهَبُ; لَحَظَ *to look at*, يَلْحَظُ; طَرَحَ *to throw*, يَطْرَحُ. Not a few, however, conform to the rule, particularly when the second radical is خ or غ; as شَعَرَ *to perceive, know*, يَشْعُرُ; قَعَدَ *to sit*, يَقْعُدُ; طَعَنَ *to transpierce*, يَطْعُنُ; زَعَمَ *to say*, يَزْعُمُ; طَلَعَ *to ascend*, يَطْلُعُ; صَلَحَ *to be sound, right, good*, يَصْلُحُ; بَلَغَ *to attain to, reach*, يَبْلُغُ; نَفَخَ *to blow*, يَنْفُخُ; شَخَبَ *to flow*, يَشْخُبُ; رَجَعَ *to return*, يَرْجِعُ; نَزَعَ *to draw or pull away*, يَنْزِعُ; شَخَرَ *to bray*, يَشْخِرُ. Some verbs have two

W.   8

A   forms; as نَعَقَ *to croak,* يَنْعَقُ; مَنَحَ *to give as a present,* يَمْنَحُ;

نَكَحَ *to marry,* يَنْكَحُ; نَطَحَ *to butt,* يَنْطَحُ; سَلَخَ *to flay,* يَسْلَخُ;

دَبَغَ *to tan,* يَدْبَغُ; صَبَغَ *to dye,* يَصْبَغُ; فَرَغَ *to be at leisure, to

have done with,* يَفْرَغُ; and even three, as نَحَتَ *to cut or hew,*

يَنْحَتُ; رَجَحَ *to incline* (of a scale of a balance), يَرْجَحُ; نَبَعَ *to

gush out,* يَنْبَعُ.

B   REM. *b.* Verbs of the form فَعَلَ denoting superiority, فَعَلَ

اَلدَّالُّ عَلَى ٱلْغَلَبَة (see § 43, *a*), always have *ḍamma* (the grammarian

el-Kisā'ī alone admitting *fetḥa* with a guttural), as شَعَرَهُ *he excelled

him in composing poetry,* يَشْعُرُهُ; فَخَرَهُ *he surpassed him in glory,*

يَفْخُرُهُ; unless they be primæ rad. و, med. rad. ى, or tert. rad. ى,

when they take *kesra,* as وَعَدَهُ *he outbid him in promising,* يَعِدُهُ;

خَارَهُ *he excelled him in goodness,* يَخِيرُهُ; رَمَاهُ *he surpassed him in

shooting with arrows,* يَرْمِيهِ.

C   REM. *c.* Excessively rare are cases like رَكَنَ *to incline to, lean

upon,* يَرْكَنُ, which is probably a combination of the two forms

يَرْكُنُ, رَكِنَ, and رَكَنَ يَرْكُنُ. See § 175, rem. *b.*

92. When the second radical of the Perf. has *kesra,* the Imperf.

takes *fetḥa;* as عَلِمَ *to know,* يَعْلَمُ; شَرِبَ *to drink,* يَشْرَبُ; حَزِنَ *to

be sorrowful,* يَحْزَنُ; مَرِضَ *to be sick,* يَمْرَضُ; سَلِمَ *to be safe,* يَسْلَمُ.

REM. *a.* A few verbs may retain in the Imperf. the *kesra* of

the Perf., as حَسِبَ *to think or suppose,* يَحْسَبُ or يَحْسِبُ; نَعِمَ

D   *to be green and flourishing,* يَنْعَمُ; بَئِسَ *to be in distress or poverty,*

يَبْئَسُ or يَبْأَسُ. See also §§ 142 and 146.

REM. *b.* Very rare are cases like حَضِرَ *to be present,* يَحْضُرُ;

رَكِنَ *to incline to, lean upon,* يَرْكُنُ; فَضِلَ *to be in excess, abound,*

يَفْضُلُ; نَعِمَ *to be affluent, comfortable,* يَنْعُمُ; بَرِئَ *to be clear, quit,* or *innocent of,* بَيْرُوّ or بَيْرَأ. The most common example of this kind A is a verb med. و, viz. مَاتَ, *to die* (for مَوِتَ, 1st p. sing. Perf. مِتُّ), يَمُوتُ.—Similar cases in Syriac and Hebrew, *Comp. Gr.* p. 180*.

93. When the second radical of the Perf. has *ḍamma*, that vowel is retained in the Imperf.; as حَسُنَ *to be beautiful,* يَحْسُنُ; شَرُفَ *to be high, noble,* يَشْرُفُ; بَلُدَ *to be dull or stupid,* يَبْلُدُ.

REM. With the above forms compare the Heb. יִכְתֹּב, יִשְׁלַח, B יִכְבַּד. In Heb., however, verbs in *o* usually take *a* in the Imperf., as יִשְׁכַּב, יִקְטַן, whereas in Arabic instances like لَبُبْتُ *I became wise,* دَمُمْتُ *I became ugly,* شَرُرْتُ *I became bad,* أَشَرُّ، أَدَمُّ، أَلَبُّ, are very rare. Some authorities admit the forms أَشَرُّ، أَدَمُّ، أَلَبُّ.

94. The difference between the Perf. and Imperf. in regard to their inflexion is, that the marks of the numbers, genders, and persons, are only *suffixed* to the Perf.; whereas they are both *suffixed* and *prefixed* to the Imperf., more generally the latter. C

REM. *a.* In the Perf. the *act* is placed conspicuously in the foreground, because completed; in the Imperf. the *agent*, because still occupied in the act (see § 77, rem. *a*). If we look upon the root قتل as primarily conveying the abstract idea of "killing," we may regard قَتَلْتُ as meaning "killing-of-me" (i.e. done by me), "my killing," = "I have killed;" and أَقْتُلُ as meaning "I-killing," = "I am killing."

REM. *b.* In the Imperf. the pronominal *prefixes* mark the state D or tense, and to some extent the gender; whilst the *suffixes* serve solely to indicate the gender. Thus, the 2d pers. sing. masc. تَكْتُبُ is sufficiently distinguished from the 3d pers. sing. masc. يَكْتُبُ by the form of the temporal prefix; but to distinguish the 2d pers. sing. masc. from its fem. a suffix is necessary, and accordingly we get masc. تَكْتُبُ, fem. تَكْتُبِينَ.

---

* [Anbārī, *Nozhat ěl-alibbā* p. 459 states from personal observation in Yèmèn and Ḥigāz that in some dialects every verb فَعَلَ makes يَفْعَلُ and يَفْعُلُ.—De G.]

A   REM. *c.* In the active voice of the first form, the prefixes of the Imperfect are pronounced with *fĕtḥ.* But a pronunciation with *kĕsr* instead of *fĕtḥ* is regarded as admissible and was used by some of the old Arabs with any of the preformatives except ي, save in the case where the next consonant has *ḍamma* (verbs med. و). That is, one must not say أَقُومُ, تَقُومُ, إِقُمْ for إِقُمْ etc. nor يَعْلَمُ for يَعْلَمُ; but on the other hand the pronunciation نِعْبُدُ and نِسْتَعِينُ in Sūra i. 4, and إِعْبُدْ in Sūra xxxvi. 60 are recognized as

B   legitimate dialectic variations of the usual نَعْبُدُ etc. In one case, إِخَالُ for أَخَالُ, *I suppose,* the pronunciation with *kĕsr* is generally preferred. The tribe of Kĕlb used *kĕsr* even with the prefix ي (يِعْلَمُ). Dialectically, too, the vowel of the prefix might be assimilated to a following *ḍamm,* as in نُعْبُدُ for نَعْبُدُ.

95. The *Indicative* of the Imperf. is distinguished by the third radical having *ḍamma,* the *Subjunctive* by its having *fĕtḥa;* as Indic.

C   يَكْتُبُ, Subj. يَكْتُبَ. The *Jussive* is denoted by the *absence* of any vowel with the third radical, as يَكْتُبْ; whence it is sometimes called the apocopated Imperfect.

REM. *a.* The *ḍamma* and *fĕtḥa* of the Indicat. and Subjunct. Imperf. in the verb, correspond to the *ḍamma* and *fĕtḥa* of the Nom. and Accus. in the noun (see § 308); for the Imperf. is closely akin to the noun, and its government in the Subjunct. falls under the same category with the government of the noun in the Accus. Hence the technical name of the Imperf., أَلْمُضَارِعُ, because it

D   *resembles* the noun. [The Indicative is called أَلْمَرْفُوعُ, the Subjunctive أَلْمَنْصُوبُ, and the Jussive أَلْمَجْزُومُ.]

REM. *b.* The peculiar meaning of the Jussive has brought along with it the rejection of the final vowel, which seems originally to have been *i.* At least the poets make use of the form يَقْتُلِ in rhyme. [Cf. vol. ii. § 247.]

96. The forms of the Indicat. which end in نِ and نَ reject these syllables in the Subjunct. and Jussive, because the genders, numbers, and persons are distinctly indicated even after their omission. The

2d and 3d pers. plur. fem. are exceptions, for in them ن is retained, A because it is absolutely necessary in order to mark the gender. Compare يَكْتُبُونَ, يَكْتُبُوا, with كَتَبُوا; يَكْتُبَانِ, يَكْتُبَا, with كَتَبَا; and تَكْتُبِينَ, تَكْتُبِى, with كَتَبْتِ.

97. The *Energetic* is formed by adding the termination ـَنَّ or ـَنْ (called by the grammarians اَلنُّونُ ٱلْمُوَكَّدَةُ, or *the corroborative n*) to the Jussive. If the Jussive ends in *i* or *ū*, the fĕtḥa of ـَنَّ or ـَنْ is elided, and the long vowel of the verbal form shortened, because it is in a shut syllable : يَكْتُبُنَّ, يَكْتُبُنْ, from تَكْتُبِى; تَكْتُبِنَّ, تَكْتُبِنْ, from يَكْتُبُوا; etc. In the dual, the first fĕtḥa of ـَنَّ is absorbed by the ـا B of the termination, and the second weakened into a kĕsra through the influence of the same long vowel : تَكْتُبَانِّ, يَكْتُبَانِّ, from يَكْتُبَا, تَكْتُبَا. In the 2d and 3d pers. plur. fem. the fĕtḥa of the verb unites with the initial fĕtḥa of ـَنَّ into a long *ā*, and in consequence the second fĕtḥa of ـَنَّ becomes kĕsra : يَكْتُبْنَانِّ (3) from يَكْتُبْنَ (3).

REM. *a.* The syllable ـَنْ of the second Energetic is appended only to those persons which have, in the first Energetic, a short vowel before نّ; and not to the dual, because its forms would then C coincide with those of the singular, nor to the fem. plur., apparently because the sound of the syllable نَنْ (يَكْتُبْنَنْ) was disagreeable to the ear.

REM. *b.* Before an *ĕlifu 'l-waṣl* (§ 19) the *n* of the termination ـَنْ is rejected (§ 20, rem. *c*), as لَا تُهِينَ ٱلْفَقِيرَ, *despise not the poor*, for تُهِينَنْ, from أَهَانَ, IV. of هَانَ.

REM. *c.* The syllable ـَنْ is often written ـًا, and pronounced D in pause ـَا. Compare the Hebrew Energetic or Cohortative in הָ-, *Comp. Gr.* p. 194.

98. The *Imperative* (ٱلْأَمْرُ *the order* or *command*) may be described as formed from the Jussive by rejecting the prefix of the 2d pers. sing. Hence it has always the same characteristic vowel as the Jussive ; but, since it begins with two consonants, it takes, according to § 26, a short

A prosthetic vowel. When the second radical is pronounced with *fétha* or *kèsra*, this vowel is *kèsra;* when with *damma*, it is *damma*. E.g. اُكْتُبْ, اِضْرِبْ, اِفْعَلْ.

REM. *a.* Regarding the elision of the prosthetic vowel (اِ), see § 19, *b*; and on the orthography ا and اِ, in cases where that elision does not take place, § 19, rem. *d.*

REM. *b.* Fétha is never employed as a prosthetic vowel.

B REM. *c.* As an Imperative the Arabs also use the indeclinable form قَتَالِ; as حَضَارِ *be present!* حَذَارِ *beware!* نَزَالِ *alight!* سَمَاعِ *listen!* تَرَاكِ *let alone!* دَبَابِ *creep along!* نَعَآءِ *announce the death of—!* from نَعَى. This corresponds to the Hebrew *Infinitive absolute* קָטוֹל (ō for ā, and the final short vowel dropped), which is also used in the same way; as זָכוֹר *remember!* In quadriliterals this form is very rare, the only examples mentioned being

C قَرْقَارِ = قَرْقِرْ بِٱلرَّعْدِ, *let thy thunder crash,* and عَرْعَارِ, *come and play the game called 'ar'ara.* Occasionally it seems to take its meaning from one of the derived conjugations, as خَرَاجِ *bring out!* دَرَاكِ *overtake!* = أَدْرِكُوا, أَخْرِجُوا, Imper. IV.

99. The same remarks apply to the energetic forms of the Imperative as to those of the Imperf. (§ 97).

D ⟨[REM. The common phrase اِضْرِبَا عُنُقَهُ, *strike off his head,* is sometimes pointed without tènwîn (اِضْرِبَا) and is then explained by the grammarians as a dual used in an intensive sense (تَثْنِيَة عَلَى التَّوْكِيد, cf. vol. ii. § 35, *a*, rem. *b*) in addressing a single person. Similarly Ḳor'ān 1. 23, أَلْقِيَا with a various reading أَلْقِيَنْ.—De G.]

---

* [And again the phrase عنقت عَقاقِ Ṭab. i. 1842, l. 15 is parallel to the Hebrew use of the Inf. Abs. with the finite verb.— De G.]

2. *The Passive Voice of the First Form in the Strong*   A
   Verb.—Table II.

100. The Perf. and Imperf. Passive are distinguished from the corresponding tenses of the Active by a change of vowels. In the Perf. Pass. the *first* radical has *ḍamma*, and the *second* radical *kèsra*. In the Imperf. Pass. the *prefixes* take *ḍamma*, and the *second* radical *fètḥa*.

REM. The vocalisation of the Passive remains always the same, whatever be the vowel of the second radical in the Perf. and Imperf. Active.

101. There is no special form to express the Imperative Passive,   B the Jussive being used instead.

3. *The Derived Forms of the Strong Verb.—Table III.*

102. The second radical of the Perf. Act. is pronounced with *fètḥa* in *all* the derived forms.

103. The second radical of the Imperf. Act. is pronounced with *fètḥa* in the *fifth* and *sixth* forms, with *kèsra* in the rest.   C

REM. The Imperfects of the ninth and eleventh forms, يَقْتَلّ and يَقْتَالّ, are contractions for يَقْتَلِلُ and يَقْتَالِلُ. This may be seen from the Jussives يَقْتَلِلْ and يَقْتَالِلْ, and the Imperatives اِقْتَلِلْ and اِقْتَالِلْ. See §§ 106 and 120.

104. In the *second*, *third*, and *fourth* forms, the *prefixes* of the Imperf. Act. are pronounced with *damma*, in the rest with *fètḥa*.

105. The characteristic èlif of the fourth form disappears when   D another letter is prefixed ; as يُقْتَلُ, not يُاقْتَلُ, from أَقْتَلَ.

[REM. But we find قِدْرٌ مُوَّتُفَاةٌ, *a pot set on the fire*, and also يُوَّتفَيْن, Sîbawèih, i. 9, 1. 21, where the ا is treated like the و of يَهْرِيق, § 118, rem. *b.*—De G.]

106. The ninth and eleventh forms were originally اِفْعَلَلَ and اِفْعَالَلَ. But, by a rule of the language (see § 120), if the last radical

A in such words has a vowel, the preceding radical loses its vowel, and the two are combined into one letter with tèśdìd ; e.g. اِصْغَرَّ for اِصْغَرَرَ, يَصْغَرُّ for يَصْغَرِرُ. If the last radical has no vowel, the word remains uncontracted ; as اِصْغَرِرْ, يَصْغَرِرْ, اِصْغَرَرْتَ (see § 120).

107. The formation of the Perf. and Imperf. Passive in the derived forms is exactly analogous to that in the ground-form.

> REM. *a.*   The Imperfects Pass. of the first and fourth forms are identical.

B
> REM. *b.*   The Imperfects Pass. of the fifth and sixth forms are distinguished from their Imperfects Act. only by the vowel of the prefixes, which is *ḍamma* instead of *fètḥa*.

108.   Since the idea of the Perf. Pass. is expressed by pronouncing the first radical with ḍamma, and the idea of the third form by lengthening the vowel of the first radical, there results in the Passive of the third form (in which both ideas are united) the form قُوتِلَ ; and hence in the Pass. of the sixth, تُقُوتِلَ.

C   **109.**   In the Perf. Pass. of the fifth and sixth forms, not only is the fètḥa of the first radical changed into ḍamma, but also the fètḥa of the characteristic ت (which expresses the reflexive idea of these forms) ; e.g. تُقُوتِلَ, تُقُتِّلَ. In like manner, in the Perf. Pass. of the seventh, eighth, and tenth forms, not only is the first radical, or the characteristic ت, pronounced with ḍamma, but also the prosthetic ĕlif ; e.g. أُسْتُقْتِلَ, اُقْتُتِلَ, اُنْقُتِلَ. Compare § 98 and rem. *a.*

D   **110.**   The ninth and eleventh [to fifteenth] forms, being neutral in their signification, have of course no passive (see § 73).

111.   When the verbal root begins with ش, س, ز, ذ, د, ج, ث, ت, ص, ض, ط, or ظ, the characteristic ت of the fifth and sixth forms occasionally (in the Ḳor'ân frequently) loses its vowel, and unites with the first radical to form a double letter. The forms thus originated take a prosthetic ĕlif, when they happen to commence with two consonants (compare § 54). E. g. اِزَّيَّنَ, اِدَّارَأَ, اِدَّثَّرَ, اِثَّاقَلَ, اِثَّايَعَ,

A. تَسَاقَطَ, تَزَيَّنَ, تَدَارَأَ, تَدَثَّرَ, تَقَاتَلَ, تَتَايَعَ for اطَّيَّرَ, اشَّمَّرَ, اسَّمَّعَ, اسَّاقَطَ, يَتَزَكَّى, يَزَّكَّى, يَصَّدَّقُ, يَطَّهَّرُ, تَطَيَّرَ: يَذَّكَّرُ, يَتَذَكَّرُ for يَتَزَكَّى, يَتَطَهَّرُ, يَتَصَدَّقُ. The language in its later stages admits this in all verbs of the fifth and sixth forms, merely rejecting the vowel of the preformative تَ; as اتَّنَفَّسَ for تَنَفَّسَ, *to take breath*.

REM. See § 48, rem. *b*, and compare such Hebrew forms as הֹפָּטַר, חֻזְּקָה, הִדַּבֵּר; *Comp. Gr.* p. 110 *seq.*

B. **112.** The تَ of the fifth and sixth forms is sometimes omitted in those persons of the Imperf. Act. to which تَ is prefixed (2d pers. sing. du. and plur. masc. and fem., 3d pers. sing. and du. fem.); e.g. تَقَدَّمُونَ, تَبَاعَدُ, تَحَمَّلُ, تَكَسَّرُ for تَقَدَّمُونَ, تَبَاعَدُ, تَحَمَّلُ, تَكَسَّرُ [and necessarily تَتَايَعُ for تَتَايَعُ (*Fāik* i. 130)—De G.]. These shortened forms are sufficiently distinguished by the fèthas of the prefixed تَ and of the second radical from the same persons in the active voice of the second and third forms (تَبَاعَدُ, تُكَسَّرُ); and by C the fètha of the prefixed تَ from the same persons in the passive of the second and third forms (تَبَاعَدُ, تُكَسَّرُ).

113. Verbs of which the first radical is ا, و, ى, ر, ل, or ن, have no seventh form in classical Arabic, but use the fifth or eighth, or the passive of the first, instead. In the (so far as we know) solitary example of the seventh form from a verb beginning with ن,—namely انَّمَسَ, *to lie concealed*,—the characteristic ن is united by tèśdīd to the first radical.

REM. *a.* Some grammarians regard انَّمَسَ as being of the eighth D form, by assimilation for انْتَمَسَ.

REM. *b.* In modern Arabic such forms as انْأَخَذَ, انْأَطَرَ (*Kāmil*, p. 569, note i.), انْوَلَدَ, انْوَجَدَ, انْصَرَ, انْرَضَّ, are of common occurrence.

114. If the first radical is م, the characteristic ن of the seventh form often unites with it into مّ; as انْمَحَقَ or امَّحَقَ from مَحَقَ,

A اِنْمَحَى or اِمَّحَى from مَحَا, اِنْمَعَطَ or اِمَّعَطَ from مَعَطَ, اِنْمَلَسَ or

اِمَّلَسَ from مَلَسَ, اِنْمَلَصَ or اِمَّلَصَ from مَلَصَ.

REM. These forms are sometimes assigned to the eighth form ;

اِمَّحَقَ for اِمْتَحَقَ. اِمَّحَى for اِمْتَحَى, اِمَّرَطَ for اِمْتَرَطَ, etc.

115. If the first radical be د or ذ, the characteristic ت of the

eighth form unites with the initial د into دّ, with the initial ذ into

تّ or ذّ. E.g. اِتَّبَعَ, for اِتْتَبَعَ, from تَبِعَ ; اِتَّأَرَ or اِئْتَأَرَ, for اِتْتَأَرَ, from

ثَأَرَ ; اِتَّرَدَ or اِتْرَدَ from ثَرَدَ ; اِتَّغَرَ or اِتْثَغَرَ from ثَغَرَ.

B   REM. The same assimilation is sometimes extended to the

letter س, as اِسَّمَعَ, for اِسْتَمَعَ, from سَمِعَ.

116. If the first radical be د, ذ, or ز, the characteristic ت of the

eighth form is changed into د, which unites with an initial د into دّ,

and with an initial ذ into دّ or ذّ. E.g. اِزْدَجَرَ, for اِزْتَجَرَ, from زَجَرَ ;

اِزْدَادَ, for اِزْتَادَ, from زَادَ ; اِدَّرَكَ, for اِدْتَرَكَ, from دَرَكَ ; اِدَّرَى, for اِدْتَرَى,

C from دَرَى ; اِدَّعَى, for اِدْتَعَى, from دَعَا ; اِدَّخَرَ or اِذَّخَرَ, for اِدْتَخَرَ, from

ذَخَرَ ; اِدَّرَعَ or اِذَّرَعَ, for اِذْتَرَعَ, from ذَرَعَ ; اِدَّكَرَ or اِذَّكَرَ, for اِذْتَكَرَ,

from ذَكَرَ.

REM. *a.* Whether the form with دّ or ذّ is to be preferred,

depends upon usage ; for instance, اِدَّكَرَ and اِذَّكَرَ are preferable to

اِذَّخَرَ and اِذَّكَرَ, but Lane gives in his Lexicon only اِدَّرَقَ, اِدَّبَجَ, and

اِدَّرَى. The unassimilated اِذْدَكَرَ is also said to occur, as well as

D اِذْدَرَى.

REM. *b.* Some grammarians extend this assimilation to the

letter ز, as اِزَّانَ, for اِزْدَانَ, from زَانَ.

REM. *c.* The letter ت is sometimes changed into د after an

initial ج ; e.g. اِجْدَمَعَ, اِجْدَرَّ, اِجْدَرَّ, instead of the usual اِجْتَزَّ,

اِجْتَمَعَ, اِجْتَزَّ, from جَمَعَ, جَرَّ, جَزَّ.

117. If the first radical be ص, ض, ط, or ظ, the characteristic A
ت is changed into ط, which unites with initial ط into طّ, with initial
ظ into طّ or ظّ, and occasionally with initial ض into ضّ. E.g. اصْطَبَغَ,
اطَّرَدَ, اطَّبَخَ, from صَبَغَ, صَفا, صَلَى; صَلَحَ, اصْطَلَحَ, اصْطَلَى, اصْطَفَى
اطَّعَنَ, اطَّلَبَ, from طَبَخَ, طَرَدَ, طَعَنَ, طَلَبَ; اظَّلَمَ, اطَّلَمَ, or اظْطَلَمَ,
from ظَلَمَ; اظَّأَرَ, or اظْطَأَرَ, from ظَأَرَ; اظَّعَنَ, اظَّلَمَ, اظَّهَرَ, from ظَعَنَ,
ظَهَرَ, ظَفَرَ; اضْطَرَبَ, or اضَّرَبَ, from ضَرَبَ; اضْطَجَعَ, or اضَّجَعَ, from
ضَجَعَ; اضْطَرَّ, اضْطَلَعَ, from ضَرَّ, ضَلَعَ.

REM. *a.* The letter ص sometimes assimilates the following ط; B
as اصَّبَرَ, اصَّفَى, اصَّلَى, اصَّلَحَ, اصَّادَ, for اصْطَبَرَ, etc.

REM. *b.* From ضَجَعَ the form اطَّجَعَ also occurs.

[**117*.** If the second radical be ت the characteristic ت of the
eighth form may lose its vowel and unite with it. The first radical
then necessarily assumes a vowel, either *a* or *i*, and the helping vowel
ا is unnecessary and disappears. Thus for اسْتَتَرَ we may have سَتَّرَ
or سِتَّرَ; Imperf. يَسَتَّرُ, يِسِتَّرُ or يِسَتَّرُ or even يَسْتَّرُ (with a furtive *kesra*
to the first radical); Part. act. مُسَتَّرُ (مُسِتَّرُ); Inf. سِتَّارُ (see § 202, C
rem. *a*). Similar forms from verbs whose second radical is د, ذ, ص or
ط occur (or are recorded as variants) in the Ḳor'ân (*Sûr.* x. 36, ix. 91,
ii. 19, xxxvi. 49).]

4. *The Quadriliteral Verb.—Table IV.*

118. The four forms of the quadriliteral verb follow throughout D
their inflexion the second, fifth, seventh and ninth forms of the
triliteral (see §§ 69—72).

REM. *a.* The ت, which is prefixed to certain persons in the
Imperf. Act., is omitted in the second form of the quadriliteral
verb, just as in the fifth form of the triliteral (see § 112).

REM. *b.* As mentioned in § 45, rem. *d*, words like هَرَاقَ (for
أَرَاقَ), *to pour out*, and هَيْمَنَ, *to believe*, are treated as quadriliterals:

A The latter is inflected exactly like قَمْطَرٌ, but the former is irregular: Imperf. يُهَرِيقُ, Imperat. هَرِقْ, Nom. act. هَرَاقَةٌ, Perf. Pass. هُرِيقَ. The form أَهْرَاقَ, Imperf. يُهْرِيقُ, is also used.—The tenth form of طَاعَ, viz. اِسْتَطَاعَ, *to obey,* is sometimes shortened into اِسْطَاعَ or اِسْتَاعَ, Imperf. يَسْطِيعُ or يَسْتِيعُ, and then converted into أَسْطَاعَ, Imperf. يُسْطِيعُ. [Also, in verse, we find مُسْطَارٌ for مُسْتَطَارٌ.]

B 5. *Verbs of which the Second and Third Radicals are Identical.—Table V.*

119. These verbs are usually called *verba mediæ* or *secundæ radicalis geminatæ* (ع"ع). The Arab grammarians name them اَلْفِعْلُ الْأَصَمُّ, *the solid verb,* or اَلْفِعْلُ الْمُضَاعَفُ, *the doubled verb.*

120. They differ from other strong verbs in two points.

(*a*) When both the first and third radicals have vowels, the C second radical rejects its vowel, and unites with the third, so as to form a double letter, which is marked with téšdīd. E.g. فَرَّ *to flee,* for فَرَرَ; شَقَّ *to split* or *cleave,* for شَقَقَ; مَسَّ *to touch,* for مَسَسَ: شَمَّ *to smell,* for شَمِمَ; حَبَّ *to become dear* (*to one*), for حَبُبَ; لَبَّ *to become wise* or *intelligent,* for لَبُبَ.

(*b*) If the third radical has a vowel, but the first is without one, the second radical throws back its vowel upon the first, and then D combines with the third, so as to form a double letter. E.g. يَجِلُّ for يَجْلِلُ, يَمُدُّ for يَمْدُدُ, يَمَلُّ for يَمْلَلُ. But if the third radical has no vowel, the second retains its vowel, and no contraction takes place; as فَرَرْتُ، مَلِلْتُ، لَبُبْتُ، يَفْرِرْ، يَمْدُدْ.

REM. *a.* Transitive verbs of this class, of the form فَعَلَ, have damma in the Imperfect, with the exception of six, which also admit kèsra; viz. بَتَّ *to sever* or *separate entirely, make decisive* or *absolute,* رَمَّ *to repair,* شَدَّ *to make hard* or *firm, tie firmly,* عَلَّ *to water* (camels) *a second time*, نَمَّ *to spread abroad* or *divulge secretly*, هَرَّ *to abhor, detest*, Imperf. يَهَّتُ or يَهِتُّ, etc. One verb has only kĕsra, viz. حَبَّ *to love* (instead of the common IV. أَحَبَّ), Imperf. يَحِبُّ.

REM. *b.* Uncontracted verbs of the forms فَعِلَ and فَعُلَ sometimes occur; as صَكِكَ *to be knock-kneed* or *weak in the hocks*, مَشِشَ *to have a swelling* [splint] *on the pastern* (of a horse), أَلِلَ *to smell badly*, ضَبِبَ *to abound in lizards* (ضَبّ), لَحِحَ *to be sore* (of the eye), قَطِطَ *to be curly*, حَكِكَ *to have its hoof worn at the edges* (of a horse, etc.); لَبُبَ *to be wise* or *intelligent*, دَمُرَ *to be ugly*, شَرُرَ *to be bad*, فَكُكَ *to be silly, in one's dotage*, عَزُزَ *to have narrow orifices of the teats* (of a she-camel, ewe, etc.).

REM. *c.* Forms like ظَلِلْتَ, مَدَدْتَ, فَرَرْتَ, are, however, sometimes contracted in different ways.—1. The second radical is dropped, along with its vowel, or else its vowel is transferred to the first radical; as, رَدْتَ, رَدْنَ, for رَدَدْتَ, رَدَدْنَ, أَحَسْتَ for أَحْسَسْتَ, مَسْتُ for مَسِسْتُ (compare the Aramaic form ظَلْتُ, ظَلِلْتُ, for ظَلِلْتَ or ظَلْتَ (בַּזּוֹת for בָּזַזְתְּ) [also يَزِفْنَ for يُزْفِنَ, يَقْرِرْنَ for يَقْرِرْنَ etc.*].
2. The third radical is united with the second, and a vowel-sound inserted before the pronominal suffix. This may be either (*a*) the diphthong ـَـيْ, as قَصَّيْتَ for قَصَصْتُ, اِسْتَسْرَيْتَ for اِسْتَسْرَرْتُ, a form which is not uncommon in the fifth conjugation, as تَسَرَّيْتَ, تَلَعَّيْتَ, تَقَضَّيْتَ, تَظَنَّيْتَ for تَلَعَّعْتُ, تَقَضَّضْتُ, تَظَنَّنْتَ, تَسَرَّرْتَ (compare in the Hebrew Imperf. תְּסֻבֵּינָה for תִּסְבָּבְנָה); or (*b*) the long vowel ـَا, as مَدَّاتَ for مَدَدْتَ (compare in Hebrew סַבּוֹת, where ō = ā). The form described under 2 *a* is the usual one in modern Arabic, but in N. Africa *ai* becomes *i*, as *reddīt* for رَدَّيْتَ. Such forms as أَحَسَّيْتَ for أَحْسَسْتَ also occur.—*Comp. Gr.* p. 227 *seq.*

---

* [See De Goeje, *Gloss.* to Ibn al-Faķih s.v. زَقّ.]

A   **121.**   In the Jussive, however, the second radical not unfrequently throws back its vowel upon the first, and combines with the third, in which case the doubled letter necessarily takes a supplemental vowel (§ 27). In verbs that have *a* or *i* in the Imperf., this vowel may be either *fetḥa* or *kesra*; in those that have *u*, it may be any one of the three vowels. E.g. يَعَضَّ or يَعَضِّ, يَمَلَّ or يَمَلِّ, for يَعْضَضْ, يَمْلَلْ; يَرِدَّ, يَرُدَّ, or يَرِدِّ, يَمَدَّ, يَمَدِّ, or يَحْبِبْ يَفْرِرْ, for يَحِبَّ or يَحِبِّ, يَفِرَّ or يَفِرِّ يَفُرَّ or يَرُدِّ, for يَرْدُدْ يَمْدُدْ*.

B   **122.**   Those persons of the Imperative in which the third radical has a vowel (sing. fem., dual, and plur. masc.), sometimes do not follow the rule given in § 120, *b*, but keep the second radical apart from the third; as اِفْرِرِى, اِفْرِرَا, اِفْرِرُوا. When the usual contraction takes place, the prosthetic ĕlif is obviously no longer necessary, and therefore the Arabs say فِرِّى, فِرَّا, فُرُّوا—not اِفْرِرِّى, اِفْرَرَّا, اِفْرَرُّوا,—instead of اِفْرِرِى, etc. The masc. sing. undergoes exactly the same contraction as the Jussive (§ 121), rejecting at the same time the prosthetic اۤ; e.g. عَضَّ for اِعْضَضْ, فِرَّ for اِفْرِرْ, مُدَّ for اُمْدُدْ.

C   REM.   If the verb has a suffix, the choice of the supplemental vowel depends to some extent upon that of the suffix; say رُدَّه (رُدّه), عَضَّهُ (عَضّه), but رُدَّهَا, عَضَّهَا, not رُدَّهَا, عَضَّهَا. In the *waṣl* (§ 20) say رُدَّ الْقَوْمَ or رُدِّ الْقَوْمَ.

123.   The same rules that apply to the Active of the first form, apply also to its Passive, and to the third, fourth, sixth, seventh, D eighth, and tenth forms. But in the second, fifth, ninth, and eleventh, the second or third radical cannot be united with the other, because it is already doubled. Consequently فَرَّرَ, تَفَرَّرَ, اِفْرَرَّ, and اِفْرَارَّ, undergo no contraction. [But cf. § 120, rem. *c*, for Conj. V.]

---

* [The uncontracted forms are said to belong to the dialect of Ḥigāz, the contracted to that of Tamīm, *Faik* ii. 566.—De G. Cf. Sībawĕih ii. 443.]

Rem. In the Passive some of the Arabs substituted kĕsra for A damma, as حِلَّ for حُلَّ (contracted from حُلِلَ), whilst others gave the vowel of the first radical a sound between those of kĕsra and damma (technically called اَلْاِشْمَامُ, *giving the one vowel a scent or flavour of the other*), as رُدَّ, شُدَّ, *rüdda, šüdda* (with the German *ü* or French *u*), instead of *rudda, sudda.*

124. In the third, sixth, and eleventh forms, a long vowel, namely *ā*, precedes the double consonant, which is allowed in the case of *fĕtḥa* alone (§ 25, rem.). However, the uncontracted forms, B such as مُصَافَّةٌ, يُمَادِدُ, يُسَابِبُ, شَاحَحَ, شَاقَقَ, حَاجَجَ, قَاصَصَ, سَارَرَ, مُحَاجَجَةٌ, not unfrequently occur. Forms like تَفُورِرَ, فُورِرَ, and اِفْرِيرَأْ, are not contracted.

125. The Jussive of the derived forms may undergo exactly the same contraction as the Jussive of the ground-form, by throwing back the vowel of the second radical upon the first, combining the second radical with the third, and giving the double letter an auxiliary vowel. E.g. أُزِلَّهُ for أُزْلِلْهُ, أُقِلَّهُ for أُقْلِلْهُ, the 1st pers. sing. Juss. of the fourth C form of ذَلَّ and قَلَّ.

C. The Weak Verb.

126. Weak Verbs (*verba infirma*) are those in which one of the radicals is subject, on account of its weakness, to transformation or rejection; and which consequently differ more or less, in some parts of their inflexion, from strong verbs (see §§ 82 and 83). D

127. The weak letters are اْ, و, and ى.

128. There are two sorts of weak verbs.

(*a*) Those that have among their radicals a moveable ĕlif or hĕmza, the weakest of the gutturals. These are called *verba hĕmzata.*

(*b*) Those that have among their radicals one of the weak consonants و and ى, which approach very nearly in their nature to the vowel-sounds *u* and *i*. These are more particularly called *weak verbs.*

A   REM. The Arab grammarians do not reckon the *verba hĕmzata* among the *weak verbs*, restricting this appellation to those that contain a و or ى (§ 83, rem.).

129. In a root there may be two, or even three weak letters ; as رَأَى, وَقَى, أَوَى. Verbs that have two weak radicals are said to be *doubly weak;* those that have three, to be *trebly weak.* These may be reckoned as forming a third class of weak verbs.

1. *Verbs that have a Hĕmza among their Radicals (Verba Hĕmzata).—Tables VI., VII., VIII.*

B   **130.** These are divided into three classes, according as the hĕmza is the first, second, or third radical (verba primæ, mediæ, ultimæ radicalis hĕmzatæ). The following sections point out wherein they differ from the strong verbs.

131. If the ĕlif with hĕmza and ǵĕzma, at the end of a syllable (أْ), be preceded by one of the heterogeneous vowels ḍamma and kĕsra, it is converted, after the ḍamma, into و with hĕmza (ؤ); after the kĕsra, into ى with hĕmza (ئ). Hence بُرِئْتُ for بُرِئْتُ, 1st pers. sing. Perf.

C   Pass. of بَرَأ ; يُوْئَرُ for يَأْئَرُ, 3d pers. sing. masc. Imperf. Pass. I. or IV. of أَئَرَ; دَنُوْتَ and شَئِنْتَ for دَنَأْتَ and شَنَأْتَ, 2d pers. sing. masc. Perf. Act. of دَنُؤَ and شَئِنَ, for دَنَأ and شَنَأ (see § 133).

132. The و and ى represent in these cases the sound to which the hĕmza inclines through the influence of the preceding vowel*.

---

* [This is a convenient formula, and cannot well be improved upon without reference to the history of the Arabic language and writing, a
D consideration that lay quite beyond the scope of the native systematic grammarians, to whose method of exposition this work, for good practical reasons, is closely conformed. But from an historical point of view, when we consider the cases when *hĕmza* Is expressed by ؤ, ئ or by ء alone without a *kursī*, or supporting letter, we must distinguish between two pronunciations—that indicated by the consonants alone, which in the oldest times were written without any supplementary signs, and that indicated by the later points, such as ء. It is known

The hèmza is retained, not only to show their origin from ‍ﺍ, but also to A remind us that the syllables ‍ﺅَ and ‍ﺉٍ are not to be confounded in pronunciation with ﻮُ, ū, and ‍ﻲٍ, ī. The ḍamma and kèsra remain *short*, whilst ﺅ and ﺉ are pronounced like ‍ﺍ itself; that is to say, at the commencement of a syllable, with the spiritus lenis between the preceding syllable and the vowel that accompanies the hèmza (as ﺩَﻧُﻮ, *danu-'a*, not *danu-wa*); at the end of a syllable, with a slight emphasis and resting of the voice upon the soft breathing (as ﺷَﻨِﺌْﺖَ, *sani'-ta*, not *sanī-ta*).

REM. *a.* In modern Arabic, hèmza in the middle and at the B end of words has so completely disappeared, that ﺅ and ‍ﺉ, when preceded and followed by vowels, become ﻭ and ﻱ; except when the former has ḍamma (ﻮُ) and the latter kèsra (‍ﻲٍ), as explained in §§ 133–4. The modern Arab also pronounces ‍ﺅَ and ‍ﺉٍ like the long vowels ﻮُ ū and ‍ﻲٍ ī. Even in the ancient language, especially among the poets, we find traces of a softer pronunciation, or total rejection, of the hèmza [ﺗَﺨْﻔِﻴﻒُ ﺍﻟْﻬَﻤْﺰَﺓ § 17, *b*, rem. *b*] ; and hence the custom, at the present day, of resolving the verba C tert. rad. hèmzatæ into verba *tertiæ yā*, as ﻗَﺮﻯ for ﻗَﺮَﺃ, *to read*, ﻳَﻘْﺮﻯ for ﻳَﻘْﺮَﺃ, ﻗَﺮِﻯ for ﻗَﺮَﺃْﺕُ. This change has already begun in Hebrew, and is almost universal in Aramaic.

---

that the people of the Ḥiǵāz in the time of Mohammed gave up the original guttural sound of *hèmza* in very many cases where the other Arabs still preserved it. Now the rules of Arabic orthography were mainly fixed by the Ḳor'ān, which was originally written down in the D Ḥiǵāz in accordance with the local pronunciation. This pronunciation did not ultimately prevail over the Arabic area, but the old orthography could not lightly be tampered with, having the character of a sacred tradition. The first scribes wrote ﺟﺎﻙ, ﺟﻴﺖ, ﺑﻮﺱ, because they said *bawusa, ǵīta, ǵāka* (or nearly so). The pronunciation that prevailed, however, was *ba'usa, ǵi'ta, ǵā'aka* and this was expressed, without touching the old consonants, by writing ﺟﺎﺀَﻙَ, ﺟِﺌْﺖَ, ﺑَﻮُﺱَ. Rules for writing hèmza as ﺅ, ﺉ or ء are therefore really rules for preserving the old guttural ', in cases where it was already lost or transformed by the first scribes of the Ḳor'ān.]

A   REM. *b.* The hèmza gèzmatum over و and ى falls away after an èlif hèmzatum, because of the impossibility of pronouncing it (§ 17, *b*, rem. *b*). Hence اِيسِرْ, not اِئْسِرْ, Imperat. of أَسَرَ; اِيذَنْ, not اِئْذَنْ, Imperat. of أَذِنَ; أُومُلْ, not أُؤْمُلْ, Imperat. of أَمَلَ; اِيتَمَرَ, not اِئْتَمَرَ, 3d pers. sing. Perf. Act. VIII. of أَمَرَ; أُوتُمِنَ, not أُؤْتُمِنَ, 3d pers. sing. Perf. Pass. VIII. of أَمِنَ, all with èlif

B   conjunctionis (هَمْزَةُ ٱلْوَصْلِ); أُومِنَ, not أُؤْمِنَ, 3d pers. sing. Perf. Pass. IV. of أَمِنَ; إِيمَانٌ, not إِئْمَانٌ, Infin. IV. of أَمِنَ; أُوثِرُ, not أُؤْثِرُ, 1st pers. sing. Imperf. Act. IV. of أَثَرَ, all with èlif separationis (هَمْزَةُ ٱلْقَطْعِ).—When a word of this sort, beginning with the èlif conjunctionis, comes into the waṣl, the èlif conjunctionis falls away in pronunciation, though it may be retained in writing. In Imperatives, when preceded by وَ or فَ, *and*, it is usually rejected; as

C   وَأْتَمِرُوا, وَأْسِرْ, فَأْذَنْ, فَأْمُلْ, فَأْتِ (from اِيتِ, Imper. of أَتَى *to come*), فَأْتَمِنْ. In other cases it is retained, and the radical hèmza is left in its altered form (ئ, ؤ); as فَٱئْتَزَرَتْ *fa'tazarat*, بَعْدَ ٱئْتِلَافٍ *ba'dä'tilāfin*, ٱئْتِنَا ٱلْهُدَى *èlhudä'tinā*, يَقُولُ ٱئْذَنْ *yaküla'dan*, ٱلَّذِى ٱئْتُمِنَ (also written أُوؤْتُمِنَ) *èlladï'tumina*. In later times the pronunciation was softened in some of these cases by rejecting the hèmza and lengthening the preceding vowel; e. g. *èlhudätinā*, *yakülüdan*, *èlladïtumina* (as if written ٱلْهُدَاتِنَا, يَقُولُودَنْ, ٱلَّذِيتُمِنَ).

D   REM. *c.* ا is always retained after fètḥa in the ancient language, as يَأْسِرُ; but in modern Arabic it passes into the èlif of prolongation, as يَاكُلُ, يَامُرُ, for يَأْكُلُ, يَأْمُرُ. [And so even of old in Mecca, Nöldeke *Gesch. d. Qoráns*, p. 250, 257, whence with *scriptio defectiva* (§ 6, rem. *a*) such variations as يَلْتُكُمْ for يَأْلِتْكُمْ Süra xlix. 14.] Those who used the form تَعْلَمُ (see § 94, rem. *c*) also said تِيثَمُ for تِئْثَمُ, from أَثِمَ.

133. In the same way, ‍ا passes into ‍ؤ or ‍ئ, when it is pronounced A with damma or kèsra and preceded by fètha, or with fètha and preceded by damma or kèsra; and into ‍ئ, when it is pronounced with kèsra and preceded by damma (see § 17, *b*). E. g. بُؤُس, for بَأُس, *to be brave;* يُلَائِمُ, for يُلَاءِمُ or يُلَاإِمُ, *it agrees with,* Imperf. III. of لَأَمَ;

اِلْتَئِمُ, for اِلْتَأِمُ, *agree with, be reconciled to,* Imperat. VIII. of لَأَمَ; دَنُؤَ, for دَنُأَ, *to be mean, worthless;* يُؤَثِّرُ, for يَأَثِّرُ, *an impression is made,* Imperf. Pass. II. of أَثَرَ; اِلْتِئَامُ, for اِلْتِأَامُ, Infin. VIII. of لَأَمَ; سُئِلَ *he B was asked,* for سُأِلَ, Perf. Pass. of سَأَلَ; لُوئِمَ *peace is made (between them),* for لُوأِمَ, Perf. Pass. III. of لَأَمَ.

Rem. At the end of a word, ‍ا, pronounced with damma and preceded by fètha, is usually left unchanged; as يَقْرَأُ from قَرَأَ, يَهْنَأُ from هَنِئَ. يَبْرَأُ Imperf. Pass. II. of بَرِئَ, instead of يَقْرُؤُ, يَهْنُؤ, يَبْرُؤ. But the latter form is commonly used before the accusative suffixes, as يَقْرُؤُه.

134. Finally, ‍ا pronounced with damma or kèsra (‍ا or ‍إ), becomes C ‍ؤ or ‍ئ at the beginning of a syllable which is preceded by a syllable ending in a consonant. E.g. يَبْؤُس, for يَبْأُس, Imperf. of بَؤُس; بَؤُس, مَسْؤُول, for مَسْأُول, Pass. Particip. of سَأَلَ; يَنْئِمُ, for يَنْأِمُ, Imperf. of نَأَمَ, *to groan, to twang;* يَلْئِمُ, for يَلْأِمُ, *he acts stingily and meanly,* Imperf. IV. of لَؤُمَ; اِسْتَلْئِمُ, *put on armour,* Imperat. X. of لَأَمَ.

Rem. ‍ا at the beginning of a word remains unchanged, except in the cases stated in § 135. E.g. إِئَارٌ, أُثِرَ. D

135. At the beginning of a word, if an èlif productionis follows the radical ‍ا, the two èlifs are combined into one, which is written either with mèdda alone, or with mèdda accompanied by a hèmza to the right of the èlif, or sometimes with hèmza and a perpendicular fètha (see § 6, rem. *a*); as آمَرَ, آءَمَرَ, or أَأْمَرَ, for أَأْمَرَ, *to consult,* III. of

A اَمَرَ *to order.* The same thing takes place when a radical ا with ǧèzma (اْ) is preceded by an èlif hèmzatum with fètḥa (compare § 132, rem. *b*) ; as اَاْثَرَ, آثَرَ, or اُاْثَرَ اُثَرَ, for اُاْثَرَ, *to prefer,* IV. of اَثَرَ. In old Mss. we often find اَاْثَرَ, اَاْمَرَ.

136. In a more modern stage of the language, èlif hèmzatum with fètḥa passes into و, when preceded by fètḥa and followed by an
B èlif of prolongation (compare § 17, *b*, rem. *b*) ; as تَاَامَرُوا, تَوَامَرُوا, for or تَاَامَرُوا, *they deliberated together,* 3d pers. plur. Perf. Act. VI. of اَمَرَ ; تَوَاخَيَا, for تَاَاخَيَا or تَاَخَيَا, *the two became intimate friends,* from اَخَا (for اَخَوَ).

> REM. The same change sometimes takes place even with the
> initial èlif of the third form ; as وَاخَى, وَازَى *to be intimate with,*
> *to be opposite* or *parallel to,* وَاسَى *to console,* وَاكَلَ *to eat along with,*
> C   for اَاخَى, etc. It commenced, of course, in the Imperf. and the
> Nomina agentis and actionis, where, according to § 17, *b*, rem. *b*,
> و took the place of ؤ ; as مُوَاسٌ, يُوَاسِى, and مُوَاسَاةٌ.

137. The verbs اَخَذَ *to take,* اَمَرَ *to order,* and اَكَلَ *to eat,* reject
the first radical in the Imperat., making خُذْ, مُرْ, and كُلْ.

138. When preceded by و or فَ, *and,* the Imperative مُرْ generally recovers its radical èlif, وَامُرْ or وَمُرْ ; but not so خُذْ and كُلْ,
D which make only وَكُلْ, فَكُلْ. For the rule as regards other verba
prim. rad. hèmz., see § 132, rem. *b* ; and on the Imperative of اَتَى, *to
come,* see also § 175, rem. *a.*

139. The first radical of اَخَذَ is assimilated in the eighth form
to the characteristic ت of that form ; اِتَّخَذَ, for اِاْتَخَذَ (§ 132, rem. *b*),
to take for oneself.

> REM. *a.* The same assimilation sometimes takes place in اَزَرَ,
> *to put on one the article of dress called* اِزَارٌ, and اَجَرَ, *to give wages,*
> which makes اِيتَزَرَ or اِتَّزَرَ, *to put on an 'izār,* and اِيتَجَرَ or اِتَّجَرَ, *to*

give alms, to receive wages; still more rarely in اَمِنَ, *to be safe,* A

اِتَّمَنَ, for اِيتَمَنَ, *to trust or confide in,* and اَهَلَ, *to marry,* اِتَّهَلَ, for

اِيتَهَلَ, *do.*—The tenth form of اَخَذَ may also lose its ělif and be

written اِسْتَخَذَ.

REM. *b.* From the above assimilated forms are derived the

secondary radicals تَخِذَ, *to take,* and تَجَرَ, *to trade* (see § 148,

rem. *b*). Compare in Syriac ܐܙ̈ܕܒܢ, ܐܙ̈ܕܗܪ, ܐܙ̈ܕܗܢ; and with B

اِسْتَخَذَ, اِهَبْمَهِ, if from the rad. اِبْهَ.

140. Verba med. hèmzatæ are occasionally inflected like verba med.

rad. و et ى (§ 149, etc.), and take an ělif of prolongation instead of the

radical hèmza with fětḥa. This is particularly the case with the verb

سَأَلَ *to ask,* which has سَالَ for سَأَلَ, 2d pers. sing. m. سُلْتَ [not سَلْتَ],

يَسَلُ for يَسْأَلُ, سَلْ for اِسْأَلْ (Imperat.), Perf. Pass.

سِيلَ.—Sometimes the ělif hèmzatum is elided, its vowel being trans-

ferred to the preceding (previously vowelless) consonant. E. g. يَسَلُ C

for يَسْأَلُ, from سَأَلَ; يَرَى for يَرْأَى, from رَأَى *to see;* اَلَّكَ *to send,* for

اَلْأَكَ, whence مَلَكُ, for مَلْأَكُ, *an angel* (מַלְאָךְ).

REM. *a.* The Imperative سَلْ makes in the fem. سَلِى, du سَلَا,

plur. سَلُوا, not سَالِى, etc. When preceded by وَ and فَ, we may

say وَاْسَأَلْ or وَسَلْ, فَاْسَأَلُوا (§ 21, *d,* rem. *b*), or فَسَلُوا.

REM. *b.* The elision of the ělif occasionally happens in Hebrew,

and in Syriac it is the rule; see *Comp. Gr.* p. 46, p. 282.   D

2. *Verbs which are more especially called Weak Verbs* (§ 128, *b*).

141. These likewise fall into three classes, according as the

letter و or ى is the first, second, or third radical (verba primæ,

secundæ, tertiæ rad. و et ى).

A   A. *Verbs of which the First Radical is* و *or* ي (*verba primæ*
rad. و *et* ي).—*Table LX.*

142. Those verbs primæ rad. و, which have *kèsra* as the characteristic vowel of the Imperf. and Imperat., reject the و in these forms. E.g.
وَلَدَ *to bear children,* Imperf. يَلِدُ for يَوْلِدُ, Imper. لِدْ for اِيلِدْ (اِوْلِدْ);
وَعَدَ *to promise,* Imperf. يَعِدُ for يَوْعِدُ, Imper. عِدْ for اِيعِدْ (اِوْعِدْ).

B

REM. *a.*   Eight verbs primæ rad. و, of the form فَعَلَ, have in
the Imperf. يَفْعِلُ instead of يَفْعَلُ (contrary to the rule laid down
in § 92), and hence elide their first radical; وَثِقَ *to trust or confide
in,* يَثِقُ; وَرِثَ *to inherit,* يَرِثُ; وَرِعَ *to abstain from (what is un-
lawful),* يَرِعُ; وَرِمَ *to swell,* يَرِمُ; وَرِيَ *to be firm and hard* (of fat),
يَرِي; وَثِقَ *to be in good condition and handsome,* يَفِقُ; وَلِيَ *to be
near, to be in charge of,* يَلِي; وَمِقَ *to love,* يَمِقُ. Of these وَرِعَ has
also dialectically the form يَوْرَعُ, and a few more admit both forms;
C   e.g. وَحِرَ *to be angry with, full of hatred of,* يَحَرُ، يَوْحَرُ *to be
rough and broken* (of ground), وَغِرَ *to be hot, angry,* يَغَرُ، يَوْغَرُ, يَغَرُ;
وَلِهَ *to be stupefied with grief, to be melancholy,* يَلِهُ، يَوْلَهُ;
وَهِلَ *to be cowardly, to forget,* يَهِلُ، يَوْهَلُ.

REM. *b.*   The Imperat. عِمْ in the phrases عِمْ صَبَاحًا *good
morning!* عِمْ مَسَاءً *good evening!* seems to come from وَعِمَ, but is
in reality from نَعِمَ, Imperf. يَنْعِمُ, *to be happy, comfortable.* This is
D   the solitary instance in Arabic of the loss of the initial *n* in the
Imperat. of verbs פ״נ, which is so common in Heb. and Aram.

143.   But those verbs primæ rad. و, which have fètḥa or ḍamma
as the characteristic vowel of the Imperf. and Imperat., retain the و
in these forms.   E.g. وَجَرَ or وَجِلَ *to be afraid,* يَوْجَرُ or يَوْجَلُ, اِيجَرْ
or اِيجَلْ (for اِوْجَرْ or اِوْجَلْ); وَجِعَ *to be in pain,* يَوْجَعُ; وَحِلَ *to stick*

in the mud, يَوْحَلُ وَبِقَ; *to perish*, يَوْبَقُ وَبُوَ; *to be visited by the mur-* A *rain*, يَوْبُو وَبُلَ; *to be unwholesome* or *insalubrious*, يَوْبُلُ وَضُوَ; *to be clean and fair*, يَوْضُوَ. The same is the case with those verbs which are at once primæ rad. و and mediæ rad. geminatæ; as وَدَّ (for وَدِدَ) *to love*, يَوَدُّ for يَوْدَدُ, ايدَدْ for اوْدَدْ.

REM. In verbs primæ rad. و, of which the second and third radicals are strong, and in which the Imperf. has fĕtḥa, some Arabic dialects change the و into ا or ى. E.g. يَاجَلُ and يَيْجَلُ, for يَوْجَلُ, B from وَجِلَ, *to be afraid*; يَاجَعُ and يَيْجَعُ or يَيْجَعُ, for يَوْجَعُ, from وَجِعَ, *to be in pain*; يَاهَمُ and يَيْهَمُ, for يَوْهَمُ, from وَهِمَ, *to make a mistake*. Others even use the forms يِيجَلُ, يِيجَعُ, and يِيهَمُ.

144. In a few verbs, of which the eight following are those that most commonly occur, the initial و is dropped in the Imperf. and Imperat., notwithstanding that the characteristic vowel of these forms C is fĕtḥa.

وَدَعَ *to let alone,*	يَدَعُ,	دَعْ.
وَذَرَ *to let alone,*	يَذَرُ,	ذَرْ.
وَزَعَ *to restrain,*	يَزَعُ,	زَعْ.
وَسِعَ *to be wide* or *spacious,*	يَسَعُ,	سَعْ.
وَضَعَ *to put down* or *place,*	يَضَعُ,	ضَعْ. D
وَطِئَ *to trample upon,*	يَطَأُ,	طَأْ.
وَقَعَ *to fall,*	يَقَعُ,	قَعْ.
وَهَبَ *to give,*	يَهَبُ,	هَبْ.

REM. *a.* The reason why the و is elided in these verbs probably is, that the fĕtḥa of the Imperf. and Imperat. owes its existence only to the fact of the second or third radical being in each case a guttural or semiguttural (ر).

REM. *b.* وَدَعَ and وَذَرَ are not used in the Perf.

A   **145.** In those forms in which a kèsra or damma precedes a vowelless و, the و is changed into ى or و productionis, according to the preceding vowel. Hence اِيْجَلْ, اِيْدَدْ, for اُوْجَلْ, اُوْدَدْ, Imperat. I.; اِيرَاقٍ for اُورَاقٍ, Perf. XI.; اِسْتِيدَاعٌ, إِيدَاعٌ, for اِسْتِوْدَاعٌ, إِوْدَاعٌ, Infin. IV. and X.; يُوجِبَ for يُوْجِبَ, Imperf. Act. IV.; أُوجِبَ, أُسْتُودِعَ, for أُوجِبَ, أُسْتُودِعَ, Perf. Pass. IV. and X.

REM. In the Passive of verbs primæ rad. و, the و is sometimes changed into ﺍ, on account of a certain repugnance of the Arabs to

B   the sound of the syllable وُ; e.g. أُقِّتَ, for وُقِّتَ, *it is fixed* or *determined* (of time); أُحِىَ, for وُحِىَ, *it is revealed.*

146. Verbs primæ rad. ى are inflected in almost all their forms like the strong verbs; e.g. يَسَرَ *to play at hazard,* or *to be gentle, easy,* يَفَعَ *to ascend* (a hill), *to be grown up,* يَقِظَ; بَيْسَرُ *to be awake,* يَقِظَ *do.,* بَيْقَظُ; يَنَعَ *to become ripe,* بَيْنَعُ or بَيْنِعُ.

C   REM. يَبِسَ, *to be dry,* has بَيْبَسُ or بَيْبِسُ, and يَئِسَ, *to despair,* بَيْئَسُ or بَيْئِسُ. See § 92, rem. *a.* Dialectic varieties are يَابَسُ, for بَيْبَسُ, and يَائَسُ or بِيَأْسُ, for بَيْأَسُ. See § 143, rem.

147. In those forms in which a kèsra or damma precedes a vowelless ى, the ى is changed into ى or و productionis, according to the preceding vowel. Hence ايِسَرُ for ايْسَرُ, Imperat. I.; إِيسَارُ and اِسْتِيسَارُ, for إِيسَارُ and اِسْتِيسَارُ, Infin. IV. and X.; يُوسِرُ, يُوقِظُ, for بَيْسِرُ,

D   بَيْقِظُ, Imperf. Act. IV. of يَسَرَ and يَقِظَ.

148. In the eighth form, و and ى are assimilated to the characteristic ت, producing تّ for وْت and يْت; as اِتَّعَدَ, for اِيْتَعَدَ (اِوْتَعَدَ), *to receive a promise;* اِتَّسَرَ, for اِيْتَسَرَ (اِيْتَسَرَ), *to play at hazard.*

REM. *a.* Sometimes, however, although many grammarians disapprove of it, و and ى are not assimilated to the ت, but pass after fètha, damma, and kèsra, into the homogeneous letters of prolongation, ١, و ى. E.g. اِتَّصَلَ for اِوْتَصَلَ, اِتَّعَدَ for اِوْتَعَدَ (§ 145), A اِتَّسَرَ for اِيْتَسَرَ, اُوتُسِرَ for اُيْتُسِرَ (§ 147), in the Perf.; يَاتَصِلُ for يَوْتَصِلُ, يَاتَعِدُ for يَوْتَعِدُ, يَاتَسِرُ for يَيْتَسِرُ, in the Imperf. Compare § 139, and rem. *a.*

Rem. *b.* From these assimilated forms are derived secondary radicals; such as تَجَّهَ to *turn oneself towards, to face;* تَخَّمَ *to suffer from indigestion;* تَسَّعَ *to be wide or spacious;* تَقَّى *to fear* (God); تَلَدَ *to be born in one's house* (of a slave), *to be hereditary, inherited,* B *or long possessed;* تَكَّلَ *to rely upon;* تَلِهَ *to be stupefied by grief, to be melancholy;* تَلَا, or تَلَى, *to follow;* and in the fourth form, أَتْكَأَ *to make one lean, to prop him up;* أَتْلَجَ *to insert;* أَتْهَمَ *to suspect a person.* Compare § 139, rem. *b.*

Rem. *c.* For the inflection of verbs of this class in the cognate languages, see *Comp. Gr.* p. 234 *seq.*

B.　*Verbs of which the Second Radical is* و *or* ى (*verba*　　C *mediæ radicalis* و *et* ى).—*Tables X.—XIII.*

149. Verba mediæ rad. و et ى (called by the Arab grammarians اَلْفِعْلُ ٱلْأَجْوَفُ, *the hollow verb*) differ from strong verbs only in the first, fourth, seventh, eighth, and tenth forms. The following sections indicate the principal points of difference.

150. If the first radical is without a vowel, and the third has one, the vowel of the second radical is thrown back upon the first, and the و or ى is changed into that letter of prolongation which is homogeneous to the vowel that the first radical has now assumed. E.g.　　　D

يَقْوُلُ, *he says,*	becomes	يَقُولُ, Imperf. Act. I.
يَسْيِرُ, *he goes,*	,,	يَسِيرُ, do.
يَخْوَفُ, *he is afraid,*	,,	يَخَافُ, do.
يَهْيَبُ, *he is afraid,*	,,	يَهَابُ, do.
يُقْوَلُ, *it is said,*	,,	يُقَالُ, Imperf. Pass. I.
يُقْيَلُ, *pardon is granted,*	,,	يُقَالُ, Imperf. Pass. IV.

W.　　　　　　　　　　　　　　　　　　　11

A   يَقْوُمُ, *he remains,*   becomes   يَقِيمُ, Imperf. Act. IV.

يُلْيِنُ, *he softens,*   „   يُلِينُ,   do.

أَقْوُمُوا, *remain,*   „   أَقِيمُوا, Imperat. Plur. IV.

أَلْيِنُوا, *soften,*   „   أَلِينُوا,   do.

أَقْوَمَ, *he remained,*   „   أَقَامَ, Perf. Act. IV.

أَلْيَنَ, *he softened,*   „   أَلَانَ,   do.

B   يَسْتَقْوُمُ, *he stands upright,*   „   يَسْتَقِيمُ, Imperf. Act. X.

اُسْتُلْيِنَ, *he was thought gentle,*   „   اُسْتُلِينَ, Perf. Pass. X.

يُسْتَقْيَلُ, *pardon is asked,*   „   يُسْتَقَالُ, Imperf. Pass. X.

151. But if the third radical loses its vowel, the long vowels ـَا, ـِى و, ـُو, are changed into the corresponding short ones, because a shut syllable does not admit of a long vowel (§ 25). E.g.

C   يَقُلْ, for   يَقُولُ   (يَقْوُلُ), Jussive Act. I.

يَسِرْ   „   يَسِيرُ   (يَسْيِرُ),   do.

يَخَفْ   „   يَخَافُ   (يَخْوَفُ),   do.

يُقَلْ   „   يُقَالُ   (يُقْوَلُ), Jussive Pass. I.

يُقِمْ   „   يُقِيمُ   (يُقْوِمُ), Jussive Act. IV.

أَقِلْ   „   أَقِيلُ   (أَقْيِلُ), Imperat. IV.

أَقِمْ   „   أَقِيمُ   (أَقْوِمُ),   do.

D   أَقَمْتَ   „   أَقَامْتَ   (أَقْوَمْتَ), 2d p. sing. m. Perf. Act. IV.

أُقِدْتَ   „   أُقِيدْتَ   (أُقْوِدْتَ),   do.   Pass. IV.

اُسْتُلِنْتَ   „   اُسْتُلِينْتَ   (اُسْتُلْيِنْتَ),   do.   Pass. X.

أَقَمْنَ   „   أَقَامْنَ   (أَقْوَمْنَ), 3d p. plur. f. Perf. Act. IV.

أَقِمْنَ   „   أَقِيمْنَ   (أَقْوِمْنَ), 2d p. plur. f. Imperat. IV.

REM.   يَكُنْ, for يَكُونُ, Jussive of كَانَ, *to be,* is sometimes still farther abbreviated, especially by the poets, into يَكُ.

152. In consequence of the changes produced by the operation A of the two preceding rules, the Imperative of the first form loses its prosthetic ‍ (see §§ 98 and 122). E.g.

أَقْوُلْ becomes successively أَقُولْ, أَقُلْ, قُلْ.

اسِيرْ   ,,   ,,   اسِيرْ, اسِرْ, سِرْ.

اخْوَفْ   ,,   ,,   اخَافْ, اخَفْ, خَفْ.

اهْيَبْ   ,,   ,,   اهَابْ, اهَبْ, هَبْ.

أُقْوُلُوا   ,,   ,,   أُقُولُوا, قُولُوا.   B

اسْيِرُوا   ,,   ,,   اسِيرُوا, سِيرُوا.

اخْوَفُوا   ,,   ,,   اخَافُوا, خَافُوا.

اهْيَبُوا   ,,   ,,   اهَابُوا, هَابُوا.

153. If three open syllables follow one another in immediate succession, the first of which has fèt̤ha and the last any vowel, then the و or ى of the middle syllable is changed into ĕlif productionis, without any regard to the nature of the vowel that accompanies it. C E.g.

قَوَمَ becomes قَامَ, Perf. Act. I.

خَوِفَ   ,,   خَافَ,   do.

طَوُلَ   ,,   طَالَ,   do.

سَيَرَ   ,,   سَارَ,   do.

هَيِبَ   ,,   هَابَ,   do.

انْقَوَدَ   ,,   انْقَادَ, Perf. Act. VII.

يَنْقَوِدُ   ,,   يَنْقَادُ, Imperf. do.   D

اقْتَوَدَ   ,,   اقْتَادَ, Perf. Act. VIII.

ازْدَيَدَ   ,,   ازْدَادَ,   do.

يَزْدَيِدُ   ,,   يَزْدَادُ, Imperf. do.

Rᴇᴍ. The forms زِيَلَ and كِيدَ are mentioned as being dia-lectically used instead of زَالَ (for زَيِلَ), *to cease*, and كَادَ (for كَوِدَ), *to be near* or *on the point of*.

A   **154.** But if the vowel of the first syllable be ḍamma, and the
و or ى is accompanied by kèsra, the ḍamma is elided and the kèsra
substituted in its place, in consequence of which the و or ى becomes
ى productionis. E.g.

قُوِلَ   becomes   (قوْلَ)   قِيلَ,   Perf. Pass. I.

سُيِرَ   „   (سِيْرَ)   سِيرَ,   do.

اُسْتُوِقَ   „   (اُسْتِوْقَ)   اُسْتِيقَ,   Perf. Pass. VIII.

B   اُخْتُيِرَ   „   (اُخْتِيْرَ)   اُخْتِيرَ,   do.

REM. *a.* Instead of غيضَ ,(سوق)، سِيقَ (قول)، حِيلَ (حول)، سِيقَ (سوق)، غيضَ
(غيضَ), and the like, some Readers of the Ḳor'ān give the vowel *ī*
an إِشْمَامُ الضَّمِّ حَرَكَةٌ بَيْنَ الضَّمِّ, *a scent* or *flavour of the u-sound*
(وَالْكَسْرِ), that is to say, they pronounce it with the sound of the
German *ü* in *hüten* or the French *u* in *lune* (compare § 123, rem.),
ḳūla, ḥūla, sūḳa, ǧūḍa.

C   REM. *b.* Some of the Arabs take another method of forming
the Passive, namely by rejecting the vowel of the و or ى, and
changing those letters into و productionis; as قُوِلَ (for قُولَ, قُوِلَ),
(اُخْتُيِرَ، اُخْتِيرَ), for اُخْتُورَ (بِيعَ، بُوعَ (for بِيعَ) بُوعَ (for حُوكَ، حُوكَ) حُوكَ (for).
The verb سَالَ, for سَأَلَ (see § 140), is said to admit of the forms
سُولَ ,سِيلَ, *sūla,* and سُولَ.

REM. *c.* In forms like اُخْتِيرَ، اُسْتِيقَ, some assimilate the vowel
D   of the prosthetic èlif to the following *ī*, اُسْتِيقَ، اِخْتِيرَ, pronouncing
i or *ü*.

155. If the first radical has fètḥa and the third is without a
vowel, three cases arise.

(*a*) The second radical is و or ى with fètḥa. In this case the
second radical is elided along with its vowel, but its influence is strong
enough to change the fètḥa of the first radical into ḍamma, if it was و,
and into kèsra, if it was ى. E.g.

قُمْتَ   for   قَوَمْتَ,   2d pers. sing. m. Perf. Act. I.

سِرْتَ   „   سَيَرْتَ,   do.

(b) The second radical is و with ḍamma or ى with kèsra. In this **A** case the second radical is elided along with its vowel, as in *a*, but its influence is sufficient to change the fèṭḥa of the first radical into the homogeneous vowel. E.g.

طُلْتَ for طُوُلْتَ, 2d pers. sing. m. Perf. Act. I.

هُبْتَ „ هَيِبْتَ, do.

(c) The second radical is و with kèsra. In this case the same elision takes place, but the influence of the characteristic vowel *i* suffices to change the fèṭḥa of the first radical into kèsra. E.g. **B**

خِفْتَ for خَوِفْتَ, 2d pers. sing. m. Perf. Act. I.

مِتَّ „ مَوِتَّ (مَوِتْتَ), do.

156. In the Perfect Passive of the first, seventh, and eighth forms, if the third radical loses its vowel, the ى productionis (§ 154) is shortened into kèsra, according to § 25. E.g.

بِعْتَ for بِيعْتَ (بُيِعْتَ), 2d pers. sing. m. Perf. Pass. I.

لِمْتَ „ لِيمْتَ (لُوِمْتَ), do. **C**

اُسْتُقْتَ „ اُسْتِيقْتَ (اُسْتُوِقْتَ), do. VIII.

REM. *a.* In verbs mediæ rad. ى, and in those mediæ rad. و of the form فَعِلَ, the 1st and 2d pers. m. and fem. sing. dual and plural Perf. Act. and Pass. are identical in form; e.g. بُعْتُ for بَيَعْتُ (§ 155, *a*) and بِيعْتُ; خِفْتَ for خَوِفْتَ (§ 155, *c*).

REM. *b.* Those who pronounce in the 3d pers. ḳāla, bū‘a, etc., **D** say in the 1st and 2d persons ḳūltu, bü‘tu, etc.; whilst those who prefer قُولَ, بُوعَ, say بُعْتُ, قُلْتُ. [The prophet himself in the *ḥadīth al-waḥy* says فَبُهِلْتُ.—De G.]

157. Most verba mediæ rad. و take ḍamma, and most verba mediæ rad. ى kèsra, as the characteristic vowel of the Imperf.; e.g. from زَالَ (زَوَلَ), *to move away,* comes يَزُولُ (يَزْوُلُ); from نَالَ (نَوَلَ), *to give in a present,* يَنُولُ (يَنْوُلُ); from طَالَ (طَوُلَ), *to be long,* يَطُولُ (يَطْوُلُ, § 93); from زَانَ (زَيَنَ), *to adorn,* يَزِينُ (يَزْيِنُ); from سَارَ (سَيَرَ),

A *to go*, يَسِيرُ (يَسْيِرُ). But in some, which are of the form فَعِلَ, the Imperf. takes fètḥa (§ 92) ; e.g. from زَالَ (زَيِلَ), *to cease*, comes يَزَالُ (شَوِیَ), ; from نَالَ (نَيِلَ), *to get, obtain*, يَنَالُ (يَنْيَلُ) ; from شَاءَ *to wish*, يَشَاءُ (يَشْيَأُ) ; from خَافَ (خَوِفَ), *to fear*, يَخَافُ (يَخْوَفُ) ; from نَامَ (نَوِمَ), *to sleep*, يَنَامُ (يَنْوَمُ). مَاتَ, *to die*, has usually the form مُتُّ (for مَوِتُّ, مَوِتْتُ, Heb. מֵת, Syr. ܡܝܬ) in the Perfect, and أَمُوتُ (Heb. יָמוּת, Syr. ܢܡܘܬ) in the Imperfect, though مُتُّ, يَمَاتُ, and

B also يَمِيتُ, are mentioned by the lexicographers.

158. In verba mediæ rad. و et ى, of which the third radical is ت or ن, these letters combine with an initial ت or ن in the pronominal suffixes so as to form تّ and نّ. E.g. مُتُّ, مُتُّمْ, مِتُّ, for مُتُّتْ, from مَاتَ (موت) *to die*; بَتُّ, for بِتُّتْ, from بَاتَ (بيت) *to pass the night*; صُنُّ, for صُنْنُ, and يَصُنَّ, for يَصُنْنَ, from صَانَ (صون) *to guard*; بِنَّا, for بِنْنَا, and يَبِنَّ, for يَبْيِنَّ, from بَانَ (بين) *to be separate.* See § 90, rem. *a, b, c.*

159. In the Passive of the third and sixth forms of verba med. rad. و, the و productionis (§ 108) does not coalesce with the second radical into ٓو, for, if it did, the peculiar feature of these forms would be effaced, and they would become identical in appearance with the second and fifth (قُوِّلَ and تَقُوِّلَ). Hence we write قُووِلَ, تَقُووِلَ, not

D تَقُوِّلَ, قُوِّلَ. For the same reason, no coalition takes place in the same forms of verba mediæ rad. ى, which are always written, for example, بُويِعَ and تُبُويِعَ. See § 11, rem. *a.*

160. Some verba mediæ rad. و, and a few mediæ rad. ى, of the form فَعِلَ, are inflected throughout like strong verbs; as أَوِدَ *to be curved* or *bent*, Imperf. يَأْوَدُ ; سَوِدَ *to be black*, Imperf. يَسْوَدُ, IV. أَسْوَدَ ; عَوِرَ *to be one-eyed*, Imperf. يَعْوَرُ, IV. أَعْوَرَ ; صَوِفَ *to be woolly*, Imperf.

حَوِلَ ; يَصْوَفُ to squint, Imperf. يَحْوَلُ, IV. أَحْوَلَ ; عَوِزَ to be wanting, A
Imperf. يَعْوَزُ, IV. أَعْوَزَ ; صَيِدَ to have a particular disease (صَيَدٌ, the
glanders), said of a camel, Imperf. يَصْيَدُ ; جَيِدَ to have a long, slender
neck, Imperf. يَجْيَدُ ; غَيِدَ to be tender and flexible, Imperf. يَغْيَدُ ; هَيِفَ
to have a slender waist, Imperf. يَهْيَفُ.

161. Some verba mediæ rad. و et ى follow in the fourth form
either the strong or the weak inflection. E.g. أَثَابَ or أَثْوَبَ, to reward,
from ثَابَ to return; أَرَاحَ or أَرْوَحَ, to perceive the smell or odour of a B
thing, from رَاحَ do.; أَغَامَ or أَغْيَمَ, to be cloudy, from غَامَ do.; أَخَالَ or
أَخْيَلَ, to watch a rain-cloud, from خَالَ.

162. A few verba mediæ rad. و have only the strong inflection in
the eighth form, used to denote reciprocity; as اجْتَوَرَ to be neighbours,
from the rad. جَارَ ; ازْدَوَجَ to pair, to marry or intermarry, from the
rad. زَاجَ ; اعْتَوَرَ to borrow, from the rad. عَارَ ; اعْتَوَنَ to help one another, C
from the rad. عَانَ.

163. Many verba mediæ rad. و admit in the tenth form of either
inflection, but they generally prefer the weak, with the exception of a
few, [chiefly denominatives], which almost always adopt the strong.
E.g. اسْتَجَابَ or اسْتَجْوَبَ, to give an answer, grant a prayer, from the
rad. جَابَ ; اسْتَصَابَ or اسْتَصْوَبَ, to consider right, from the rad. صَابَ ;
اسْتَقْوَسَ to be bent with age, from قَوْسٌ a bow; اسْتَنْوَقَ to become like a D
she-camel (نَاقَةٌ). Similarly, from verba med. rad. ى, اسْتَتْيَسَ to become
like a he-goat (تَيْسٌ); اسْتَفْيَلَ to become like an elephant (فِيلٌ).

REM. a. On اسْطَاعَ or اسْتَاعَ, shortened from اسْتَطَاعَ, to obey, to
be able to do, X. of طاع, and on the secondary أَسْطَاعَ, see § 118,
rem. b.

REM. b. On the formation of the nomina agentis et patientis of
the first form from verba med. rad. و et ى, see §§ 240–1.

REM. c. For the inflection of verbs ע״ו and ע״י in Hebrew and
Aramaic see Comp. Gr. p. 242 seq.

A   *C.   Verbs of which the Third Radical is* و *or* ى (*verba tertiæ radicalis* و *et* ى ; اَلْفِعْلُ ٱلنَّاقِصُ *the defective verb*).—*Tables XIV.—XVIII.*

164.   These verbs are of five kinds ; namely :—

(*a*)   Verba tertiæ rad. و of the form فَعَلَ ; as غَزَا to *make a foray* or *raid*, for غَزَوَ (§ 167, *a*, β, a).

(*b*)   Verba tertiæ rad. ى of the form فَعَلَ ; as رَمَى to *throw*, for رَمَىَ (§ 167, *a*, β, a).

B   (*c*)   Verba tertiæ rad. و of the form فَعِلَ ; as رَضِىَ to *be pleased with*, for رَضِوَ (§ 166, *a*).

(*d*)   Verba tertiæ rad. ى of the form فَعِلَ ; as خَزِىَ to *be ashamed*.

(*e*)   Verba tertiæ rad. و of the form فَعُلَ ; as سَرُوَ to *be noble*.

165.   There are three things to be noticed regarding the third radical of these verbs ; namely, that it retains its power as a consonant, C   or it resolves itself into a vowel, or it is elided.

166.   At the commencement of a syllable, one of two things takes place. Namely :—

(*a*)   The third radical maintains its power as a consonant between the vowels ă—ā (ـَوَا, ـَيَا), ŭ--ă (ـُوَ), ŭ—ā (ـُوَا), ĭ—ă (ـِيَ), ĭ—ā (ـِيَا) ; as also when the preceding syllable ends with a consonant. E.g. غَزَوْا ,رَمَيَا ,سَرُوَتْ ,سَرُوَا ,سَرُوَ ,يَغْزُو ,يَغْزُوَانِ ; رَضِيَا ,رَضِيَ ,تَرْمِى ,تَرْمِيَانِ ; غَزْوٌ, D   رَمْىٌ ,رِضْوَانٌ.   The letter و between the vowels ĭ—ă (ـِوَ) and ĭ—ā (ـِوَا) always passes into ى ; as غُزِىَ ,رَضِىَ, for رَضِوَ ,غُزِوَ.   The letter ى is never found between the vowels ŭ—ă, ŭ—ā.

REM.   In the first and second classes, the 3d pers. fem. sing. and dual of the Perf. Act. I. and II. might have been رَمَيَتْ, غَزَوَتَا, غَزَوَتْ, رَمَيَتَا, etc., after the analogy of رَضِيَتْ, خَزِيَتْ, and سَرُوَتْ ; but the Arabs followed in the sing. the masc. forms غَزَا, رَمَى (§ 167, *a*, β, a), and, not being able to say غَزَاتْ and غَزَاتْ or رَمَيْتْ (§ 25), they substituted غَزَتْ and رَمَتْ.   In the dual, on the other hand, where they might have said غَزَزَتَا and رَمَاتَا, they followed the received fem. sing. A in adopting غَزَتَا and رَمَتَا. The form رَمَاتَا is said to occur dialectically, but is condemned by the grammarians.

(*b*)   The third radical is elided between a short vowel and the long vowels *ī* and *ū*, and the two vowels are contracted in one of two ways.

α.   Into a long vowel; namely ـُوُو into ـُو, as سَرُوا for سَرُوُوا, and يَغْزُونَ for يَغْزُوُونَ and يَغْزُوُوا ; رَضُوا ـُيُو into ـُو, as for and يَرْمُونَ for يَرْمِيُونَ and يَرْمِيُوا ; ـُوِى into ـِى, as B رَضِيوا, and تَغْزِينَ for تَغْزُوِينَ and تَغْزُوِى, أُغْزِى for أُغْزُوِى ; ـِيى into ـِى, as أَرْمِى for , and تَرْمِى for تَرْمِيِينَ and تَرْمِيِى, ارْمِى for .

REM.   The 2d pers. sing. fem. Imperat. أُغْزِى may be pronounced either *'uǵzī*, with the pure sound of the *u* (as in the masc. *'uǵzu*), or *'iǵzī*, with the إِشْمَامِ (see §§ 123, rem., and 154, rem. *a*), owing to the influence of the *ī* in the second syllable.

β.   Into a diphthong; namely ـَوُو into ـَوْ, as غَزَوْا for غَزَوُوا ; C ـَيُو into ـَوْ, as رَمَوْا for رَمَيُوا, يَرْضَوْنَ and يَرْضَوْا for يَرْضَيُونَ and ـَيى into ـَىْ, as يَغْزَوْنَ and يَغْزَوْا for يَغْزَيُونَ and يَغْزَيُوا ; يَرْضَيْوا, تَغْزَىْ for and تُغْزَىْ and تُغْزَيْنَ for تُغْزَيِينَ and تَرْضَيْنَ, تَرْضَيِى for and ارْضَيْى, تُغْزَيِى for ارْضَيِى and تُغْزَيِينَ.

167.   At the end of a syllable, the third radical is either vocalised or elided.   It may stand at the end of a syllable either naturally, as in فَعَلْتَ = غَزَوْتَ, or after dropping a short vowel, as in يَرْمِى for D يَفْعَلُ = يَرْمِىُ.   Hence arise the following cases.

(*a*)   α.   When standing naturally at the end of a syllable, the third radical is vocalised in two ways.

(a)   If the preceding vowel be homogeneous (ـُ or ـِ), و and ى become letters of prolongation, that is to say, ـُوْ *uw* and ـِىْ *iy* pass into ـُو *ū* and ـِى *ī*. E.g. سَرُوْتَ for سَرُوْتَ, خَزِيْتَ for خَزِيْتَ, رَضِيْتَ for رَضِيْتَ (from رَضِوَ for رَضِوَ, according to §§ 166, *a*, and 168).

A   (b)   If the preceding vowel be heterogeneous (َ), it forms with

و and ى the diphthongs ـَوْ and ـَىْ.   E.g. غَزَوْتَ, *gazauta*, for

gazawta; رَمَيْتَ, *ramaita*, for *ramayta*.

β. When the third radical stands at the end of a syllable, not
naturally, but in consequence of a short vowel having been dropped
(ـَوْ for ـَوَ, ـَىْ for ـَىَ and ـُىْ, ـُوْ for ـُوُ, ـِىْ for ـِىُ), it is
vocalised in three different ways.

    (a) ـَوْ *aw* and ـَىْ *ay* become *ā*, but for the sake of distinction
B   we write اـ for *aw*, and ـَى (§ 7, rem. *b*) for *ay*. E.g. غَزَا for غَزَوَ,

بُرْمَى for رَمَيَ, يُغْزَى for يُغْزَىَ and يُغْزَىُ، يُرْمَى for يَرْمَىَ and يُرْمَىُ.

    (b) ـُوْ *uw* becomes ـُو *ū*; as يَسْرُو, يَغْزُو for يَغْزُوُ، يَسْرُوُ.

    (c) ـِىْ *iy* becomes ـِى *ī*; as تَرْمِى for تَرْمِىُ.

(*b*) The third radical is elided :—

    α. When standing naturally at the end of a syllable. This
C   happens in the Jussive and Imperative, in which the signification of
the form produces the abbreviation. E.g. يَغْزُ، اُغْزُ, for يَغْزُوْ)،

اُغْزُو (اُغْزُوْ)؛ اِرْمِ، يَرْمِ، اِرْمِ, for يَرْمِى (يَرْمِىْ) اِرْمِى (اِرْمِىْ)؛ يَرْضَ، اِرْضَ،

for يَرْضَى (يَرْضَىْ) اِرْضَى (اِرْضَىْ)*.

β. When it does not naturally stand at the end of a syllable.
This happens in the nomina agentis, فَاعِلٌ (§ 80), مُفْعِلٌ، مُفَعِّلٌ, etc.
(see § 236), before the tenwīn of damma and kesra. These vowels are
elided at the same time, but the tenwīn is thrown back upon the kesra
D   of the second radical. E.g. رَامٍ for رَامِىٌ and رَامِى؛ غَازٍ for غَازِىٌ and

غَازِى (غَازِوٌ، رَاضِوٌ، § 166, *a*)؛ رَاضٍ for رَاضِىٌ and رَاضِى؛

مُغْنٍ for مُغْنِىٌ and مُغْنِى؛ مُغْنٍ for مُغَنِّىٌ and مُغَنِّى؛ etc.

168. It has been already mentioned (§ 166, *a*) that when the
third radical is و, it passes between the vowels *i—u* (ـِوُ) and *i—ā*

---

* [At the end of a sentence the final vowel of the Imperative is
often protected by a *o*, as اُمْضِهْ *go on*, اُدْنُهْ *approach*. The Jussive is
sometimes treated in the same manner (comp. Vol. ii. § 230). D. G.]

(وَا‍ـ) into ى. After ى has been introduced in this manner into the A
3d pers. sing. masc. Perf., it maintains itself throughout the whole
inflection, as far as the above rules permit. Consequently, we get
from رَضَى (for رَضِوَ) the forms تَرْضَيْتَ, رَضِيتَ, يَرْضَى, اِرْضَى; from
غُزِىَ, غُزِيتَ, تَغْزَيْنَ.

169. Final و is changed into ى in all the derived forms of the
verb; as غُزِى, رَاضَى, أَغْزَى, تَجَلَّى, تَرَاضَى, اِنْجَلَى, اِغْتَزَى, اِسْتَرْضَى.   B

REM. The ninth and eleventh forms conform to this rule, instead of contracting the two wāws into وّ. The Arabs say اِرْعَوَى *to*
abstain or *refrain*, for اِرْعَوَوَ, and not اِرْعَوَّ (اِفْعَلَّ, see § 59, rem. *a*).

170. In the nomina patientis, مَفْعُولٌ (§ 80), of verba tertiæ
rad. و, the و of the long vowel ـُو *ū* coalesces with the radical و
into وّ; as مَغْزُوٌّ for مَغْزُووٌ. In verba tertiæ rad. ى, the influence of
the third radical converts this secondary و into ى, the two coalesce
into يّ, and, in consequence, the preceding ḍamma becomes kèsra;   C
as مَرْمِىٌّ for مَرْمُوىٌ, مَرْمُوىٌ. Such verbs as رَضِىَ, in which the final ى
stands for و (§ 166, *a*), admit of either form, though مَرْضِىٌّ is far more
common than مَرْضُوٌّ.

REM. *a.* The form مَغْزِىٌّ is occasionally found in verba tert.
rad. و, instead of مَغْزُوٌّ; e.g. أَرْضٌ مَسْنِيَّةٌ or أَرْضٌ مَسْنُوَّةٌ, *irrigated*
land, from سَنَا *to irrigate*, Imperf. يَسْنُو; أَنَا اللَّيْثُ مَعْدِيًّا عَلَيْهِ وَعَادِيًا,
I am (like) the lion, whether attacked or attacking, from عَدَا عَلَى *to*   D
run at, to attack, Imperf. يَعْدُو (عَادِىٌ in rhyme for عَادِيًا).

REM. *b.* For verbs final و and ى as compared with the corresponding forms in the other Semitic dialects see *Comp. Gr.* p. 255 *seq.*

3. *Verbs that are Doubly and Trebly Weak* (§ 129).

171. Doubly weak verbs are divisible into two classes, each of
which comprises several varieties. The *first class* consists of those
which have both an élif hèmzatum and a و or ى among their radicals;
the *second* of those in which the letter و or ى occurs twice.

A   REM.   There is no triliteral verb that has more than one radical hèmza.

172.   Of the first class there are three sorts :—

(*a*)   Verba hèmzata and primæ rad. و or ى ;

(*b*)   Verba hèmzata and secundæ rad. و or ى ;

(*c*)   Verba hèmzata and tertiæ rad. و or ى.

Each of these admits of two varieties, according to the position of the êlif hèmzatum.

B   **173.**   The first sort consists of (α) verba secundæ rad. hèmzatæ, as وَأَر to *frighten;* and (β) verba tertiæ rad. hèmzatæ, as وَدَأَ to *smooth,* وَطِئَ to *tread upon.* Such words follow in their inflection both the classes to which they belong ; e.g. Imperf. يَثِرُ, يَدَأَ, يَطَأُ (§§ 132—3, and 142, 144).

REM.   The Imperf. of يَئِسَ, to *despair,* is يَيْئِسُ, more rarely يَيْئَسُ or يِيْأَسُ, [also يَائَسُ and يَايَسُ]; its Imperat. ايْأَسُ, rarely ايْئِسُ. See § 146, rem.

C   **174.**   The second sort is divided into (α) verba primæ rad. hèmzatæ, as آبَ or ءآبَ (for أَوَبَ) to *return,* آلَ or ءآلَ (for أَوَلَ) to *return;* and (β) verba tertiæ rad. hèmzatæ, as سَاءَ (for سَوَءَ) to *illtreat,* جَاءَ (for جَيَأَ) to *come,* شَاءَ (for شَيِءَ) to *wish.* Each variety unites the peculiarities of the two classes to which it belongs.

	a.		β.	
Perf. 3d p. s.	ءآبَ	سَاءَ	جَاءَ	شَاءَ
2d p. s.	أُبْتَ	سُؤْتَ	جِئْتَ	شِئْتَ
Imperf.	يُووبُ	يَسُوءُ	يَجِيءُ	يَشَاءُ
Imper.	أُبْ	سُوْ	جِيْ	شَأْ
Perf. pass.	إِيبَ	سِيءَ	جِيءَ	شِيءَ

D

175.   The third sort is divided into (α) verba primæ rad. hèmzatæ, as أَتَى to *come,* أَبَى to *refuse,* أَسِى to *grieve* or *mourn;* and (β) verba secundæ rad. hèmzatæ, as نَأَى to *be far off,* صَأَى to *utter a cry.* They are treated in their inflection like the two classes of verbs to which they belong.

α. اَتَى, اَتَتْ, اَتَيْتَ ; يَاْتِى ; ايتِ (§ 132, rem. *b*) ; اْتِ. A

اَبَى, اَبَتْ, اَبَيْتَ ; يَاْبَى ; ايبَ ; اْبَ.

β. نَاَى, نَاَتْ, نَاَيْتَ ; يَنْاَى ; انْاَ ; نَاَءْ.

REM. *a.* The Imperat. of the verb اَتَى is not unfrequently
shortened into تِ (compare § 137, and the Syriac form ܬܐ), which,
at the end of a sentence, is written تِهْ. The same thing holds good
in pause of all imperatives that consist of only one letter; as رَهْ for B
رَ, from رَاَى *to see* (§ 176) ; فِهْ for فِ, from وَفَى *to keep faith* (§ 177).

REM. *b.* The verb اَبَى, imperf. يَاْبَى, is an example of the rare
forms mentioned in § 91, rem. *c.* Lexicographers mention the forms
يَاْبِى, يِئْبَى and بِئْبَى [§ 94, rem. *c*], as being occasionally used.

176. The ělif hěmzatum of the verb رَاَى is almost always elided
in the Imperf. and Imperat.

Imperf. Indicative.　　　C

	3. m.	3. f.	2. m.	2. f.	1. c.
S.	يَرَى	تَرَى	تَرَى	تَرَيْنَ	اَرَى
D.	يَرَيَانِ	تَرَيَانِ	تَرَيَانِ	تَرَيَانِ	
P.	يَرَوْنَ	يَرَيْنَ	تَرَوْنَ	تَرَيْنَ	نَرَى

Jussive.

S.	يَرَ	تَرَ	تَرَ	تَرَىْ	اَرَ	D
D.	يَرَيَا	تَرَيَا	تَرَيَا	تَرَيَا	
P.	يَرَوْا	يَرَيْنَ	تَرَوْا	تَرَيْنَ	نَرَ

Imperative.

S. m. رَ or رَهْ (§ 175, rem. *a*), f. رَىْ ; D. c. رَيَا ; P. m. رَوْا, f. رَيْنَ.

REM. *a.* The Perf. Act. of رَاَى almost always retains the hěmza,
which may however be transposed, رَآءَ ; [for رَاَيْتُ some say رَيْتُ].
The Imperf. يَرْاَى and the Imperat. ارْاَ are used dialectically.

A   REM. *b.* The Perf. Pass. is رُئِيَ (like رُمِيَ) or, by transposition,

رِيَ*. In the Imperf. Pass. the hèmza is elided, just as in the Active

voice; e. g. يُرَأُ, يُرَ, for يُرَى.

REM. *c.* In the fourth form, when it signifies *to show*, the hèmza

is always elided : أَرَى, أَرَتْ, أَرَيْتَ; يُرِي : يُرِ; أَرِ. Otherwise it is

retained.

B   **177.** Of the second class, in which و or ي occurs twice, there

are two sorts : (*a*) those in which و or ي is the first and third

radical, as وَقَى to *guard*, وَلِيَ to *be near*, وَجِيَ to *be sorefooted* (of

a horse); and (β) those in which و or ي is the second and third

radical, as شَوَى to *roast*, قَوِيَ to *be strong*, حَيِيَ (for حَيِوَ) to *live*,

عَيِيَ to *have an impediment in one's speech*.

178. The first sort follows in its inflection the verbs of the two

C classes primæ and tertiæ rad. و or ي. E.g.

وَقَى,   وَقَتْ,   وَقَيْتَ ;   يَقِى ;   قِ or قِهْ (§ 175, rem. *a*).

وَلِيَ,   وَلِيَتْ,   وَلِيتَ ;   يَلِى ;   لِ or لِهْ.

وَجِيَ,   وَجِيَتْ,   وَجِيتَ ;   يَوْجَى ;   إِيجَ (for اوْجَ).

179. In the second sort, the second radical undergoes no change

whatever. E.g.

شَوَى,   شَوَتْ,   شَوَيْتَ ;   يَشْوِى ;   اِشْوِ.

D   قَوِيَ ,   قَوِيَتْ,   قَوِيتَ ;   يَقْوَى ;   اِقْوَ.

حَيِيَ,   حَيِيَتْ,   حَيِيتَ ;   يَحْيَا ;   اِحْىَ.

عَيِيَ,   عَيِيَتْ,   عَيِيتَ ;   يَعْيَا ;   اِعْىَ.

REM. *a.* We write يَحْيَا, يَعْيَا, not يَحْيِيَ, يَعْيِيَ, to prevent the

union of two ي, and also, in the former case, to distinguish the

Imperf. of حَيِيَ from the proper name يَحْيَى *Yaḥyà* (John).

REM. *b.* حَيِيَ admits (1) of the *contraction* of the two ي, (*a*) in

those persons of the Perf. I. in which the second ي has a vowel, as

---

* [A more recent form is رُوِّيَ; see the Gloss. to Tabarî. D. G.]

حَىَّ for حَوِىَ; (*b*) in the Imperf. I., as يَحْيَيْنَ, يَحْيَى, يَحَىَّ; (*c*) in the A
nomen actionis II. (§§ 80 and 202, rem.), تَحِيَّةٌ for تَحْيِيَةٌ; (2) of the
elision of the second ى in the Perf. and Imperf. X., when it signifies *to feel shame*, as اسْتَحَى, يَسْتَحِى, for اسْتَحْيَا.يَسْتَحْيِى — عَيِىَ-
also admits of being contracted into عَىَّ, and يَعْيَا into يَعَىَّ.—The
forms حَىَّ and عَىَّ are said to occur (compare § 123, rem., and § 153,
rem.).

180. Trebly weak verbs are divisible into two classes; namely B
(*a*) those in which one radical is hèmza and the other two و or ى;
and (*b*) those in which all the three radicals are و or ى.

REM. We pass over the second class, as it seems to consist of
only one verb, which is hardly ever used; viz. يَيَّا to *write the
letter* ى.

181. Verbs of the first class are of two sorts, namely (a) those in
which the hèmza is the first radical, as أَوَى to *betake oneself to, to
repair to*; and (β) those in which the hèmza is the second radical, C
as وَأَى to *promise*. The former are inflected like أَسَرَ and شَوَى (§ 179),
e.g. ايو, يَأْوِى, أَوَيْتَ, أَوَتْ, أَوَى; the latter like سَأَلَ and وَقَى (§ 178),
e.g.

Perfect.

	3. m.	3. f.	2. m.	2. f.	1. c.
S.	وَأَى	وَأَتْ	وَأَيْتَ	وَأَيْتِ	وَأَيْتُ
D.	وَأَيَا	وَأَتَا	وَأَيْتُمَا	وَأَيْتُمَا		D
P.	وَأَوْا	وَأَيْنَ	وَأَيْتُمْ	وَأَيْتُنَّ	وَأَيْنَا

Imperf. Indicative.

	3. m.	3. f.	2. m.	2. f.	1. c.
S.	يَأى	تَأى	تَأى	تَأْيِنَ	أَأى
D.	يَأْيَانِ	تَأْيَانِ	تَأْيَانِ	تَأْيَانِ	
P.	يَأْوُنَ	يَأْيِنَ	تَأْوُنَ	تَأْيِنَ	نَأى

A

Jussive.

	3. m.	3. f.	2. m.	2. f.	1. c.
S.	يَ	تَ	تَ	تَاي	أَ
D.	يَايَ	تَايَ	تَايَ	تَايَ	
P.	يَأُوا	يَايِنَ	تَأُوا	تَايِنَ	نَ

Imperative.

B   S. m. إِ or اِ (§ 175, rem. *a*), f. اِي; D. c. اِيَا; P. m. اُوا, f. اِينَ.

APPENDIX A.

I. *The Verb* لَيْسَ.

182. The negative substantive verb لَيْسَ, *he is not*, has no Imperf. or Imperat., and is inflected like verba mediæ rad. و et ي.

	3. m.	3. f.	2. m.	2. f.	1. c.
S.	لَيْسَ	لَيْسَتْ	لَسْتَ	لَسْتِ	لَسْتُ
C D.	لَيْسَا	لَيْسَتَا	لَسْتُمَا	لَسْتُمَا	لَسْنَا
P.	لَيْسُوا	لَسْنَ	لَسْتُمْ	لَسْتُنَّ	لَسْنَا

REM. *a*. لَيْسَ is con.pounded of لا, *not*, and the unused أَيْسَ* = Heb. יֵשׁ, *he is*, Aramaic אִית׳, אִית, ܐܝܬ; originally a substantive, signifying *being, existence*, as in the phrase لَا يَعْرِفُ أَيْسَ مِنْ لَيْسَ, *he does not know what is from what is not*. [Therefore the suffix of the 1st person sing. added to لَيْسَ is not only لَيْسَنِى (and لَيْسَ إِيَّاى), but also لَيْسِى (§ 185, rem. *a*, Vol. ii. § 186, *e*)] The Assyrian seems also to have the word *isu*, with its negative *lā isu*, in the double sense of ‘to be’ and ‘to have’.

REM. *b*. Instead of لَيْسَ we find occasionally [as in the Kor’ānic phrase وَلَاتَ حِينَ مَنَاصٍ] the indeclinable لَاتَ, which corresponds to the Aramaic ܠܝܬ, לֵית, לַיִת, compounded of לָא and אִית, ܐܝܬ.

---

* [Or rather لِيَس according to Nöldeke, *Mand. Gramm.* p. 293, note 5.]

II. *The Verbs of Praise and Blame.* A

183. The *verbs of praise and blame* (أَفْعَلُ ٱلْمَدْحِ وَٱلذَّمِّ) are
نِعْمَ, *to be good*, and بِئْسَ, *to be bad.* They are used as exclamations,
and are generally indeclinable, though the fem. نَعْمَتْ and بِئْسَتْ
(and, it is said, the dual نَعْمَتَا, نَعْمَمَا, and the plur. نِعْمُوا, نِعْمْنَ) occur.
[The following noun must be defined by the article or a dependent
genitive, as: نِعْمَ ٱلصَّاحِبُ زَيْدٌ, *Zèid is an excellent companion*, lit. B
excellent is the companion Zèid, or else the indefinite accusative must
be used نِعْمَ صَاحِبًا زَيْدٌ, *excellent as a companion is Zèid.*]

REM. *a.* Instead of نِعْمَ we may say نَعْمَ, نَعِمَ, and نَعِمَ, which
last is obviously the original form. In like manner بِئْسَ admits of
the forms بَئِسَ, بَأْسَ, and بَئِسَ. If followed by مَا, we may write
نِعْمَ مَا or بِئْسَمَا, and نِعْمَ مَا or, by contraction, نِعِمَّا.

REM. *b.* These forms are to be explained as follows. (1) Every C
Arabic verb of the form فَعَلَ or فَعُلَ may also be pronounced فَعْلَ;
as رَضِيَ for رَضْيَ, بَذِخَ for بَذْخَ, دَبِرَ for دَبْرَ, ضَجِرَ for ضَجْرَ, عَلِمَ for عَلْمَ, for
قَصُرَ, قَرُبَ for قَرْبَ, حَسُنَ for حَسْنَ, شَهِدَ for شَهْدَ, and شَهُدَ for شَهْدَ, رَضِيَ for
كَرُمَ for كَرْمَ, قَصُرَ for قَصْرَ,—a contraction which is sometimes extended
to the passive فُعِلَ, as مُطِيَ for مُطْيَ (from مَطَا). Hence نِعْمَ and
بِئْسَ become نَعْمَ and بَأْسَ. (2) If the second radical be guttural,
its vowel, instead of being elided, may be transferred to the first D
radical; as شَهِدَ for شِهْدَ, ذَهِبَ for ذِهْبَ. Hence نِعْمَ for نَعِمَ, بِئْسَ
for بَئِسَ. (3) The form فِعْلَ, which has been thus attained, may
take an additional kèsra to lighten the pronunciation (فِعِلَ); as
ذِهِبَ, شِهِدَ. Hence نِعِمَ, بِئِسَ [or rather, according to *Comp. Gr.*
p. 166, شَهِدَ becomes شِهِدَ by assimilation of the vowels, and the
latter may then be shortened to شِهْدَ, as the former may be shortened

A   to شُهِدَ]. -These observations cast light on the peculiar form of intransitive verbs in Æthiopic ; as *gabra* ("to do") for *gabĭra* (compare عَمِلَ), and, when the second radical is guttural, *mĕhra* ("to have pity upon," رَحِمَ) for *maḥĭra*, *sĕhna* ("to be hot," سَخِنَ) for *saḥĭna* or *saḥŭna*, see *Comp. Gr.* l.c.

REM. c.   Other verbs of this class are حَبَّ or حُبَّ, *to be pleasing or charming* (contracted from حَبُبَ)*; حَسُنَ, usually contracted into

B   حُسْنَ, *to be good* or *excellent ;* سَاءَ, *to be bad* or *evil ;* بَعُدَ, commonly contracted into بَعْدَ, *to be far off ;* and سَرُعَ or سُرُعَ, *to be quick* (contracted from سَرُعَ). The first of these is frequently combined with the demonstrative ذَا (§ 340), and forms the indeclinable حَبَّذَا, *lovely, charming,* or *excellent, is* ——.

III.   *The Forms expressive of Surprise or Wonder.*

184.   The Arabic language possesses two forms of expression,

C   called by the native grammarians أَفْعَالُ التَّعَجُّبِ or *verbs of surprise or wonder.* The one is the 3d pers. sing. masc. Perf. Act. IV., preceded by مَا (مَا التَّعَجُّبِيَّةُ *the mā expressive of surprise*), and followed by the accusative of the object that causes surprise ; as مَا أَفْضَلَ زَيْدًا, *what an excellent man Zĕid is!* The other is the 2d pers. sing. masc. Imperat. IV., followed by the preposition بِ with the genitive ; as أَفْضِلْ بِزَيْدٍ, with the same signification as before.

REM. a.   The first formula literally means : *what has made Zĕid excellent?* can anything make him more excellent than he is? The

D   second : *make Z. excellent* (if you can,—you cannot make him more excellent than he is) ; or, more literally : *try (your ability at) making excellent upon* (بِ) *Zĕid.* They are, of course, indeclinable. [For أَكْثِرْ بِسَعْدٍ a poet says كَاثِرْ بِسَعْدٍ, *Ḥamāsa* p. 670; comp. § 43, rem. c. D. G.]

REM. b.   Verbs of surprise are, generally speaking, formed only from triliteral verbs in the active voice, which are capable of being fully inflected, and express an act or state in which one person may

———

*   [You say حَبَّ زَيْدٌ إِلَيْنَا and, more commonly, حَبَّ بِزَيْدٍ إِلَيْنَا, *how beloved Zĕid is to us!* D. G.]

vie with or surpass another. They cannot be formed from the A
passive voice; nor from quadriliterals; nor from verbs that are
defective in inflection, like نِعْمَ and بِئْسَ, or in meaning, like the
substantive verb كَانَ *to be* (from كَانَ زَيْدٌ قَائِمًا, *Zeid was standing
up,* we cannot say مَا أَكْوَنَ زَيْدًا قَائِمًا or أَكُونُ بِزَيْدٍ قَائِمًا); nor
from verbs like مَاتَ *to die* and فَنِيَ *to perish,* expressing an act or
state in which one agent cannot excel another; nor from negatived
verbs (as مَا عَاجَ بِالدَّوَآءِ, *he did not heed the medicine*); nor from
verbs signifying colours and defects, whence are derived adjectives B
of the form أَفْعَلُ (as سَوِدَ *to be black,* أَسْوَدُ; حَوِلَ *to squint,*
أَحْوَلُ).
The grammarians add that verbs of surprise cannot be formed from
the derived forms of the triliteral verb; but neither this limitation,
nor that with respect to the passive voice, is strictly observed (compare § 235). We find, for example, from the Passive مَا أَشْغَلَهُ, *how
much he is busied!* from شُغِلَ *to be busy;* مَا أَزْهَاهُ, *how proud or
vain he is!* from زُهِيَ *to be proud or vain;* مَا أَمْقَتَهُ عِنْدِى, *how
hateful he is to me!* from مُقِتَ *to be hated;* and from derived forms, C
especially the fourth, مَا أَعْطَاهُ, *how liberal he is!* from أَعْطَى *to
give,* IV. of عَطَا *to take in the hand;* مَا أَوْلَاهُ لِلْمَعْرُوفِ, *how liberal
he is in bestowing gratuities!* from أَوْلَى *to bestow,* IV. of وَلِىَ *to be
near;* مَا أَحْوَلَهُ, or مَا أَحْيَلَهُ, *how wily he is!* from اِحْتَالَ *to practise
an artifice or wile,* VIII. of حَالَ *to be shifted or changed;* مَا أَخْصَرَهُ,
how short, or shortened, it is! from اُخْتُصِرَ *to be shortened or abridged,* D
passive of VIII. from the rad. خصر. The rule with regard to verbs
expressing colours or defects is violated, for example, by مَا أَحْمَقَهُ,
how stupid he is! from حَمُقَ *to be stupid,* مَا أَبْيَضَ هٰذَا الثَّوْبَ, أَحْمَقُ,
how white this piece of cloth is! from اِبْيَضَّ *to be white,* أَبْيَضُ.

REM. *c.* When formed from verbs med. rad. gemin. or tert. rad.
و et ى, the verbs of surprise follow the inflection of these classes;
as مَا أَشُدَّ أَبَاهُ or مَا أَشْدِدْ بِأَبِيهِ, *how strong his father is!* مَا أَحْلَاهُ, *how
sweet it is!* مَا أَغْنَاهُ, *how rich he is!* But if formed from verba med.

rad. و et ى, they follow the inflection of the strong verb; as أَجْوِدْ بِهِ or مَا أَقْوَلَهُ, *how well he speaks !* مَا أَجْوَدَهُ or أَقْوِلُ بِهِ, *how excellent* or *generous he is !*

REM. *d.* When a verb of surprise cannot be formed directly from a root, recourse must be had to a circumlocution (compare § 235); as مَا أَنْقَى حُمْرَتَهُ, *how red it is !* مَا أَشَدَّ بَيَاضَهُ, *how pure white it is !* مَا أَكْثَرَ قَائَلَتَهُ, *what a pretty brown it is !* أَحْبِبْ بِسُمْرَتِه, *how often he takes a siesta !* مَا أَجْوَدَ جَوَابَهُ or أَجْوِدْ بِجَوَابِه, *how good his reply is !* and not مَا أَحْمَرَهُ, مَا أَبْيَضَهُ, أَسْمِرْ بِه, مَا أَقْيَلَهُ, مَا أَجْوَبَهُ or أَجْوِبْ بِه.

REM. *e.* To form the past tense of such verbs, كَانَ is prefixed to the Perfect form; as مَا كَانَ أَفْضَلَ زَيْدًا, *how excellent Zèid was !* But we may also say مَا أَفْضَلَ مَا كَانَ زَيْدٌ (literally, *what has made excellent that which Zèid was ?* What has produced the past excellence of Zèid ?).

REM. *f.* مَا أَحْسَنَهُ, *how good,* or *goodly, he is !* مَا أَمْلَحَهُ, *how handsome he is !* and less frequently مَا أَحْلَاهُ, *how sweet it is !* admit of the diminutive forms (see § 269) مَا أُحَيْسِنَهُ, مَا أُمَيْلِحَهُ, and مَا أُحَيْلَاهُ.

APPENDIX B.

The Verbal Suffixes, which express the Accusative.

185. The following are the verbal suffixes, which express the accusative :

Singular.

Masc.	Common.	Fem.
3. p. هُ *him.*		هَا *her.*
2. p. كَ *thee.*		كِ *thee.*
1. p.	نِى *me.*	

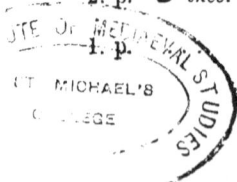

Dual.

Masc.	Common.	Fem.
3. p.	هُمَا *them both.*	A
2. p.	كُمَا *you both.*	
1. p.		

Plural.

3. p. هُمْ *them.*		هُنَّ *them.*
2. p. كُمْ *you.*		كُنَّ *you.* B
1. p. . . .	نَا *us.*	. . .

REM. *a.* The same forms serve, when appended to the noun, to express the genitive; excepting that *my* is ـِي instead of نِي (see § 317). The نْ of the suffix نِي is called by the grammarians نُونُ ٱلْوِقَايَةِ, *the guarding* or *preventive* n, because it prevents the final vowels of the verb from being absorbed by the long vowel ـِي, as happens with the noun (see § 316, *b*); and also نُونُ ٱلْعِمَادِ, *the* C *supporting* n, because it serves as a sort of prop or support to the ـِي, which is regarded as the essential portion of the suffix.

REM. *b.* The ḍamma of هُ, هُمَا, هُمْ, and هُنَّ, is changed after ـِ, ـِي, and ـَيْ, into kĕsra; as يَأْتِيهِمْ, يَأْتِيهِ, *he will come to him, to them;* اِيتِهِمَا, اِيتِهِنَّ, *come to them* (dual m. and f.), *to them* (plur. fem.); لَمْ تَرْضَيْهِ *thou* (fem.) *hast not been pleased with him.*

REM. *c.* The ـِي of the suffix 1st pers. sing. is sometimes dropped; as اِتَّقُونِ for اِتَّقُونِي, *fear me;* [comp. § 6, rem. *a*]. D

REM. *d.* Old and poetic forms are: ـِيَ and نِيَ (هِمْ or هِمُ) هُمُ هِمِ, كُمُ. See § 89, 1, rem. *c*, and § 20, *b* and *d*. [The pausal forms ـِيَهْ and نِيَهْ, see Vol. ii. § 228, rem. *b*. Instead of كَ some dialects have شْ; see Lane and the *Moḥît.* D. G.]

REM. *e.* The Hebrew and Aramaic suffixes, in general, closely resemble those of the *modern* Arabic; see *Comp. Gr.* p. 153 *seq.*

A 186. Some forms of the verb are slightly altered by the addition of the accusative suffixes.

(*a*) Those persons which end in the élif otiosum (see § 7, rem. *a*), reject it before the suffix, as being no longer necessary (since it was added only to prevent the possibility of the termination ـُوـ being in some cases mistaken for the conjunction وَ, *and*); as نَصَرُوا *they helped,* نَصَرُونِى *they helped me.*

B (*b*) The final consonant of the 2d pers. masc. plur. Perf. retains before the suffixes, to avoid cacophony, the long ḍamma which it had in an older stage of the language; as رَأَيْتُمْ *ye have seen,* رَأَيْتُمُونِى *ye have seen me.* The same thing takes place with the accusative suffix of the 2d pers. masc. plur. كُمْ, when it is followed by another suffix (see § 187); as يُرِيكُمُوهُمْ *he shews them to you.*

(*c*) The 2d and 3d pers. masc. plur. Imperf. occasionally reject

C the termination نَ before the suffixes نِى and نَا; as تَأْمُرُونِى for تَأْمُرُونَنِى, *ye order me**, تَقْلُونَا for تَقْلُونَنَا, *ye hate us,* يَجِدُونِى for يَجِدُونَنِى, *they will find me.* The same thing happens to the 2d pers. sing. fem.; as تُشَوِّقِينِى, *thou makest me long,* for تُشَوِّقِينَنِى.

(*d*) The vowel ـَ in the termination of the 2d pers. fem. sing. Perf. is sometimes lengthened before the suffixes; as كَسَرْتِيهِ · for كَسَرْتِهِ, *thou hast broken it.*

D (*e*) The ى of the 3d pers. masc. sing. Perf. in verba tertiæ rad. ى, may be retained before the suffixes, or (which is far more usual) be changed into ١; as رَمَيِهُ (§ 7, rem. *c*) or رَمَاهُ, *he threw, or shot, at him.*

[* In Sūra xxxix. 64 a third reading is recorded, viz. تَأْمُرُونِّى, and there are similar variations in other passages. So also with verbs third نْ we occasionally find such contractions as مَكَّنِى for مَكَّنَنِى (Sūr. xviii. 94), تَأْمَنَّا for تَأْمَنُنَا (Sūr. xii. 11).]

[REM.   In case of the suffixes ‌كَ, ‌كُمْ etc. being affixed to the A Jussive of a verb tertiæ ‌كَ, the two ‌كَ are assimilated; the latter loses its ǵezma, the ‌كَ of the suffix takes tešdîd, as يُدْرِكُّمْ.]

187.   A verbal form may take two suffixes, provided they do not indicate one and the same person.   These two may both be appended to the verb, the suffix of the 1st pers. naturally preceding that of the 2d or 3d, and the suffix of the 2d pers. that of the 3d.   E.g. أَعْطَانِيكَ, أَعْطَانِيهِ, *he gave thee, it, to me*; أَعْطَيْتُكَهُ, *I gave it to thee*; يَكْفِيكَهُمْ, *he will suffice thee against them* (will be sufficient to protect thee B against them); أَنُلْزِمُكُمُوهَا, *shall we compel you (to receive) it?*

[REM.   Combinations like أَعْطَاهَاهُ, *he gave him to her*, أَعْطَاهُوهَا, *he gave her to him*, are legitimate but rare.   (Note the orthography in the latter case.)   But أَعْطَاهُهُ is not used; see § 189, rem. *a*.]

188.   Sometimes, however, we find the pronominal object expressed, not by the accusative suffixes attached to the verb, but by the genitive suffixes appended to the word إِيَّا *'iyâ* (which never occurs alone).   The following are the compound pronouns thus formed :

	Masc.	Common.	Fem.
		Singular.	C
3. pers.	إِيَّاهُ		إِيَّاهَا
2. pers.	إِيَّاكَ	. . .	إِيَّاكِ
1. pers.	. . .	إِيَّايَ	
		Dual.	
3. pers.	. . .	إِيَّاهُمَا	D
2. pers.	. . .	إِيَّاكُمَا	
1. pers.	. . .	. . .	. . .
		Plural.	
3. pers.	إِيَّاهُمْ	. . .	إِيَّاهُنَّ
2. pers.	إِيَّاكُمْ	. . .	إِيَّاكُنَّ
1. pers.	. . .	إِيَّانَا	

A   REM. *a.*   The suffix of the 1st p. sing. is in this case ــِيَ, instead of ـِيَ, because all nouns ending in ـِي take that form.   See § 317, rem. *a.*

REM. *b.*   For the linguistic affinities of إِيَّا (dialectically هِيَّا) in the other Semitic languages, see *Comp. Gr.* p. 112 *seq.*

189.   These suffixes compounded with إِيَّا are used in two cases.

(*a*)   Very frequently, but not always (see § 187), when two suffixes B would otherwise have to be appended to the same verb; as أَعْطَانِى إِيَّاهُ, instead of أَعْطَانِيهِ, *he gave it to me.*

(*b*)   When the pronoun is, for the sake of emphasis, placed before the verb; as إِيَّاكَ نَعْبُدُ وَإِيَّاكَ نَسْتَعِينُ, *Thee* (none but Thee) *we worship, and to Thee we cry for help.* Compare in Heb. הָאוֹתִי לֹא־תִירָאוּ, Jerem. v. 22.

C   REM. *a.*   The suffix attached to إِيَّا is always that which would occupy the second place, if appended to the verb.   In certain cases this form alone is used, either for the sake of precision or of euphony.   Thus, *he gave me to him* must be worded أَعْطَاهُ إِيَّاىَ, to distinguish it from أَعْطَانِيهِ *he gave him to me;* but it is euphony which requires أَعْطَاهُ إِيَّاهُ, *he gave it to him,* instead of أَعْطَاهُهُ.

REM. *b.*   A very strong emphasis is expressed by prefixing the D pronoun with إِيَّا, and at the same time appending the pronominal suffix to the verb; as وَإِيَّاىَ فَاتَّقُونِ, *Me therefore, fear Me.*

II. THE NOUN.

190.   The Noun, اَلِاسْمُ, *nomen,* is of six kinds.

(*a*)   The *nomen substantivum,* or Substantive, more especially designated اَلِاسْمُ, and also اَلْمَوْصُوفُ, or اَلْمَنْعُوتُ, *qualificabile,* that is, a word which admits of being united with a descriptive epithet (adjective).

(*b*) The *nomen adjectivum*, or Adjective, ٱلصِّفَةُ, ٱلْوَصْفُ, or ٱلنَّعْتُ, A quality, *descriptive epithet*.

(*c*) The *nomen numerale*, or Numeral Adjective, ٱسْمُ ٱلْعَدَدِ, *the noun of number*.

(*d*) The *nomen demonstrativum*, or Demonstrative Pronoun, ٱسْمُ ٱلْإِشَارَةِ, *the noun of indication*, that is, by which some object is pointed out.

(*e*) The *nomen conjunctivum*, or Relative Pronoun, ٱلْاِسْمُ ٱلْمَوْصُولُ B or ٱلْمَوْصُولُ ٱلْاِسْمِيُّ, *the noun that is united (with a relative clause)*, as opposed to ٱلصِّلَةُ, *the relative clause itself*.

(*f*) The *pronomen*, or Personal Pronoun, ٱلضَّمِيرُ or ٱلْمُضْمَرُ, *the word by which something is concealed or kept in, and so conceived of by, the mind*, as opposed to ٱلظَّاهِرُ or ٱلْمُظْهَرُ, *that which is apparent or manifested*, the substantive to which the pronoun refers. It is also C called ٱلْكِنَايَةُ, ἀντωνυμία.

REM. *a.* Of the pronouns we have already treated in part in §§ 84—89 and 185—189, and some further remarks regarding them will be given in § 317. The numeral adjectives and the demonstrative and relative pronouns will be handled separately, after the nouns substantive and adjective (see §§ 318—353). The nouns substantive and adjective we shall treat of together, because, in regard to form, they are identical in almost every respect.

REM. *b.* The names of the pronoun, ٱلضَّمِيرُ and ٱلْمُضْمَرُ, are D elliptical expressions, for ٱلضَّمِيرُ بِهِ and ٱلْمُضْمَرُ بِهِ, as the above translation shows.

--- --- ---

A
A. THE NOUNS SUBSTANTIVE AND ADJECTIVE.

1. *The Derivation of Nouns Substantive and Adjective, and their different Forms.*

191. Nouns are divisible, in respect of their origin, into two classes, *primitive* and *derivative.* The primitive nouns are all substantives; as رَجُلٌ *man*, فَرَسٌ *horse*, عَيْنٌ *eye*, مَآءٌ *water.* The derivative nouns may be substantives or adjectives, and are either

B *deverbal*, that is, derived from verbs, as تَقْسِيمٌ *division* (from قَسَمَ to divide), مِفْتَاحٌ *a key* (from فَتَحَ to open), مَرِيضٌ *sick* (from مَرِضَ to be sick); or *denominative*, that is, derived from nouns, as مَأْسَدَةٌ *a place which abounds in lions* (from أَسَدٌ *a lion*), إِنْسَانِىٌّ *human* (from إِنْسَانٌ *a human being*), كُلَيْبٌ *a little dog* (from كَلْبٌ *a dog*). At a later period, nouns were formed, in the language (or rather jargon) of the philosophical schools, from pronouns and particles (we might call

C them *departiculative*), as أَنَانِيَّةٌ *egotism* (from أَنَا *I*), كَيْفِىٌّ *qualitative*, and كَيْفِيَّةٌ *quality* (from كَيْفَ *how?*).

REM. *a.* In such Arabic Lexicons as are arranged according to the etymological principle, a verb is frequently given as the etymon of what are really primitive nouns, and a comparison of the meaning of the two shows that the former is in fact the derivative

' word. Thus مَآءٌ, *water*, is not derived from مَاهَ, *to be full of water*,

D which is given in the Dictionaries as its root, but, conversely, مَاهَ is a denominative verb, formed from مَآءٌ; nor is فَرُسَ, *to be skilled in horsemanship*, the root of فَرَسٌ, *a horse*, but a denominative from it.

REM. *b.* By the native grammarians nouns are classified as follows.

(1) اِسْمٌ جَامِدٌ, *a noun that is stationary* or *incapable of growth*, one that is not itself a nomen actionis or infinitive, nor derived from a nom. act., and which does not give birth to a nom. act. or verb,

as رَجُلٌ *a man,* بَطَّةٌ *a duck;* opposed to اسْمٌ مُشْتَقٌّ, *a noun that is* A
derived from a nom. act. or verbal root, as كَاتِبٌ *a writer,* قَتِيلٌ
slain.

(2) اسْمٌ مُجَرَّدٌ, i.e. مُجَرَّدٌ عَنِ الزِّيَادَةِ, *a noun that is bare of any*
accessory or *increment,* which comprises merely the letters of the
root and no more, as عِلْمٌ *knowledge,* سَفَرْجَلٌ *a quince;* opposed to
اسْمٌ مَزِيدٌ فِيهِ, *a noun that is augmented* by additional letters, as
عَلَّامَةٌ *a very learned man,* اِحْرِنْجَامٌ *the being gathered together in* B
a mass.

(3) اسْمٌ عَلَمٌ, or اسْمُ عَلَمٍ, *a proper name,* the distinctive mark
of an individual; opposed to اسْمُ جِنْسٍ, *a generic* or *common noun,*
designating a whole kind or genus (γένος, ܓܢܣܐ).

(4) The اسْمُ الْجِنْسِ may be either (*a*) اسْمُ عَيْنٍ, a noun
denoting *a concrete object,* as رَجُلٌ *a man,* فَرَسٌ *a horse;* or (*b*) اسْمُ
مَعْنًى, a noun denoting *an abstract idea,* as عِلْمٌ *knowledge,* جَهْلٌ C
ignorance. The same terms may be applied to adjectives; رَاكِبٌ,
riding, is an اسْمُ عَيْنٍ, but مَفْهُومٌ, *understood,* an اسْمُ مَعْنًى.

(5) The اسْمُ الْعَلَمِ may be either (*a*) عَلَمٌ جِنْسِىٌّ, *a proper name*
applicable to every individual of a whole kind, as أُسَامَةُ *the lion,*
جَعَارِ *the female hyæna* (like "Puss" for the cat, "Renard" for the
fox); or (*b*) عَلَمٌ شَخْصِىٌّ, *a proper name applicable to only one* D
individual of a kind, as دَاحِسٌ and الْغَبْرَآءُ, *names of horses,* قَرُوبٌ,
the name of a camel, سَعْدٌ، عَوْفٌ، ثَعْلَبَةُ, *names of men,* أُمَيْمَةُ,
الْخَنْسَآءُ, *names of women.*

(6) The اسْمُ الْعَلَمِ may also be either (*a*) an اسْمٌ, or *name,* in
its strictest sense, as عَمْرُو، جَعْفَرُ، بُثَيْنَةُ; or (*b*) a كُنْيَةٌ, i.e. a name
compounded with أَبُو, *father of,* as أَبُو الْعَبَّاسِ, or أُمّ, *mother of,* as
أُمّ كُلْثُومِ, or اِبْنُ, *son of,* as اِبْنُ حَيَّانَ, or اِبْنَةُ or بِنْتُ, *daughter of,*

A   as بِنْتُ هِنْدٍ ; or (c) a لَقَبٌ, *a surname*, which may be either a
nickname (نَبَزٌ), as بَطَّة *Duck* or *Bottle*, أَنْفُ ٱلنَّاقَةِ *Camel's-nose*,
بَبَّة *Bebba* (imitation of a sound), or an honourable epithet, as
شَمْسُ, زَيْنُ ٱلْعَابِدِينَ, *the pride* or *glory of those that worship* (God),
ٱلْمَعَالِى, *the sun of virtues.* The كُنْيَة is also employed in reference
to animals, as أَبُو, أَبُو أَيُّوبَ, *Job's father*, the "patient" camel; أَبُو
ٱلْحُصَيْنِ, *the father of the little fort*, the fox; أُمُّ عَامِرٍ, *the female
hyœna*; ٱبْنُ عِرْسٍ, *the weasel*; بِنْتُ طَبَقٍ, *the tortoise.*

B   (7) An ٱسْمُ عَلَمٍ may likewise be either (a) مُفْرَدٌ, *simple*,
consisting of a single word, as عَنْتَرَةُ, أَوْسٌ ; or (b) مُرَكَّبٌ, *compounded.* The مُرَكَّبٌ may be either (a) إِسْنَادِىٌّ, *predicative*, when
the words that compose it constitute a جُمْلَة or proposition, as
بَرَقَ نَحْرُهُ (his throat shone), تَأَبَّطَ شَرًّا (he carried mischief under his
arm), شَابَ قَرْنَاهَا (her two locks became gray); or (β) a mixed
compound, مُرَكَّبٌ مَزْجِىٌّ, which is not a proposition (غَيْرُ جُمْلَةٍ), as

C   بَعْلَبَكُّ, Baʻal-bèk, مَعْدِيكَرِبُ, Maʻdī-karib, سِيبَوَيْهِ, Sība-wèih ; or
(γ) مُضَافٌ وَمُضَافٌ إِلَيْهِ, a substantive governing another in the
genitive, as عَبْدُ مَنَافٍ, ٱمْرُؤُ ٱلْقَيْسِ, أَبُو ذُوَيْبٍ, أُمُّ كُلْثُومٍ.

(8)   Finally, an ٱسْمُ عَلَمٍ may be either (a) مُرْتَجَلٌ, *improvised*,
extemporised, impromptu, existing only as a proper name, as عِمْرَانُ.
فَقَعَسُ, حَيْوَةُ ; or (b) مَنْقُولٌ, *transferred* from some other use, *tro-*

D   *pical.* The latter class is of six kinds, viz. (a) مَنْقُولٌ عَنِ ٱسْمِ عَيْنٍ
as فَضْلٌ, مَنْقُولٌ عَنِ ٱسْمِ مَعْنًى, as نَوْرٌ (a bull), أَسَدٌ (a lion); (β)
(excellence), إِيَاسٌ (giving, gift); (γ) مَنْقُولٌ عَنْ صِفَةٍ, as حَاتِمٌ,
يَشْكُرُ, شَمَّرُ, مَنْقُولٌ عَنْ فِعْلٍ, as نَائِلَةُ (bestowing); (δ) (judging),
; (ε) مَنْقُولٌ عَنْ صَوْتٍ, as بَبَّةُ (see above, 6, c); إِصْمِتْ, تَغْلِبُ, يَحْيَى
and (ζ) مَنْقُولٌ عَنْ مُرَكَّبٍ (see above, 7, b).

192.   Deverbal nouns are divisible into two principal classes; A namely:—

(*a*)   *Nomina verbi* or *nomina actionis,* أَسْمَآءُ ٱلْفِعْلِ (*infinitives*).

(*b*)   *Nomina agentis,* أَسْمَآءُ ٱلْفَاعِلِ, and *nomina patientis,* أَسْمَآءُ ٱلْمَفْعُولِ, (*participles*).

The nomina verbi are by their nature substantives, but have come to be used also as adjectives; the nomina agentis et patientis are by their nature adjectives, but have come to be used also as B substantives.

193.   Connected with the nomina verbi are the four following classes of deverbal nouns.

(*a*)   *Nomina vicis,* أَسْمَآءُ ٱلْمَرَّةِ, nouns that express the doing of an action *once.*

(*b*)   *Nomina speciei,* أَسْمَآءُ ٱلنَّوْعِ, nouns of *kind* or *manner.*

(*c*)   *Nomina loci et temporis,* أَسْمَآءُ ٱلْمَكَانِ وَٱلزَّمَانِ, also called *nomina vasis,* أَسْمَآءُ ٱلظَّرْفِ, nouns of *place* and *time.*   C

(*d*)   *Nomina instrumenti,* أَسْمَآءُ ٱلْآلَةِ, nouns denoting the *instrument.*

194.   Denominative nouns are divisible into six classes; namely:—

(*a*)   *Nomen unitatis vel individualitatis,* اِسْمُ ٱلْوَحْدَةِ, the noun that denotes *the individual.*

(*b*)   *Nomen abundantiæ vel multitudinis,* اِسْمُ ٱلْكَثْرَةِ, the noun D that denotes the place where anything is found in *abundance.*

(*c*)   *Nomen vasis,* اِسْمُ ٱلْوِعَاءِ, the noun that expresses the *vessel* which contains anything.

(*d*)   *Nomen relativum,* ٱلِٱسْمُ ٱلْمَنْسُوبُ or ٱلنِّسْبَةُ (lit. *the referred noun, the reference* or *relation*), a particular class of derivative adjectives.

A (e) *Nomen abstractum qualitatis,* اِسْمُ ٱلْكَيْفِيَّةِ, the abstract noun of quality (see § 191).

(*f*) *Nomen deminutivum,* اَلِٱسْمُ ٱلْمُصَغَّرُ or اَلتَّصْغِيرُ (lit. *the lessened noun, the lessening*), the *diminutive*.

a. THE DEVERBAL NOUNS.

(a) *The Nomina Verbi.*

195. The nomina verbi, اَسْمَآءُ ٱلْفِعْلِ, are abstract substantives,
B which express the action, passion, or state indicated by the corresponding verbs, without any reference to object, subject, or time.

> REM. The nomen verbi is also called اَلْمَصْدَرُ (lit. *the place
> whence anything goes forth, where it originates*), because most Arab
> grammarians derive the compound idea of the finite verb from the
> simple idea of this substantive. We may compare with it the
> Greek Infinitive used with the article as a substantive.

196. The nomina verbi, which may be derived from the ground-
C form of the ordinary triliteral verb, are very numerous. The following
is a nearly complete list of them, the rarest forms being included
within brackets.

1. فَعْل, as ضَرْبٌ, رَدَّ, عَجْزٌ, فَهْمٌ, قَوْلٌ, سَيْرٌ, غَزْوٌ, جَرْىٌ.

2. فَعَل, as طَلَبٌ, هَرَبٌ, جَلَبٌ, نَظَرٌ, كَرَمٌ, عَمَلٌ, سَخَطٌ, فَرَحٌ, شَلَلٌ, جَوًى.

3. فَعِل, as كَذِبٌ, ضَحِكَ, حَرِمٌ, سَرِقٌ, حَلِفٌ.

D 4. فِعْل, as حِفْظٌ, عِلْمٌ, ذِكْرٌ, فِسْقٌ.

5. فَعَل, as كَبَرٌ, عِظَمٌ, صِغَرٌ, ثِقَلٌ, سِمَنٌ, رِضًى.

6. فُعْل, as جُبْنٌ, شُغْلٌ, زُهْدٌ, شُكْرٌ, شُرْبٌ, سُخْطٌ, وُدَّ.

7. فُعَل, as هُدًى, سُرًى.

8. فَعْلَة, as رَحْمَة, كُثْرَة, غَيْرَة, حَيْرَة.

9. فَعَلَة, as غَلَبَة, ضَبَعَة, عَظَمَة, شَكَاة.

A

10. فَعِلَة, as سَرِقَة.

11. فَعلَة, as نُشْدَة, عِصْمَة, حِمْيَة.

12. فَعلَة, as سُمْرَة, أُدمَة.

[13. فُعلَّة, as غُلُبَّة (also written غَلُبَّة).]

[13*. فِعلَّة, as جِبِلَّة.]

14. فَعْلَى, as تَقْوَى, دَعْوَى.

[15. فَعَلَى, as مَرَطَى, جَمَزَى.]

B

16. فِعْلَى, as ذِكْرَى.

17. فُعْلَى, as رُجْعَى, بُشْرَى.

[18. فُعَلَّى, as غُلُبَّى (or غِلِبَّى).]

[19. فَعْلَاء, as رَهْبَاء, رَغْبَاء.]

[19*. فُعْلَاء, as رُهْبَاء.]

[20. فَعْلَانُ, as زَيْدَانُ, شَنْآنُ, لَيَّانُ.]

21. فَعَلَانُ, as شَنَآنُ, نَزَوَانُ, هَيَجَانُ, جَوَلَانُ, طَوَفَانُ, خَفَقَانُ.

C

22. فِعْلَانُ, as رِضْوَانُ, نِسْيَانُ, حِرْمَانُ.

23. فُعْلَانُ, as كُفْرَانُ, غُفْرَانُ, شُكْرَانُ, رُجْحَانُ.

[24. فَعَلُوت, as رَهَبُوت, رَحَمُوت, جَبَرُوت.]

[24*. فَعَلُوتَى, as رَهَبُوتَى, رَحَمُوتَى, جَبَرُوتَى.]

25. فَعَالٌ, as رَوَاحٌ, نَفَاذٌ, نَفَادٌ, ذَهَابٌ, فَسَادٌ, صَلَاحٌ.

26. فِعَالٌ, as إِبَاء, نِفَار, شِرَاد, إِيَب, قِيَام, نِكَاح, حِجَاب, كِتَاب.

D

27. فُعَالٌ, as نُعَاب, نُعَاق, أُرَاز, مُشَاء, زُكَام, سُعَال, سُؤَال, مُزَاح.

28. فَعَالَة, as زَهَادَة, ضَخَامَة, جَزَالَة, فَصَاحَة, نَظَافَة, ظَرَافَة.

29. فِعَالَة, as صِيَانَة, عِبَادَة, سِفَارَة, كِتَابَة.

[30. فُعَالَة, as حُفَارَة, بُغَايَة.]

31. فَعَالِيَة, as رَكَانِيَة, عَلَانِيَة, طَمَاعِيَة, كَرَاهِيَة.

A   32.   فَعُولٌ, as قَبُولٌ, وَلُوعٌ, وَقُودٌ؛ وَضُوءٌ.

    33.   فُعُولٌ, as لُزُومٌ, قُدُومٌ, جُحُودٌ, غُدُوٌّ, وُرُودٌ, دُخُولٌ, خُرُوجٌ.

[33*.   فَعُولَةٌ, as الْوُكَةٌ.]

    34.   فُعُولَةٌ, as سُهُولَةٌ, صُعُوبَةٌ, عُذُوبَةٌ.

[35.   فُعُولِيَّةٌ, as خُصُوصِيَّةٌ, لَصُوصِيَّةٌ.]

[36.   فُعُولِيَّةٌ, as جُهُولِيَّةٌ, خُصُوصِيَّةٌ, شُيُوخِيَّةٌ.]

    37.   فَعِيلٌ, as صَهِيلٌ, ذَمِيلٌ, أَزِيزٌ, نَعِيبٌ, نَعِيقٌ, صَهِيلٌ, رَحِيلٌ.

B   38.   فَعِيلَةٌ, as شَكِيَّةٌ, حَمِيَّةٌ.

    39.   مَفْعَلٌ, as مَحْبَسٌ, مَدْخَلٌ, مَحْمَلٌ, مَفَرٌّ.

    40.   مَفْعِلٌ, as مَكِيرٌ, مَوْثِقٌ, مَرْجِعٌ, مَوْعِدٌ, مَسِيرٌ, مَصِيرٌ, مَحِيضٌ, مَجِىءٌ.

[41.   مَفْعَلٌ, as مَهْلَكٌ.]

    42.   مَفْعَلَةٌ, as مَحْمَدَةٌ, مَرَمَّةٌ, مَوَدَّةٌ, مَرْضَاةٌ.

    43.   مَفْعِلَةٌ, as مَحْمِدَةٌ, مَرْجِعَةٌ, مَعْرِفَةٌ, مَوْجِدَةٌ, مَسِيرَةٌ, مَأْوِيَةٌ, مَرْثِيَةٌ.

C [44.   مَفْعُلَةٌ, as مَهْلُكَةٌ, مَقْدُرَةٌ.]

[Rem. For the forms with prefix *ma-*, 39—44, the so-called مَصْدَرٌ مِيمِىٌّ, see further §§ 208, 221, rem. *c*, and the remarks to §§ 222—225.]

197. *All* these nouns cannot, however, be formed from *every* triliteral verb. The majority of verbs admit of but one form, very few of more than two or three. What these are, must be learned D from the Lexicon.

198. The five forms, which are most frequently used, are:

1. فَعْلٌ,   2. فَعَلٌ,   28. فَعَالَةٌ,   33. فُعُولٌ,   34. فُعُولَةٌ.

(*a*) فَعْلٌ is the abstract noun from *transitive* verbs of the forms فَعَلَ and فَعِلَ; as قَتَلَ *to kill*, قَتْلٌ *killing* or *being killed* (§ 201); فَهِمَ *to understand*, فَهْمٌ *understanding*, *insight*; خَطِفَ *to snatch*, خَطْفٌ.

(*b*) فُعُولٌ is the abstract noun from *intransitive* verbs of the form A قَعَدَ ; as قَعَدَ and جَلَسَ *to sit,* قُعُودٌ and جُلُوسٌ *sitting;* خَرَجَ *to go out,* خُرُوجٌ *going out.*

(*c*) فَعَلٌ is the abstract noun from *intransitive* verbs of the form فَعِلَ (§§ 38 and 92); as فَرِحَ *to be glad,* فَرَحٌ *joy;* مَرِضَ *to be sick,* مَرَضٌ *sickness.*

(*d*) فَعَالَةٌ and فُعُولَةٌ are the abstract nouns from verbs of the form فَعُلَ; as جَزُلَ *to be thick and large, to be of sound judgment,* جَزَالَةٌ *firmness* or *soundness of judgment;* سَرُوَ *to be generous,* B سَرَاوَةٌ *generosity;* خَشُنَ *to be rough,* خُشُونَةٌ *roughness;* سَهُلَ *to be smooth,* سُهُولَةٌ *smoothness.*

Rem. The abstract nouns of verbs which express FLIGHT, or REFUSAL, usually take the form 26. فِعَالٌ; as نَفَرَ, فَرَّ, شَرَدَ, *to flee,* جَمَحَ ; شِرَادٌ, نِفَارٌ, فِرَارٌ *to become refractory, to run away* with his rider (of a horse), نَارَ ; جِمَاحٌ *to flee from, shun with horror,* نِوَارٌ ; أَبَى *to refuse,* إِبَاءٌ. Those that express SICKNESS or AILMENT of any C kind have 27. فُعَالٌ, as عَطَسَ *to sneeze,* عُطَاسٌ ; سَعَلَ *to cough,* سُعَالٌ ; VIOLENT or CONTINUOUS MOTION, 21. فَعَلَانٌ, as طَارَ *to fly,* طَيَرَانٌ ; جَرَى *to run,* جَرَيَانٌ ; خَطَرَ *to lash* the tail, *to brandish,* خَطَرَانٌ ; بَرَقَ *to gleam,* بَرَقَانٌ ; وَمَضَ *to flash,* وَمَضَانٌ ; خَفَقَ *to palpitate,* خَفَقَانٌ ; CHANGE OF PLACE, 37. فَعِيلٌ, as رَحَلَ *to travel,* رَحِيلٌ ; دَبَّ *to creep,* دَبِيبٌ ; رَسَمَ *to gallop* (of a camel), رَسِيمٌ ; ذَمَلَ *to trot* (of a camel), ذَمِيلٌ ; وَجَفَ *to be agitated, palpitate, run quickly,* وَجِيفٌ ; D بَرَقَ *to gleam,* بَرِيقٌ ; وَمَضَ *to flash,* وَمِيضٌ ; SOUND, 27. فُعَالٌ and 37. فَعِيلٌ, as نَعَبَ *to croak,* نُعَابٌ and نَعِيبٌ ; شَقَبَ *to sob, to bray,* نَهَتَ, نَبِيتٌ ; صَهَلَ *to neigh,* صَهِيلٌ : نَهَقَ *to bray,* نُهَاقٌ and شَهِيقٌ ; *to roar,* نُهَاتٌ and نَبِيتٌ : صَاحَ *to cry out,* صُيَاحٌ ; صَرَخَ *to cry out* for help, صُرَاخٌ ; نَبَحَ *to bark,* نُبَاحٌ ; بَكَى *to weep,* بُكَاءٌ ; عَوَى *to*

A   howl, عُوَآءٌ; ثَغَا to bleat, ثُغَآءٌ; رَغَا to grumble (of a camel), رُغَآءٌ; OFFICE, TRADE or HANDICRAFT, 29. فَعَالَةٌ, as خَلَفَ to succeed, خِلَافَةٌ the office of successor (خَلِيفَةٌ) or caliph, the caliphate; أَمَرَ to be chief or emīr, إِمَارَةٌ the office of emīr; وَلِيَ to be in charge or command of, وِلَايَةٌ, governorship; نَابَ to take one's place, act as deputy, نِيَابَةٌ deputyship; كَتَبَ to write, كِتَابَةٌ the office of secretary; خَاطَ to sew, خِيَاطَةٌ the trade of tailor; تَجَرَ to trade, تِجَارَةٌ trade, traffic.

B   **199.**   If the middle radical of a verb can be pronounced with two or three vowels, and its signification varies accordingly, that verb may have several abstract nouns, one for each form and meaning of the Perfect.   Thus, فَرَقَ, to part, divide, has فَرْق, but فَرِقَ, to be afraid, فَرَقٌ; جَهَرَ, to be plain, open or public, has جَهْرٌ or جِهَارٌ, but جَهِرَ, to be unable to see in the sunlight, جَهَرٌ, and جَهُرَ, to be loud, جَهَارَةٌ; شَرَفَ, to surpass or excel in rank or nobility, has شَرْفٌ, but شَرِفَ, to be

C   high or prominent, شَرَفٌ, and شَرُفَ to be exalted, noble or eminent, شَرَافَةٌ or شَرَفٌ.

200.   If a verb has only one form, but several different significations, it often has different abstract nouns, one of which is peculiar to, or more generally used in, each of its meanings.   E.g. حَكَمَ, to judge, has حُكْمٌ, but when it signifies to curb (a horse), حَكَمٌ; خَرَّ, to fall prostrate, has خَرٌّ or خُرُورٌ, but when it means to sound like rushing

D   water, خَرِيرٌ; رَفَعَ, to be exalted or noble, has رِفْعَةٌ, but in the sense of to have a loud voice, رَفَاعَةٌ; وَجَدَ, to find, usually has وِجْدَانٌ, but when it means to be wealthy, جِدَةٌ, and to be moved by love, grief or anger, وَجْدٌ.

201.   The nomina verbi are used both in an active and a passive sense; as قَتْلُهُ his killing (another) or his being killed himself; لَا تُفْسِدُوا فِى ٱلْأَرْضِ بَعْدَ إِصْلَاحِهَا work no evil upon the earth after

its having been well ordered; فِى هٰذِهِ ٱلسَّنَةِ أَظْهَرَ ٱلْمَأْمُونُ ٱلْقَوْلَ بِخَلْقِ A
ٱلْقُرْآنِ *in this year el-Ma'mūn publicly adopted the doctrine of the*
Ḳor'ān's having been created.

REM. There are also nomina verbi that have always a passive
signification; as سُرُورٌ *joy, gladness,* from سُرَّ *to be glad;* وُجُودٌ
existence, from وُجِدَ *to be found, to exist* (see § 200)*.

202. The nouns formed from the derived forms of the strong
triliteral verb are as follows.

II. 1. تَفْعِيلٌ. B

2. تَفْعِلَةٌ, as تَبْصِرَةٌ, تَفْرِقَةٌ, تَكْمِلَةٌ, تَقْدِمَةٌ, تَكْرِمَةٌ, تَذْكِرَةٌ,
    تَزْكِيَةٌ, تَذْكِيَةٌ, تَجْزِئَةٌ, تَهْنِئَةٌ, تَضِرَّةٌ, تَسِرَّةٌ.

[3. تَفْعُلَةٌ, as تَضُرَّةٌ, تَسُرَّةٌ, تَهْلُكَةٌ]

4. تَفْعَالٌ, as تَكْرَارٌ, تَرْدَادٌ, تَصْدَاقٌ, تَبْتَانٌ, تَبْطَالٌ, تَصْبَالٌ,
    تَسْيَارٌ, تَطْوَافٌ, تَجْوَالٌ, تَوْمَاضٌ.

[5. تِفْعَالٌ, as تِمْثَالٌ, تِبْكَاءٌ, تِشْرَابٌ, تِمْشَاءٌ, تِلْقَاءٌ, تِبْيَانٌ, C
    تِنْضَالٌ. Of these examples some allow only the two
    first, pointing the others as examples of تَفْعَالٌ.]

[6. فِعَّالٌ, as كَذَّابٌ, كَلَّامٌ, عَلَّامٌ, فِسَّارٌ, خِرَّاقٌ, قِدَّامٌ, قِضَّاءٌ,
    حِمَّالٌ, كِبَّارٌ.]

[7. فِعِّيلَى, as حِثِّيثَى, خِصِّيصَى, خِلِّيفَى, قِلِّيلَى, خِطِّيبَى,
    رِمِّيَّا, قِتِّيتَى, فِخِّيرَى, دِلِّيلَى, مِكِّيثَى.] D

[8. فِعِّيلَاءٌ, as خِصِّيصَاءٌ, مِكِّيثَاءٌ.]

To these may be added تَفْعُولٌ, as تَبْلُوكٌ. Here the vowel of the

---

* وُجُودٌ is also employed in the active signification; see the Gloss.
to Bibl. Geogr. viii. and Lane. D. G.]

A first syllable seems to have been assimilated to that of the second; تَفْعُول for تُفْعُول.

III. 1. مُفَاعَلَةٌ. 2. فِعَالٌ.

[3. فِيعَالٌ, as ضِيرَابٌ (قِيتَالٌ). [4. فَعَّالٌ, as قِتَّالٌ ,مِرَآءٌ.]

IV. إِفْعَالٌ.

V. 1. تَفَعُّلٌ. [2. تِفْعَّالٌ, as تِكِلَّامٌ ,تِمِلَّاقٌ ,تِنْقَامٌ.]

B VI. 1. تَفَاعُلٌ. [2. تَفَاعَلٌ, as تَفَاوَتٌ.]

[3. تَفَاعِلٌ, as تَفَاوِتٌ.]

VII. اِنْفِعَالٌ. VIII. 1. اِفْتِعَالٌ. [2. فِعَّالٌ, as قِتَّالٌ ,سِتَّارٌ.]

IX. اِفْعِلَالٌ. X. اِسْتِفْعَالٌ.

XI. اِفْعِيلَالٌ. XII. اِفْعِيعَالٌ.

XIII. اِفْعِوَّالٌ. XIV. اِفْعِنْلَالٌ.

C XV. اِفْعِنْلَآءٌ.

REM. *a.* In II. the form فَعَّالٌ is the original infinitive, but تَفْعِيلٌ is by far the most common; تَفْعِلَةٌ is chiefly used in verba tert. rad. hemz. and tert. rad. و et ى (in which latter the form تَفْعِيلٌ is excessively rare, as تَنْزِيٌّ from نَزَّا); . فِعِّيلَ and فِعِّيلَاّ are 'usually ascribed to I., but as their use is لِقَصْدِ ٱلْمُبَالَغَةِ, *to express energy* or *intensity,* [or *frequency,*] they seem as deserving of a

D place here as تَفْعَالٌ [which in like manner differ from the infin. of I., only by expressing greater energy or frequent repetition]. These forms with tešdīd are akin to the Heb. infin. absol. קַטּוֹל (קָטוֹל ,קַטּוֹל), to Heb. substantives like שִׁלּוּם, and to the Eastern Aramaic infin. קַטּוֹלֵי; whereas تَفْعَالٌ ,تَفْعِيلٌ, تُفْعُولٌ and تَفْعُلَةٌ are, strictly speaking, the infinitives, not of فَعَّلَ, but of an obsolete تَفْعَلَ, akin to שִׁפְעֵל ,הִתְפַּעֵל ,הִתְפַּעֵל, and are represented in the cognate dialects by such substantives as תַּבְלִית, תַּגְמוּל, תַּנְמוּל, תַּכְרִיךְ, A

תַּבְנִית, תַּרְבּוּת, ܐ݁ܘܺ݁ܨ ܴ݁ ، ܠ ، etc.*—In III.

فِعَال is the original infinitive, which the great majority of the Arabs shortened into فَعَال, whilst some compensated the loss of the long vowel by doubling the following consonant, فَعَّال. The most common form of all is مُفَاعَلَة ([in form identical with the] pass. particip. fem.).—In V. the original form is تَفَعَّال. which has however been almost entirely supplanted by تَفَعَّل.—In VIII. those B Arabs alone use فَعَال, who shorten the Perf. and Imperf. into فَعَل, يَفْعَل, or فَعَّل, يَفَعِّل, etc. in the cases mentioned in § 117*.— The form تَفْعَال is sometimes ascribed to III., as تَنْضَال ; تَرْمَآء; and (تَرَامَوْا) رِمِّيَّا, (تَبَاجَرُوا) هِجِّيرَى, (تَحَاجَرُوا) حِجِّيزَى to VI., as فَعِيلَى.

[Rem. *b.* For the مَصْدَر مِيمِيّ of the derived conjugations see § 227, rem.]

203. The nouns formed from the quadriliteral verbs are :— C

I. 1. فَعْلَلَة, as سَلْقَاة, بَيْطَرَة, جَهْوَرَة, حَوْقَلَة, سَرْهَفَة, دَحْرَجَة, قَلْقَلَة, زَلْزَلَة.

 2. فِعْلَال, as قَلْقَال, زِلْزَال, سِلْقَآء, حِيقَال, بِسِرْهَاف, دِحْرَاج.

 [3. فَعْلَال, as قَلْقَال, زَلْزَال.]

II. تَفَعْلُل, as تَدَحْرُج.

III. افْعِنْلَال as احْرِنْجَام. D

IV. افْعِلَّال, as اطْمِئْنَان, اقْشِعْرَار. [The irregular form طُمَأْنِينَة is rather to be considered as a substantive, اسْمُ مَصْدَرٍ.]

Rem. In I. فَعْلَلَة is the common form, whilst the employment of فِعْلَال depends upon the *usus loquendi* (like that of فَعَال in III.

* [Barth, *Nominalbildung*, § 180 disapproves of this theory. D. G.]

A   of the triliteral verb). The form فَعْلَالٌ seems to be restricted to reduplicated verbs, like زُلْزَلَ.—A variation of the fourth form is presented to us in the word طِعَّانٌ, *mutual thrusting and stabbing with lances* = تَطَاعُنٌ, which comes from اِطْعَنَّ = طَعْنَنَ.

204. The abstract nouns of the verba mediæ rad. geminatæ are formed according to the rules given in § 120. Hence مَدٌّ for مَدْدٌ, مَرَدٌّ for مَرْدَدٌ (from رَدَّ), تَغَرَّةٌ for تَغْرِرَةٌ (from the second form of غَرَّ).

B   REM. *a.* Those nouns, of which the first and second radicals are pronounced with fètḥa, undergo no contraction; as سَدَدٌ, عَلَلُ, مَلَلُ, غَصَصٌ.

REM. *b.* The nouns of the third and sixth forms may either be contracted or not; as مُهَادَةٌ or مُهَادَدَةٌ, تَسَابُبٌ or تَسَابٌّ. See § 124.

205. The formation of nouns from the verba hèmzata takes place C according to the rules laid down in §§ 131—136.

206. Those verba primæ rad. و, that reject the و in the Imperf. and Imperat. (§§ 142 and 144), drop it also in the verbal noun. E.g.

عِدَةٌ	from	وَعَدَ	Imperfect	يَعِدُ	Imperat.	عِدْ
عِظَةٌ	„	وَعَظَ	„	يَعِظُ	„	عِظْ
دَعَةٌ	„	وَدَعَ	„	يَدَعُ	„	دَعْ
زِنَةٌ	„	وَزَنَ	„	يَزِنُ	„	زِنْ
دِيَةٌ	„	وَدَى	„	يَدِى	„	دِ

D

The termination ةٌ, with which these nouns are furnished, is a compensation for the lost radical.

REM. *a.* Not a few verba primæ rad. و, however, have nouns of the form فَعْلٌ, though they drop the first radical in the Imperf.; e.g. وَجْنٌ ,يَجِنُ ,وَجَنَ ; وَجْرٌ ,يَجِرُ ,وَجَرَ. Others have both forms;

e.g. وَضَعَ، يَضَعُ، وَضْعٌ and ضَعَةٌ; زِنَةٌ، وَزَنَ، يَزِنُ، وَزْنٌ and A
عِدَةٌ and وَعْدٌ.

REM. *b.* Initial و, if pronounced with ḍamma or kèsra, may be
changed into أ (see § 145, rem.), as إِجْدَانٌ، أُجُودٌ, for وُجَدَانٌ وُجُودٌ.

REM. *c.* In nouns from verba primæ rad. و, this radical is
changed into ى, if it be without a vowel, and kèsra precede; as
إِيجَابٌ for إِوْجَابٌ, from the fourth form of وَجَبَ; اِسْتِيفَآءٌ for
اِسْتِوْفَآءٌ, from the tenth of وَفَى. See § 145. B

REM. *d.* Compare in Hebrew, שֶׁבֶת ,(רִבָּה) רֶשֶׁת לֶדֶת (לֵדָה),
דַּעַת, from יָלַד ,יָרֵשׁ ,יָשַׁב ,יָדַע; עֵדָה (עִדָּה),(עֻלְצָה),
שֵׁנָה (שִׁנָה), from יָשֵׁן ,יָעֵץ ,יָעֵד. Corresponding forms in Syriac
are ܝܰܠܕܐ (rad. ܝܠܕ), ܝܕܰܥܬܐ (rad. ܝܕܥ).

207. Nouns derived from verba mediæ rad. و et ى are subject to C
the same irregularities as those verbs (§ 150, etc.).

208. If the noun from a verb mediæ rad. و or ى be of the form
فَعْلٌ, the و or ى remains unchanged; as سَيْرٌ، قَوْلٌ. In the form فُعُولٌ
from verba med. و, the و may be changed into ؤ, as حَوُولٌ، ثُوُوبٌ,
دُوُورٌ، رُوُوبٌ، غُوُورٌ، سُوُورٌ, for ثُوُوبٌ, etc. Verba med. ى of the form
فَعَلَ, Imperf. يَفْعَلُ (see § 157), frequently take kèsra in the مَصْدَر مِيمِي,
as مَزِيدٌ، (مَبْيِتٌ for) مَبِيتٌ, مَجِيءٌ، مَبِيعٌ، مَجِيٍّ (or by assimilation مَجِيٌّ),
مَعِيشٌ، مَصِيرٌ، مَسِيرٌ, and the like. [See § 223, rem.] D

209. If the letter و, pronounced with fètḥa, be preceded by kèsra,
it is converted into ى; as قِيَامٌ for قِوَامٌ, from قَامَ; صِيَانَةٌ for صِوَانَةٌ,
from صَانَ; اِنْقِيَادٌ and اِقْتِيَادٌ for اِنْقِوَادٌ and اِقْتِوَادٌ, from the seventh and
eighth forms of قَادَ. Except in the third form, where it remains

A unchanged; as عِوَانٌ, سَاوَرَ from ثِوَارٌ from قَاوَرَ, جِوَارٌ from جَاوَرَ, سِوَارٌ from from نَاوَأَ, عَاوَنَ, قِوَامٌ from قَاوَمَ, لِوَامٌ from لَاوَمَ, نِوَآءٌ from نَاوَأَ.

210. Peculiar to verba mediæ rad. و et ى is the nominal form فَعْلُولَةٌ, in which ى always takes the place of the second radical; as (كون) كَانَ from كَيْنُونَةٌ, قَادَ (قود) from قَيْدُودَةٌ, دَامَ (دوم) from دَيْمُومَةٌ, شَاخَ from شَيْخُوخَةٌ, بَانَ (بين) from بَيْنُونَةٌ, سَادَ (سود) from سَيْدُودَةٌ,

B (شيخ), صَيْرُورَةٌ from صَارَ (صير), غَابَ (غيب) from غَيْبُوبَةٌ, قَيْلُولَةٌ from قَالَ (قيل).

Rem. Some grammarians regard فَعْلُولَةٌ as the original form. The impossible صَيْرُورَةٌ, شَيْخُوخَةٌ, were, they say, first changed into صِيرُورَةٌ, شِيخُوخَةٌ, and then altered, on account of the discord between ī and ū in successive syllables, into صَيْرُورَةٌ, شَيْخُوخَةٌ. Others look upon فَعْلُولَةٌ as a contraction for فَيْعَلُولَةٌ, so that

C دَيْمُومَةٌ was originally دَيْمُومَةٌ, by assimilation دَيْمُومَةٌ, and then shortened دَيْمُومَةٌ (like مَيْتٌ for مَيِّتٌ); but there is no verbal form فَيْعَلَّ, with which such a nomen verbi could be connected. The rare substantive forms سُودَدٌ (or سُؤْدُدٌ) from سَادَ, to be chief or ruler, and عُوطَطٌ from عَاطَ to desire the male (of a she-camel); the cognate forms فَوْضَى, فَيْضُوضَى, فَوْضُوضَآءُ and فَوْضُوضَى and فَيْضُوضَآءُ, فَيْضِيضَآءُ and فَيْضِيضَ, mixture, confusion; and the analogy of the

D Aramaic verbal form פְּעַלְעֵל (as כַּרְכֵּר, כַּרְדֵּם) and the Heb. פִּעְלֵל (as רוֹמֵם, קוֹמֵם, כּוֹנֵן, בּוֹנֵן),—all combine to prove that فَعْلُولَةٌ comes directly from a quadriliteral فَعْلَلَ.

211. In nouns of the fourth and tenth form of verba mediæ rad. و et ى, the second radical is elided, after throwing back its vowel upon the vowelless first radical; and the termination ة‍ is appended to the noun by way of compensation (compare § 206). E.g. إِفْيَادٌ and إِفَادَةٌ for إِقْوَامٌ and إِقَامَةٌ; اِسْتِقْوَامٌ and اِسْتِقَامَةٌ for اِسْتِفْوَادٌ and اِسْتِفَادَةٌ and اِسْتِفْيَادٌ.

REM. Nouns of the fourth form without the ة very rarely A occur; e.g. إِقَام in the Ḳorʾān, Sūr. xxi. 73 (for إِقْوَام, إِقْأَام or إِقْأَام);

إِرَآء (for إِرْئَاء) from أَرَى *to make* or *let see, to show* (§ 176, rem. c).

212. In nouns formed from verba tertiæ rad. و et ى, the third radical is retained, when the second immediately precedes it and is vowelless; as غِشْيَان, رِضْوَان, فَرْيٌ, زَهْوٌ, رَمْيٌ, غَزْوٌ. If the second radical be و and the third ى, an assimilation takes place in the form فَعْلٌ, as حَيٌّ, زَيٌّ, طَيٌّ, لَيٌّ, for حَوْىٌ, زَوْىٌ, طَوْىٌ, لَوْىٌ.

213. In nouns from verba tertiæ rad. و et ى of the forms فَعَلٌ, B فِعَلٌ, and فُعَلٌ, the third radical (which in this case always [if the root be of the latter, often if it be of the former class,] assumes the form of ى) rejects its ḍamma, throws back the tènwīn upon the fètḥa of the second radical, and becomes quiescent. E.g. جَلًى for جَلَىٌ, سُرًى for سُرَىٌ, (رِضَوٌ), رِضًى for رِضَىٌ, لَظًى for لَظَىٌ [or رِضًا for رِضَاً], هُدًى for هُدَىٌ (compare § 167, a, β, and b, β).

214. In nouns from verba tertiæ rad. و of the form فَعَلَة, the و C is changed, after the elision of its fètḥa, into ẻlif productionis; as شَكَاةٌ for شَكَوَةٌ, زَكَاةٌ for زَكَوَةٌ, حَيَاةٌ for حَيَوَةٌ, صَلَاةٌ for صَلَوَةٌ.

REM. a. We often find, however, the (etymologically more correct) orthography زَكٰوةٌ, حَيٰوةٌ, صَلٰوةٌ (§ 7, rem. d).

REM. b. In the same way as حَيَاةٌ for حَيَوَةٌ, we find مَرْضَاةٌ for مَرْضَيَةٌ, مَرْئَاةٌ for مَرْئَيَةٌ, (مَرْضَوَةٌ) etc.

215. If the noun from a verb tertiæ rad. و be of the form D فُعُولٌ or فُعُولَةٌ, the و productionis of the second syllable combines with the radical و into وّ; as عُلُوٌّ, دُنُوٌّ, for عُلُوْوٌ, دُنُوْوٌ. But, if these forms come from verba tertiæ rad. ى, the و productionis is changed, through the influence of the third radical, into ى, and combines with it into يّ, whilst, at the same time, the ḍamma of the second radical becomes a kèsra; as مُضِىٌّ, رُقِىٌّ, أُوِىٌّ, for رُقُوىٌ, أُوُوىٌ, رُقُوىٌ,

A مُضْوِى (compare § 170). A further assimilation of the vowel of the first syllable sometimes takes place, as اِتِى for أُتِى, اوِى for أُوِى, عِتِى for عُتِى; just as in the plural of substantives we find عِصِى, قِسِى, دِلِى, for عُصِى, دُلِى, قُسِى, from قَوْس, عَصَا, دَلْو.

216. If the noun from a verb tertiæ rad. ى be of the form فَعِيل, the ى productionis of the second syllable combines with the B radical ى into ِّى; as هَوِى for هَوِيِى, from هَوَى. In the same form from verba tertiæ rad. و, the third radical is converted into ى, and combines in the same manner with the ى productionis into ِّى.

217. In the nomina verbi of the forms فَعَال, فِعَال, and فُعَال, the third radical of verba tertiæ rad. و et ى is changed into hèmza; as خَفَاءٌ, بِنَاءٌ, بُكَاءٌ. The same thing takes place in the verbal nouns of the fourth, seventh, and following forms, as اِرْتِجَاءٌ, اِنْجِلَاءٌ, اِعْطَاءٌ, C اِحْوِوَاءٌ, اِسْتِدْعَاءٌ, اِرْعِوَاءٌ; and in that of the third, when it has the form فِعَال, as نِدَاءٌ from نَادَى. This change is caused by the preceding long fètha.

218. The nomina verbi of the second form of verba tert. rad. و et ى always take the form تَفْعِلَة (§ 202, rem.), as تَسْلِيَة, تَعْزِيَة. In those of the fifth and sixth forms, the influence of the third radical D (always ى, § 169) converts the damma of the penult syllable into kèsra, and the syllables ـِى are contracted into ـ (according to § 167, *b*, *β*). Hence تَجَلٍّ for تَجَلُّىٌ, (تَجَلُّىٌ), تَوَالٍ for تَوَالُىٌ (تَوَالُىٌ).

(β) *The Nomina Vicis or Nouns that express the Doing of an Action once.*

219. That an act has taken place *once* (مَرَّة), the Arabs indicate by adding the feminine termination ة to the verbal noun. For this

purpose the form فَعْل is always selected in the first form of the A
triliteral verb, تَفْعِيل in the second, and فَعْلَال in the first form of
the quadriliterals. E.g. تَقْلِيَةٌ, فَرَّةٌ, فَرْحَةٌ, شُرْبَةٌ, ضَرْبَةٌ, قَعْدَةٌ, نَصْرَةٌ,
اِسْتِنْشَاقَةٌ, اِكْرَامَةٌ, اِحْزَانَةٌ, تَقَلُّبَةٌ, تَغَافُلَةٌ, اِنْكِشَافَةٌ, اِلْتِفَاتَةٌ, تَرْوِيحَةٌ,
دِحْرَاجَةٌ, اِقْشِعْرَارَةٌ, تَدَحْرُجَةٌ, the act of helping, sitting down, striking,
drinking, rejoicing, fleeing, turning over, giving rest, vexing, honouring,
rolling over, neglecting, being uncovered, turning round, inhaling or B
snuffing, rolling, being rolled, shuddering, once. These nouns are
called أَسْمَآءُ ٱلْمَرَّةِ, *nomina vicis*, or nouns that express the doing of an
action once.

REM. *a.* Nouns of this sort, derived from weak verbs, do not
differ in form from those of the strong verbs; as عَدْوَةٌ, قَوْمَةٌ, وَعْدَةٌ,
أَتْيَةٌ, رَمْيَةٌ, لَقْيَةٌ from وَعَدَ, قَامَ, عَدَا, أَتَى, رَمَى, لَقِيَ.

REM. *b.* If the verbal noun happens to end in ةٌ, the feminine C
termination ةٌ cannot, of course, be appended to it, and the single-
ness of the action can only be expressed by adding the adjective
وَاحِدَةٌ *one*, as رَحِمَهُ رَحْمَةً وَاحِدَةً, *he had pity* or *compassion upon
him once;* and so with عَيْنَةٌ, تَسْلِيَةٌ, مُقَاتَلَةٌ, إِقَامَةٌ, اِسْتِعَانَةٌ, دَحْرَجَةٌ.

REM. *c.* From these nouns a dual and a plural may be formed
to express the doing of the act twice or oftener; as du. نَصْرَتَانِ,
pl. نَصَرَاتٌ.

REM. *d.* Other verbal nouns are but rarely used in this way; D
as حِجَّةٌ, رُوْيَةٌ, لِقَآءَةٌ, إِتْيَانَةٌ, *the act of going on a pilgrimage, seeing,
meeting, coming, once.*

(γ) *The Nomina Speciei or Nouns of Kind.*

220. The اِسْمُ ٱلنَّوْعِ or *noun of kind*, has always the form فِعْلَةٌ,
and indicates the manner of doing what is expressed by the verb;
as جِلْسَةٌ, رِكْبَةٌ, قِعْدَةٌ, طِعْمَةٌ, قِتْلَةٌ, مِيتَةٌ, نِيمَةٌ, *manner, mode,* or

A way of sitting, riding, sitting, eating, killing, dying, sleeping. E.g.

هُوَ حَسَنُ ٱلْكِتْبَة *he is good as to his manner of writing, he writes a*

good hand, قُتِلَ قِتْلَةَ سَوْءٍ *he was killed in a miserable way,* بِئْسَتِ ٱلْمِيتَة

't is a wretched death!

> REM. *a.* The nom. speciei may, like the nom. verbi and nom.
> vicis, be used in a passive sense, as صِرْعَة, *way of being thrown* (from
> horseback), e.g. سُوءُ ٱلِٱسْتِمْسَاكِ خَيْرٌ مِنْ حُسْنِ ٱلصِّرْعَة, *to sit fast*

B *badly is better than to be thrown easily.* Sometimes too it takes the
meaning of one of the derived forms of the verb; as عِذْرَة *manner of*
excusing oneself, from ٱعْتَذَرَ *to excuse oneself;* خِمْرَة *mode of veiling*
oneself, from ٱخْتَمَرَت *she put on the* خِمَار *or yashmak;* عِمَّة *way of*
putting on a turban, from تَعَمَّمَ *or* ٱعْتَمَّ *to put on a turban* (عِمَامَة).

> REM. *b.* If the nom. verbi has the form فُعْلَة, we must have
C recourse to a circumlocution to express the idea of the nom. speciei;
as حَمَيْتُهُ حِمْيَةَ ٱلْمَرِيض *I made him observe a regimen like a sick*
man, نَشَدْتُهُ نِشْدَةَ ٱلنَّفِيس *I searched for it as for something precious;*
or else نَشَدْتُهُ نَوْعًا مِنَ ٱلنِّشْدَة, حَمَيْتُهُ نَوْعًا مِنَ ٱلْحِمْيَة. So too with
the derived forms of the verb, أَكْرَمْتُهُ إِكْرَامَ ٱلصَّدِيقِ *I honoured*
him as a friend is honoured, or أَكْرَمْتُهُ نَوْعًا مِنَ ٱلْإِكْرَامِ.

D (δ) *The Nomina Loci et Temporis or Nouns of Place and Time.*

221. The nouns called أَسْمَاءُ ٱلظَّرْفِ (*nomina vasis*), or أَسْمَاءُ
ٱلْمَكَانِ وَٱلزَّمَانِ (*nomina loci et temporis*), are formed after the analogy
of the Imperfect Active of the first form of the verb, by substituting
the syllable مَ for the prefixes, and giving the second radical *fètha*,
if the Imperfect has *fètha* or *ḍamma*, but *kèsra*, if the Imperfect has
kèsra. E.g. مَشْرَب *a place for drinking, a reservoir* or *water-trough,*
from شَرِب *to drink,* imperf. يَشْرَب; مَنْهَل *the time* or *place for watering*

(*camels*), from نَهَل *to drink*, imperf. يَنْهَل ; مَصْرَع *the time when*, or A
place where, one is thrown down or *slain*, from صَرَع *to throw down*,
imperf. يَصْرَع ; مَكْتَب *a place where writing is taught, a school*, from
كَتَب *to write*, imperf. يَكْتُب ; مَخْرَج and مَدْخَل, *a place of egress* and
ingress, from خَرَج *to go out*, imperf. يَخْرُج, and دَخَل *to go in*, imperf.
يَدْخُل ; مَجْلِس *the place where*, or *time when, several persons sit, room,
assembly, party*, from جَلَس *to sit*, imperf. يَجْلِس ; مَقْصِد *the place
aimed at* or *made for*, from قَصَد *to aim at, make for*, imperf. يَقْصِد. B

Rem. *a.* These nouns are called أَسْمَآء ٱلظَّرْف, because *time* and
place are, as it were, the *vessels* in which the act or state is contained.

Rem. *b.* Twelve of these nouns, though derived from verbs in
which the characteristic vowel of the Imperfect is *damma*, take, notwithstanding, *kèsra*; viz.

1. مَجْزِر *the place where animals are slaughtered, slaughterhouse* or C
   shambles.

2. مَرْفِق .... *whereon one rests, the elbow.*

3. مَسْجِد .... *of prostration in prayer, a mosque.*

4. مَسْقِط .... *where anything falls.*

5. مَسْكِن .... *where one dwells, habitation.*

6. مَشْرِق .... *where the sun rises, the east.* D

7. مَطْلِع .... *of ascent* or *rising.*

8. مَغْرِب .... *where the sun sets, the west.*

9. مَفْرِق .... *of division*, in particular, *where the hair divides
   in different directions, the crown of the head.*

10. مَنْبِت .... *where a plant grows.*

A   11.   مَنْخَر   *the place where the breath passes through the nose, the nostril.*

12.   مَنْسَك   *where a sacrifice is offered during a religious festival.*

Of these, nos. 5, 7, 9, 11, and 12, may be pronounced with *fètḥa*, and the same license is extended by some grammarians to all the rest.   Instead of مَنْخَر some say مِنْخَر, مُنْخُر, and even مُنْخُور.

The verb جَمَعَ, *to collect*, which has *fètḥa* in the imperf., also makes

B   مَجْمَع or مَجْمِع, *a place of collecting, meeting or assembling.* The vowel of the first syllable is variable in مَخْدَع, also مُخْدَع and مِخْدَع, *a place of hiding or concealment, a small room or closet.* See § 228, rem. *a*; and compare the variations in مُجْسَد *a garment worn (by a woman) next the skin*; مُصْحَف *a book, a copy of the Kor'ān*; and مُطْرَف *a robe with ornamental borders.*

C   REM. *c.*   The kèsra of the second syllable distinguishes in many cases the nomina temp. et loci from the مَصْدَر مِيمِى, which, as a general rule, takes fètḥa in the second syllable.   Thus مَجْلَس, مَفَرّ, مَضْرَب, مَحْبِس, مَحْمَل, are nomina verbi or infinitives; whilst مَفِرّ, مَضْرِب, مَحْبِس, مَحْمِل, مَجْلِس, are nomina temporis or loci.

REM. *d.*   This class of nouns exists in the other Semitic 'languages.   In Hebrew, the vowel of the first syllable has fre-

D   quently been weakened into ֶ and ִ; as מַשְׁאָב מִצָּב מֵצַב (מַנְצָב),

(מֶחֱסָן) מִזְבֵּחַ (מִחְצָו), מִדְבָּר (מֶרְכָּב) מֶרְכָּב, (מָקוֹם) מָקוֹם.

222.   Nouns of time and place, formed from verba primæ rad. و et ى, retain the first radical, even though it be rejected in the Imperfect of the verb (§§ 142, 144), and have invariably *kèsra* in the second syllable.   E.g. مَوْرِد *watering-place*, from وَرَدَ *to go down (to draw water)*, imperf. يَرِدُ; مَوْعِد *the time* or *place of a promise* or *appointment, fixed time* or *place*, from وَعَدَ *to promise*, imperf. يَعِدُ;

مَوْضِع the *place where anything is put, a place,* from وَضَع *to put down,* A
to place, imperf. يَضَع ; مَوْجِل a *place that is dreaded,* from وَجِل *to be afraid,* imperf. يَوْجَل ; مَوْحَل a *slough* or *quagmire,* from وَحِل *to stick in the mud,* imperf. يَوْحَل ; مَيْسِر a *game at hazard,* from يَسَر *to play at hazard,* imperf. يَيْسِر.

REM. Here the مَصْدَر مِيمِى should, strictly speaking, have the same form as the nomina loci et temp., but the grammarians give B some examples with fĕtḥa in the second syllable, as مَوْضَع, مَوْحَل.

223. Those formed from verba mediæ rad. و et ى undergo changes analogous to those suffered by the Imperfect of the verb (§ 150); that is to say, after the second radical has taken fĕtḥa or kĕsra, according to § 221, this vowel is thrown back upon the vowelless first radical, and the و or ى is changed into the homogeneous letter of prolongation (ا or ى). E.g. مَقَام (مَقْوَم) *place of standing, place,* from قَامَ *to stand,* imperf. يَقُوم (يَقْوُم) ; مَغَاص (مَغْوَص) *diving-place,* C from غَاص *to dive,* imperf. يَغُوص (يَغْوُص) ; مَخَاف (مَخْوَف) and مَهَاب (مَهْيَب), a *place that is dreaded,* from خَاف *to fear,* imperf. يَهَاب (يَهْيَب), and هَاب *to fear,* imperf. مَقِيل (مَقْيِل) *place of resting at mid-day,* from قَالَ *to sleep at mid-day,* imperf. يَقِيل (يَقْيِل).

REM. The مَصْدَر مِيمِى has in this case regularly the form with ā in the second syllable, as مَآب, مَآل, مَعَاد, *return* (from آب for D أَوَب, etc.), مَشَاع *being divulged* or *published* (from شَاع for شَيَع); but many verba med. ى take in preference the form with ī, as مَسَال, or مَسِيل, مَحَاض, or مَحِيض, مَبَاع or مَبِيع, مَبَات or مَبِيت, مَمَال or مَمِيل, مَقَال or مَقِيل, مَكَال or مَكِيل, مَعَاش or مَعِيش. See § 208.

224. Those formed from verba tertiæ rad. و et ى violate the rule laid down in § 221, for they always take fĕtḥa in the second syllable,

A whatever be the vowel of the Imperfect. In regard to their contraction, they follow the analogy of the verbal nouns فَعَل from the same verbs (§ 213). E.g. مَنْجًى (مَنْجَىٌ, مَنْجَوٌ) *place of refuge*, from نَجَا *to escape*, imperf. يَنْجُو; مَرْعًى (مَرْعَىٌ) *pasture-ground*, from رَعَى, *to pasture* or *graze*, imperf. يَرْعَى; مَثْوًى (مَثْوَىٌ) *the place where one stops*, from ثَوَى *to stop*, imperf. يَثْوِى; مَأْوًى (مَأْوَىٌ) *do.*, from أَوَى *to go* or *resort to a place*, imperf. يَأْوِى; مَطْوًى (مَطْوَىٌ) *a fold*, from

B طَوَى *to fold*, imperf. يَطْوِى; مَثْنًى (مَثْنَىٌ) *a bend*, from ثَنَى *to bend*, imperf. يَثْنِى.

REM. The مَصْدَر مِيمِى has the same form, as مَجْرًى from جَرَى, imperf. يَجْرِى; مَسْرًى from سَرَى, imperf. يَسْرِى.

225. Nouns of time and place not unfrequently take the feminine

C form ـَة; as مَشْغَلَة *time* or *place of occupation, business*; مَشْرَعَة *the place where cattle, etc., are watered*; مَضْرِبَة *the part of a sword with which the blow is struck, the edge*; مَنْزِلَة *a halting-place, a station*; مَغَارَة (مَغْوَرَة) *a cave*; مَرْعَاة (مَرْعَيَة) *pasture-ground*. If derived from a strong verb, the second rad. frequently has in this case *damma* instead of *fětha*; as مَقْبُرَة *cemetery*, مَشْرُبَة *place for drinking, banqueting-room*, مَشْرَعَة *watering-place*. Some nouns have even three

D forms; as مَشْرُقَة *a place where one suns oneself* or *sits in the sunshine*, مَهْلَكَة *a place where people perish, a desert*. Peculiar is مَظِنَّة *the place where a thing is supposed to be*, from ظَنَّ *to think, suppose*, imperf. يَظُنُّ.

REM. The مَصْدَر مِيمِى is liable to the same variations, though مَفْعَلَة is the normal form, as مَسْغَبَة *hunger*. For example: مَحْمَدَة,

مَذَمَّةٌ, in preference to مَحْمَدَةٌ; مَذِمَّةٌ, مَظْلَمَةٌ, مَعْتَبَةٌ, مَغْفَرَةٌ, مَرْثِيَةٌ A

or مَقْدُرَةٌ, مَأْرُبَةٌ; مَعْذُرَةٌ; مَحْمِيَةٌ; (مَرْثِيَةٌ) مَرْثَاةٌ.

226. Some nouns of time and place, derived from verba primae
rad. و et ى, take the form مِفْعَالٌ (see § 228). E.g. مِيلَادٌ *time of
birth*, from وَلَدَ *to bear*; مِيعَادٌ *appointed time* [or *place*] for the
fulfilment of a promise, from وَعَدَ *to promise*; مِيقَاتٌ *appointed time*
[or *place* for the performance of some action], from وَقَتَ *to fix a time*. B

REM. From the strong verb this form is very rare, as مِشْرَاقٌ or
مِشْرِيقٌ = مَشْرَقَةٌ; but in Æthiopic it is the usual form from all verbs,
as *mĕsrăk* = مَشْرِقٌ, *mĕ'răb* = مَغْرِبٌ, *mĕr'ăy* = مَرْعًى.

227. The nouns of time and place from the derived forms of
the triliteral verb, or from the quadriliteral, are identical in form
with the *nomina patientis* or passive participles. E.g. مُصَلًّى *a place* C
of prayer (صَلَّى *to pray*); مُصْبَح, مُمْسًى, *the time of entering upon
the morning or evening* (أَصْبَحَ, أَمْسَى, *to enter upon the time of morning
or evening*); مُخْرَج, مُدْخَل *the place through which*, or *the time when,
one is made to enter* (أَدْخَلَ *to make one enter*) or *go out* (أَخْرَجَ *to make
go out*); مُنْصَرَف *place or time of returning* (انْصَرَفَ *to return*); مُجْتَمَع
a place where things are collected (اجْتَمَعَ *to be collected*); مُلْتَقًى *place* D
or time of meeting (الْتَقَى *to meet*); مُسْتَهَلّ *the first day of the month*
(اُسْتُهِلَّ الْهِلَالُ *the new moon appeared*); مُدَحْرَج *a place where one
rolls anything* (دَحْرَجَ *to roll*); مُحْرَنْجَم *a place where* (camels) *are
crowded together* (احْرَنْجَمَ *to be gathered together in a crowd*).

REM. The same form is also used as a مَصْدَرٌ مِيمِيّ from
the derived forms of the triliteral verb and from the quadriliteral;
e.g. مُجَرَّب *the being tried* or *tested* = تَجْرِيبٌ or تَجْرِبَةٌ; مُنَدًّى *the*

A   *letting* (camels) *graze in the interval of their being watered* ‑ تَنْدِيَة ;
تَمْزِيق = *the rending in pieces* ; مُمَزَّق   مُوَقَّى *the guarding carefully* =
تَوْقِيَة ; مُقَاتَل *fighting* = قِتَال or مُقَاتَلَة ; مُغَار *the making a raid or*
foray = إِغَارَة ; مُصَاب *affliction* = إِصَابَة ; مُنْقَلَب, مُتَقَلَّب *turning or*
tossing to and fro = تَقَلُّب, اِنْقِلَاب ; مُتَحَامَل *the pressing heavily on,*
wronging = تَحَامُل ; مُصَلْصَل *to make a clashing or ringing sound =*
صَلْصَلَة ; إِلَى ٱللّٰه مِنْهَا ٱلْمُشْتَكَى وَٱلْمُعَوَّل, *to God is (our) complaint of*
this event (وقيعة) *and (on Him) is (our) reliance.*

B   (ε) *The Nomina Instrumenti or Nouns that indicate the*
Instrument.

228. The nouns which denote the instrument that one uses
in performing the act expressed by a verb, are called in Arabic
أَسْمَاء ٱلْآلَة, *nomina instrumenti.* They have the forms مِفْعَل, مِفْعَال,
and مِفْعَلَة, and are distinguished from the nouns of place and time
C by the kèsra with which the prefixed م is pronounced. When derived
from verba med. rad. و et ي, they remain uncontracted. E.g. مِبْرَد,
a file, from بَرَد, *to file* ; مِبْضَع, *a lancet,* from بَضَع, *to cut ;* مِشْرَط *and*
مِشْرَاط, *a lancet ;* مِقْرَاض, *a pair of scissors ;* مِفْتَح or مِفْتَاح, *a key ;*
مِسْرَح *and* مِسْرَحَة, *a comb ;* مِحْجَمَة, *a cupping-glass ;* مِكْنَسَة *and*
مِكْنَسَة, *a broom ;* مِقَصّ (for مِقْصَص), *a pair of scissors ;* مِسَلَّة, *a*
D *packing-needle ;* مِثْرَة, *an iron instrument for marking* a camel's foot
(from أَثَر) ; مِيثَرَة, *a pad placed under a horse's saddle* (from وَثَر) ; مِيسَم,
a branding-iron (from وَسَم) ; مِيزَان, *a balance or pair of scales* (from
وَزَن) ; مِرْوَح *and* مِرْوَحَة, *a fan ;* مِقْوَد, *a bridle or halter ;* مِرْوَد, *a small*
probe for applying kohl to the eyes ; مِخْيَط, *a needle ;* مِصْيَد *and*
مِصْيَدَة, *a net or snare ;* مِرْقَاة (for مِرْقَيَة), *a staircase or ladder ;* مِصْفَاة,
a strainer ; مِكْوَاة, *a branding-iron or cautery.*

REM. *a.* A very few have the form مُنْخُلٌ or مُفْعَلٌ ; as مُنْخُلٌ, A
a sieve; مُنْصَلٌ, *a sword;* مِغْزَلٌ - مُغْزَلٌ, *a spindle;* مُسْعَطٌ - مِسْعَطٌ,
an instrument for introducing medicine into the nose; مُدُقُّ - مِدَقُّ,
a pestle or mallet; مُجْمَرٌ - مِجْمَرٌ, *a censer.* The form مَغْزَلٌ is
also used.

REM. *b.* The corresponding Hebrew nouns have ⌣ and ⌣, as
well as ⌣, in the first syllable; e.g. מַפְתֵּחַ ,מוֹלֵד ,מֶלְקָחַיִם ,מִזְרָק, B
מְזַמְּרָה.

(ζ) *The Nomina Agentis et Patientis.*

229. The nouns which the Arab Grammarians call أَسْمَآءُ ٱلْفَاعِلِ,
nomina agentis, and أَسْمَآءُ ٱلْمَفْعُولِ, *nomina patientis,* are *verbal* C
adjectives, i.e. adjectives derived from verbs, and nearly correspond in
nature and signification to what we call *participles.*

REM. These verbal adjectives often become in Arabic, as in
other languages, substantives.

230. The verbal adjectives, derived from the first form of the
triliteral verb, have two principal forms, namely, the nomen agentis,
فَاعِلٌ, and the nomen patientis, مَفْعُولٌ. E.g. كَاتِبٌ *writing, a scribe*
or *secretary,* from كَتَبَ *to write;* مَكْتُوبٌ *written, a letter,* from كُتِبَ ; D
خَادِمٌ *serving, a servant,* from خَدَمَ *to serve,* مَخْدُومٌ *served, a master,*
from خُدِمَ ; حَاكِمٌ *judging, a judge,* from حَكَمَ *to judge;* كَائِنٌ *being,*
from كَانَ *to be;* مَوْجُودٌ *found, existing,* from وُجِدَ, *to be found, to*
exist; مَجْنُونٌ *mad, a madman,* from جُنَّ, *to be possessed, to be mad.*

REM. *a.* When formed from فَعَلَ and the *transitive* فَعِلَ (as
رَهِبَ *to fear,* رَكِبَ *to ride on,* عَلِمَ *to know,* مَسَّ *to touch*), these
nomina agentis are not only real participles, indicating a temporary,

A transitory or accidental action or state of being, but also serve as adjectives or substantives, expressing a continuous action, a habitual state of being, or a permanent quality; e.g. كَاتِبٌ, خَادِمٌ, حَاكِمٌ (see above), عَالِمٌ *a scholar,* رَاهِبٌ *an ascetic.* But if from the *intransitive* فَعِلَ and from فَعُلَ, they have only the participial sense, the adjectival being expressed by one or other of the nominal forms enumerated in § 231. Thus فَارِحٌ or جَاذِلٌ *being glad,*

B *rejoicing,* جَابِنٌ *being cowardly,* جَائِدٌ *being liberal,* ضَائِقٌ *being narrow* or *confined,* are participles; the adjectives which indicate the corresponding permanent qualities or characteristics are فَرِحٌ and جَذِلٌ or جَذْلَانُ, *gladsome, cheery,* جَبَانٌ *cowardly,* جَوَادٌ *bountiful, generous,* and ضَيِّقٌ *narrow.* [Comp. however § 232, rem. *b.*]

REM. *b.* The nomen agentis فَاعِلٌ is said to be used occasionally in place of the nomen verbi or actionis, as in the phrase قُمْ قَائِمًا,

C for قُمْ قِيَامًا; but this is more frequently the case with the nomen patientis (compare § 227, rem.) مَفْعُولٌ. E.g. جَهْدٌ = مَجْهُودٌ, *labour, effort, one's utmost;* حَلْفٌ = مَحْلُوفٌ, *swearing, an oath;* رَدٌّ = مَرْدُودٌ, *giving* or *sending back, rejection;* عَقْلٌ = مَعْقُولٌ *understanding, intelligence;* شَعْرٌ = مَشْعُورٌ, *knowledge, perception;* وَعْدٌ = مَوْعُودٌ, *promising, a promise;* يُسْرٌ = مَيْسُورٌ *affluence,* opposed to عُسْرٌ = مَعْسُورٌ,

D , *penury, distress;* رَفْعٌ = مَرْفُوعٌ, *to trot quickly* (of a camel); وَضْعٌ = مَوْضُوعٌ *to trot easily* (do.); خَفْضٌ = مَخْفُوضٌ, *to go gently* (do.); حُصُولٌ = مَحْصُولٌ, *being in existence, being got* or *acquired;* جَلَادَةٌ = مَجْلُودٌ, *hardiness, sturdiness, endurance.* The fem. مَفْعُولَةٌ is likewise occasionally so used, as مَصْدُوقَةٌ = مَوْعُودَةٌ, مَشْعُورَةٌ مَحْلُوفَةٌ; صِدْقٌ, *the telling of the truth,* opposed to كِذْبٌ = مَكْذُوبَةٌ, *lying;* and also a cognate form مَفْعُولَاءُ, as مَشْعُورَاءُ, مَحْلُوفَاءُ.

REM. *c.* Conversely, the nomen actionis is sometimes used instead of the nomen agentis and patientis, or as an adjective. E.g. كَلَّمْتُهُ مُشَافَهَةً, أَتَيْتُهُ رَكْضًا, *I came to him riding hard,* = رَاكِضًا;

I spoke to him face to face (lit. *lip to lip*), – مُشَافِهًا ; لَقِيتُهُ عِيَانًا , A

I met him face to face (lit. *eye to eye*), – مُعَايِنًا ; قَتَلْتُهُ صَبْرًا , *I slew*

him in cold blood (lit. *bound, confined* or *held, so that he could not*

resist or *escape*), = مَصْبُورًا ; رَجُلٌ عَدْلٌ , اِمْرَأَةٌ عَدْلٌ , رِجَالٌ عَدْلٌ ,

a just man, a just woman, just men, = عَادِلٌ ; عَادِلَةٌ , عَدُولٌ ; مَاءٌ غَوْرٌ ,

water which sinks into the ground, غَائِرٌ , دِرْهَمٌ ضَرْبُ ٱلْأَمِيرِ , *a*

dirham struck by the emir, = مَضْرُوبُ ٱلْأَمِيرِ ; هُمْ خَلْقُ ٱللّٰهِ , *they are* B

the creatures (lit. *the creation*) *of God,* = مَخْلُوقُ ٱللّٰهِ .

REM. *d.* فَاعِلٌ is the Aram. קָטֵל, קָֽטְלָא, and Heb. קֹטֵל (with

ō for ā). The form مَفْعُولٌ does not occur in either of these

languages, the Heb. using instead of it קָטוּל = فَعُولٌ, and the

Aram. קְטִיל = فَعِيلٌ (see § 232, rem. *c*).

231. Besides these, there are other verbal adjectives derived

from the first form of the verb, and called صِفَاتٌ مُشَبَّهَةٌ بِأَسْمَاءِ ٱلْفَاعِلِ C

وَٱلْمَفْعُولِ, *adjectives which are made like, or assimilated to, the par-*

ticiples, viz. in respect of their inflection. Of these the following

are the principal.

1.	فَعْلٌ	9.	فَعَالٌ
2.	فَعَلٌ	10.	فُعَالٌ
3.	فَعِلٌ	11.	فَعِيلٌ
4.	فَعُلٌ	12.	فَعُولٌ
5.	فِعْلٌ	13.	فَعْلَانُ
6.	فُعْلٌ	14.	فَعْلَانٌ
7.	فُعُلٌ	15.	فُعْلَانٌ
8.	فُعَلٌ	16.	أَفْعَلُ

D

232. Most of these adjectives come from neuter verbs, and

express, partly, a quality inherent and permanent in a person or

A thing,—which is their most usual signification (see § 38),—and, partly, a certain degree of intensity. Examples: 1. صَعْبٌ *difficult*, from صَعُبَ; سَهْلٌ *easy*, from سَهُلَ; عَذْبٌ *sweet*, from عَذُبَ; ضَخْمٌ *large*, from ضَخُمَ; طَفْلٌ *tender*, from طَفُلَ; شَهْمٌ *strong, hardy, acute, clever*, from شَهُمَ; شَأْزٌ *rough, rugged*, from شَئِزَ; قَذْرٌ *unclean*, from قَذِرَ. 2. بَطَلٌ *brave*, from بَطُلَ; حَسَنٌ *handsome*, from حَسُنَ; قَذَرٌ from قَذِرَ. 3 and 4. جَذِلٌ, *glad*, from جَذِلَ, فَرِحَ; فَرِحٌ *glad*, from فَرِحَ; أَشِرٌ, بَطِرٌ *proud*,

B *self-conceited and insolent*, from أَشِرَ and بَطِرَ; وَجِعٌ *in pain*, from وَجِعَ; حَبِطٌ *having a swollen stomach*, from حَبِطَ; دَنِسٌ *dirty*, from دَنِسَ; رَدٍ; شَجٍ, جَوٍ (for شَجِىٌ, جَوِىٌ) *in grief*, from شَجِىَ, جَوِىَ; (for رَدِىٌ) *perishing*, from رَدِىَ; حَفٍ *having his foot or hoof chafed*, from حَفِىَ; وَجٍ do., from وَجِىَ; فَطِنٌ *clever, intelligent*, from فَطِنَ; يَقِظٌ, يَقْظٌ *awake*, from يَقِظَ; حَزِنٌ, حَزْنٌ *sorry*,

C from حَزِنَ; نَدِسٌ, حَذِرٌ, حَذُرٌ *timid, cautious, wary*, from حَذِرَ; نَدِسٌ, *intelligent*, from نَدِسَ; عَجِلٌ, عَجُلٌ *quick, in haste*, from عَجِلَ; قَذِرٌ, قَذُرٌ from قَذِرَ; خَشِنٌ *rough, harsh*, from خَشُنَ; طَهِرٌ *clean, pure*, from طَهُرَ. 5. خِرْقٌ *liberal;* طِفْلٌ, *small, young*, from طَفُلَ *to be tender;* جِلٌّ *large, coarse, fat*, from جَلَّ; دِقٌّ *fine, thin*, from دَقَّ. 6 and 7. صُلْبٌ *hard*, from صَلُبَ; حُلْوٌ *sweet*, from حَلُوَ; مُرٌّ *bitter*, from مَرَّ; غُمْرٌ, غُمُرٌ *inexperienced, untaught*, from غَمُرَ; جُنُبٌ *polluted*, from

D جُنُبَ. 8. حُطَمٌ *breaking, crushing, bruising*, from حَطَمَ; غُدَرٌ *perfidious, treacherous*, from غَدَرَ *to forsake, abandon, betray;* لُبَدٌ *remaining in one place, abundant*, from لَبَدَ; زُكَنٌ *knowing*, from زَكِنَ. 9. جَبَانٌ *cowardly*, from جَبُنَ; شُجَاعٌ *brave*, from شَجُعَ; جَوَادٌ *liberal*, from جَادَ; حَصَانٌ *chaste*, from حَضُنَتْ; كَهَامٌ *blunt*, from كَهُمَ, كَهَمَ. 10. شُجَاعٌ *brave*, from شَجُعَ; ضُخَامٌ *large*, from

قُرَاتُ ; صُخُمٌ كُرَامٌ noble, from كُرُمَ ; حُسَانٌ handsome, from حَسُنَ : A
sweet (of water), from فُرُتَ ; حُرَاقٌ salt (of water), from حَرَقَ to burn ;
بَخِيلٌ .11 .[طُوَالٌ long, tall, from طَالَ ; قُدَارٌ] a cook, from قَدَرَ to cook].
stingy, niggardly, from بَخُلَ ; كَثِيرٌ much, many, numerous, from كَثُرَ ;
شَرِيفٌ noble, from شَرُفَ ; كَرِيمٌ noble, from كَرُمَ ; ضَعِيفٌ weak, from
ضَعُفَ ; ثَقِيلٌ heavy, from ثَقُلَ ; غَلِيظٌ thick, coarse, from غَلُظَ ; طَوِيلٌ
long, tall, from طَالَ ; رَحِيمٌ compassionate, merciful, from رَحِمَ ; سَلِيمٌ B
safe, from سَلِمَ ; سَقِيمٌ ,مَرِيضٌ sick, from سَقِمَ ,مَرِضَ ; خَفِيفٌ light,
agile, from خَفَّ ; جَلِيلٌ great, glorious, from جَلَّ ; دَقِيقٌ small, slender,
paltry, from دَقَّ. 12. أَكُولٌ gluttonous, from أَكَلَ ; كَذُوبٌ addicted
to lying, from كَذَبَ ; صَدُوقٌ veracious, from صَدَقَ ; قَوُولٌ or قَوُّولٌ
talkative [or ready to speak], from قَالَ ; [فَعُولٌ] ready to do, from
عَطُوفٌ ; دَفُوعٌ pushing, thrusting or kicking violently, from دَفَعَ ; [فَعَلَ]
moved by affection or pity, from عَطَفَ ; جَسُورٌ daring, from جَسَرَ ; C
جَهُولٌ ignorant, foolish, from جَهِلَ ; حَصُورٌ continent, impotent, from
حَصَرَ. 13. سَكْرَانُ drunk, from سَكِرَ ; غَضْبَانُ angry, from غَضِبَ ;
عَطْشَانُ ,ظَمْآنُ thirsty, from عَطِشَ ,ظَمِئَ ; جَوْعَانُ ,غَرْثَانُ hungry,
from غَرِثَ ,جَاعَ ; شَبْعَانُ satisfied with food, from شَبِعَ ; رَيَّانُ satisfied
with drink, from رَوِيَ ; خَزْيَانُ ashamed, from خَزِيَ. 14. نَدْمَانُ
repentant, from نَدِمَ. 15. عُرْيَانُ naked, from عَرِيَ. 16. أَبْلَجُ having D
a clear space between the eyebrows, bright, open, cheerful in countenance,
from بَلِجَ ; أَشَمُّ having a high, straight nose, from شَمَّ ; أَهْيَفُ having
a slender waist, from هَيِفَ ; (ذَقَنَ) having a long chin ; أَلْأَقَنُ
humpbacked, from حَدِبَ ; أَعْوَرُ one-eyed, from عَوِرَ ; أَحْوَلُ squinting,
from حَوِلَ ; أَصَمُّ deaf, from صَمَّ ; أَحْمَقُ foolish, stupid, from حَمِقَ,
حَمْقَى ; أَخْرَقُ unskilful, clumsy, stupid, from خَرِقَ ; أَشْنَعُ unseemly,
ugly, foul, from شَنُعَ ; أَحْمَرُ red, أَسْوَدُ black, أَبْيَضُ white, أَصْفَرُ yellow.

A   REM. *a.* As is shown by the above examples, the forms فُعْلٌ and فَعِيلٌ are principally derived from فَعِلَ; فَعَلٌ and فُعُلٌ come respectively from فَعِلَ intrans. and فَعَلَ, though the distinction is not always observed; فَعْلَانُ is principally formed from فَعِلَ intrans.; فَعَّالٌ and فُعَالٌ mainly from فَعَلَ; أَفْعَلُ chiefly from فَعِلَ intrans., sometimes from فَعَلَ.

B   REM. *b.* فَاعِلٌ is rarely used as a verbal adjective from فَعِلَ intrans. or فَعُلَ (see § 230, rem. *a*); e.g. آمِنٌ *safe, secure,* = أَمِينٌ or أَمِنٌ, from أَمِنَ; سَالِمٌ, *safe, sound,* = سَلِيمٌ, from سَلِمَ; عَاقِرٌ *barren,* from عَقَرَتْ; حَامِضٌ *sour, acid,* from حَمُضَ or حَمِضَ.

REM. *c.* فَعِيلٌ, when derived from *transitive* verbs, has usually a *passive* sense; as قَتِيلٌ *slain* = مَقْتُولٌ; جَرِيحٌ *wounded* = مَجْرُوحٌ;

C   ذَبِيحٌ *slaughtered, a victim,* = مَذْبُوحٌ; خَضِيبٌ *dyed* = مَخْضُوبٌ; كَحِيلٌ *rubbed with kohl* = مَكْحُولٌ; أَسِيرٌ *bound, a prisoner,* = مَأْسُورٌ. The same is sometimes the case with فَعُولٌ, as رَكُوبٌ *ridden upon,* حَلُوبٌ *milked**.

REM. *d.* Adjectives of the forms فَعِيلٌ and فَعُولٌ, but more especially the latter, often indicate, as shown by some of the above examples, either a very high degree of the quality which their subject possesses, or an act which is done with frequency or violence

D   by their subject; and hence they are called أَبْنِيَةُ ٱلْمُبَالَغَةِ, *intensive forms.* The form فَعِيلٌ is dialectically pronounced فِعِيلٌ, especially if the second radical be a guttural, as كَبِيرٌ, سَعِيدٌ, رَحِيمٌ, شَهِيدٌ; and so also in substantives, as بَعِيرٌ, رَغِيفٌ, شَعِيرٌ, كَرِيمٌ, جَلِيلٌ, ٱلْمَسِيحُ.

---

* [رَسُولٌ does not belong to this class; according to the native scholars, it is originally a nomen actionis like قَبُولٌ, meaning *message.* Hence, as in the case of Latin *nuntius,* it got the signification of *bearer of a message.* D. G.]

Rem. *e.*   Many of these forms exist in Hebrew and Aramaic. A
For example, in the former, فَعَل, as حَدَث - חֲדַשׁ; فَعِل, as רָשָׁע ··
فَعَال, as וְגִל, וְגֵר, גָּדוֹל (ō for ā); فَعُل, as דֶּסֶם, دَسِم فَعَل, as
צָעִיר, אָסִיר, فَعِيل as עָצוּם, אָסוּר.

233.   From verbal adjectives of the form فَاعِل, as well as from
some others, is derived an adjective فَعَّال, which approaches very
nearly in meaning to فَعُول and فَعِيل, since it adds to the signification B
of its primitive the idea of intensiveness or of habit. Hence it is
called اِسْمُ ٱلْمُبَالَغَة, *the noun of intensiveness.* E.g. أَكَّال *eating,*
a glutton, = أَكُول; كَاذِب *lying,* كَذَّاب *a (habitual) liar,* = كَذُوب;
دَافِع *pushing, thrusting, repelling,* دَقَّاع *pushing, etc., violently,* =
دَفُوع; سَائِل *asking,* سَتَّال *importunate, a beggar,* = سَوُّول; شَارِب *drinking,*
شَرَّاب *drinking much, addicted to wine,* = شَرُوب; عَالِم *knowing, learned,* C
عَلَّام *very learned;* بَاك *weeping,* بَكَّاء *weeping much;* هَائِب *fearing,*
هَيَّاب *timid.*

Rem. *a.*   The nouns which indicate professions and trades have
usually this form; as عَطَّار *a druggist,* طَبَّاخ *a cook,* خَبَّاز *a baker,*
خَيَّاط *a tailor,* نَجَّار *a carpenter,* سَقَّاء *a water-carrier,* جَنَّان *a*
gardener, رَءَّاس *a seller of sheeps' heads,* صَرَّاف *a money-changer or*
banker, بَنَّاء *a builder or architect,* حَمَّال *a porter.* Compare in
Hebrew and Aram. סַבָּל, מַלָּח, טַבָּח, גַּנָּב, חַטָּא, etc.   D

Rem. *b.*   Other intensive adjectives, less common than فَعَّال, are
1. فُعَّال, 2. فِعِّيل, 3. فُعُول or فُعُّول, 4. فُعَّل, and 5. فَاعُول; as
1. حُسَّان, وُضَّاء, *very handsome,* كُرَّام *very noble,* كُبَّار *very large,*
قُرَّاء *one who devotes himself to reading (the sacred writings),* دُقَّاع
a strong propeller or repeller, a great rush (of water or of people);
2. خُمِّير, سِكِّير, شِرِّيب, *addicted to wine, drunken,* ضِلِّيل *going astray,*

A *wandering;* عَرِيض *fond of opposition,* فَخِير *boastful,* صِدِّيق *exceedingly veracious,* خِرِّيق *very liberal,* صَرِيع *one who throws down often or violently, a wrestler;* دِرِّى؟ *glistening intensely* (also دُرِّى؟, the only instance of the form فُعِّيل, except مُرِّيق); 3. فَرُوق *timid,* قَيُّوم *everlasting,* سَتُوق or سُتُوق *bad* (of money), سَبُوح or سُبُوح *all-pure, all-glorious,* قَدُّوس or قُدُّوس *most holy;* 4. قَلَّب، حُوَّل،

B فَارُوق *shifting, turning, knowing, cunning,* خُلَّب *deceitful;* 5. *timid,* جَاسُوس *a spy.*—On the other hand, مِفْعَل، مِفْعَال, and مِفْعِيل, are, strictly speaking, substantives (nomina instrumenti, § 228), but used metaphorically as adjectives to mean "doing something like a machine, mechanically, and therefore invariably (habitually)." E.g. مِدْفَع *thrusting or pushing much,* مِزْحَم *pushing or pressing much,* مِصَدَم *a brave warrior,* مِحْرَب، مِحْرَاب, *do.,*

C مِطْعَن، مِطْعَان, *thrusting with the spear,* مِهْذَر، مِهْذَار, *talking nonsense,* مِطْعَم، مِطْعَام, *eating much or giving much to eat, hospitable,* مِقْوَل، مِقْوَال, *talkative, eloquent,* مِفْرَاح *cheerful,* مِذْعَان *docile, tractable,* مِحْرَاق *very liberal,* مِقْدَام *advancing boldly, daring,* مِكْسَال *slothful,* مِذْكَار *bearing male children,* مِنْثَاث *bearing female children,* مِعْطَاء؟ *very liberal,* مِكْثَار، مِكْثِير, *very talkative,* مِعْطَار,

D مِعْطِير, *using perfumes,* مِسْكِين *mean, poor* (מִסְכֵּן),—*.(מַחְסֶב) Similar, too, is the use of such forms as تَفْعَال or تِفْعَال، تِفْعَلَة, and تِفْعَّال, which are abstract substantives (nomina actionis, § 202) used concretely; e.g. تِلْعَاب، تِلْعَاب، تَلْعَاب, *given to play or sport;* تِلْقَام، تِلْقَام, *swallowing big morsels, greedy;* تَضْرَاب *covered by the stallion* (of a she-camel), تِلْقَاع *talking much and foolishly,* تِكْذَاب *mendacious,* تِلْمَاظ *fickle,* تِقْوَلَة *loquacious,* تِعْلِمَة *very learned.*

---

* [To this class belongs also مُنْتِن، مُنْتَن، مِنْتِن *stinking.* D. G.]

REM. *c.* Nearly all these adjectives and quasi-adjectives admit A of being strengthened in their meaning by the addition of the termination ة‑, which is here used, as the grammarians say, لِلْمُبَالَغَة, *to signify intensiveness*, or لِتَأْكِيدِ ٱلْمُبَالَغَة, *to strengthen the idea of intensiveness*. For example, from فَاعِلٌ comes فَاعِلَةٌ, as رَاوٍ *one who hands down poems or historical facts by oral tradition*, رَاوِيَةٌ; دَاهٍ *crafty*, دَاهِيَةٌ; دَاعٍ *calling or summoning, an emissary or missionary*, دَاعِيَةٌ; بَاقِعَةٌ *clever, crafty*; خَائِنَةٌ *treacherous, faithless;* B بَاقِرَةٌ *a deep investigator* (compare in Heb. קֹהֶלֶת from קָהַל);

from فَعْلٌ, فَعْلَةٌ, as حُطَمَةٌ *breaking in pieces, crushing to bits*, طُلَعَةٌ *always on the watch*, صُرَعَةٌ *throwing down or prostrating often*, سُوَلَةٌ *asking often, begging*, ضُحَكَةٌ *prone to laughter*, قُوَلَةٌ *loquacious*, نُوَمَةٌ *given to sleep*, لُوَمَةٌ *abusive*, عُيَبَةٌ *finding fault;* from فَعِيلٌ, فَعِيلَةٌ, as كَرِيمَةٌ, عَقِيلَةٌ, *noble, excellent;* from فَعُولٌ, فَعُولَةٌ, as مَنُونَةٌ *taunting (one) with favours (conferred on him)*, كَذُوبَةٌ *lying*, مَلُولَةٌ *tired of, disgusted with*, فَرُوقَةٌ, هَيُوبَةٌ *timid;* from فَعَّالٌ, C فَعَّالَةٌ, as عَلَّامَةٌ *very learned*, نَسَّابَةٌ *a great genealogist*, رَحَّالَةٌ *a great traveller*, فَهَّامَةٌ *very quick of comprehension*, وَقَّاعَةٌ *ill-natured, slanderous*, قَوَّالَةٌ *very talkative*, جَمَّاعَةٌ *a great collector*, صَنَّاجَةٌ *an excellent player on the cymbals or harp* (صَنْجٌ); from فُعَّالٌ, فُعَّالَةٌ, as ضُرَّاعَةٌ *prostrating or throwing down very often*, كُرَّامَةٌ *very generous or noble*, لُقَّاعَةٌ *talking much and rashly or foolishly;* from فِعِّيلٌ, فِعِّيلَةٌ, as خِلِّيفَةٌ *very contrarious;* from فَعُولٌ, فَعُولَةٌ, as فَرُوقَةٌ *very timid;* from فَاعُولٌ, فَاعُولَةٌ, as حَاذُورَةٌ *very wary or cautious*, D فَارُوقَةٌ *very timid;* from مِفْعَالٌ, مِفْعَالَةٌ, as مِلْحَادَةٌ *very unjust*, مِقْدَامَةٌ *very bold in attacking*, مِهْذَارَةٌ *talking much and sillily;* from تَفْعَالٌ, تَفْعَالَةٌ, as تَلْعَابَةٌ *addicted to play or sport*, تَقْوَالَةٌ *loquacious*, تَعْلَامَةٌ *very learned*, تَعْجَابَةٌ *causing great wonder or marvel*, تَلْقَامَةٌ *swallowing big morsels, greedy* (the cognate form تِفْعِيلَةٌ also occurs, as

A تَلْعِيبَةٌ *much addicted to play or sport*); from تِفْعَالٌ, تِفْعَالَةٌ as تِلْعَّابَةٌ *much addicted to play or sport*, تِلْقَامَةٌ *swallowing huge morsels, very greedy*, تِلْقَاعَةٌ *talking much and foolishly*.

Rem. *d.* Besides the forms incidentally noticed above, others of these intensive adjectives occur in Hebrew and Aramaic; for example, فَعُولٌ, as רַחוּם, חַנּוּן, and فَعِيلٌ, but with the purer vowel *a* in the first syllable (فَعِيلٌ), as עַלִּין, צַדִּיק, אַבִּיר, ܣܰܓ݁ܺܝܐ,

B ܚܰܟ݁ܺܝ݂ܡ. Other forms are without exact equivalents in Arabic, as יָלוֹד (قُدُّوسٌ), עַזּוּז (coming nearest to גִּבּוֹר = جَبَّارٌ, שִׁכּוֹר = سِكِّيرٌ = Aram. ܠܰܚܕ݁ܳܐ); (فَعُولٌ); and especially the form קְטִיל, as גִּבֵּן (= أَخْرَسُ) חֵרֵשׁ (= אֵוֵר) עִוֵּר (= أَعْوَرُ), חִגֵּר (= حَدِبٌ), which may be viewed as an intensive of فَعِلٌ (קְטִיל for קַטֵּל, קַטֵּל = فَعِلٌ).

C **234.** From verbal adjectives with three radicals*, or with three radicals and a letter of prolongation, are derived adjectives of the form أَفْعَلُ, which have the signification of our comparative and superlative, and are therefore called اِسْمُ التَّفْضِيلِ, *the noun of preeminence*, or أَفْعَلُ التَّفْضِيلِ, *the form 'af'alu denoting preeminence.* E.g. عَذْبٌ, *sweet*, أَعْذَبُ, *sweeter, sweetest*; حَسَنٌ *beautiful*, أَحْسَنُ, *sweeter, sweetest*; أَحْلَى, حُلْوٌ *more or most beautiful*; قَبِيحٌ *ugly*, أَقْبَحُ *uglier, ugliest*; جَلِيلٌ *great, glorious*, أَجَلُّ *more or most glorious.*

D Rem. *a.* In the superlative sense, these adjectives must always have the article, or else be in the construct state, as ٱلْمَدِينَةُ ٱلْعُظْمَى *the greatest city*, كُبْرَى ٱلْمُدُنِ *the largest of the cities.*

---

* [A rare exception to this rule is أَعْلَتُ *bitterer*, as derived from عَلْقَمٌ *anything bitter*, spec. *the colocynth*, according to 'Ibn Dureïd, *Kitâb el-istikâk*, 53, l. 6, 98, l. 16 *seq.* In the *Lisân*, however (xii. 142), it is differently explained. R. S.]

Rem. *b.* Of this form there remain only a very few traces in A Hebrew, none in Aramaic. Such are: אָכְזָב *lying, false* (of a stream that dries up in summer), from כָּזַב = כָּאזِب ; אַכְזָר *fierce, cruel,* perhaps connected with كَاسِر *breaking in pieces*; אֵיתָן (for אֵיתָן) *lasting, perennial,* = وَاتِن ; and even these have lost their original signification, and are used as simple adjectives.

235. No اِسْمُ التَّفْضِيلِ can, according to strict rule, be formed B from the verbal adjectives of the passive voice and the derived forms of the verb, nor from verbal adjectives that denote colours or deformities, because they are themselves of the form أَفْعَلُ (compare § 184, rem. *b*). If we wish to say that one person surpasses another in the qualities expressed by such adjectives, we ought to prefix to the corresponding abstract or verbal nouns the comparatives أَشَدُّ *stronger,* أَحْسَنُ *more beautiful,* أَجْوَدُ *more excellent,* أَقْبَحُ *uglier,* خَيْرٌ *better,* شَرٌّ *worse,* and the like. E.g. أَشَدُّ حُمْرَةً (*stronger as to redness*) *redder;* C أَحْسَنُ تَعْلِيمًا وَتَأْدِيبًا (*more excellent as to teaching and training*) *a better teacher and trainer;* أَجْوَدُ مِنْهُ جَوَابًا (*more excellent than he as to answering*) *more ready than he in answering,* or *giving a better answer than he;* أَسْرَعُ انْطِلَاقًا (*more quick as to departing*) *departing more quickly;* أَقْبَحُ عَوَرًا *more deformed by blindness of one eye.* This form of expression is sometimes employed where a simple comparative might have been used; as ثُمَّ قَسَتْ قُلُوبُكُمْ مِنْ بَعْدِ ذَلِكَ فَهِيَ كَالْحِجَارَةِ أَوْ أَشَدُّ قَسْوَةً, *then, after that, your hearts became hard,* D *like stones, or even harder* (lit. *stronger as to hardness*), where أَشَدُّ قَسْوَةً = أَقْسَى (el-Ḳorān ii. 69).—As a matter of fact, however, the strict rules laid down by the grammarians are constantly violated by usage. (*a*) Examples of أَفْعَلُ formed from the derived forms of the verb, especially from IV.: أَطْهَرُ *more cleansing* or *purifying* (أَكْثَرُ تَطْهِيرًا), from طَهَّرَ *to cleanse* or *purify,* II. of طَهُرَ *to be clean* or *pure;* أَصْفَى لِ

A *making clearer* or *purer*, from صَفَّى *to clarify* or *clear*, II. of صَفَا *to be clear*; أَسْلَمُ لِ *preserving better*, from سَلَّمَ, II. of سَلِمَ *to be safe*; أَقْوَمُ لِ *confirming* or *establishing better*, from أَقَامَ, IV. of قَامَ *to stand upright*; أَثْبَتُ لِ *making more firm* or *sure*, from أَثْبَتَ, IV. of ثَبَتَ *to be firm*; أَخْوَفُنِى عَلَى *causing me greater alarm about*, from خَوَّفَ or أَخَافَ, II. or IV. of خَافَ *to fear*; أَعْوَنُ عَلَى *giving more help towards*, from أَعَانَ *to help*, IV. of عَانَ; أَذْهَبُ لِ *making depart more quickly*,

B from أَذْهَبَ, IV. of ذَهَبَ *to go away*; أَرْخَاهُمَا لِ *that of the two which relaxes*, or *loosens, more*, from أَرْخَى, IV. of رَخُوَ or رَخِيَ *to be flaccid* or *flabby*; أَبْقَى لِ *causing to last longer*, أَبْقَى عَلَى *more merciful to*, from أَبْقَى, IV. of بَقِيَ *to remain, last*; أَهْيَبُ لِ *inspiring more fear* or *respect*, from أَهَابَ, IV. of هَابَ *to fear*; أَنْصَفُ مِنْ *more just than*, from أَنْصَفَ *to be just*, IV. of نَصَفَ *to take the half, reach the middle*; أَطْوَلُ لِ *causing to last longer*, from أَطَالَ, IV. of طَالَ *to be long*;

C أَحْيَى لِ *preserving alive better*, from أَحْيَى, IV. of حَيِيَ *to live*; أَظَلُّ مِنْ *giving more shade than*, from أَظَلَّ *to give shade*, IV. of ظَلَّ; أَجْوَدُ لِ *causing to be better*, from أَجَادَ, IV. of جَادَ *to be good, excellent*; أَعْطَى لِ *giving more freely*, from أَعْطَى *to give*, IV. of عَطَا; أَوْلَى لِ; أَكْرَمُ لِ *bestowing more liberally*, from أَوْلَى *to bestow*, IV. of وَلِيَ;

D *showing greater honour to*, from أَكْرَمَ, IV. of كَرُمَ *to be noble*; أَفْلَسُ مِنْ *more desert than*, from أَقْفَرَ *to be desert*, IV. of قَفَرَ; أَقْفَرُ مِنْ *poorer than*, from أَفْلَسَ *to be poor*, IV. of فَلَسَ; أَحْوَلُ مِنْ *more crafty than*, from اِحْتَالَ, *to be crafty*, VIII. of حَالَ; أَقْوَدُ مِنْ *more easily led*, or *more docile, than*, from اِنْقَادَ, VII. of قَادَ *to lead*.   (β) Examples of أَفْعَلُ *formed from the passive voice* : أَهْيَبُ, أَخْوَفُ, أَخْشَى, *more feared*

or *formidable;* أَحْمَدُ *more praiseworthy* or *commendable;* أَعْرَفُ *better* A
known; أَلْوَمُ *more deserving of blame;* أَسَرُّ *more glad of* or *pleased by;*
أَعْذَرُ *more to be excused;* أَوْجَدُ *more readily found;* أَشْغَلُ *more occupied;* أَزْهَى *prouder* (زُهِىَ *to be proud*); أَمْقَتُ *more hated* or *hateful;*
أَعْنَى بِ *more occupied with* (عُنِىَ or VIII. . .اِعْتَنَى); أَخْصَرُ *shorter* (from
اُخْتُصِرَ, pass. of VIII.). (γ) Examples of أَفْعَلُ from words denoting
colours or defects: أَبْيَضُ مِنْ *whiter than;* أَسْوَدُ مِنْ *blacker than;*
أَحْمَقُ مِنْ *more stupid than.* B

236. The verbal adjectives formed from the active and passive
voices of the derived forms of the triliteral verb, and from the quadriliteral verb, are the following.

Triliteral Verb.

	Act.	Pass.		Act.	Pass.	
II.	مُفَعِّلٌ	مُفَعَّلٌ	VII.	مُنْفَعِلٌ	مُنْفَعَلٌ	C
III.	مُفَاعِلٌ	مُفَاعَلٌ	VIII.	مُفْتَعِلٌ	مُفْتَعَلٌ	
IV.	مُفْعِلٌ	مُفْعَلٌ	IX.	مُفْعَلٌّ		
V.	مُتَفَعِّلٌ	مُتَفَعَّلٌ	X.	مُسْتَفْعِلٌ	مُسْتَفْعَلٌ	
VI.	مُتَفَاعِلٌ	مُتَفَاعَلٌ	XI.	مُفْعَالٌّ		

Quadriliteral Verb. D

I.	مُفَعْلِلٌ	مُفَعْلَلٌ	III.	مُفْعَنْلِلٌ	مُفْعَنْلَلٌ
II.	مُتَفَعْلِلٌ	مُتَفَعْلَلٌ	IV.	مُفْعَلِلٌّ	مُفْعَلَلٌّ

REM. a. The characteristic vowel of the second and third
radicals is the same in all these verbal adjectives as in the corresponding Imperfects, excepting the active participles of the fifth
and sixth forms of the triliteral verb and the second form of the

A   quadriliteral, in which the second and third radicals have $\smile$ instead
of $\angle$.

REM. *b.* The preformative م takes in Arabic the vowel $\angle$, in
Heb. and Aram. $\smile$ (e.g. מִתְקַטֵּל ,מְהַקְטִיל ,מְהֻקְטָל - מְהַקְטִיל מַקְטִיל =
"מֵהַת), but the Æthiopic seems to have retained the original
vowel in its prefix **ማ**: *ma*, as **ማዐምጽ** (maʿámmĕz) *oppressor*

B   (חֹמֵץ ,חֹמֵץ); **ማኰንን**: (makwánnĕn) *judge* (מְכוֹנֵן); **ማናፊቅ**:
(manáfĕk) *sceptic, heretic* (مُنَافِق); **ማርዐድ**: (márʿed) *causing to
tremble, dreadful* (מַרְעִיד ,مُرْعِد); **ማፍሪ**: (máfrī) *fruitful*
(מַפְרֶה); **ማስታምሕር**: (mastámḥĕr) *imploring mercy* (مُسْتَرْحِم);
ማተርጕም: (matárgwĕm) *an interpreter* (مُتَرْجِم).

237.   In the formation of verbal adjectives from verba mediæ
C   rad. geminatæ, the rules laid down in § 120 are to be observed.   Hence
مَادّ becomes مَادّ (see § 13, rem.); أَشَدُّ ,أَشْدَدُ ; مُضِلٌّ ,مُضْلِل ; etc.

238.   In the formation of verbal adjectives from the verba hèmzata, the rules laid down regarding those verbs (§§ 131-6) are to be
observed.   Hence we write آثِرٌ for أَأْثِرٌ (§ 135), سَائِل for سَاإِل (§ 133),
مُؤْثِرٌ for مُؤْثِرٌ (§ 133), مَأْثِرٌ for مُؤَاثِرٌ ,لَإِيمٌ for لَئِيمٌ ,رَأُوفٌ for رَؤُوفٌ or رَؤُوف
مَأْثِرٌ (§ 131).

D   REM. *a.* أ preceded by kèsra becomes ئ; as هَانِئٌ for هَانِئٌ.

REM. *b.* Final hèmza, preceded by $\bar{i}$ and $\bar{u}$, admits of assimilation; as رَدَى؟ or رَدِيٌّ ,رَدِيٌّ؟ or دُرِّيٌّ ,دُرِّيٌّ؟ or مَقْرُوء ,مَقْرُوٌّ.   See § 17, *b*,
rem. *b.*

239.   In the formation of verbal adjectives from verba primæ
rad. ى, the rule laid down in § 147 must be observed; as مُوسِرٌ for
مَيْسِر.

240. In the nomina agentis of the first form of verba mediæ A rad. و et ى, the place of the middle radical is occupied by a ى with hèmza (arising, according to § 133, out of أ); as قَائِلٌ (for قَاوِلٌ), سَائِرٌ (for سَاوِرٌ), instead of قَاوِلٌ, سَايِرٌ.

REM. *a.* This rule does not apply to the verbs mentioned in § 160, which retain their middle radical unchanged; as صَايِدٌ, عَاوِرٌ.

REM. *b.* The form قَائِمٌ admits in certain words of being con- tracted into قَامٌ (compare the Heb. קָם for קָוֶם), as شَاكٌ for شَائِكٌ, B in the phrase شَاكُ ٱلسِّلَاحِ or شَائِكُ ٱلسِّلَاحِ, *bristling with weapons;* مَاهٌ for مَائِهٌ, in the phrase مَاهُ ٱلْفُؤَادِ or مَائِهُ ٱلْفُؤَادِ, *water-hearted, cowardly, stupid;* هَارٌ *feeble,* for هَائِرٌ; هَاعٌ لَاعٌ *timid or greedy,* for هَائِعٌ لَائِعٌ; شَاهٌ *sharp (of sight),* for شَائِهٌ; سَاسٌ *corroded or decayed* (of a tooth), for سَائِسٌ; طَاعٌ *obedient,* for طَائِعٌ; طَافٌ *going about,* for طَائِفٌ; طَانٌ *clayey,* for طَائِنٌ*. Sometimes the second radical C is transposed; as شَاطِ, جَالِ, لَاعِ, هَارِ, مَاهِى ٱلْفُؤَادِ, شَاكِى ٱلسِّلَاحِ, لَاثِ, شَاهِ.

REM. *c.* In the form فَعُولٌ the medial و is usually changed into ؤ; as نَوُومٌ, صَوُولٌ, قَوُولٌ, for نَوُومٌ, صَوُولٌ, قَوُولٌ.

241. In the nomina patientis of the first form of verba mediæ rad. و, the middle radical is elided, after throwing back its ḍamma D upon the preceding vowelless letter; as مَخُوفٌ, for مَخْووفٌ, from مَخْووفٌ. The same thing takes place in verba mediæ rad. ى, with this difference, that (to indicate the elision of the radical ى) the ḍamma is changed into kèsra, and, in consequence, the و productionis into a ى; as مَبِيعٌ, instead of مَبُوعٌ, from مَبْيوعٌ.

---

* [A poet even allows himself to say سَارُهَا for سَائِرُهَا (from سَيَرَ); see Abū Zèid, *Nawādir*, 26 infra. D. G.]

A   REM. The forms مَصْوُونٌ ,مَدْوُوفٌ, and مَقْوُودٌ, are said to be used dialectically. From verba med. ي the uncontracted forms are more common, but still rare; as مَخْيُوطٌ ,مَدْيُونٌ ,مَزْيُوتٌ, مَبْيُوعٌ for مَخِيطٌ ,مَبِيعٌ, مَغْيُومٌ ,مَكْيُولٌ, etc.

242. Verbal adjectives of the form فَعِيلٌ, derived from verba mediæ rad. و et ي, become by transposition فَيْعِلٌ, and then pass into فَيِّلٌ, which is in its turn frequently shortened into فَيْلٌ. E.g. مَيِّتٌ

B   or مَيْتٌ, *dead,* for مَيْوِتٌ مَيِّتٌ (مَاتَ); [عَيِّلٌ *dependent for sustenance,* for عَيْوِلٌ (عَال)]; لَيِّنٌ لَيِيْنٌ, *soft, easy,* for لَيْنٌ or لَيِّنٌ; (لَانَ); هَيِّنٌ or هَيْنٌ, *easy, contemptible* (هَوِينٌ); نَيِّفٌ or نَيْفٌ, *exceeding* (نَوِيفٌ); نَيِّرٌ, *bright* (نَوِيرٌ); سَيِّئٌ, *wicked* (سَوِى؟); بَيِّنٌ, *clear* (بَيِينٌ); خَيِّرٌ, *good* (خَيِيرٌ). The verb قَامَ has قَوِيمٌ in the sense of *straight, right, tall,*

C   and قَيِّمٌ in that of *having charge of, managing.*

243. Verbal adjectives from the derived forms of verba mediæ rad. و et ي follow the same rules as their Imperfects.

REM. The learner should observe that the participles of III. and VI. of verba med. ي are written and pronounced with ي, and on no account with hèmza; e.g. مُتَبَايِنٌ ,يُبَايِنٌ ,يَتَبَايَنُ, like مُبَايِنٌ, and not مُبَائِنٌ ,مُتَبَائِنٌ.

D   244. The nomina agentis et patientis of the first form of verba ultimæ rad. و et ي have already been mentioned (§ 167, b, β, and § 170). Verbal adjectives of the forms فَعُولٌ and فَعِيلٌ are treated according to the same rules as the nomina patientis (§ 170); e.g. عَدُوٌّ *hostile, an enemy,* بَغِىٌّ *a harlot,* سَرِىٌّ *generous, noble,* صَبِىٌّ *a boy,* سَبِىٌّ *captive,* for عَدُووٌ ,بَغُوىٌ ,سَرِيوٌ ,صَبِيوٌ, سَبِيىٌ.

245. In all adjectives derived from verba tertiæ rad. و et ي,

if the second radical be pronounced with fètḥa, the ى and و (which A
is converted into ى) reject their vowel or tènwīn, and assume the
nature of the èlif maksūra (§ 7, rem. *b*).   If the form be one that
admits of complete declension, the tènwīn is transferred to the second
radical.   According to this rule are formed : (*a*) the nomina patientis
of the derived forms, as مُعْطًى for مُعْطَى ، مُوَلًّى for مُوَلَّى ، (مُعْطُوْ);
(*b*) adjectives of the form أَقْعَلُ ، as أَرْمًى for أَرْمَى ، أَبْكًى for أَبْكَى ،
أَرْضًى for (أَرْضُوْ) ، أَحْلًى for أَحْلَى ، (أَحْلَوْ).   Compare § 167, *a*,
β, a, and *b*, *β*.

b. THE DENOMINATIVE NOUNS.   B

(*a*) *The Nomina Unitatis or Nouns that denote the Individual.*

246. The أَسْمَاءُ ٱلْوَحْدَةِ ، or nouns of individuality, designate one
individual out of a genus, or one part of a whole that consists of
several similar parts.   They are formed, like the analogous nomina
vicis (§ 219), by adding the termination ـَة to the nouns that express
the genus or whole.   E. g. حَمَامَةٌ *a pigeon* (*male* or *female*), from
حَمَامٌ *pigeons*, with the article, ٱلْحَمَامُ *, the genus pigeon* or *the whole* C
number of pigeons spoken of ; بَطَّةٌ *a duck* or *drake,* from بَطٌّ *the duck ;*
بَقَرَةٌ *one head of cattle* (*bull* or *cow*), from بَقَرٌ *cattle ;* ثَمَرَةٌ *a fruit,* from
ثَمَرٌ *fruit ;* تَمْرَةٌ *a date,* from تَمْرٌ *dates ;* بَصَلَةٌ *an onion,* from بَصَلٌ *the*
onion ; ذَهَبَةٌ *a bit of gold, a nugget,* from ذَهَبٌ *gold ;* تِبْنَةٌ *a straw,*
from تِبْنٌ *straw*.*

REM. *a.* The use of the nom. unit. is almost entirely restricted,
as the above examples show, to created things or natural objects. D

---

* [A peculiar application of the اسْمُ ٱلْوَحْدَةِ is its use for *a dish* or
portion of any food, as أُرْزَةٌ *a dish of rice,* سَمَكَةٌ *a dish of fish* (èl-
Mubarrad 173, l. 4), لَحْمَةٌ *a portion of meat,* جُبْنَةٌ *a portion of cheese,*
etc.   Comp. Gloss. Fragm. Add. 129.   This ة is called اَلتَّاءُ لِلتَّخْصِيصِ
(Zamaḫšarī, *Fāïḳ,* i. 331, 417, ii. 323.   D. G.]

A Examples of artificial or manufactured objects are very rare; e.g.

لَبِنَة or لِبْنَة *a brick*, from لَبِنٌ or لِبْنٌ *bricks;* سَفِينَة *a ship* or *boat*,

from سَفِينٌ *shipping, boats.*

REM. *b.* Similar forms in Heb. are: שְׂעָרָה, שֵׂעָר ;נִצָּה, נֵץ;

שִׁירָה, שִׁיר ;אֳנִיָּה, אֳנִי; שׁוֹשַׁנָּה, שׁוֹשָׁן.

(β) The Nomina Abundantiæ vel Multitudinis.

B **247.** The أَسْمَاءُ ٱلْكَثْرَةِ, or nouns of abundance, designate the place where the object signified by the noun from which they are formed, is found in large numbers or quantities. They have the form مَفْعَلَة, and are, consequently, a mere variety of the nouns of place (§ 221). E.g. مَسْبَعَة, مَذْأَبَة, مَأْسَدَة, *a place abounding in lions* (أَسَد), wolves (ذِئْب), beasts of prey (سَبُع); مَفْعَاة or مَحْوَاة, مَحْيَاة, *a place abounding in snakes* (حَيَّة), vipers (أَفْعَى); مَقْثَأَة, مَبْطَخَة, *a bed of melons* (بِطِّيخ), cucumbers (قِثَّاء); مَرْمَنَة, *a place where pomegranates*

C (رُمَّان) *grow abundantly.*

REM. *a.* From quadriliterals this formation is rare; as مَثْعَلَة, مَعْقَرَة, *a place abounding in foxes* (ثَعْلَب, שׁוּעָל), scorpions (عَقْرَب).

REM. *b.* Sometimes the fem. participle of the fourth form is used in this sense, with or without أَرْض; as مُضَبَّة, مُجْعَلَة, *(a place) abounding in lizards* (ضَبّ), black beetles (جُعَل), مُقْثَأَة *(a spot)*

D *producing cucumbers.* Similarly from quadriliterals, مُثْعَلِبَة, مُعْقَرِبَة, مُحَرْبِئَة, مُوَرْنِبَة *(a place)* abounding in foxes, scorpions, chamæleons (حَوْرَبَاء), hares. Also from XII. مُغْلَوْلِبَة *(a spot)* producing many trees.

REM. *c.* The use of nouns of the form مَفْعَلَة to indicate the cause of a certain state or feeling, is only a tropical application of their ordinary meaning; as ٱلْوَلَدُ مَجْبَنَةٌ مَبْخَلَةٌ *children are a cause of cowardice and niggardliness* (in their parents); مَطْيَبَةٌ، مَحْسَنَةٌ، A مَجْبَنَةٌ, *a cause of good health, joy or happiness, evil or ill-feeling;* مَجْلَبَةٌ لِلسَّقَامِ *a cause of bringing on or producing disease;* ٱلْفَكَاهَةُ مَقْوَدَةٌ إِلَى ٱلْأَذَى *joking leads to annoyance;* and the like.

(γ) *The Nomina Vasis or Nouns denoting the Vessel which contains anything.*

248. The nomina vasis, أَسْمَاءُ ٱلْوِعَاءِ, have the same form as the nomina instrumenti (§ 228); e.g. مِثْبَرٌ *a needle-case,* from إِبْرَةٌ *a needle;* B مِحْلَبٌ *a milk-pail,* from حَلَبٌ or حَلِيبٌ *milk;* مِلْبَنٌ *a milk-pail,* from لَبَنٌ *milk,* or *a brick-mould,* from لِبْنَةٌ *a brick;* مِبْوَلَةٌ *a urinal,* from بَوْلٌ *urine;* مِبْزَقَةٌ *a spittoon,* from بُزَاقٌ *saliva.*

REM. A very few take the form مُفْعُلٌ or مُفْعُلَةٌ (see § 228, rem.); as مُدْهُنٌ or مُدْهُنَةٌ *an oil-jar,* from دُهْنٌ *oil;* مُحْرَضَةٌ = *a vessel for keeping* حُرْضٌ, i.e. the plants from which alkali or potash is obtained; مُكْحُلَةٌ *a phial for keeping kohl or eye-salve* C (كُحْلٌ), to be carefully distinguished from مِكْحَلٌ, *the mīl* (مِيلٌ) or *instrument with which it is applied to the eye.*

(δ) *The Nomina Relativa or Relative Adjectives.*

249. The relative adjectives, ٱلْأَسْمَاءُ ٱلْمَنْسُوبَةُ, or simply ٱلنِّسَبَاتُ (*relationes*), are formed by adding the termination ـِيٌّ to the words D from which they are derived, and denote that a person or thing belongs to or is connected therewith (in respect of origin, family, birth, sect, trade, etc.). E.g. أَرْضِيٌّ *earthly,* from أَرْضٌ *the earth;* شَمْسِيٌّ *solar,* from شَمْسٌ *the sun;* جَوِّيٌّ *aërial,* from جَوٌّ *the air, the sky;* حَسَنِيٌّ *descended from el-Ḥasan* (ٱلْحَسَنُ); تَمِيمِيٌّ *belonging to the tribe of Temīm* (تَمِيمٌ); دِمَشْقِيٌّ *born or living at Damascus* (دِمَشْقُ);

A مِصْرِيٌّ *Egyptian*, from مِصْرُ *Egypt*; سَعْدِيٌّ *a freedman of Sa'd* (سَعْدُ);
عِلْمِيٌّ *scientific*, from عِلْمُ *knowledge, science*; حِسِّيٌّ *relating to sense*
(حِسٌّ), *perceptible by one of the senses*; عَقْلِيٌّ *intellectual*, from عَقْلُ
the intellect; شَرْعِيٌّ *legal, legitimate*, from شَرْعُ *the law*; عُرْفِيٌّ *according*
to common use and wont (عُرْفُ); قِيَاسِيٌّ *according to analogy* (قِيَاسُ);
مَجُوسِيٌّ *belonging to, or one of, the Maǧūs or fire-worshippers*
B (اَلْمَجُوسُ); مَالِكِيٌّ *belonging to, or one of, the sect of Mālik* (مَالِكٌ);
طَوِيلِيٌّ from طَوِيلُ *long*; خَيْرِيٌّ from خَيْرُ *good*; إِنِّيٌّ from إِنَّ *truly*,
verily.

REM. *a.* The nomina relativa are chiefly formed from substantives and adjectives, but in more modern Arabic, and especially in
the language of the schools, also from the other kinds of nouns,
and even from particles (see § 191).

REM. *b.* The nomina relativa derived from adjectives properly
express "belonging to the class designated by such and such an
C adjective." [However, in such words as أَتَاوِيٌّ ,خَارِجِيٌّ ,أَحْمَرِيٌّ,
دَوَّارِيٌّ the termination يّ has, according to some, a corroborative or
intensifying force (لِلْمُبَالَغَةِ). D. G.]

REM. *c.* This termination is common in Heb. (m. ◌ִי, f. ◌ִיָּה
and ◌ִית), as יִשְׂרְאֵלִי *Israelite*, עִבְרִי *Hebrew*, נָכְרִי *strange.* In
Æthiopic, *ī* is generally used to form certain adjectives which are
derived from other adjectives, as ḥarrāsī: (ḥarrāsī) *a ploughman*,
D ooḥZ: (maḥḥārī) *compassionate*, from the obsolete ḥZ·ñ:
(= חֲרָת, חָרֵשׁ) and ooḥZ:; whilst *āwī* and *āy* are the
usual relative terminations, as ooZP: (mĕdrāwī) *terrestrial*,
ḥZñ·PñP: (krĕstīyānāwī) *Christian*, ḥPP: ('aiyāwī) or
ḥPP: ('aiyāy) *like* (from ḥP: 'ay, *of what kind? which?*). The
Aram. has the last of these forms, viz. ◌ַ◌ִי, ◌ָ◌ַ◌, in general use; as
מִצְרָי *Egyptian*, מַדְנְחָי *eastern.*

250. In forming the nomina relativa, the primitive nouns undergo A various changes in regard to the auxiliary consonants, to the final radicals و and ی, and to the vocalisation.

I. *Changes of the Auxiliary Consonants.*

251. The feminine terminations ة_, يَ_, and ـيَة, are rejected;

as مَكَّة *Mekka,* مَكِّيٌّ; ٱلْبَصْرَةُ *el-Basra,* بَصْرِیٌّ; ٱلْكُوفَةُ *el-Kūfa,* كُوفِيٌّ; إِفْرِيقِيَةُ *Africa,* إِفْرِيقِيٌّ; صِقْلِيَةُ *Sicily,* صِقْلِيٌّ; مَلَطْيَةُ *Malatya,* مَلَطِيٌّ; B ٱلسُّنَّة *the corpus of traditions relating to the ways and habits of Muhammad,* سُنِّيٌّ; [ٱلشِّيعَةُ *the party of Alī,* شِيعِيٌّ *;] ٱلْقِبْلَةُ *the kibla* or *direction of Mekka,* to which the Muslim turns in praying, قِبْلِيٌّ; كُوَّةٌ *a window,* كُوِّیٌّ; خَاصِّیٌّ *refined,* عَامِّیٌّ *vulgar,* from ٱلْخَاصَّةُ *distinguished persons, the higher classes,* and ٱلْعَامَّةُ *the common people, the vulgar;* عِدَةٌ *a promise,* عِدِیٌّ; زِنَةٌ *weight, measure,* زِنِیٌّ. C

REM. In the case of nouns which, like عِدَةٌ, have lost their first radical, if the third radical be a weak letter, the first ought to be restored and the second to take fètḥa; as شِيَةٌ (from وَشَى), [وَشَوِیٌّ or] وَشَوِیٌّ (on the second و see §§ 258 and foll.). The forms وَشِیِیٌّ [or وَشِیِیٌّ] are mentioned by the grammarians, and also the very irregular عَدَوِیٌّ from عِدَةٌ, [and شِيَوِیٌّ from شِيَةٌ (Ḥammād in 'Anbārī's *Nozhat ̇el-'alibbā* 52. D. G.]. D

252. 1, (*a*) The feminine termination ـیٰ is rejected in nouns that have *four* or more letters, besides the ی; as حُبَارَی *a bustard,* حُبَارِیٌّ; جُمَادَی *Gumādā,* the name of two months, جُمَادِیٌّ. (*b*) But if the nouns ending in ـیٰ fem. have only *three* letters besides the

---

* [Lane has شِيعِیٌّ; of this form, however, only a single instance has been mentioned in the T. A. D. G.]

A ى, two cases are to be distinguished. (*a*) If the second letter has a vowel, the ى is rejected; as جَمَزَى *a swift ass*, جَمَزَى; بَرَدَى *Baradā*, the name of a river, بَرَدَى. (*β*) If the second letter is without a vowel, the ى may either be rejected (which is preferable), or changed into و; as حُبْلَى *pregnant*, حُبْلِىٌّ or حُبْلَوِىٌّ; قُرْبَى *relationship*, قُرْبِىٌّ or قُرْبَوِىٌّ; اَلدُّنْيَا *the (present) world*, دُنْيِىٌّ or دُنْيَوِىٌّ.—
2, (*a*) The letter ى is likewise rejected in nouns that contain *four* or more letters besides the ى, if it belongs neither to the root nor
B to the feminine termination, but is what the Arab grammarians call أَلِفُ ٱلْإِلْحَاق or *the appended ălif* (i. e. which serves to give to the word to which it is appended the form of a quadriliteral or quinqueliteral word, e.g. ذِفْرَى to give it the form of دِرْهَم, قُوبَآءَ to assimilate it to (قُرْطَاس); as حَبَرْكَى *a bug or tick*, حَبَرْكِىٌّ; قَبَعْثَرَى *a big, stout camel*, قَبَعْثَرِىٌّ; بَاقِلَّى, *the bean*, بَاقِلَّى or بَاقِلِّىٌّ. (*b*) But if such
C nouns have only *three* letters besides the ى, it may either be changed into و (which is preferable), or rejected altogether; as عَلْقَى *a sort of heath*, عَلْقِىٌّ or عَلْقَوِىٌّ; أَرْطَى *a sort of shrub or small tree*, أَرْطَوِىٌّ.

REM. In 1, *b*, *β*, and 2 *b*, a third form is admissible, viz. أَرْطَاوِىٌّ, عَلْقَاوِىٌّ, دُنْيَاوِىٌّ, قُرْبَاوِىٌّ, حُبْلَاوِىٌّ, ـَاوِىٌّ, but دُنْيَائِىٌّ, with hèmza, is a vulgarism.

D **253.** The terminations ـِىٌّ and ـِيَّة of relative adjectives fall away when new relative adjectives are to be formed from them; as جَعْفِىٌّ *belonging to* Mèkkī, Gu'fī (مَكِّىٌّ, جُعْفِىٌّ, names of men); شَافِعِىٌّ *a* Šāfi'*ite, one of the sect of* ĕs-Šāfi'ī (اَلشَّافِعِىٌّ); مَرِىٌّ *belonging to* Almeria (اَلْمَرِيَّة) *in Spain*; إِسْكَنْدَرِىٌّ *a native of Alexandria* (اَلْإِسْكَنْدَرِيَّة). Similarly, from substantives like كُرْسِىٌّ *a chair, a seat*, and بَرْدِىٌّ *a bullrush*, the relative adjectives are كُرْسِىٌّ and بَرْدِىٌّ.

254. The plural terminations ـُونَ and ـَاتٌ, and the dual termination ـَانٍ, are rejected ; as اِثْنَانِ *two,* اِثْنِىٌّ *relating to two, dualistic;* A اَلْحَرَمَانِ *the two ḥarams* (or sacred territories of Mèkka and èl-Medina), اَلْمُسْلِمُونَ ; قَيْسَىٌّ *two men named Ḳais,* قَيْسَانِ ; حَرَمِىٌّ *the Muslims,* هِنْدَاتٌ ; زَيْدِىٌّ *men of the name of Zèid,* زَيْدُونَ ; مُسْلِمِىٌّ *women of the name of Hind,* هِنْدِىٌّ ; عَرَفَاتُ '*Arafāt,* the name of a place, عَرَفِىٌّ.

REM. *a.* It need hardly be remarked that this rule does not apply to proper names ending in ـَانٌ and ـُونٌ, as عِمْرَانُ '*Imrān,* زَيْدُونِىٌّ ; خَلِيلَانِىٌّ ; خَلِيلَانُ *Ḥalīlān,* زَيْدُونُ *Zèidūn,* عِمْرَانِىٌّ. B

REM. *b.* It is only in later times that such forms are possible as عِشْرِينِىٌّ, from عِشْرُونَ *twenty,* instead of عِشْرِىٌّ ; مِئِينِىٌّ, from مِئُونَ, plur. of مِئَةٌ *a hundred,* for مِئَوِىٌّ ; اِثْنَيْنِىٌّ *dualistic,* from اِثْنَانِ *two,* instead of تَنَوِىٌّ or اِثْنِىٌّ.

REM. *c.* Foreign names of towns, ending in ـِينٌ, sometimes change this termination in Arabic into ـُونَ, at other times retain C it. In the former case the termination is rejected, in the latter it is preserved ; as قَنَّسْرُونَ *Ḳinnèsrīn,* قَنَّسْرِىٌّ, but قَنْسْرِينُ ,قَنْسْرِينِىٌّ ; نَصِيبُونَ *Nisībis,* نَصِيبِىٌّ, but نَصِيبِينُ ,نَصِيبِينِىٌّ ; يَبْرُونَ *Yèbrīn,* يَبْرِىٌّ, but يَبْرِينُ ,يَبْرِينِىٌّ.

REM. *d.* Some proper names, chiefly foreign, are very irregular in their formations ; e.g. اَلْبَحْرَيْنِ ,بَحْرَانِىٌّ ; دَارِيًّا ,دَارَانِىٌّ ; اَلْحِيرَةُ D ; حَارِىٌّ ,بَغْشُورُ ,بَغَوِىٌّ ,اَلرَّىُّ ,رَازِىٌّ إِصْطَخْرُ, إِصْطَخْرَزِىٌّ ; (اَلشَّاهِجَانُ) مَرْوُ ,مَرْوَزِىٌّ ,اَلْقَيْرَوَانُ ,قَرَوِىٌّ ,سِجِسْتَانُ ,سِجْزِىٌّ ; لَرِسْتَانُ ,لُرِّىٌّ ,طَبَرِسْتَانُ ,طَبَرِيَّةُ ; طَبَرِىٌّ *Tiberias,* طَبَرَانِىٌّ ,أَذَرِبَيْجَانُ, أَذَرِىٌّ or أَذَرِبِىٌّ. We may, however, use حِيرِىٌّ ,إِصْطَخْرِىٌّ ,مَرَوِىٌّ, قَيْرَوَانِىٌّ, سِجِسْتَانِىٌّ.—حَرَّانُ makes either حَرَّانِىٌّ or حَرْنَانِىٌّ :

A   دَرَاوَرْدِىُّ or دَرَابَجِرْدُ دَرَابَجِرْدُ has دَرَاوَرْدِىُّ, as well as the regular formation;

مَانِى *Manes* makes مَنَانِىُّ ,مَنَوِىُّ and مَانِىُّ. D. G.]

REM. *e.*   Quite peculiar are: تِهَامِ (with the art. اَلتِّهَامِى), fem. تِهَامِيَة, from تِهَامَة, *Tihāma*; شَامِ (with the art. اَلشَّامِى), fem. شَامِيَة, from اَلشَّامُ *Syria*; and يَمَانٍ (with the art. اَلْيَمَانِى), fem. يَمَانِيَة, from اَلْيَمَنُ *el-Yemèn*; instead of تِهَامِىُّ ,شَامِىُّ, and يَمَنِىُّ, which

B   are also used. The forms تِهَامِىُّ ,شَامِىُّ, and يَمَانِىُّ likewise occur. Comp. the words ثَمَانٍ, رَبَاعٍ and شَنَاحٍ (= شَنَاحِىُّ).

255. The letter ى in words of the forms فَعِيلَة and فُعَيْلَة, when not derived from verba mediæ rad. geminatæ or infirmæ (و or ى), is rejected, the kèsra of فَعِيلَة being at the same time changed into fètḥa*;

C   as فَرِيضَة *a statute*, فَرَضِىُّ; جَزِيرَة *an island*, or اَلْجَزِيرَة *Mesopotamia*, جَزَرِىُّ; اَلْمَدِينَة *el-Medina*, مَدَنِىُّ; سَفِينَة *a ship*, سَفَنِىُّ; جُهَيْنَة ,ضُبَيْعَة (tribes), جُهَنِىُّ ,ضُبَعِىُّ. But, if they come from verba mediæ rad. geminatæ or mediæ و vel ى, they remain unchanged; as حَقِيقَة *reality*, حَقِيقِىُّ; حَدِيدَة *a piece of iron, an iron tool*, حَدِيدِىُّ; قُلَيْلَة *a small jug*, قُلَيْلِىُّ.—In the forms فَعِيل and فُعَيْل, the ى is rejected only when

D   the third consonant of the radical is و or ى; as عَدِىُّ ,غَنِىُّ (tribes), غَنَوِىُّ ,عَلِىُّ ,قُصَىُّ (men), عَدَوِىُّ ,غَنَوِىُّ ,عَلَوِىُّ ,قُصَوِىُّ. Otherwise it remains unchanged, as تَمِيم (a tribe), تَمِيمِىُّ; عَقِيل (a man), عَقِيلِىُّ; زَبِيد (a town), زَبِيدِىُّ; نُمَيْر ,عُقَيْل (tribes), عُقَيْلِىُّ ,نُمَيْرِىُّ.

---

* [According to Zamaḫšarī, *Fāik* i. 160 the same thing happens to the و of the form فَعُولَة, as in شَنَئِىُّ (شَنَاىٌ) from شَنُوءَة, غَضَبِىُّ from غَضُوبَة. Comp. also *Mufaṣṣal* 90, 1. 7 and Sībawèih ii. 66, § 319. D. G.]

REM. *a.* There are, however, exceptions to these rules. E.g. A
طَبِيعَةٌ nature, طَبِيعِىٌّ ; مَدِينَةٌ *a city,* مَدِينِىٌّ (to distinguish it from
مَدَنِىٌّ belonging to *el-Medina*), جَزِيرِىٌّ belonging to *Algeziras* in
Spain (to distinguish it from جَزَرِىٌّ *Mesopotamian*); سَلِيمِىٌّ, عَمِيرِىٌّ,
from قُرَيْشٌ, سَلِيمَةٌ عَمِيرَةٌ (tribes); خُرَيْبِىٌّ from خُرَيْبَةٌ (a place);
ثَقِيفٌ, عَتِيكٌ ; فُقَمِىٌّ, سُلَمِىٌّ, هُذَلِىٌّ, قُرَشِىٌّ (tribes), فُقَيْمٌ, سُلَيْمٌ, هُذَيْلٌ
(tribes), ثَقَفِىٌّ, عَتَكِىٌّ ; خَرِيفٌ *autumn,* خَرَفِىٌّ.—نَبِىٌّ, *a prophet,* B
makes نَبَوِىٌّ, from the assimilated form نَبِىٌّ.

REM. *b.* Words of the form فَعْلٌ (for فَعِيلٌ, § 242) from radicals
mediæ و et ى, reject the second ى along with its vowel kèsra, or in
other words follow the shorter form فَعْلٌ ; as سَيّدٌ *a lord or master,*
سَيْدِىٌّ ; طَيّبٌ *good,* طَيْبِىٌّ. But طَيّءٌ (a tribe) has طَائِىٌّ.—The
same remark applies to every penultimate double ى with kèsra
(يّ); as أَسْوَدُ, dimin. of أَسْوَدُ, *black,* أَسَيْدِىٌّ ; حُمَيّرٌ, dimin. of حِمَارٌ, C
an ass, حُمَيْرِىٌّ. [But أُسَيّدٌ as a tribal name has أُسَيّدِىٌّ.]

256. The ى productionis of the nomen patientis in verba tertiæ
ى may be rejected, and the radical ى changed into و, whilst the kèsra
of the second radical becomes fèṭḥa; as مَرْمِىٌّ *thrown,* مَرْمَوِىٌّ. But
many grammarians prefer to reject both the ى productionis and the
radical ى, so that the relative adjective coincides in form with the
nomen patientis, مَرْمِىٌّ. D

257. Lastly, the و productionis in the form فَعُولَةٌ, derived from
verba tertiæ و (§ 244), is rejected, and the second radical takes fèṭḥa
instead of ḍamma; as عَدُوَّةٌ, *a female enemy,* عَدَوِىٌّ. Many, however,
form عَدُوِّىٌّ from both عَدُوٌّ and عَدُوَّةٌ.

A II. *Changes of the Final Radicals و and ى.*

258. The *ʾalif maksūra* (ا or ى, § 7, rem. *b*), as the third radical of a *triliteral* noun, is changed into و before adding the termination ـِيٌّ; as فَتًى *a youth*, فَتَوِيٌّ; رَحًى *a mill*, رَحَوِيٌّ; عَصًا *a staff*, عَصَوِيٌّ; قَذًى *a mote*, قَذَوِيٌّ. But if the noun has *four* letters, the final ى (ا does not occur in such words in good Arabic) may either be changed

B into و, which is the better form, or be rejected; as أَعْشَى *purblind*, أَعْشَوِيٌّ; مَلْهًى *play*, or مَلْهًى *a musical instrument*, مَلْهَوِيٌّ or مَلْهِيٌّ; مَعْنًى *meaning*, مَعْنَوِيٌّ or مَعْنِيٌّ. If the noun contains *five* or more letters, the ى is always rejected; as مُصْطَفًى *chosen*, مُصْطَفِيٌّ.—The same rules apply to the final ى of radicals tertiæ و et ى, which falls away in some nouns after kèsra (see § 167, *b*, β); but it must be borne in mind that the missing ى is to be counted as one of the letters

C of the word, and also, if it be changed into و, that the kèsra always becomes fètha. E.g. عَمٍ (for عَمِيٌ) *blind*, عَمَوِيٌّ; شَجٍ (for شَجِيٌ) *sorrowful*, شَجَوِيٌّ; قَاضٍ (for قَاضِيٌ) *a judge*, قَاضَوِيٌّ (which is the preferable form) or قَاضَوِيٌّ; مُعْتَدٍ (for مُعْتَدِيٌ), مُشْتَرٍ (for مُشْتَرِيٌ), مُسْتَعْلٍ (for مُسْتَعْلِيٌّ, مُشْتَرِيٌّ, مُعْتَدِيٌّ).

D REM. *a.* The addition of the feminine termination ةٌ does not affect the rule of formation; as دَوَاةٌ *an inkhorn* or *writing-case*, دَوَوِيٌّ *one who carries an inkhorn*; حَمَاةٌ *Ḥamā* (חֲמָת), حَمَوِيٌّ; اَلشَّرَاةُ, a district in Palestine, شَرَوِيٌّ; مِرْقَاةٌ *a ladder*, مِرْقَوِيٌّ; حَانَاةٌ or حَانِيَةٌ *a wine-shop*, حَانَوِيٌّ or حَانِيٌّ *a vintner*.

REM. *b.* Such forms as دَوَاتِيٌّ for دَوَوِيٌّ, مَعْنَاوِيٌّ for مَعْنَوِيٌّ, and مُصْطَفَوِيٌّ for مُصْطَفِيٌّ, are modern and corrupt.

259. The hèmza of the termination اَاءٌ (the *álif mèmdūda*, § 23, A rem. *a*), is always changed into و; as عَذْرَاءُ *a virgin*, عَذْرَاوِیٌّ; اَلْبَیْضَاءُ (a town in Persia), بَیْضَاوِیٌّ; خُنْفَسَاءُ *the black beetle*, خُنْفَسَاوِیٌّ; زَكَرِیَّاءُ *Zachariah*, زَكَرِیَّاوِیٌّ. But in the termination آءٌ, whether the hèmza be sprung from an original radical و or ی, or be not a radical but merely the so-called هَمْزَةُ الْاِلْحَاقِ (see § 252, 2, *a*), it may either be retained unaltered (which is better) or be changed into و; as تَاءٌ the letter B *ta*, رِدَاءٌ *a garment*, كِسَاءٌ *a robe*, سَمَاءٌ *the heaven*, تَائِیٌّ, رِدَائِیٌّ, كِسَائِیٌّ, سَمَائِیٌّ, or سَمَاوِیٌّ, كِسَاوِیٌّ, رِدَاوِیٌّ, تَاوِیٌّ; عِلْبَاءٌ *a large sinew in the neck*, حِرْبَاءٌ *a male chameleon*, بَاقِلَّاءٌ *the bean*, عِلْبَائِیٌّ, حِرْبَائِیٌّ, بَاقِلَّائِیٌّ, or عِلْبَاوِیٌّ, حِرْبَاوِیٌّ, بَاقِلَّاوِیٌّ. On the contrary, if the hèmza be an original ا, it always remains unaltered; as قَرَّاءٌ (rad. قَرَأَ), قَرَّائِیٌّ.

REM. The termination اَاءٌ is very rarely dropped in proper C names; as جَلُولَاءُ, حَرُورَاءُ (places), حَرُورِیٌّ, جَلُولِیٌّ.—In a few cases too the letter ن is substituted for the hèmza; as رَوْحَاءُ (a place), رَوْحَانِیٌّ; بَهْرَاءُ (a tribe), بَهْرَانِیٌّ; صَنْعَاءُ (a city in ĕl-Yèmèn), صَنْعَانِیٌّ; with which compare the Hebrew forms שִׁילֹנִי, גִּילֹנִי, from שִׁילֹה, גִּילֹה.

260. Primitive defective substantives, i.e. those which have lost D their third weak radical,—as أَبٌ, أَخٌ, حَمٌ, لُغَةٌ, لِثَةٌ, etc.,—necessarily recover it only in cases where it reappears in the dual and plural; but if this reappearance be not necessary, the third radical may be omitted in the relative adjective. In all cases where the third radical is restored, it appears as و, whether it was originally ی or not. E.g. أَبٌ (for أَبَوٌ, dual أَبَوَانِ) *a father*, أَبَوِیٌّ; أَخٌ (for أَخَوٌ, du. أَخَوَانِ) *a brother*, أَخَوِیٌّ; حَمٌ (for حَمَوٌ) *a husband's father or brother*, حَمَوِیٌّ;

A لُغَةٌ (rad. لغو) *a dialect,* لُغَوِىٌّ ; لِثَةٌ (rad. لثى) *the gum,* لِثَوِىٌّ ; مِئَةٌ (rad. مأى) *a hundred,* مِئَوِىٌّ ; أَمَةٌ (rad. امو) *a female slave,* أَمَوِىٌّ ; سَنَةٌ (rad. سنو) *a year,* سَنَوِىٌّ ; ابْنٌ (for بَنَىٌ, du. ابْنَانِ) *a son,* ابْنِىٌّ or بَنَوِىٌّ ; اسْمٌ (rad. سمو) *a name,* اسْمِىٌّ or سُمَوِىٌّ (from سُمٌ); أَنْتَ (rad. سته) *podex,* or اسْتِىٌّ or سَتَهِىٌّ (from سَتَهٌ) or سَهِىٌّ (from سَهٌ); يَدٌ (for يَدْىٌ, du. يَدَانِ) *a hand,* يَدِىٌّ or يَدَوِىٌّ ; دَمٌ *blood,* دَمِىٌّ or دَمَوِىٌّ ; غَدٌ *to-*

B *morrow,* غَدِىٌّ or غَدَوِىٌّ.

REM. *a.* أُخْتٌ, *a sister,* and بِنْتٌ, *a daughter,* make أُخْتِىٌّ and بِنْتِىٌّ, as well as أَخَوِىٌّ and بَنَوِىٌّ. — شَفَةٌ, *a lip,* has the three forms شَفَوِىٌّ, شَفَهِىٌّ, or شَفِىٌّ ; حِرٌ, *vulva,* makes حِرِىٌّ or حِرَحِىٌّ (from حِرْحٌ).— شَاةٌ (شَاءٌ) has شَاوِىٌّ, شَاهِىٌّ and شَائِىٌّ.

REM. *b.* Where the original form was فَعْلٌ, some retain the C *gezm*; as حِرْحِى, سُمْوِى, غَدْوِى, دَمْوِى, يَدْيِى.

261. The third radical و or ى of the forms فُعْلٌ and فُعْلَةٌ is retained unchanged; as نَحْوٌ *grammar,* نَحْوِىٌّ *a grammarian*; ظَبْىٌ *a gazelle,* ظَبْيِىٌّ ; غَزْوَةٌ *a foray,* غَزْوِىٌّ ; رِشْوَةٌ *a bribe,* رِشْوِىٌّ ; عُرْوَةٌ *a handle,* عُرْوِىٌّ ; قَرْيَةٌ *a village,* قَرْيِىٌّ ; دُمْيَةٌ *an image,* دُمْيِىٌّ. But

D if the final ى of فُعْلَةٌ be changed into و, the second radical takes fetḥa, as قَرَوِىٌّ, دُمَوِىٌّ, قَنَوِىٌّ, from دُمْيَةٌ, قَرْيَةٌ, and قِنْيَةٌ *a possession*; a rule which is extended by some to words in which the third radical was originally و, as غَزَوِىٌّ, رِشَوِىٌّ, عُرَوِىٌّ, from غَزْوَةٌ, etc.—If the second radical in such nouns be a و or ى, combining with the third radical into ىّ, this ىّ is resolved into its original consonants, the second radical takes fetḥa, and final ى is converted into و; as طَىٌّ (for طَوْىٌ) *a fold,* طَوَوِىٌّ ; حَىٌّ (for حَيْىٌ) *living,* حَيَوِىٌّ ; لَيَّةٌ *a twist* or *turn,* لَوَوِيٌّ ; حَيَّةٌ *a snake,* حَيَوِيٌّ.—In words of the form A فَعَالَةٌ, final و is retained, as شَقَاوَةٌ *misery,* شَقَاوِيٌّ ; but final ى is changed into hèmza, as سِقَايَةٌ *a drinking-ressel,* سِقَائِيٌّ, عَظَايَةٌ *a sort of lizard,* عَظَائِيٌّ.—Words of the form آيَةٌ *a sign,* ثَايَةٌ *a place where cattle, etc., rest at night,* رَايَةٌ *a banner,* make آئِيٌّ, آيِيٌّ, or آوِيٌّ, etc.

REM. *a.* بَدْوٌ, *a desert,* makes irregularly بَدَوِيٌّ (instead of B بَدْوِيٌّ) *an inhabitant of the desert, a Bèdawî.*

REM. *b.* Nouns of the forms فُعَيْلَةٌ, فَعِيلٌ, فُعَيْلٌ, فَعِيلَةٌ, etc. from verba tertiæ rad. و et ى, reject the ى productionis and change a radical ى into و; as غَنِيٌّ : غَنَوِيٌّ ; ضَرِيَّةٌ *(a town),* ضَرَوِيٌّ ; قُصَيٌّ, قُصَوِيٌّ ; أُمَيَّةٌ *(a man's name),* أُمَوِيٌّ *(rarely* أُمَيِّيٌّ, and, though very incorrectly, أُمَوِيٌّ).* See §§ 255–6.

III. *Changes in the Vocalisation.*

262. In the forms فَعِلٌ and فَعِلَةٌ, the kèsra of the middle radical is changed into fètḥa ; as مَلِكٌ *a king,* مَلَكِيٌّ ; كَبِدٌ *the liver,* كَبَدِيٌّ ; شَقِرَةٌ *(a tribe),* شَقَرِيٌّ ; نَمِرٌ, صَدِفٌ *(tribes),* نَمَرِيٌّ, صَدَفِيٌّ. So also in فُعِلٌ, as اَلدُّئِلُ *(a tribe),* دُوَلِيٌّ. But in فِعِلٌ, the kèsra may be retained, as إِبِلٌ *camels,* إِبِلِيٌّ or إِبَلِيٌّ.

REM. In nouns that consist of more than three consonants, the vowel of the penultimate letter is not altered. From تَغْلِبُ *(a tribe)* and يَثْرِبُ *(the ancient name of èl-Medîna)* the forms تَغْلِبِيٌّ and يَثْرِبِيٌّ are admissible, though تَغْلِبِيٌّ and يَثْرِبِيٌّ are preferred ; أَنْبَجَانِيٌّ, مَنْبِجٌ makes مَنْبَجَانِيٌّ and أَذْرِعَىٌّ, as well as مَنْبِجِيٌّ ; أَذْرِعَاتٌ.

A   **263.** Kèsra or ḍamma of the penultimate consonant is changed into fètḥa in all forms in which a و or ى has been rejected, or in which a final ى has been changed into و; as غَنِىٌّ; جَزَرِىٌّ, اَلْجَزِيرَةُ, غَنَوِىٌّ (see the preceding §§).

Rem. Of rare and arbitrary changes, such as بَصْرِىٌّ from اَلْبَصْرَةُ, حَرَمِىٌّ from اَلْحَرَمُ *the sacred territory of Mèkka,* دَهْرِىٌّ from

B دَهْرٌ *time,* إِمْسِىٌّ from أَمْسِ *yesterday,* a grammar can take no account.

  264. If a relative adjective is to be formed from a proper name which is compounded of *two words,* the following points must be attended to.—A. If the two words form a proposition (مُرَكَّبٌ إِسْنَادِىٌّ or تَرْكِيبٌ إِسْنَادِىٌّ), as تَأَبَّطَ شَرًّا (*he carried mischief under his arm,* the nickname of a celebrated poet and warrior), بَرَقَ نَحْرُهُ (*his throat*

C *shone*)*—or are contracted into one compound word (مُرَكَّبٌ مَزْجِىٌّ, *mixed compound*) as مَعْدِيكَرِبُ, a man's name, بَعْلَبَكُّ, قَالِيقَلَا, the towns of *Ba'albèk* and *Ḳālīḳalā,*—then the second word is omitted, and the termination ـِىٌّ appended to the first; as تَأَبَّطِىٌّ, بَرَقِىٌّ, مَعْدِىٌّ, بَعْلِىٌّ, قَالِىٌّ.—B. If the first word is in the status constructus, governing the second in the genitive, two cases arise. (1) If the governing word be

D one of the nouns أَبٌ *father,* اِبْنٌ *son,* أُمٌّ *mother,* or بِنْتٌ *daughter,* it is rejected, and ـِىٌّ appended to the governed word; as بَكْرِىٌّ, أَبُو بَكْرٍ; اِبْنُ الزُّبَيْرِ, أَزْرَقِىٌّ; اِبْنُ الْأَزْرَقِ, بَيْهَسِىٌّ; أَبُو بَيْهَسَ, حَنَفِىٌّ; أَبُو حَنِيفَةَ, زُبَيْرِىٌّ. (2) If the first word be any other than these four, two secondary cases arise. (*a*) If the idea of definiteness through the status constructus still exists in the consciousness of the speaker,—as

---

  * Compare the nickname of one of the Earls of Douglas, *Archibald Bell-the-cat.*

in غُلَامُ حُسَيْنٍ, *the slave of Hosein,*—the first word is rejected, and A
the second takes ـِيٌّ; as حُسَيْنِيٌّ. (*b*) But if the idea of definiteness
is no longer present to the mind of the speaker, then: (*a*) in cases
where no uncertainty can arise as to the person intended, ـِيٌّ is
attached to the first word, and the second is omitted; as فَخْرُ ٱلدِّينِ,
عُبَيْدِيٌّ, عُبَيْدُ ٱللّٰهِ ; نِظَامِيٌّ, نِظَامُ ٱلْمُلْكِ ; تَقَوِيٌّ, تَقِيُّ ٱلدِّينِ ; فَخْرِيٌّ ;
تَيْمِيٌّ, تَيْمُ ٱللَّاتِ ; أَنْفِيٌّ (*Camel's-nose,* nickname of a man), أَنْفُ ٱلنَّاقَةِ ; B
عَبْدِيٌّ, عَبْدُ ٱلْقَيْسِ ; مَرْئِيٌّ or مَرْؤِيٌّ, ٱمْرُؤُ ٱلْقَيْسِ ; سَعْدِيٌّ, سَعْدُ ٱلْعَشِيرَةِ ;
[وَادِيٌّ, وَادِي ٱلْقُرَى] ; but (*β*) if uncertainty might arise by so doing,
the first is omitted, and the termination added to the second; as
وَادِي ; مَنَافِيٌّ, عَبْدُ مَنَافٍ ; أَشْهَلِيٌّ, عَبْدُ ٱلْأَشْهَلِ ; مُطَّلِبِيٌّ, عَبْدُ ٱلْمُطَّلِبِ
ٱلْحِجَارَةِ, *Guadalaxara* in Spain, حِجَارِيٌّ. أَزْدُ شَنُوءَةَ (a tribe) makes
شَنَوِيٌّ or شَنَائِيٌّ (from the assimilated form شَنُوَّةَ).

Rem. *a.* In the case of the مُرَكَّبَاتٌ مَزْجِيَّةٌ, some allow a C
double formation, from both parts of the word; e.g. from رَامَهُرْمُزُ,
رَامِيٌّ هُرْمُزِيٌّ. In later times it became very common to form the
nisba from the whole compound word, as بَعْلَبَكِّيٌّ, رَامَهُرْمُزِيٌّ ; and
this license was extended to innumerable names which fall under
the class B. For example: from بَيْتُ سَوَا, بَيْتَسَوَانِيٌّ, with the
article ٱلْبَيْتَسَوَانِيٌّ ; from تَلُّ عُكْبَرَا and تَلُّ مَنَّسَ, تَلَّعُكْبَرِيٌّ and D
تَلَّمَنَّسِيٌّ ; from دَارُ ٱلْقُطْنِ, دَارَقُطْنِيٌّ ; from عَيْنُ زَرْبَى, عَيْنَزَرْبِيٌّ ; from
مَرْوُ ٱلرُّوذِ, دَيْرَعَاقُولِيٌّ ; from دَيْرُ ٱلْعَاقُولِ ; from نَهْرُ تِيرَى, نَهْرَتِيرِيٌّ ; from
وَادِيٓ آشَى, *Guadix* in Spain, وَادِي آشَ ; from مَرْوَرُوذِيٌّ ; from
عَبْدُ ٱلْمَلِكِ, عَبْدَمَلِكِيٌّ ; from تَاجُ ٱلْمُلْكِ, تَاجَمُلْكِيٌّ. To this stage of
the language, too, belong such words as ذُو ٱلنُّونِ from ذُنُونِيٌّ (*a*

A family in Spain); بُوْمَالِكِىّ from أَبُو مَالِكٍ ; بَلْعَدَوِيَّةٌ *a woman of the Benū ʿAdī* (§ 21, *c*, footn.)]; بُوْجَدِىّ *an ignoramus* (Fr. *abécédaire*), from ابجد *'abuǵed*, the first four letters of the alphabet (§ 32).

> REM. *b.* In many cases falling under B, 2, *b*, *a* and *β*, strange forms arise by the rejection of some consonants, or the combination into one word of a few letters (generally four) selected from the two nouns. E.g. حَضْرَمِىّ from حَضْرَمَوْت *Haḍramaut* ; عَبْدَرِىّ

B from عَبْدُ ٱلدَّارِ (a family in Mèkka); عَبْقَسِىّ from عَبْدُ ٱلْقَيْسِ (a tribe); رَعَنِىّ from عَبْدُ شَمْسٍ (a tribe); عَبْشَمِىّ from رَأْس عَيْنٍ *Rās-ʿain* ; شُرُنْبُلَالِىّ from شُبْرَى بُلُولَةَ (a village in Egypt); ٱلطَّبَرْخَزِىّ, the name of a poet, whose mother was from طَبَرِسْتَانُ, and his father from خُوَارِزْمُ.

265. A relative adjective is never formed, in classical Arabic, from the plural, even where the sense might seem to demand it, but

C always from the singular; e.g. فَرَضِىّ *acquainted with the divine institutions,* from فَرِيضَةٌ, plur. فَرَائِضُ ; حَصِيرِىّ *a seller of mats,* from حَصِيرٌ, plur. حُصُرٌ ; صَحَفِىّ *one who makes mistakes in reading manuscript,* also *a learner* or *student,* from صَحِيفَةٌ *a written sheet, a letter, a book,* plur. صُحُفٌ or صَحَائِفُ. Such plurals, however, as are either really proper names, or approximate to them in sense, are excepted ;

D e.g. كِلَابٌ ; أَنْمَارِىّ (plur. of نَمِرٌ *a leopard*) the tribe of *'Anmār,* (plur. of كَلْبٌ *a dog*), the tribe of *Kilāb,* كِلَابِىّ ; هَوَازِنُ (a tribe), ٱلْمَدَائِنُ ; مَعَافِرِىّ (a tribe), مَعَافِرُ (the name of a city, *Ctesiphon,* properly the plur. of مَدِينَةٌ), مَدَائِنِىّ ; ٱلْأَنْصَارُ *the Helpers* (of Muḥammad, epithet of the tribes of *êl-'Aus,* ٱلْأَوْسُ, and *êl-Hazraǵ,* ٱلْخَزْرَجُ, at êl-Medīna), أَنْصَارِىّ ; ٱلْأَعْرَابُ *the Arabs of the desert,*

أَعْرَابِىّ; [ٱلْأَحْلَاف the *confederate tribes,* أَحْلَافِى, as 'Omar is called in a A tradition ; ٱلْأَبْنَآء *the Persian colonists in el-Yèmèn,* أَبْنَاوِىّ. D. G.]

Rem. In more modern Arabic, on the contrary, a host of relative adjectives are formed from the plurals of nouns that indicate the object with which a person usually occupies himself in his trade, studies, etc. E.g. أَنْمَاط (plur. of نَمَط) *rugs,* أَنْمَاطِى *a maker* or *seller of rugs;* كُتُب (plur. of كِتَاب) *books,* كُتُبِى *a bookseller;* حُصُر (plur. of حَصِير) *mats,* حُصُرِى *a maker* or *seller of mats;* قَوَارِير (plur. of قَارُورَة) *glass bottles,* قَوَارِيرِى *a dealer in* B *bottles;* مَنَاخِل (plur. of مُنْخُل) *sieves,* مَنَاخِلِى *a maker* or *seller of sieves;* سَاعَات (plur. of سَاعَة) *watches,* سَاعَاتِى *a watchmaker;* مَشَاعِلِى *a bearer of the cresset called* مَشْعَلَة ; خَرَائِط (plur. of خَرِيطَة) *pouches* or *bags,* خَرَائِطِى *one who makes* or *sells them;* جَرَائِح (pl. of جَرِيحَة) *wounds,* جَرَائِحِى *a surgeon;* صِفَات (pl. of صِفَة) *qualities, attributes,* صِفَاتِى *one who recognises in God attributes distinct from* C *His essential nature;* صَحَفِى = فَرَائِضِى ; فَرَضِى ; صُحَفِى.—Similar forms in Syriac, of early date, are ܢܶܩܦܳܝ, *belonging to women,* from ܢܶܩܦܳܐ, plur. of ܐܰܢ̱ܬܬܳܐ, *a woman,* and ܨܰܘܪܳܢܳܝ from ܨܰܘܪܳܐ, plur. of ܨܰܘܪܳܐ.

266. Biliteral particles may double their second consonant or D not, at pleasure, if it be a strong letter ; as كَمْ *how much?* كَمِّى or كَمِى ; *not,* لَمْ, لَمِّى or لَمِى. But if the second consonant be weak, the opinions of grammarians differ. In the case of و, the simple doubling is permitted, as لَوْ *if,* لَوِّى ; or else a fètha is inserted between the two wāws, as لَوَوِى. In the case of ى, this latter form is alone admissible, the second ى being changed into و ; as كَىْ *that,* كَيَوِى ; فِى *in,*

A فَيَوِيٌّ. If the second letter be a quiescent êlif, there is inserted between it and the termination ـِيٌّ a hèmza, which may be changed into a و ; as لَا *not*, لَآءِيٌّ or لَاوِيٌّ. The pronoun مَا *what?* forms مَآئِيٌّ and مَاهِيٌّ.

267. We have seen above (§§ 231, 232) that the termination ـَانُ or ـَانٌ in adjectives is one of those which imply a certain degree B of intensity; and a few examples of rarer forms may here be given, as تَيَّهَانٌ *daring, reckless;* صِفْتَانٌ or صِفْتَانٌ, *strong, robust;* جُلْبَانٌ *clamorous, vociferous;* إِنْفُخَانٌ *corpulent;* أُسْحُلَانٌ or مُسْحُلَانٌ *tall or straight-haired;* مَلْكَعَانٌ *vile, sordid;* كُذُبْذُبَانٌ and مَكْذَبَانٌ *or* مَكْذَبَانَةٌ, *mendacious.* Hence we may form from many nouns a relative adjective ending in ـَانِيٌّ, as the grammarians say, لِتَأْكِيدِ النِّسْبَةِ, *to strengthen the relation;* e.g. from مَنْظَرٌ, *aspect, appearance,* C the ordinary nisba is مَنْظَرِيٌّ, but حَسَنُ ٱلْمَنْظَرِ=is مَنْظَرَانِيٌّ *good-looking.* So: شَعْرَانِيٌّ *having much or long hair* (شَعْرٌ), لِحْيَانِيٌّ *having a long beard* (لِحْيَةٌ), جُمَّانِيٌّ *having a large head of hair* (جُمَّةٌ), رَقَبَانِيٌّ *bull-necked* (رَقَبَةٌ *the neck*), جُسْمَانِيٌّ *large in the body* (جِسْمٌ), إِنْفُخَانِيٌّ *corpulent,* إِسْحِلَانِيٌّ *tall or long-bearded,* مُسْحُلَانِيٌّ *tall or straight-haired,* [حَوْصَلَانِيٌّ *having a large crop or craw* (حَوْصَلَةٌ), D صَيْدَلَانِيٌّ *smiting with the evil eye* (from نَفْسٌ in the sense of *eye*), or صَيْدَنَانِيٌّ *a drugseller* (from original صَنْدَلَانِيٌّ *seller of ṣandalwood,* Fleischer, *Kl. Schr.* i. 245, n. 1). D. G.] In later times this termination was more extensively employed, both in common speech and in scientific writings (in the latter, perhaps, under the influence of the Aramaic); e.g. فَاكِهَانِيٌّ *a fruiterer,* بَاقِلَانِيٌّ *one who sells beans,* سِمْسِمَانِيٌّ *one who sells sesame,* instead of فَاكِهِيٌّ, بَاقِلِيٌّ, or بَاقِلَائِيٌّ

بَاقِلَاوِيٌّ, and جَوَّانِيٌّ ; سِمْسِيٌّ *inner, interior, private,* بَرَّانِيٌّ *outward,* A external, *public* ; فَوْقَانِيٌّ *upper,* تَحْتَانِيٌّ *lower* ; رُوحَانِيٌّ *spiritual* (ذَمْلُمَد), نَفْسَانِيٌّ *relating to the soul,* (لِصْعُلُمَد), جَسَدَانِيٌّ *corporeal,* نُورَانِيٌّ *relating to light,* رَبَّانِيٌّ *learned and devout* (רַבָּן).

REM. A form expressing intensiveness, and applicable exclusively to the members of the body, is فُعَالِيٌّ ; as رُوَاسِيٌّ *having a* B *large head;* عُضَادِيٌّ, أَذَانِيٌّ, أَنَافِيٌّ, *having a large or long nose, ears,* *arms;* أَيَارِيٌّ, سُتَاهِيٌّ. Another rare form is exemplified by شُدْقَمٌ and سُتْهُمٌ = أَشْدَقُ and أَسْتَهُ.

(ϵ) *The Abstract Nouns of Quality,* أَسْمَاء ٱلْكَيْفِيَّة.

268. The feminine of the relative adjective serves in Arabic C as a noun to denote the abstract idea of the thing, as distinguished from the concrete thing itself; and also to represent the thing or things signified by the primitive noun as a whole or totality. It corresponds therefore to German substantives in *heit, keit, schaft, thum,* and to English ones in *head, dom, ty,* etc. E.g. ٱلْإِلِهِيَّة [and ٱلْأُلُهَانِيَّة D. G.] *the divine nature, Godhead* (ٱلْإِلَه *God*) ; إِنْسَانِيَّة *humanity* (إِنْسَانٌ *a human being*) ; ٱلرُّبُوبِيَّة *Lordship, Godhead* (ٱلرَّبُّ) ; رَجُولِيَّة *manhood;* [خُصُوصِيَّة or خُصُوصِيَّة *particularity*] ; وَصْفِيَّة,ٱسْمِيَّة. D *substantivity, adjectivity,* from ٱسْمٌ, *a substantive,* and وَصْفٌ, *an adjective;* (مُتَمَكِّن أَمْكَنُ) أَمْكَنِيَّة *the belonging to the fully-inflected class of nouns;* مَاهِيَّة *substance, quiddity* (مَا *what?*) ; مَآئِيَّة *wateriness* (مَآءٌ *water*) ; جَمْعِيَّة *totality;* شَاعِرِيَّة *what constitutes the being a poet, the poetic mind* or *temperament;* مَفْهُومِيَّة *the capability of being understood, intelligibility;* ٱلْحَنَفِيَّة *what constitutes being a Ḥanĕfite, the school of*

A   *the Ḥanéfites;* اَلنَّصْرَانِيَّة *Christendom, the Christian religion;* اَلْيَهُودِيَّة *Judaism.*

   REM. In a few cases the termination ـُوت, borrowed from the Aramaic ܢ݁ـ, is similarly employed; as لَاهُوت *divinity,* (ܐܠܳܗܽܘܬ),
نَاسُوت *humanity* (ܐ݈ܢܳܫܽܘܬ), مَلَكُوت *kingdom* (מַלְכוּת, ܡܰܠܟܽܘܬ),
جَبَرُوت *pride, haughtiness, omnipotence,* etc. [These nouns are, in Arabic, of the masculine gender.]

B   (ζ) *The Diminutive.*

   269. The diminutive, اَلِاسْمُ ٱلْمُحَقَّرُ or اَلتَّصْغِيرُ or اَلِاسْمُ ٱلْمُصَغَّرُ, and
or اَلتَّحْقِيرُ, when formed from a *triliteral* noun (اَلتَّكْبِيرُ or اَلِاسْمُ ٱلْمُكَبَّرُ),
takes the form فُعَيْلٌ; as رَجُلٌ *a man,* رُجَيْلٌ; كَلْبٌ *a dog,* كُلَيْبٌ;
عَمْرٌو *'Amr* (a man's name), عُمَيْرٌ; جَبَلٌ *a hill,* جُبَيْلٌ. When the
noun is *quadriliteral,* it takes the form فُعَيْعِلٌ; as عَقْرَبٌ *a scorpion,*

C عُقَيْرِبٌ; دِرْهَمٌ *a dirham,* دُرَيْهِمٌ; مَسْجِدٌ *a mosque,* مُسَيْجِدٌ; أَرْطًى *a
kind of tree,* أُرَيْطِ (for أُرَيْطِىٌ). When the noun is *quinqueliteral,* but
the fourth letter *weak,* the diminutive is فُعَيْعِيلٌ; as عُصْفُورٌ *a sparrow,*
عُصَيْفِيرٌ; مِفْتَاحٌ *a key,* مُفَيْتِيحٌ.

   REM. *a.* The diminutive is used, not merely in its literal sense,
but also to express endearment (as بُنَىٌّ, أُخَىٌّ, أُبَىٌّ) or contempt (as

D عُدَىٌّ), and even enhancement (لِلتَّعْظِيمِ, as دُوَيْهِيَةٌ *a great misfortune,*
سُنَيَّةٌ *a terrible year of drought* or *dearth,* خُيَيْرٌ *the very best,* صُدَيِّقٌ
a special friend), [اَلدُّهَيْمَاءُ *a very black calamity, a severe trial*].

   REM. *b.* In forming a diminutive, it is not usual to fall back
upon the root-consonants. On the contrary, the servile letters are
generally taken into account, as long as the word does not exceed
the form فُعَيْعِلٌ; as أَزْرَقُ *blue,* أُزَيْرِقُ; مِعْطَفٌ *a mantle,* مُعَيْطِفٌ.
See however § 283.

REM. *c.* The first syllable of the form فُعَيْل is occasionally A pronounced with kèsra instead of ḍamma, when the second radical of the primitive is ى; as شِيَيْخ, بِيَيْب, نِيَيْب، شِيَىْ، بِيَيْت for بُيَيْت، (شِيَىْ، شُيَيْخ، نُيَيْب from بَيْت، شَىْ، شَيْخ، and نَاب (for نَيَب).

REM. *d.* Traces of this diminutive form in Aramaic are עוּלֵימָא ,ܕܟ݂ܣܡܐ, *a youth* (غُلَيِّم, from غُلَام), and ܚ̇ܘܪܠܐ *a fawn* (غُزَيِّل, from غَزَال). In Hebrew we may perhaps consider as such, זְעֵיר *little, a little* (صُغَيِّر), פְּלֵיטָה *a band of fugitives*, שְׁפִיפֹן *the cerastes, a sort of snake* (سُفّ), and אֲמִינוֹן (from אַמְנוֹן, a con- B temptuous diminutive, like اَلْأُحَيْمِلُ. If so, the vowel ־ִי must be regarded as a weakening of ־ֵי (orig. ־ַי), like גְּלֵית for גְּלָית (גָּלִיִתְ). This view derives some confirmation from the modern pronunciation of North Africa, where, for example, قُفَيْفَة, the diminutive of قُفَّة, *a basket*, is sounded *k'fifè* or *g'fifè*,—in post-biblical Hebrew קְפִיפָה and קוּפָּה.

REM. *e.* Diminutives may be formed not only from nouns C (substantive or adjective), but also (1) from the demonstrative pronoun ذا and its derivatives, as well as the relative pronoun اَلَّذى; (2) from certain prepositions, which are, however, obviously substantives in the accusative, as قُبَيْلَ *a little before,* بُعَيْدَ *a little after,* فُوَيْقَ *a little above,* دُوَيْنَ *a little below, a little nearer than,* etc.; and (3) from a few of the verbs of surprise or wonder (§ 184, rem. *f*). On the other hand, they cannot be formed from nouns D which have already the measure of a diminutive, as جُمَيْلٌ, *a kind of small bird,* كُمَيْتٌ *a bay horse.*

270. When the noun contains *five* letters, of which the fourth is *strong,* or more than five, the diminutive فُعَيْعِل is commonly formed from the first four, and the rest are rejected; as سَفَرْجَلٌ *a quince,*

A عُنَيْكِبٌ. a spider, عَنْكَبُوتٌ ; عُنَيْدِلٌ a nightingale, عَنْدَلِيبٌ ; سُفَيْرِجٌ
But if there be among the consonants several servile letters, these are
rejected, or some of them ; as إِسْتَبْرَقٌ thick gold-brocade, أُبَيْرِقٌ ;

مُتَدَحْرِجٌ rolling oneself, دَحْرِجٌ ; مُسْتَكْمِلٌ trying to render perfect,
مُكَيْمِلٌ ; مُخْتَارٌ chosen, مُخَيِّرٌ (for مُخَيِّيرٌ), and not مُخَيْتِرٌ ; مُقْعَنْسِسٌ
having a hump in front, مُقَيْعِسٌ.

B   REM. *a.* The rule as to quinqueliterals like سَفَرْجَلٌ is not
always strictly observed. Thus جَحْمَرِشٌ *a fat, lazy, old woman,*
فَرَزْدَقٌ *a burnt cake,* and قِذَعْمِلٌ *a big camel or a little, ugly woman,*
are said to make either جُحَيْمِرٌ, فُرَيْزِدٌ, قُذَيْعِمٌ, or فُرَيْزِقٌ, جُحَيْمِرِشٌ,
قُذَيْعِلٌ.

    REM. *b.* If there be more servile consonants than must neces-
sarily be cut off, their relative importance for the signification of
the word is taken into account in choosing which is to be retained.

C   In مُسْتَكْمِلٌ, for example, م is preserved in preference to س or ت,
because it indicates the participial form. But if all the consonants
are of equal value, we may select which we please, and therefore
the diminutive of عَلَنْدًى, *a sort of thorn,* is either عُلَيْنِدٌ or عُلَيْدٌ
(for عُلَيْدِىٌّ) ; of قَلَنْسُوَةٌ, *a sort of cap,* قُلَيْنِسَةٌ or قُلَيْسِيَةٌ ; of حَبَنْطًى,
short and big-bellied, حُبَيْطٌ or حُبَيْنِطٌ (for حُبَيْطِىٌّ).

    REM. *c.* The termination ـَانٌ, when appended to nouns of four
D or more letters, is not rejected, but remains attached to the diminutive, which is formed out of the preceding consonants ; as زَعْفَرَانٌ
saffron, زُعَيْفِرَانٌ ; أُفْعُوَانٌ *a male snake,* أُفَيْعِيَانٌ.

    REM. *d.* Nouns containing five or more consonants do not
exceed the form فُعَيْعِلٌ, as قَرَعْبَلَانَةٌ *a tick,* قُرَيْعِبَةٌ ; and therefore a
word which consists of four radical and one or more servile consonants, rejects the latter at once (except in the cases specified in
rem. *b,* and in § 269). In place of the rejected consonants, however,

ى may be inserted immediately before the last letter; as سُفَيْرِيج, A
مُكَيْمِيل, عُنَيْكِيبٌ, and the like.

271. The feminine terminations ـَة, ـَى, and اَـٓ; the relative
termination ـِىّ; the ending اـَن in adjectives of which the feminine
is فَعْلَى, and in proper names; the dual and plural terminations ـَان,
ـُونَ, and ـَاتٌ; and the second syllable of the plural form أَفْعَال;
are all disregarded. The diminutives must be formed out of the B
preceding consonants, and these terminations added to them. E.g.
قَلْعَةٌ *a castle,* قُلَيْعَة; طَلْحَة (a man's name), طُلَيْحَة; مَسْلَمَة (a man's
name), مُسَيْلِمَة; سَلْمَى (a woman's name), حُبْلَى *pregnant,* حُبَيْلَى; سُلَيْمَى;
حَمْرَآ *red,* حُمَيْرَآ; عَبْقَرِىّ (from a place called عَبْقَر, supposed
to be inhabited by the *ginn*) *demoniacal, mighty, perfect,* عُبَيْقِرِىّ;
بَصْرِىّ *belonging to* el-Baṣra, بُصَيْرِىّ; سَكْرَان (fem. سَكْرَى) *drunken,* C
سُكَيْرَان; سَلْمَان (a man's name), سُلَيْمَان; مُسْلِمَان *two Muslims,*
مُسَيْلِمَان; مُسْلِمَات *Muslim women,* مُسْلِمُونَ *Muslims,* مُسَيْلِمُونَ;
مُسَيْلِمَات; أَبْيَات *verses,* أَجْمَال *camels,* أَصْحَاب *companions,* أَلْفَاظ *words,*
أَبْيَيَات, أَلْيَفَاظ, أَصَيْحَاب, أُجَيْمَال.

REM. *a.* The fem. ـَى is rejected, when the noun consists of
five letters, the third of which is strong, or of more than five; as D
قَرْقَرَى *the back,* قُرَيْقِر; لُغَيْزَى *a riddle,* لُغَيْغِيزٌ. But if, in the quinqueliteral noun, the third letter be a weak servile, either it, or the
ى, may be omitted; as حُبَارَى *a bustard,* حُبَيْرَى or حُبَيِّرٌ (for
حُبَيِّر).

REM. *b.* Other plurals, besides أَفْعَال, of the class called
جُمُوع القِلَّة (see § 307) form their diminutives regularly; viz.
فِعْلَة, as وِلْدَة *children,* وُلَيْدَة; غِلْمَة *boys, slaves,* غُلَيْمَة; أَفْعُل, as

A   أَكْلُب *dogs*, أُكَيْلِبُ; أَضْلُع *ribs*, أُضَيْلِع; and أَفْعِلَة, as أُجَيْرِبَة *bags*,

أَصْبِيَة; أَجَيْرِبَة; أَعْمِدَة *pillars*, أُعَيْمِدَة; أَغْلِمَة *boys, slaves*, أُغَيْلِمَة;

children, أُصَيْبِيَة. In regard to the جُمُوعُ ٱلْكَثْرَة (see § 307), two

courses may be adopted. We may fall back on the singular, adding

to its diminutive the appropriate plural termination; e.g. شُعَرَاءُ

poets, شُوَيْعِرُونَ, from شُوَيْعِرٌ, شَاعِرٌ (see § 277); دُورٌ *houses*, دُوَيْرَاتٌ,

B   from دَارٌ, دُوَيْرَة (see § 274). Or we may have recourse to the

جَمْعُ ٱلْقِلَّة, if such exist; e.g. فَتًى, فُتَيٌّ, from فُتْيُونَ *youths*, فِتْيَانٌ,

or فُتَيَّة, from the plural فِتْيَة; أَذِلَّاءُ *base fellows*, ذُلَيِّلُونَ, from

ذَلِيل, ذُلَيِّل (see § 278), or أُذَيْلَة (for أُذَيْلِلَة), from the plural أَذِلَّة

(for أَذْلِلَة).

272. The termination ـَانْ in *triliteral* nouns, of which the femi-

C   nine is *not* فَعْلَى, and which are not proper names, is regarded as

radical, and consequently the diminutive takes the form فُعَيْعِلٌ; as

سُلْطَانٌ *power, a sultan*, سُلَيْطِينٌ; سِرْحَانٌ *a wolf*, سُرَيْحِينٌ;

a devil, شُيَيْطِينٌ; رَيْحَانٌ *sweet basil*, رُوَيْحِينٌ.

273. Proper names, consisting of two words (see § 264), form

their diminutives from the *first* word, the second remaining unchanged;

D   as عَبْدُ ٱللّٰه *'Abdu 'llāh*, عُبَيْدُ ٱللّٰه *'Obèidu 'llāh*; مَعْدِيكَرِبُ, مُعَيْدِيكَرِبُ;

حَضْرَمَوْتُ, حُضَيْرَمَوْتُ; بَعْلَبَكُّ, بُعَيْلَبَكُّ.

274. If a diminutive be formed from a *triliteral feminine* noun,

which has not however a feminine termination, ـَة is added to the

diminutive, provided that the primitive has no nomen unitatis (§ 246).

E. g. هِنْدُ (a woman's name), هُنَيْدَة; شَمْسُ *the sun*, شُمَيْسَة; دَارٌ *a house*,

دُوَيْرَة; سِنٌّ *a tooth*, سُنَيْنَة; إِبِلٌ *camels*, أُبَيْلَة; غَنَمٌ *a flock of sheep* or

goats, غُنَيْمَة; عَيْنٌ *an eye or fountain*, عُيَيْنَة or عِيَيْنَة (see § 269, rem. *c*).

But if the primitive has a nomen unitatis, ة‍َ is not appended to the A diminutive, in order to avoid ambiguity. E.g. شَجَرٌ *trees*, شُجَيْرٌ, but شَجَرَةٌ *a tree*, شُجَيْرَةٌ; بَقَرٌ *cattle*, بُقَيْرٌ, but بَقَرَةٌ *an ox or cow*, بُقَيْرَةٌ.

REM. *a.* The diminutives of the fem. cardinal numbers, from 3 to 10 inclusive, do not take ة‍َ for the same reason; e.g. خَمْسٌ *five* (fem.), خُمَيْسٌ, but خَمْسَةٌ *five* (masc.), خُمَيْسَةٌ. But see § 319, rem. *a.*

REM. *b.* If the noun contains more than three consonants, ة‍َ is not added to the diminutive.

REM. *c.* There are a few exceptions to the rules of this § and rem. *b.* For example, حَرْبٌ, *war*, makes حُرَيْبٌ; دِرْعٌ *a coat of mail*, دُرَيْعٌ; ذَوْدٌ, *a herd of she-camels*, ذُوَيْدٌ; عَرَبٌ *Arabs*, عُرَيْبٌ; عَرُوسٌ *a bride*, عُرَيْسٌ; نَعْلٌ *a shoe*, نُعَيْلٌ; قَوْسٌ, *a bow*, قُوَيْسٌ; قَلُوصٌ *a young she-camel*, قُلَيِّصٌ, D. G.]; whilst قُدَّامٌ, *the front*, and قَوْمٌ.(وُرَيِّئَةٌ)— *the rear or back*, have قُدَيْدِيمَةٌ, and وُرَيِّئَةٌ (for وَرَآءٌ) *one's people or tribe*, which is masc. and fem., has قُوَيْمٌ or قُوَيْمَةٌ; C but رَهْطٌ and نَفَرٌ, though also of both genders, seem to make only رُهَيْطٌ and نُفَيْرٌ. عُرْسٌ, *a wedding-feast*, is usually masculine, and therefore has عُرَيْسٌ. بَحْرٌ *a sea*, which is masc., makes بُحَيْرَةٌ.

275. The double consonants in nouns formed from verba mediæ rad. geminatæ are resolved; as تَلٌّ *a hill*, تُلَيْلٌ; طَسٌّ *a cup* (Fr. *tasse*), طُسَيْسٌ; مُدَّةٌ *time*, مُدَيْدَةٌ.

276. If the second radical be a weak letter, and have been D changed by the influence of the vowels into another, the original letter is restored in forming the diminutive. E.g. بَابٌ (بَوَبٌ) *a door*, بُوَيْبٌ; نَابٌ (نَيَبٌ) *an eye-tooth or canine tooth*, نُيَيْبٌ; رِيحٌ (رِوْحٌ) *wind*, رُوَيْحٌ; مُوسِرٌ (مُيْسِرٌ) *rich*, مُيَيْسِرٌ; قِيمَةٌ (قِوْمَةٌ) *price, value*, قُوَيْمَةٌ; رُوَيْحَةٌ; مِيزَانٌ (مِوْزَانٌ) *a pair of scales*, مُوَيْزِينٌ.

A   Rem. شَيْءٌ, *a thing,* commonly makes شُوَيٌّ (for شُوَيْءٌ), and vulgarly شُوَيَّةٌ, instead of شُيَيْءٌ. From بَيْتٌ *a house,* شَيْخٌ *an old man,* عَيْنٌ *an eye* or *fountain,* بَيْضَةٌ *an egg,* and ضَيْعَةٌ *a farm,* may be formed ضُوَيْعَةٌ, بُوَيْتٌ, شُوَيْخٌ, عُوَيْنَةٌ, بُوَيْضَةٌ, and ضُوَيْعَةٌ, but the regular forms are preferable. Conversely, عِيدٌ, *a festival,* though derived from the radical عود, makes عُيَيْدٌ, following the plural أَعْيَادٌ.

277. If the second letter be either a servile ělif, or an ělif, the B origin of which is unknown, it is changed into و; as شَاعِرٌ *a poet,* شُوَيْعِرٌ; دَاهِيَةٌ *a calamity,* دُوَيْهِيَةٌ; فَارِسٌ *a horseman,* فُوَيْرِسٌ; خَاتَمٌ *a signet-ring,* خُوَيْتِمٌ; صَابَةٌ *a certain bitter tree,* صُوَيْبَةٌ.

Rem. *a.* Words of the form فَاعِلٌ, in which the initial letter is و, change it into أ in forming the diminutive; e.g. وَاصِلٌ, أُوَيْصِلٌ, not وُوَيْصِلٌ. In other cases this change is optional, as in أُرَيْقٌ for C   وُرَيْقٌ, formed according to § 283 from أَوْرَقُ.

Rem. *b.* Words of the form of دُوَيْبَّةٌ sometimes substitute ‑ٮ for ‑ِيْ, to lighten the pronunciation, as دُوَابَّةٌ and شُوَابَّةٌ, the latter for شُوَيْبَّةٌ, from شَابَّةٌ *a young woman.* [Comp. § 13, rem.]

278. If the third letter be weak, it coalesces with the preceding ى of the diphthong ‑َيْ into ىّ; as غُلَامٌ *a youth, a slave,* غُلَيِّمٌ; ظَلِيمٌ *a male ostrich,* ظُلَيِّمٌ; أَكُولٌ *a glutton,* أُكَيِّلٌ; طَعَامٌ *food,* طُعَيِّمٌ; عَصًا *a* D   *brook,* جُدَيِّلٌ; أَسْوَدُ *black,* أُسَيِّدُ; فَتًى *a youth,* فُتَيٌّ; عَصًا *a stuff,* عُصَيَّةٌ; رَحًى *a mill,* رُحَيَّةٌ; عُرْوَةٌ *a handle,* عُرَيَّةٌ.

Rem. *a.* The forms جُدَيْوِلٌ and أُسَيْوِدٌ are also used.

Rem. *b.* In words of which the second and third radicals are contracted into ىّ, these letters must be separated, and treated according to this rule and § 276; e.g. طَىٌّ *a fold* (طُوَىٌّ), طُوَىٌّ; حَيَّةٌ *a snake,* (حُيَيَّةٌ), حُيَيَّةٌ.

279. A quadriliteral or quinqueliteral, of which the last two A letters are *weak*, rejects one of them; as يَحْيَى *Yaḥyā* (*John*), يُحَىّ (for يُحَيِّى); أُحَىّ *black*, (for أُحَيِّى); صَبِىّ *a boy*, صُبَىّ (for صُبَيِّى); عَدُوّ *an enemy*, عُدَىّ (for عُدَيِّى); عَطَآءٌ *a gift, pay*, عُطَىّ (for عُطَيِّى); سَمَآءٌ *the sky* or *heaven*, سُمَيَّةٌ; إِدَاوَةٌ *a small water-skin*, أُدَيَّةٌ (for أُدَيِّيَةٌ); مُعَاوِيَةُ (a man's name), مُعَيَّةٌ (for مُعَيِّيَةٌ).

Rem. Instead of أُحَىّ, some say أُحَيْوٍ (accus. أُحَيْوِىَ, like B أُسَيْوِدٌ, § 278, rem. *a*), others أُحَيٍّ (accus. أُحَيَّى, for أُحَيِّيَى, like مُعَاوِيَةُ, § 278), and others still, but irregularly, أُحَىّ.—From the forms مُعَيْوَةٌ and مُعَيَّةٌ are also said to be in use.

280. The infinitives of verba primae و, which reject the first radical and take the fem. termination ة‍ in exchange (§ 206), resume C the و in their diminutives; as عِدَةٌ *a promise*, وُعَيْدَةٌ; جِدَةٌ *affluence*, وُجَيْدَةٌ; شِيَةٌ *being spotted, spots*, وُشَيَّةٌ.

Rem. They are distinguished by the ة from the diminutives of the form فَعْلٌ in the same verbs; such as وُعَيْدٌ from وَعْدٌ, etc.

281. Nouns which have lost their third radical,—whether they have the fem. termination ة‍ or not,—recover it in the diminutive. D E.g. أَبٌ *a father* (ابو), أُبَىّ; أَخٌ *a brother* (اخو), أُخَىّ; دَمٌ *blood*, دُمَىّ; يَدٌ *a hand*, يُدَيَّةٌ; حِرٌ *vulva*, حُرَيْحٌ; مَآءٌ *water*, مُوَيْهٌ and مُوَىّ; شَاةٌ *a sheep* or *goat*, شُوَيْهَةٌ; شَفَةٌ *a lip*, شُفَيْهَةٌ; أَمَةٌ *a maidservant*, أُمَيَّةٌ; لُغَةٌ *a dialect*, لُغَيَّةٌ; سَنَةٌ *a year*, سُنَيْهَةٌ and سُنَيَّةٌ; هَنَةٌ *a thing*, هُنَيَّةٌ, هُنَيْهَةٌ, and هُنَيَّةٌ.

Rem. *a.* فَمٌ, *mouth*, of which the radical is فُوهٌ or فَوَهٌ, forms its diminutive accordingly, فُوَيْهٌ.

Rem. *b.* A lost first or second radical is not restored, if the

A   word consists of three letters, exclusive of the feminine ة; as نَاسٌ (for أُنَاسٌ) *people,* هَائِرٌ; نُوَيْسٌ هَارٌ (for هَائِرٌ, § 240, rem. *b*) *feeble,* مَيْتٌ (for شُوَيْكٌ; شَائِكٌ (for شَائِكٌ) *bristling (with weapons),* مَيْتٌ; هُوَيْرٌ (for خَيْرٌ (خَيْرٌ for) good, خُبَيِّرٌ   Otherwise the مَيِّتٌ. § 242) *dead,* خُبَيِّرٌ. مَيِّتٌ, and أُنَيِّسٌ هُوَيِّرٌ, شُوَيِّكٌ. مُيَيِّتٌ, and خُبَيِّرٌ.

[Words of the form فَاعِلٌ retain in the diminutive the termination ‑ٍ, as قُوَيْضٍ from قَاضٍ *a judge,* رُوَيْعٍ from رَاعٍ *a pastor.* D. G.]

B   **282.** Those nouns which, after having lost their third radical, take a prosthetic *élif,* reject the *élif,* and recover their original letter. E.g. اِسْمٌ *a name,* سُمَىٌّ; اِبْنٌ *a son,* بُنَىٌّ; اِسْتٌ *the anus,* سُتَيْهَةٌ.

REM.   The diminutives of أُخْتٌ *sister,* بِنْتٌ *daughter,* and هَنْتٌ *a thing,* are formed like those of أَخٌ, اِبْنٌ, and هَنَةٌ, and distinguished in the first two by the fem. termination; هُنَيَّةٌ بُنَيَّةٌ, أُخَيَّةٌ (see
C   § 281).

283. Another way of forming diminutives is to fall back upon the root. If this consists of *three* consonants, the diminutive is فُعَيْلٌ; if of *four,* فُعَيْعِلٌ (see § 269, rem. *b*). E.g. مُعَيْطَفٌ, عُيَيْفٌ; هُمَيْمٌ, هُمَيْمٌ; سُوَيْدٌ, أَسْوَدُ; قُضَىٌّ قَاضٍ, حُمَيْدٌ; حَامِدٌ; حُرَيْثٌ; حَارِثٌ; قُرَيْطِسٌ, قِرْطَاسٌ; عُصَيْفِرٌ, عُصْفُورٌ; أُرَيْقٌ or وُرَيْقٌ or وُرَيْقٌ; أَوْرَقُ; نُفَيْعٌ, نَافِعٌ; D   [مُعَيْدِىٌّ مَعَدِّىٌّ]; فُعَيْسٌ, مُقَعْنِسٌ. This sort of diminutive is called تَصْغِيرُ التَّرْخِيمِ, *the softened* or *curtailed diminutive.*

284. With regard to this kind of diminutive the following rules are to be observed. (*a*) If a masc. noun ends in ة‑, this termination falls away; e.g. حَارِثَةٌ (a name), حُرَيْثٌ. (*b*) Fem. nouns in ى‑ and اَء‑ reject these terminations and take ة‑; as حَمْرَاءُ, حُمَيْرَةٌ; حُبْلَى, حُبَيْلَةٌ.

Rem.   Very irregular diminutives are : رَجُلٌ *a man,* رُوَيْجِلٌ ; A

عُشَيَّةٌ smoke, دُخَانٌ ; دُوَيْخِنٌ ; مَغْرِبٌ sunset, مُغَيْرِبَانٌ ; عَشًى or

إِنْسَانٌ nightfall, عُشَيْشِيَة ,عُشَيْشَةٌ .عُشَيْشَانٌ ,عُشَيَّانٌ , and عُشَيْشِيَانٌ ;

a human being, أُنَيْسِيَانٌ ; لَيْلَةٌ *a night,* لُيَيْلِيَةٌ (compare the plur.

لَيَالٍ for (لَيَالِي) ; بَنُونَ *sons* (plur. of ابْنٌ).أُبَيْنُونَ ; أَصْلَانٌ (derived

from the plur. of أَصِيلٌ *the evening),* أُصَيْلاَنَ ,أُصَيْلاَلَ , and أُصَيَّالٌ.

Further, دِينَارٌ *a dînâr,* دُنَيْنِيرٌ , and دِيوَانٌ *a register, an account-book,* B

a collection of poems, a public office or bureau, دُوَيْوِينٌ , as if from

دِنَّارٌ and دِوَّانٌ (see § 305, II., rem. *b*) ; دِيبَاجٌ *brocade,* دُبَيْبِيجٌ or

دُبَيْبِيجٌ, as if from دِبَّاجٌ.

(η)   Some other Nominal Forms.

285.   (*a*) The form فُعْلَةٌ frequently means a *small piece* of C
anything ; as فِلْذَةٌ ,قِطْعَةٌ, *a piece,* كُسْرَةٌ *a fragment,* جِذْوَةٌ *a firebrand,*
a live coal, خِرْقَةٌ *a rag,* فِرْقَةٌ *a sect,* حِصَّةٌ *a portion,* خِطَّةٌ *a piece of*
land, an allotment.—(*b*) The form فُعْلَةٌ is often used to signify a *small*
quantity, such as can be contained in a place at once ; as قُبْضَةٌ *a*
handful ; أُكْلَةٌ ,لُقْمَةٌ, *a morsel, a mouthful ;* مُضْغَةٌ ,جُرْعَةٌ ,بُلْعَةٌ, *a gulp,*
a sup or sip ; شُرْبَةٌ *a draught (of water).*   It also denotes *colour ;* as
حُمْرَةٌ *redness,* صُفْرَةٌ *yellowness,* زُرْقَةٌ *a light blue,* دُكْنَةٌ *a blackish* D
brown.

286.   (*a*) The form فِعَالٌ indicates *vessels* and *implements ;* as
إِنَاءٌ ,وِعَاءٌ, *a vessel,* جِرَابٌ *a bag,* حِلاَبٌ *a milk-pail,* خِلاَلٌ *a wooden pin,*
سِقَاءٌ *a water-skin,* شِرَاكٌ *the thong or strap of a sandal,* لِبَاسٌ *a garment,*
إِزَارٌ ,رِدَاءٌ, certain garments, لِحَافٌ *a coverlet, a pelisse.*—(*b*) The form
فُعَالٌ denotes *diseases ;* as حُمَامٌ *a fever,* زُكَامٌ *a cold,* سُعَالٌ *a cough,*

A صُدَاعٌ *a headache,* طُحَالٌ, كُبَادٌ, *disease of the spleen* (طِحَالٌ), *of the liver* (كَبِدٌ)*.

287. (*a*) The form فِعَالَة indicates *a post or office;* as كِتَابَة *the post of secretary* (كَاتِبٌ): عِمَالَة, وِلَايَة, *the post of governor* (عَامِلٌ); إِمَارَة *the office of ʾemîr* (أَمِيرٌ); خِلَافَة *the caliphate;* نِيَابَة *deputyship* B (نَائِبٌ); قِيَادَة *the post of general* (قَائِدٌ); عِرَافَة *the post of inspector, centurion,* etc. (عَرِيفٌ).—(*b*) The form فُعَالَة denotes *small portions* which are broken off or thrown away; as بُرَادَة, قُرَاضَة, *filings;* بُرَايَة *chips, shavings;* قُلَامَة, قُصَاصَة, *parings;* كُنَاسَة, كُسَاحَة, قُمَامَة, *sweepings;* رُضَاضَة *brayed or pounded fragments;* كُسَارَة *broken pieces;* قُطَاعَة *cuttings;* عُجَالَة *a little food got ready in haste;* عُفَاوَة *a small quantity* C *of broth* (left in a borrowed pot, when it is returned). Some of these words admit of a masculine collective form فُعَال, indicating a larger quantity, as فُتَاتٌ, دُقَاقٌ, حُطَامٌ, كُسَارٌ, رُضَاضٌ, قُمَامٌ, بُرَآءٌ.

288. The form فَعَّالَة (the feminine of فَعَّالٌ, § 233) is frequently employed to designate (*a*) an instrument or machine, as doing something, or by means of which something is done, regularly and constantly; or (*b*) the place where something is constantly obtained or prepared. D E.g. بَرَّادَة *a vessel* or *stand for cooling water;* حَرَّاقَة *a fire-ship, a galley;* عَرَّادَة, دَبَّابَة, *engines of war;* طَرَّاحَة *a mattrass or cushion, a fishing-net;* زَرَّاقَة *a short javelin;* طَرَّادَة *a spear, a bolt;* حَرَّاضَة *a*

---

* [According to D. H. Müller (Asmaʿî's *Kitâb al-Farḳ,* p. 26 *seqq.*) the forms فُعَال, فُعَالَة and فَعِيل are often used to denote excretions, as *spittle* or *phlegm* لَغَامٌ, (رُغَامٌ) رُغَامٌ, رُؤَالٌ, لُعَابٌ, بُصَاقٌ, مُجَاجَة, مُجَاحٌ; *sweat* صُوَاحٌ, رَشِيحٌ, حَمِيمٌ, حُمَامٌ; *blood issuing from the nose* رُعَافٌ; *excrements* سُلَاحٌ; *sperma* سُلَالَة; *drippings* قُطَارَة. D. G.]

place where potash is made (by burning the plants called حُرْض) ; A
جَصَّاصَةٌ *a place where gypsum or plaster* (جِصّ) *is made;* كَلَّاسَةٌ *a*
chalk-pit or quarry (كِلْسٌ) ; مَلَّاحَةٌ *a salt-pan or salt-mine* (مِلْح) ;
قَيَّارَةٌ *a well of bitumen* (قَارٌ) ; جَبَّاسَةٌ *a place where gypsum is found*
or prepared; زَرَّاعَةٌ *a land that is sown.* Hence the tropical application
of this form to persons, as an intensive (§ 233, rem. *c*).

Rem.   As فَعَّالَةٌ has been transferred from things to persons, as
an intensive adjective, so also فَاعِلَةٌ (§ 233, rem. *c*); for سَاقِيَةٌ is B
a camel that draws water, an irrigating machine, a water-wheel;
سَانِيَةٌ, *a water-wheel* and *the camel that works it;* رَاوِيَةٌ, *a water-skin,*
a camel that carries or draws water; دَاعِيَةٌ, *a call* or *invitation;*
عَادِيَةٌ, *a hindrance, an injury;* etc.

2.   *The Gender of Nouns.*

289.   In respect of gender, Arabic nouns are divisible into *three* C
classes ; (*a*) those which are only *masculine* (مُذَكَّرٌ) ; (*b*) those which
are only *feminine* (مُؤَنَّثٌ) ; (*c*) those which are both masc. and fem.,
or, as it is usually phrased, of the *common* gender.

Rem. *a.*   None of the Semitic languages have what we call the
neuter gender.

Rem. *b.*   Feminines may be either *real* or *natural* (مُؤَنَّثٌ حَقِيقِيٌّ),
as اِمْرَأَةٌ *a woman,* نَاقَةٌ *a she-camel;* or unreal, *unnatural* (غَيْرُ
حَقِيقِيٍّ), or *tropical* (مَجَازِيٌّ), as الشَّمْسُ *the sun,* نَعْل *a shoe* or D
sandal, ظُلْمَةٌ *darkness,* بُشْرَى *good news.*

290.   That a noun is of the *fem.* gender may be ascertained
either (*a*) from its *signification,* or (*b*) from its *form.*

a.   Feminine by signification (اَلْمُؤَنَّثُ اَلْمَعْنَوِيُّ) are :—

(*a*)   All common nouns and proper names which denote females,
as أُمٌّ *a mother,* عَرُوسٌ *a bride,* عَجُوزٌ *an old woman,* [خَادِمٌ *a female*

w.   23

A *servant*]; مَرْيَمُ *Mary*, هِنْدُ *Hind*, سُعَادُ *Su'ād*, زَيْنَبُ *Zeineb* [; or that are represented as females, as شَعُوبُ *Death*, ذُكَآءُ *the Sun*].

(β) Proper names of countries and towns; because the common nouns أَرْضُ, بُقْعَةُ, مَدِينَةُ, بَلْدَةُ, and قَرْيَةُ, are feminine*; as مِصْرُ *Egypt*, مُخَا *Mocha*. Those names, however, which belong to the triptote declension, are originally masculine, as ٱلشَّأْمُ *Syria*, ٱلْعِرَاقُ

el-'Irāk, هَجَرُ, فَلْجُ, دَابِقُ, وَاسِطُ, مِنًى ; but they may also be inflected B as diptotes, and are then feminine, as وَاسِطُ, مِنَى, etc.

REM. The names of the quarters or directions, as قُدَّامُ, أَمَامُ, *the front*, خَلْفُ, وَرَآءُ, *the rear*, may also be treated as feminine, following the gender of جِهَةُ.

(γ) The names of the winds and the different kinds of fire, because the common nouns رِيحٌ, *wind*, and نَارُ, *fire*, are feminine ; as

قَبُولُ *the east wind*, دَبُورُ *the west wind*, شَمَالُ *the north wind*, جَنُوبُ C *the south wind*; سَعِيرُ, جَحِيمُ, *blazing fire*, [جَهَنَّمُ,] سَقَرُ, لَظَى *hell-fire*.

Except إِعْصَارُ *a dust-storm with whirlwinds*, which is masc.

(δ) The names of many parts of the body, especially those that are double ; as يَدُ *a hand*, رِجْلُ *a leg or foot*, عَيْنُ *an eye*, أُذُنُ *an ear*, سِنٌّ *a tooth*, كَتِفُ *a shoulder*, سَاقُ *a shank*, رَحِمُ *the womb*, إِسْتُ *the anus*.

D REM. رَأْسُ *the head*, وَجْهُ *the face*, أَنْفُ *the nose*, فَمُ *the mouth*, صَدْرُ *the breast*, ظَهْرُ *the back*, [خَدُّ *the cheek*,] and the names of the blood, muscles, sinews, and bones, are masc.; as also, in most instances, رَحِمُ, when it means *relationship*. [قَدَمُ is sometimes masc. and so كَفُّ.]

---

* [Some admit also the use of the masculine gender, because the word مِصْرُ is masc., بَلَدُ masc. or fem. See Muḳaddasī, p. 7, l. 16 *seq.* D. G.]

(ε) Collective nouns (شِبْهُ ٱلْجَمْعِ, *resembling the plural*), which A
denote living objects that are destitute of reason, and do not form a
nomen unitatis; as اِبِل *camels,* ذَوْد *a herd of she-camels,* غَنَم *sheep*
or *goats.*

b. Feminine by form (ٱلْمُؤَنَّثُ ٱللَّفْظِيُّ) are :—

(a) Nouns ending in ة‍َ; as جَنَّة *a garden,* ظُلْمَة *darkness,* حَيَاة,
or حَيْوَة, *life.*

(β) Nouns ending in ى‍َ or ا‍َ (ĕlif maksūra, § 7, rem. b), when B
that termination does not belong to the root; as دَعْوَى *a claim, a*
demand, نَجْوَى *a secret,* لَوْمَى *blame,* أُرَبَى *misfortune,* ذِكْرَى *memory,*
دِفْلَى *the oleander,* ذِفْرَى *the prominent bone behind the ear,* مِعْزَى *goats,*
بُهْمَى *barley-grass,* ٱلدُّنْيَا *the world,* رُؤْيَا *a vision or dream,* بُشْرَى *good*
news, حُمَّى *a fever.*

Rem. But those who say مِعْزًى, ذِفْرًى, دِفْلًى, and بُهْمًى, regard C
them as masculine, the ى being considered as an أَلِفُ ٱلْإِلْحَاقِ
[§ 252].

(γ) Nouns ending in اَ‍ء, when that termination does not belong
to the root; as بَيْدَاء, صَحْرَاء, *a plain* or *desert,* ضَرَّاء *harm, mischief,*
بَغْضَاء *hatred,* قَاصِعَاء *a jerboa's hole,* كِبْرِيَاء *glory* (of God), *pride* (of
man), خُيَلَاء *vainglory, arrogance,* سِيَرَاء *a sort of striped cloth.*

Rem. A few nouns ending in ة‍َ, and those verbal adjectives D
to which ة‍َ is added to intensify their signification (§ 233, rem. c),
are masc., because they apply to males; e.g. خَلِيفَة *a successor,*
deputy, or *caliph* (compare in Italian *il podestà*), عَلَّامَة *very learned,*
رَاوِيَة *a traditionary.*

291. The following is a list of nouns which are feminine, not by
form or signification, but merely by usage.

A أَرْض *the earth, the ground, the floor.*

بِئْر *a well.*

حَرْب *war.*

خَمْر *wine.*

دِرْع *a coat of mail.*

دَلْو *a bucket.*

B دَار *a house.*

رَحًى *a mill.*

رِيح *wind.*

اَلشَّمْس *the sun.*

ضَبُع *a hyæna.*

[طَاغُوت *idol.*]

عَرُوض *metre.*

C عَصًا *a staff.*

عُقَاب *an eagle.*

عَقْرَب *a scorpion.*

عِير *a caravan.*

فَأْس *an axe.*

اَلْفِرْدَوْس *Paradise.*

أَفْعَى *a viper.*

[قَدُوم *an adze.*]

كَأْس *a cup.*

[كِرْش or كَرْش *the maw.*]

مَنْجَنُون *a water-wheel.*

مَنْجَنِيق *a catapult.*

مُوسَى *a razor.*

نَار *fire.*

نَعْل *a shoe or sandal.*

نَفْس *the soul.*

نَوًى *a traveller's destination.*

REM. Of these مَنْجَنِيق, ضَبُع, رِيح, دَلْو, دَار, دِرْع, خَمْر, حَرْب and نَار, are occasionally used as masculine; whilst دِرْع *a woman's shift*, شَمْس *a collar or pendant*, and فِرْدَوْس *a garden or park*, are masculine. Those who say مُوسًى instead of مُوسَى, regard the word of course as masculine.

D **292.** Masculine or feminine are :—

(a) Collective nouns (أَسْمَاءُ الْجِنْس), chiefly denoting animals and plants, which form a nomen unitatis; e.g. حَمَام *pigeons*, شَاءٌ *sheep or goats*, بَقَر *cattle*, جَرَاد *grasshoppers, locusts*, نَحْل *bees*; شَجَر *trees*, نَخْل *palm-trees*, تَمْر *dates*; [شَعِير *barley* (gen. masc.)]; سَحَاب *clouds*, لِبْن or لَبِن *bricks*, ذَهَب *gold*. These are masc. by form, fem. by signification (اَلْجَمَاعَة *totality*).

[(*b*) Collective nouns (أَشْبَاهُ ٱلْجَمْعِ or أَسْمَاءُ ٱلْجَمْعِ), denoting A rational beings and not forming a *nomen unitatis*; e.g. قَوْمٌ *one's people or tribe,* رَهْطٌ *do.,* نَفَرٌ *a small number of men* (3—7), نَاسٌ *men* (gen. masc.), تَجْرٌ *a company of merchants,* رَكْبٌ *a company of wayfarers,* etc. But أَهْلٌ *and* آلٌ *one's family,* are masc. D. G.]

(*c*) The names of the letters of the alphabet, which are more usually feminine; as هٰذِهِ ٱلْأَلِفُ, or هٰذَا ٱلْأَلِفُ, *this* elif.

[(*d*) The nomina verbi (*maṣdar*). One may say أَوْجَعَنِى ضَرْبُكَ B and أَوْجَعَتْنِى ضَرْبُكَ *your striking caused me pain**. D. G.]

(*e*) Words regarded merely as such. These may be masculine, following the gender of لَفْظٌ, or feminine, following that of كَلِمَةٌ or لُغَةٌ. A noun may also be masculine, taking the gender of ٱسْمٌ; a verb, taking that of فِعْلٌ; and a particle, taking that of حَرْفٌ. But a particle is more usually feminine, following the gender of أَدَاةٌ. The C verb كَانَ, *to be,* seems by common consent to be taken as feminine (كَانَ ٱلنَّاقِصَةُ, كَانَ ٱلتَّامَّةُ). Such mere words are treated like proper names, and therefore do not take the article, as هٰذَا مَاءٌ or مَاءٌ هٰذِهِ, *this word* مَاءٌ (*water*).

(*f*) A considerable number of nouns, of which the following are those that most frequently occur.

[إِبْطٌ *the armpit* (gen. masc.).]	بَطْنٌ *the belly* (gen. masc.). D
إِزَارٌ *an article of dress.*	[بَعِيرٌ *camel* (gen. masc.).]
آلٌ *the mirage.*	إِبْهَامٌ *the thumb* or *great toe* (gen. fem.).
بَشَرٌ *a human being, human beings.*	ثَدْىٌ *a breast* (*mamma*).

---

* [This seems to be the explanation of صَوْتٌ being used as a fem. noun, *Ḥamāsa* 78, vs. 1, هٰذِهِ ٱلصَّوْتُ *this crying.* Comp. Lane. D. G.]

A. ثَعْلَب‎ *a fox.*

جَنَاح‎ *a wing* (gen. masc.).

حَالٌ‎ *state, condition* (gen. fem.).

حَانُوتٌ‎ *a booth, a shop.*

[خَيَالٌ‎ *a phantom.*]

أَرْنَب‎ *a hare* (gen. fem.).

دُكَّانٌ‎ *a shop.*

B [ذِرَاعٌ‎ *cubit* (gen. fem.).]

دَنُوبٌ‎ *a large bucket.*

رُوحٌ‎ *spirit, soul* [when signifying a *celestial being* always masc.]

[زُقَاقٌ‎ *a street* or *lane.*]

C زَنْدٌ‎ *the upper of the two pieces of wood, used in producing fire* (gen. masc.).

سَبِيلٌ‎ *a path, a road.*

سُرًى‎ *journeying by night.*

سِكِّينٌ‎ *a knife* (gen. masc.).

سِلَاحٌ‎ *a weapon, weapons.*

D سُلْطَانٌ‎ [prop. *authority,* hence] *power, a sovereign.*

سَلْمٌ‎ *peace.*

سُلَّمٌ‎ *a ladder.*

سَمَآءٌ‎ *the sky* or *heaven, the clouds, rain.*

[سُورٌ‎ *a wall* (gen. masc.).]

سُوقٌ‎ *a market.*

إِصْبَع‎ *a finger* (gen. fem.).

صِرَاطٌ‎ *a way, a road* (via *strata*).

صُلْح‎ *peace.*

صَاع‎ *a measure for corn, etc.*

ضُحًى‎ *the forenoon.*

ضَرَبٌ‎ *white honey.*

[ضِرْسٌ‎ *a tooth.*]

طِبَاعٌ‎ *nature, natural disposition* [gen. fem.].

طَرِيقٌ‎ *a road.*

عَجُزٌ‎ *the hinder part, the rump* [gen. fem.].

عُرْسٌ‎ *a wedding, a marriage.*

عَسَلٌ‎ *honey.*

[عَنْبَرٌ‎ *ambergris.*]

عُنُقٌ‎ *the neck.*

عَنْكَبُوتٌ‎ *a spider* (gen. fem.).

فَرَسٌ‎ *a horse* [gen. fem.].

فُلْك‎ *a ship.*

[فِهْرٌ‎ *a stone for bruising perfume.*]

قِدْرٌ‎ *a pot, a kettle* (gen. fem.).

قَفًا‎ *the nape of the neck.*

قَلِيبٌ‎ *a well.*

قَوْسٌ‎ *a bow* (gen. fem.).

كَبِدٌ‎ *the liver.*

كُرَاعٌ *the tibia* or *shin-bone.*　　　مَعًى *an intestine* (gen. masc.).　A

لِسَانٌ *the tongue.*　　　مِلْحٌ *salt* (gen. fem.).

لَيْلٌ *the night* (gen. masc.).　　　[مُلْكٌ *dominion.*]

مِسْكٌ *musk* (gen. masc.).　　　[هُدًى *the right direction.*]

REM. *a.* زَنْدٌ *the bone* (either *radius* or *ulna*) *of the fore-arm,* سَمَاءٌ *a roof* or *ceiling,* and usually عُرْسٌ *a wedding-feast,* are masculine.　B

REM. *b.* The above list, and that contained in § 291, cannot lay claim either to absolute completeness or to perfect accuracy, since the usage of the language has varied considerably at different periods. For example, in later times فَمٌ, *the mouth,* and مَرْكَبٌ, *a boat* or *ship,* are used as feminine; whilst عَضُدٌ, *the upper arm,* كَتِفٌ, *the shoulder,* [كَرِشٌ, *the maw,*] and بِئْرٌ, *a well,* become masculine. The masculine gender too preponderates in later times over the feminine in words which were anciently of both genders, as نَارٌ *fire,* كَبِدٌ *the liver.*　C

293. From most adjectives and some substantives of the mascu-
line gender, feminines are formed by adding the terminations ـَةٌ, ـَى, or ـَاءُ (§ 290, *b*).

REM. Only ـَةٌ is appended to the masculine without farther affecting the form of the word; ـَى and ـَاءُ have forms distinct from the masculine, which must be learned by practice.

294. The most usual termination, by the mere addition of which to the masculine feminines are formed, is ـَةٌ; as عَظِيمٌ *great,* عَظِيمَةٌ;　D
ضَارِبٌ *striking,* ضَارِبَةٌ; نَدْمَانُ *repentant,* نَدْمَانَةٌ; فَرِحٌ *glad,* فَرِحَةٌ; مَضْرُوبٌ *struck,* مَضْرُوبَةٌ; جَدٌّ *a grandfather,* جَدَّةٌ *a grandmother;* فَتًى (for فَتَىٌ) *a young man,* فَتَاةٌ (for فَتَيَةٌ) *a young woman.*

[REM. *a.* The hèmza of the termination اءٌ of nouns derived from verbs tertiæ و or ى may be replaced, before ة, by the radical letter, as سَمَاوَةٌ from سَمَاءٌ, سِقَايَةٌ from سِقَاءٌ, *a water-carrier,* but the

A   forms with hemza, as عَزَاءَةٌ, سَقَّاءَةٌ, are preferable; comp. *Kāmil,*
p. 87, l. 10—15, and below § 299, rem. *c*, § 301, rem. *e*.]

REM. *b.* ةٌ is a compromise in orthography between the original
تٌ, *at*, the old pausal form هٌ, *ah*, and the modern اٌ, *a*, in which
last the *a* is silent (see the footnote to p. 7 supra). This view is
confirmed by the comparison of the other Semitic languages; see
Comp. Gr. 133—137.

B   **295.**   Feminines in ىَ are formed :—

(*a*)   From adjectives of the form فَعْلَانُ, the feminine of which
is فَعْلَى; as شَبْعَانُ *sated*, غَضْبَانُ *angry*, غَضْبَى; سَكْرَانُ *drunk*, سَكْرَى;
ظَمْآنُ *thirsty*, ظَمْأَى, عَطْشَانُ *hungry*, عَطْشَى; غَرْثَانُ غَرْثَى; شَبْعَى;
خَشْيَا خَشْيَانُ *timid, fearing*, مَلْأَى; مَلْآنُ *full*, مَلْآنُ.

(*b*)   From adjectives of the form أَفْعَلُ, when they have the
superlative signification, and are defined by the article or by a fol-
C   lowing genitive, in which case the feminine is فُعْلَى; as ٱلْأَكْبَرُ *the
largest*, ٱلْكُبْرَى; ٱلْأَصْغَرُ *the smallest*, ٱلصُّغْرَى; ٱلْأَعْظَمُ *the greatest*,
ٱلْعُظْمَى; كُبْرَى ٱلْمُدُنِ *the largest of the cities*.

REM. *a.*   Adjectives of the forms فَعْلَانُ and فُعْلَانُ form their
feminine by adding ةٌ; as سَيْفَانُ *tall and slender*, سَيْفَانَةٌ; عُرْيَانُ
naked, عُرْيَانَةٌ.

D   REM. *b.*   The feminine of ٱلْأَوَّلُ (for ٱلْأَوْءَلُ or ٱلْأَوْءَلُ) *the first*,
is ٱلْأُولَى; that of آخَرُ (for أَأْخَرُ) *other, another*, أُخْرَى. The latter
word can be used indefinitely, because it is superlative only in
form, not in signification. The numeral أَحَدٌ, *one*, has إِحْدَى.

REM. *c.*   There are some feminine adjectives of the form فُعْلَى,
not superlatives, without any corresponding masculines; as أُنْثَى
female, feminine, حُبْلَى *pregnant*, رُبَّى *which has recently yeaned* (of
a ewe or she-goat).

296. Feminines in ـَآءُ are formed from adjectives of the form A
أَفْعَلُ, which have not the comparative and superlative signification; as أَصْفَرُ *yellow*, صَفْرَآءُ; أَجْهَرُ *of pleasing aspect*, جَهْرَآءُ; أَحْدَبُ *hump-backed*, حَدْبَآءُ. Many of these adjectives are not in actual use in the masculine; as هَطْلَآءُ *heavy and continuous* (*rain*), حَسْنَآءُ *beautiful*, شَوْكَآءُ *rough to the feel* (a new dress), ٱلْعَرَبُ ٱلْعَرْبَآءُ *the Arabs of pure race*.

Rem. The form فَعْلَآءُ sometimes serves as feminine to فَعْلَانُ, B
e.g. جَذْلَانُ *joyful*, جَذْلَآءُ; حَيْرَانُ *perplexed, amazed*, حَيْرَى and حَيْرَاءُ.

297. All adjectives have not a separate form for the feminine. The following forms are of both genders.

(*a*) فَعُولٌ, when it has the meaning of فَاعِلٌ (transitive or intransitive), and is attached to a substantive in the singular, or serves as predicate to a substantive or a pronoun in the singular; as C
رَجُلٌ صَبُورٌ وَشَكُورٌ *a patient and grateful man*, ٱمْرَأَةٌ صَبُورٌ وَشَكُورٌ *a patient and grateful woman*; رَجُلٌ كَذُوبٌ *a lying man*, ٱمْرَأَةٌ كَذُوبٌ *a lying woman*; كَانَتْ صَبُورًا *she was patient*; رَأَيْتُهَا صَبُورًا *I saw that she was*, or *I thought her, patient*; [بَقَرَةٌ شَبُوبٌ *a full grown antelope*]. But if no substantive or pronoun be expressed, فَعُولٌ makes a feminine فَعُولَةٌ, and also if it has the meaning of مَفْعُولٌ; as رَأَيْتُ صَبُورَةً *I saw a patient* (*woman*); مَا لَهُ رَكُوبَةٌ وَلَا حَمُولَةٌ وَلَا حَلُوبَةٌ *he has not a* D
she-camel to ride, nor one to carry loads, nor one for milking, where رَكُوبَةٌ and حَلُوبَةٌ = مَرْكُوبَةٌ and مَحْلُوبَةٌ, whilst حَمُولَةٌ = حَامِلَةٌ.

Rem. *a*. Exceptions are rare; as عَدُوٌّ *hostile, an enemy*, fem. عَدُوَّةٌ; [and again, لَا حَلُوبَ فِي ٱلْبَيْتِ *there is no milch-ewe in the tent*, as we read in the tradition of Umm Maʿbad, نَاقَةٌ ضَبُوثٌ or نَاقَةٌ ضَغُوثٌ and شَاةٌ جَزُوزٌ *a shorn sheep*. D. G.]

A [REM. *b*. Hence the fem. nouns صَعُودٌ *an acclivity,* كَوُودٌ *a mountain-road difficult of ascent,* حَدُورٌ and هَبُوطٌ *a declivity.* D. G.]

(*b*) فَعِيلٌ, when it has the meaning of مَفْعُولٌ, and under the same conditions as فَعُولٌ; e.g. عَيْنٌ كَحِيلٌ *an eye adorned with kohl,* اِمْرَأَةٌ جَرِيحٌ *a wounded woman,* فَتَاةٌ قَتِيلٌ *a murdered woman;* but رَأَيْتُ قَتِيلَةَ ٱلْحَرُورِيَّةِ *I saw (the woman) whom the Ḥarūrīs had murdered;* هٰذِهِ أَكِيلَةُ سَبُعٍ *this is (a sheep) which has been (partly)*

B *eaten by a beast of prey.* If فَعِيلٌ has the meaning of فَاعِلٌ (transitive or intransitive), it forms a feminine in ـَة; as نَصِيرٌ *a helper,* نَصِيرَةٌ; شَفِيعٌ *an intercessor,* شَفِيعَةٌ; عَفِيفٌ *temperate, chaste,* عَفِيفَةٌ; مَرِيضٌ *sick,* مَرِيضَةٌ.

REM. Exceptions in either case are rare. For example: فَعْلَةٌ خَصْلَةٌ ذَمِيمَةٌ *a praiseworthy way of acting,* = حَمِيدَةٌ مَحْمُودَةٌ;

C *blameworthy habit,* = مَذْمُومَةٌ; and, on the other hand, مِلْحَفَةٌ جَدِيدٌ *a new wrapper,* إِنَّ رَحْمَةَ ٱللّٰهِ قَرِيبٌ مِنَ ٱلْمُحْسِنِينَ *verily God's mercy is nigh unto them who do well.*

(*c*) مِفْعَالٌ, مِفْعَلٌ, and مِفْعِيلٌ, which were originally nomina instrumenti (§ 228), but afterwards became intensive adjectives (§ 233, rem. *b*), under the same conditions as فَعُولٌ and فَعِيلٌ; e.g.

D اِمْرَأَةٌ مِغْشَمٌ *an obstinate, self-willed woman;* نَاقَةٌ مِذْعَانٌ *a docile she-camel;* جَارِيَةٌ مِعْطِيرٌ, or جَارِيَةٌ مِعْطَارٌ, *a young woman who uses much perfume;* but رَأَيْتُ مِعْطَارَةً *I saw (a woman) who uses much perfume.*

REM. Exceptions are rare; as مِسْكِينٌ *poor,* مِيقَانٌ *speaking the truth,* fem. مِسْكِينَةٌ, مِيقَانَةٌ [; but اِمْرَأَةٌ مِسْكِينٌ is allowed. D. G.]

[(*d*) Those adjectives that are properly infinitives (§ 230, rem. *c* and Vol. ii. § 136, *a*) e.g. قَلْبٌ, غَمٌّ, عَدْلٌ, دَنَسٌ, جُنُبٌ, جَدْبٌ, بُورٌ, and وَعْرٌ, مَحْضٌ and some others as جَبَانٌ, عُضَالٌ etc. D. G.]

REM. Adjectives which are, by their signification, applicable to females only, do not form a feminine in ة, when they designate an action or state as natural and permanent, or, at any rate, as lasting for a certain period of time (صِفَةٌ ثَابِتَةٌ); as حَامِلٌ *pregnant,* عَاقِرٌ, *barren,* كَاعِبٌ, نَاهِدٌ, *having swelling breasts,* طَامِثٌ, حَائِضٌ, عَارِكٌ, مُعْصِرٌ [مِيلَاثٌ 'Ibn Hišām 15, last l. R. S.] *menstruating,* طَالِقٌ *divorced,* عَاطِلٌ *without ornaments,* حَاسِرٌ *with the head and bust naked,* مُرْضِعٌ *giving suck,* مُتْئِمٌ *bearing twins,* مُطْفِلٌ *having a child or a young one with her,* مُشْدِنٌ *having a fawn with her,* مُجْرٍ *having a whelp with her,* [حَصَانٌ *chaste,* رَزَانٌ *staid,* عَانِسٌ *unmarried and of middle age*] and likewise مُعَضِّلٌ, مُطَرِّقٌ, مُرَاسِلٌ. But if they designate the said action or state as beginning, actually in progress, or about to begin (صِفَةٌ حَادِثَةٌ), they form a feminine in ة; as هِيَ حَائِضَةٌ ٱلْيَوْمَ *she is menstruating to-day;* هِيَ طَالِقَةٌ غَدًا *she will be divorced to-morrow;* لِكُلِّ حَامِلَةٍ تَمَامٌ *every woman who is pregnant has her time or term;* يَوْمَ تَرَوْنَهَا تَذْهَلُ كُلُّ مُرْضِعَةٍ عَمَّا أَرْضَعَتْ *on the day when ye shall see it, every woman who is suckling* (in the act of giving suck) *shall become heedless of that which she has been suckling.*

3. *The Numbers of Nouns.*

298. Nouns have, like verbs, *three* numbers, the singular, dual, and plural (see § 81).

299. The *dual* is formed by adding ان to the singular (omitting, of course, the tenwīn); as كِتَابٌ *a book,* كِتَابَانِ; رَثَأٌ *a fawn,* or رَثَأَانِ رَثَآنِ.

Rem. *a.* If the singular ends in ـَة, ة is changed into ت (see § 294, rem.); as أُمَّةٌ *a nation,* أُمَّتَانِ. But أَلْيَةٌ *a buttock,* and خُصْيَةٌ *a testicle,* usually make أَلْيَانِ and خُصْيَانِ.

Rem. *b.* If the singular ends in a quiescent ى (ـِى or ـَى), which was originally ى *mobile* (compare § 167, *a, β, a*), it becomes so again in the dual; as فَتًى *a youth,* for فَتَىْ, فَتَيَانِ; رَحًى *a mill,* رَحَيَانِ; حِمًى *interdicted ground,* حِمَيَانِ; مَرْمًى *a butt for shooting,* مَرْمَيَانِ; فَتْوَى *a legal opinion,* فَتْوَيَانِ; حُبْلَى *pregnant,* حُبْلَيَانِ; حُبَارَى *a bustard,* حُبَارَيَانِ. From حِمًى the form حِمَوَانِ is said to occur. If the singular ends in a quiescent ا (ـِا or ـَا), which was originally و *mobile* (compare § 167, *a, β, a*), the و is restored in the dual; as عَصًا *a staff,* for عَصَوٌ, عَصَوَانِ; قَفًا *the nape of the neck,* قَفَوَانِ.—If the singular of a quadriliteral noun ends in a quiescent ى, which was originally a و, the و is *not* restored in the dual, but becomes ى *mobile,* as مِلْهًى *a musical instrument* (from لَهَوَ for لَهَوْ), مِلْهَيَانِ; أَعْشَى *purblind* (from عَشِىَ for عَشِوَ), أَعْشَيَانِ; مُسَمًّى *named* (from اِسْمٌ for سِمْوٌ), مُسَمَّيَانِ; مُرْضًى *rendered contented* (from رَضِوَ for رَضِوَ), مُرْضَيَانِ. A solitary exception seems to be مِذْرَوَانِ *the upper parts of the two buttocks,* the singular of which, if used, would be مِذْرًى.

Rem. *c.* The hèmza of the termination ـَاءُ, denoting the feminine (§ 296), becomes و; as بَطْحَاءُ *a wide water-course or bottom,* بَطْحَاوَانِ; صَحْرَاءُ *a desert,* صَحْرَاوَانِ; حَمْرَاءُ *red,* حَمْرَاوَانِ; صَفْرَاءُ *yellow,* صَفْرَاوَانِ. Forms like صَحْرَاآنِ, حَمْرَاآنِ, and even صَحْرَايَانِ, are, however, said by some to be admissible.—In the termination ـَاءُ, when sprung from a radical و or ى, the hèmza may either be retained or changed into و, though the former is preferable; as كِسَاءٌ *a dress* (for كِسَاوٌ), كِسَاآنِ or كِسَاوَانِ; رِدَاءٌ *a mantle* (for رِدَاوٌ), رِدَاآنِ or رِدَاوَانِ. Some, however, admit the forms رِدَايَانِ.

A and كَسَايَانِ (comp. § 294, rem. *a*). In the case of a هَمْزَةُ ٱلْإِلْحَاقِ (see § 259), the better course is to change it into و; as عِلْبَاءٌ, حِرْبَاءَانِ or حِرْبَاوَانِ, حِرْبَاءٌ; عِلْبَاءَانِ or عِلْبَاوَانِ. If the hèmza of ـَآءُ be radical, it cannot be changed into و; as قَرَّاءٌ (from قَرَأَ), وُضَّاءَانِ, (وَضُوُ from) وُضَّاءٌ.—In words of five or more letters, the rejection of the terminations ى and ـَآءُ is admissible; as خَوْزَلَى *a sluggish mode of walking,* خَوْزَلَانِ; زَبَعْرَى *having a hairy face,*

B قَبَعْثَرَى; قَاصِعَاءٌ *a big, stout camel,* قَبَعْثَرَانِ; زَبَعْرَانِ *a jerboa's hole,* قَاصِعَانِ; خُنْفَسَاءٌ *a black beetle,* خُنْفَسَانِ; instead of خَوْزَلَيَانِ, زَبَعْرَيَانِ, قَبَعْثَرَيَانِ, and قَاصِعَاوَانِ, خُنْفَسَاوَانِ.

Rem. *d.* If a ى has been elided in the singular after a kèsra and before a ḍamma with tènwìn (see § 167, *b*, *β*), it is restored in the dual; as رَامٍ, for رَامِيُ; رَامِيَانِ, رَاضٍ, for رَاضِيُ; رَاضِيَانِ; شَجٍ,

C for شَجِيُ; شَجِيَانِ (compare § 166, *a*).—In like manner, an elided و is restored in the dual of some words; as حَمٌ, أَخٌ, أَخُو, أَبٌ (for أَبُو), أَخَوَانِ, أَبَوَانِ, (حَمُو), حَمَوَانِ, (أَخَانِ) and ٱبْنٌ, ٱسْمٌ (for بَنَى) and ٱسْمُو) have ٱبْنَانِ, ٱسْمَانِ; بِنْتٌ or ٱبْنَةٌ makes ٱبْنَتَانِ or بِنْتَانِ. دَمٌ, يَدٌ, and فَمٌ, have يَدَانِ, دَمَانِ, and فَمَانِ, rarely يَدَيَانِ, دَمَيَانِ, still more rarely دَمَوَانِ and فَمَوَانِ. فَمِيَانِ. حَرٌ makes حِرَانِ; هَنٌ, هَنَوَانِ or هَنَانِ.

D Rem. *e.* If the third radical has been elided before ة in the singular, it is not restored; as لُغَةٌ, for لُغْوَةٌ, أَمَتَانِ; أَمَةٌ, for أَمَوَةٌ, لُغَتَانِ; لِثَةٌ, for لِثْيَةٌ, شَفَتَانِ; شَفَةٌ, for شَفْهَةٌ, لِثَتَانِ; سَنَةٌ, for سَنَهَةٌ, سَنَتَانِ; هَنَةٌ, for هَنَوَةٌ, هَنَتَانِ.

Rem. *f.* The dual is commonly employed in Arabic to signify two individuals of a class, as رَجُلَانِ *two men,* or a pair of anything, as جَلَمَانِ, or مِقَصَّانِ, *a pair of scissors.* When two objects are constantly associated, in virtue either of natural connection or opposition, a dual may be formed from one of them, which shall designate both, and the preference given to the one over the other is termed تَغْلِيبٌ, *the making it prevail over the other.* For example: أَبَوَانِ *father and mother,* from أَبٌ *father ;* أَخَوَانِ *brother and sister,* from أَخٌ *brother ;* اَلْقَمَرَانِ *the sun and moon,* from اَلْقَمَرُ *the moon ;* اَلْمَشْرِقَانِ *the east and west,* from اَلْمَشْرِقُ *the east ;* [اَلْعِرَاقَانِ *Baṣra and Kūfa ;* اَلرَّقَّتَانِ *Raḳḳa and Rāfiḳa ;* اَلْفُرَاتَانِ *the Euphrates and Tigris* *;] اَلْحَسَنَانِ *ĕl-Ḥasan and ĕl-Ḥosein,* from اَلْحَسَنُ *ĕl-Ḥasan* (the elder son of 'Alī) ; اَلْعُمَرَانِ *'Omar 'ibn ĕl-Ḥaṭṭāb and 'Abū Bĕkr,* from عُمَرُ *'Omar.* Compare in Sanskrit *pitarau,* "father and mother," *bhrātarau,* "brother and sister," *rōdasī,* "heaven and earth," *ahanī,* "day and night," *uṣāsau,* "morning and evening," *Mitrā,* "Mitra and Varuṇa," etc.

[REM. *g.* The Arabs like to designate two different objects by the dual of an adjective used as a substantive and denoting a quality that the two have in common, as اَلْأَبْرَدَانِ *the two coolest* (of things) for *morning and evening ;* اَلْأَطْيَبَانِ *the two best ones for eating and coitus ;* اَلْأَحْمَرَانِ *the two red ones for meat and wine ;* اَلْأَسْوَدَانِ *or* اَلْجَدِيدَانِ *dates and water ;* اَلْأَبْيَضَانِ *milk and water ;* اَلْأَصْغَرَانِ *the two new ones for the night and the day ;* اَلْأَجَدَّانِ *the heart and the tongue ;* اَلْكَرِيمَتَانِ *the two eyes ;* اَلْأَخْبَثَانِ *urine and dung or sleeplessness and disquietude of mind ;* اَلرَّافِدَانِ *the Tigris and Euphrates.* D. G.]

REM. *h.* The dual is sometimes formed from broken plurals (§ 300, *b*), or from أَشْبَاهُ ٱلْجَمْعِ (§ 290, *a, ε*), to designate two bodies or troops (جَمَاعَتَانِ or فِرْقَتَانِ) of the objects in question. E.g. إِبِلَانِ *two herds of camels* (إِبِلٌ), غَنَمَانِ *two flocks of sheep or*

---

* [The dual of place-names in poetry sometimes means only the two sides of the town ; see Schol. on 'Ibn Hišām, p. 121, l. 16. R. S.]

goats (غَنَمٌ), جِمَالَانِ *two herds of he-camels* (from جِمَالٌ, pl. of A

جَمَلٌ), لِقَاحَانِ *two herds of milch-camels* (from لِقَاحٌ, pl. of لِقْحَةٌ);

بَيْنَ رِمَاحَىْ مَالِكٍ وَنَهْشَلٍ *between the (collected) spears of (the tribes*

of) Mālik *and* Nahšal (from رُمْحٌ, pl. of رِمَاحٌ; ٱلْأُصُولَانِ, *the*

fundamental principles of theology (أُصُولُ ٱلدِّينِ) *and of law*

(أُصُولُ ٱلْفِقْهِ), from أُصُولٌ, pl. of أَصْلٌ *a root:* [comp. in Hebrew

הַמֹּתְנַיִם].   B

REM. *i.* Proper names of the class مُرَكَّبٌ مَزْجِىٌّ (§ 264) vary
in their mode of forming the dual. If the first part of the compound be indeclinable and the second declinable, the latter takes
the termination ـَانِ; as مَعْدِى كَرِبَانِ, مَعْدِى كَرِبُ. But if both
parts be indeclinable, as in سِيبَوَيْهِ,—or, when taken together, form
a proposition, as in تَأَبَّطَ شَرًّا,—recourse must be had to a periphrasis
with ذُو *possessor of;* as ذَوَا سِيبَوَيْهِ, ذَوَا تَأَبَّطَ شَرًّا, *two men called* C
Sībawèih *or* Ta'abbaṭa šarran. If the first part be in the status
constructus, it is simply put in the dual, as عَبْدَا مَنَافٍ *two men*
called عَبْدُ مَنَافٍ, 'Abd Menāf, أَبَوَا زَيْدٍ *two men called* أَبُو زَيْدٍ, 'Abū
Zèid, ٱبْنَا ٱلزُّبَيْرِ *two men called* ٱبْنُ ٱلزُّبَيْرِ, 'Ibnu 'z-Zubèir. But in
the case of compounds with ٱبْنٌ, أَبٌ, etc., it is allowable to put the
second part in the dual likewise, as أَبَوَا زَيْدَيْنِ.

300. There are two kinds of *plurals* in Arabic.   D

(*a*) The one, which has only a single form, is called ٱلْجَمْعُ
ٱلصَّحِيحُ, or ٱلْجَمْعُ ٱلْمُصَحَّحُ, *the sound* or *perfect plural* (*pluralis*
sanus), and جَمْعُ ٱلسَّلَامَةِ, or ٱلْجَمْعُ ٱلسَّالِمُ, *the complete* or *entire*
plural, because all the vowels and consonants of the singular are
retained in it.

(*b*) The other, which has various forms, is called ٱلْجَمْعُ ٱلْمُكَسَّرُ,

A or جَمْعُ ٱلتَّكْسِيرِ, *the broken plural* (*pluralis fractus*), because it is more or less altered from the singular by the addition or elision of consonants, or the change of vowels.

301. The pluralis sanus of masculine nouns is formed by adding the termination ـُونَ to the singular; as سَارِقٌ *a thief*, سَارِقُونَ. The pluralis sanus of feminine nouns, which end in ةٌ, is formed by changing ةٌ into ـَاتٌ, as سَارِقَةٌ, سَارِقَاتٌ; of those which do not

B end in ةٌ, by adding ـَاتٌ to the sing., as مَرْيَمُ *Mary*, مَرْيَمَاتٌ.

REM. *a.* If the singular ends in élif maksûra, with or without tènwîn (ـًى or ـَى),—or in kèsra with tènwîn (ٍ), arising out of ـٍى (§ 167, *b*, β),—or in a quiescent ى preceded by kèsra (ـِى), arising out of ـٍى,—then the rules laid down in § 166, *b*, *a* and β, and § 167, *a*, β, *c*, are to be observed. E.g. مُصْطَفًى, for مُصْطَفَى (§ 245), *chosen*, مُصْطَفَوْنَ, for مُصْطَفَيُونَ, and in the oblique cases

C قَاضٍ; مُصْطَفَيْنَ, for مُصْطَفَيِينَ; مُوسَى *Moses*, مُوسَوْنَ for مُوسَيُونَ; for قَاضِى, *a judge*, قَاضُونَ, for قَاضِيُونَ, and in the oblique cases اَلْحَافُونَ, for قَاضِيينَ; اَلْحَافِى, for اَلْحَافِيُ, *the barefooted*, for اَلْحَافِيُونَ; اَلصُّغْرَى *the smallest*, حُبْلَى ; حُبْلَيَاتٌ *pregnant*, for اَلصُّغْرَيَاتٌ ; سُمَانَى *a quail*, سُمَانَيَاتٌ.

REM. *b.* The gèzma of the middle radical in feminine substantives of the forms فَعْل and فَعْلَة, فِعْل and فِعْلَة, فُعْل and فُعْلَة,

D derived from roots which are not mediæ radicalis geminatæ or mediæ و vel ى, passes in forming the plural into a vowel, which may either be the same as that of the first syllable, or in all cases fètḥa. E.g. دَعْدٌ *Da'd*, دَعَدَاتٌ; أَرْضٌ *the earth, the ground*, أَرَضَاتٌ; جَفْنَةٌ *a dish*, جَفَنَاتٌ, قَصْعَةٌ ،قَصَعَاتٌ; عَبْلَةٌ *'Abla*, عَبَلَاتٌ (אַרָצוֹת); قَرْيَةٌ *a village*, قَرَيَاتٌ; غَدْوَةٌ *a coming in the morning*, غَدَوَاتٌ; كِسْرَةٌ *a fragment*, كِسَرَاتٌ or كِسْرَاتٌ; هِنْدٌ *Hind*, هِنْدَاتٌ or هِنَدَاتٌ; جُمْلٌ *Guml*, جُمْلَاتٌ or جُمُلَاتٌ; سِدْرَةٌ *the lotus-tree*, سِدَرَاتٌ or سِدْرَاتٌ; or

ظُلْمَةٌ ; جُمَلَاتٌ *darkness*, ظُلُمَاتٌ or ظُلَمَاتٌ ; غُرْفَةٌ *an upper chamber*, A

غُرَفَاتٌ or غُرُفَاتٌ. In the forms فُعْل and فُعْلَة, the gezma may also

be retained, as كَسْرَاتٌ, ظُلُمَاتٌ [غُرُفَاتٌ]; but in فَعْلَة this can

be done only by poetic license, as رَفْضَاتٌ from رَفْضَةٌ *looseness* or

slackness (of the joints), زَفَرَاتٌ from زَفْرَةٌ *a sigh*. Names of men of

the form فَعْلَة have likewise فَعَلَاتٌ, as طَلْحَةُ *Talha*, طَلَحَاتٌ ;

حَمْزَةُ *Hamza*, حَمَزَاتٌ. The word عُرْس or عُرُس, *a wedding* or

marriage, has عُرُسَاتٌ.—In فُعْلَة, if the third radical be و, the form B

فَعَلَاتٌ is not admissible, as ذَرْوَةٌ *a summit*, ذَرَوَاتٌ or ذُرُوَاتٌ (but not

ذَرَوَاتٌ). A rare exception is جِرْوَاتٌ from جِرْوَةٌ *a whelp*. [If the

third radical be ى, the form فَعَلَاتٌ is likewise disapproved. One

may say لِحْيَاتٌ, as كَسْرَاتٌ, but not لِحَيَاتٌ, instead of which one

uses لِحًى. R. S.]—In فُعْلَة, if the third radical be ى, the form

فُعَلَاتٌ is inadmissible, as رُقْيَةٌ *a charm*, كُلْيَةٌ *a kidney*, رُقْيَاتٌ, C

كُلْيَاتٌ (but not كُلَيَاتٌ, رُقَيَاتٌ).—If the middle radical be و or ى,

the gezma of these three forms is retained ; as جَوْزَةٌ *a nut*, جَوْزَاتٌ ;

رَوْضَةٌ *a garden*, رَوْضَاتٌ ; بَيْضَةٌ *an egg, a helmet*, بَيْضَاتٌ ; عَيْبَةٌ *a fault*,

عَيْبَاتٌ ; دِيمَةٌ (for دِيْمَةٌ) *a lasting, still rain*, دِيمَاتٌ ; بِيعَةٌ (for بِيْعَةٌ)

a church, بِيعَاتٌ ; دُولَةٌ (for دُوْلَةٌ) *a turn of fortune, a vicissitude*,

دُولَاتٌ. The vowel fètha is, however, admitted dialectically*,

especially in the form فَعَلَة, as جَوَزَاتٌ, بَيَضَاتٌ, دِيَمَاتٌ, بِيَعَاتٌ, D

دُوَلَاتٌ.—Substantives of the forms فُعْلَة, derived from verbs med.

rad. gemin. always retain the gezma ; as ذَرَّةٌ *a mote*, ذَرَّاتٌ ; شِدَّةٌ

a charge or *attack*, شِدَّاتٌ ; عِدَّةٌ *a certain number, a few*, عِدَّاتٌ ;

سُرَّةٌ *a navel*, سُرَّاتٌ. The same is the case with all adjectives, as

عِلْجَةٌ *fat* ; سَهْلَةٌ *easy*, سَهْلَاتٌ ; (ضَخْمَاتٌ not) ضَخْمَةٌ *big*, ضَخْمَةٌ

---

* [Viz. in the dialect of Hudèil, according to Zamaḥšari, *Fāik*,

i. 43. D. G.]

A   *and strong,* عِلْجَاتٌ : حُلْوَةٌ *sweet,* حُلْوَاتٌ. Exceptions are, رَبْعَةٌ *of middle stature,* رَبْعَاتٌ or رَبَعَاتٌ, and لَجْبَةٌ *having little milk* (of a sheep or goat), لَجَبَاتٌ.

Rem. *c.* If و and ى, as third radicals, reject their fètha in the fem. singular, and become quiescent before ة, passing into ١ (§ 214, and § 7, rem. *c* and *d*), they are restored in the plural along with the vowel. E.g. صَلَوةٌ or صَلَاةٌ, *prayer* (for صَلَوَةٌ), صَلَوَاتٌ ; قَنَاةٌ,

B   *a cane, spear, tube* (for قَنَوَةٌ), قَنَوَاتٌ ; فَتَاةٌ, *a young woman* (for فَتَيَةٌ), فَتَيَاتٌ ; مُرْمَاةٌ, *thrown* (for مُرْمَيَةٌ), مُرْمَيَاتٌ (compare § 167, *a,* β, a, with § 166, *a*).

Rem. *d.* If the third radical has been elided in the sing. before ةٌ, it may be restored in the plural or not, according to usage.

E.g. عِضَةٌ (for عِضْوَةٌ or عِضْهَةٌ) *a thorny tree,* عِضَوَاتٌ and عِضَهَاتٌ ; شَفَةٌ (for

C   سَنَةٌ (for سَنْوَةٌ or سَنْهَةٌ) *a year,* سَنَوَاتٌ and سَنَهَاتٌ ; شَفَةٌ (for شَفْوَةٌ) *a lip,* شَفَوَاتٌ or شَفَهَاتٌ ; أَمَةٌ (for أَمَوَةٌ) *a female slave,* هَنَاتٌ or أَمَاتٌ ; هَنَةٌ (for هَنَوَةٌ), *a thing,* هَنَوَاتٌ or أَمَوَاتٌ (for ظُبْوَةٌ) *the point of a weapon,* ظُبَاتٌ ; بُرَةٌ (for بُرْوَةٌ) *an armlet, a ring,* بُرَاتٌ ; ثُبَةٌ (for ثُبْوَةٌ) *a troop or band,* ثُبَاتٌ ; لِثَةٌ (for لِثْيَةٌ) *the gum,* لِثَاتٌ ; رِئَةٌ (for رِئْيَةٌ) *a lung,* رِئَاتٌ ; مِئَةٌ (for مِئْيَةٌ) *a hundred,* مِئَاتٌ.—بِنْتٌ or اِبْنَةٌ (for بَنْيَةٌ), *a daughter,* makes بَنَاتٌ ; and أُخْتٌ (for أَخَوَةٌ), *a sister,* أَخَوَاتٌ.

D   Rem. *e.* The hèmza in the terminations اٰءٌ and ٓاءٌ is subject to the same rules in the plural as in the dual (§ 299, rem. *c*). Hence from اٰءٌ, دَكَّاءُ, دَكَّآءٌ, بَرْقَآءُ, صَحْرَآءُ, سَمَآءُ, are formed دَكَّاوَاتٌ, صَحْرَاوَاتٌ, سَمَاوَاتٌ or سَمٰوَاتٌ, بَرْقَاوَاتٌ.—Words of five or more letters sometimes reject the terminations ى and اٰءٌ (see § 299, rem. *c*); as قَاصِعَاتٌ, قَاصِعَآءُ *a jerboa's hole,* حُبَارَيَاتٌ or حُبَارَاتٌ, حُبَارَى.

302. The pluralis sanus masc. is formed from :—

(*a*) Proper names of men (excepting those which end in ةٌ, as

طَلْحَة), their diminutives, and the diminutives of common nouns A
which denote rational beings; as عُبَيْدٌ ; عُثْمَانُونَ 'Othmān,
'Obèid (dimin. of عَبْدٌ 'Abd), رُجَيْلٌ ; عُبَيْدُونَ (dimin. of رَجُلٌ a man),
شُوَيْعِرُونَ ; شُوَيْعِرٌ (dimin. of شَاعِرٌ) an inferior poet, رُجَيْلُونَ.

(b) Verbal adjectives which form their fem. by adding ـَة.

(c) Adjectives of the form أَفْعَلُ, which have the comparative and
superlative signification. [The corroboratives of كُلٌّ viz. أَكْتَعُ ,أَجْمَعُ,
etc. have also the plur. san. masc., though by their fem. sing. جَمْعَاءُ, B
كَتْعَاءُ, etc. they might seem to belong rather to the class of
adjectives exemplified by أَصْفَرُ, etc. § 296. For the plur. fem. see
§ 304, II. 2, rem. D. G.]

(d) The relative adjectives in ـِيٌّ.

(e) The words ابْنٌ (for بَنَى) a son, عَالَمٌ one of the four classes
of created beings, أَرْضٌ the earth, أَهْلٌ one's family, إِوَزٌّ the goose,
ذُو the possessor (of a thing); which make بَنُونَ ,عَالَمُونَ ,أَرْضُونَ C
(rarely أَرَضُونَ), أَهْلُونَ ,إِوَزُّونَ and ذَوُونَ (used only in the construct
state ذَوُو, see § 340, rem. c)*.

REM. a. Adjectives, however, have the plur. sanus masc. only
when joined to substantives denoting rational beings.

REM. b. Plurales fracti are also formed from substantives and
adjectives that have the plur. sanus masc., but more especially from
adjectives when used substantively. D

REM. c. To the words enumerated under (e) may be added
عِلِّيُّونَ, the highest heavens, and أُولُو or أُلُو (construct form of

---

* In a poem of ĕn-Nābiġa (Ahlw. App. 13, vs. 5) we find تُبَّعُونَ
from تُبَّعٌ, and in the commentary on the Dīw. of Hudèil, p. 120,
last l. بُوهُونَ from بُوهٌ. We ought to mention also the expressions
عَمِلَ بِهِ ٱلْعِمِلِّينَ and بَلَغْتَ مِنَّا ٱلْبَلَغِينَ ,لَقِيتُ مِنْهُ ٱلْبَرَحِينَ.

A أُولُونَ, with the first syllable short, see § 340, rem. *c*), *possessors*, which have no singular; as also the numerals denoting the *tens*, from 20 up to 90 (§ 323). Further, حُشٌّ *a privy*, حُشُّونَ; هَنٌ *a thing*, هَنُونَ; حِرٌ *vulva*, حِرُونَ; and the rarer forms أَبُونَ, أَخُونَ, from أَبٌ and أَخٌ.

REM. *d.* Some fem. nouns in ةٌ, especially those of which the third radical (و, ي, ه) has been elided, have a plur. sanus masc., the termination ةٌ disappearing entirely; as حَرَّةٌ *a stony, volcanic*

B *district*, حَرُّونَ (and, very irregularly, أَحَرُّونَ); عِضَةٌ *a thorny tree*, عِضُونَ; رِئَةٌ *a lung*, رِئُونَ; كُرَةٌ *a ball, a sphere*, كُرُونَ; قُلَةٌ *a stick used by children at play*, قُلُونَ [cas. obliq. قِلِينَ]; سَنَةٌ *a year*, سِنُونَ. From the oblique case of this last word, viz. سِنِينَ, arises a secondary formation سِنِينٌ, [like مِئِينٌ § 325, rem. *a.* Comp. also ii. § 108].

REM. *e.* In proper names of the class مُرَكَّبٌ مَزْجِيٌّ (§ 264),

C the formation of the plural is analogous to that of the dual (§ 299, rem. *h*). Thus مَعْدِيكَرِبُ, in which the second member only is declinable, makes مَعْدِيكَرِبُونَ; but سِيبَوَيْهِ and تَأَبَّطَ شَرًّا, which are wholly indeclinable, form ذَوُو سِيبَوَيْهِ and ذَوُو تَأَبَّطَ شَرًّا, *men called Sîbawèih and Ta'abbaṭa šarran.* Construct compounds, like عَبْدُ آبَاءُ زَيْدٍ, عَبْدُو مَنَافٍ, form ابْنُ ٱلزُّبَيْرِ, أَبُو زَيْدٍ, مَنَافٍ, and أَبْنَاءُ ٱلزُّبَيْرِ, *men called 'Abd Menâf, 'Abû Zèid, and 'Ibnu 'z-Zubèir;*

D but in the case of compounds with ابْنُ, أَبٌ, etc., it is also allowable to say آبَاءُ زَيْدِينَ and the like.—It may be added that compounds with ابْنُ, when they are the names, not of persons, but of animals or other objects (see § 191, rem. *b*, 6), take the feminine plural بَنَاتٌ (from بِنْتٌ or ابْنَةٌ); e.g. ابْنُ عِرْسٍ *a weasel*, ابْنُ مَاءٍ *a water-fowl*, ابْنُ نَعْشٍ *any one of the stars in the tail of the Great Bear*, بَنَاتُ عِرْسٍ, etc.

[REM. *f.* If a word in the status constructus is put in the plural, A
the following genitive of possession may be put also in the plural,
as فِعْلُ ٱلْقَلْبِ; pl. شِبْهُ ٱلْجَمْعِ or أَشْبَاهُ ٱلْجَمْعِ or أَشْبَاهُ ٱلْجُمُوعِ
or أَصْحَابُ ٱلْبُرُدِ, صَاحِبُ ٱلْبَرِيدِ; أَفْعَالُ ٱلْقَلْبِ or أَفْعَالُ ٱلْقُلُوبِ
بَيْتُ ٱلْمَالِ; لَيَالِى ٱلْجَمْعِ has لَيْلَةُ ٱلْجُمْعَةِ; أَصْحَابُ ٱلْبَرِيدِ
بُيُوتُ ٱلْأَمْوَالِ; etc. D. G.]

303. The pluralis sanus fem. is formed from :— B

(*a*) Proper names of women, and such names of men as end in
ـَة; as زَيْنَبُ *Zeineb*, زَيْنَبَاتٌ; هِنْدُ *Hind*, هِنْدَاتٌ; عَزَّةُ *'Azza*, عَزَّاتٌ;
طَلْحَةُ *Talha* (a man's name), طَلَحَاتٌ (§ 301, rem. *b*).

REM. According to some grammarians the plur. sanus fem.
may be formed from *any* word ending in ـَة; as ظَبْيَةٌ *a gazelle*,
ظَبْيَاتٌ; قَرْيَةٌ *a village*, قَرْيَاتٌ; عَلَّامَةٌ *a very learned man*, عَلَّامَاتٌ.

(*b*) Feminine adjectives, the masculine gender of which has the C
pluralis sanus.

(*c*) Feminine nouns in ـَى and ـَآء; as حُبْلَى *pregnant*, حُبْلَيَاتٌ;
ذِكْرَى *memory*, ذِكْرَيَاتٌ; ضَرَّآءُ *distress*, ضَرَّاوَاتٌ (§ 301, rem. *e*);
حُبَارَى *a bustard*, حُبَارَيَاتٌ.

(*d*) The names of the letters, which are usually feminine (§ 292, *b*);
as أَلِفٌ *an elif*, أَلِفَاتٌ; مِيمٌ *an m*, مِيمَاتٌ.

(*e*) The names of the months; as ٱلْمُحَرَّمُ *the Moharram*, D
مُحَرَّمَاتٌ; رَمَضَانُ *Ramadān*, رَمَضَانَاتٌ; شَوَّالُ *Šauwāl*, شَوَّالَاتٌ.

(*f*) The feminine nomina verbi (§ 196), and all nomina verbi of
the derived forms (§ 202); as تَعْرِيفٌ *a definition*, تَعْرِيفَاتٌ; إِقْطَاعٌ
a feof, إِقْطَاعَاتٌ; اِصْطِلَاحٌ *a technical term*, اِصْطِلَاحَاتٌ.

REM. The nomina verbi of the second and fourth forms, when
used in a concrete sense, admit also of a pluralis fractus; as تَصْنِيفٌ,

A   تَأْلِيفٌ, *a literary composition, a book,* تَصَانِيفُ, تَوَالِيفُ (compare

§ 136); تَوَارِيخُ; تَأْرِيخٌ *a date, an era, a chronicle,* تَبَارِيحُ *distresses,*

difficulties; تَبَاشِيرُ *annunciations, prognostics;* تَعَاجِيبُ *wonders,*

marvels; إِرْجَافٌ *a false rumour,* أَرَاجِيفُ; إِسْنَادٌ *a chain or series*

of authorities, أَسَانِيدُ.

B   (*g*) Substantives of foreign origin, even when they denote persons;

as سُرَادِقٌ *an awning, a tent,* سُرَادِقَاتٌ; بِيمَارِسْتَانٌ *a hospital,*

بِيمَارِسْتَانَاتٌ; شَادُرْوَانٌ *a jet d'eau, a fountain,* شَادُرْوَانَاتٌ; أَغَا *an Aga,*

أَغَوَاتٌ; بَاشَا *a Pasha,* بَاشَوَاتٌ; أُسْتَا (for أُسْتَاذٌ) *a teacher,* أُسْتَوَاتٌ.

   (*h*) Many masc. substantives, which have no plur. fractus; and

some fem. nouns, which have not a fem. termination; as سِبَحْلٌ *a*

stout camel, سِبَحْلَاتٌ; حَمَّامٌ *a warm bath,* حَمَّامَاتٌ; جَمَادٌ *an*

C *inanimate or inorganic thing,* جَمَادَاتٌ; حَيَوَانٌ *a living thing, an*

animal, حَيَوَانَاتٌ; عَقَارٌ *landed property,* عَقَارَاتٌ; مَاجَرَى *an event*

or occurrence (lit. مَا جَرَى *what happened or occurred*), مَاجَرَيَاتٌ;

أَهْلٌ *one's family or relations,* أَهْلَاتٌ or أَهَلَاتٌ, which some, however,

derive (according to § 301, rem. *b*) from أَهْلَةٌ; عِيرٌ *a caravan of loaded*

camels, عِيرَاتٌ or عِيَرَاتٌ; سَمَاءٌ *the sky or heavens,* سَمَاوَاتٌ (though this

word is also masc.); أَرْضٌ *the earth or ground,* أَرَضَاتٌ (see § 301,

D rem. *b*); مَنْجَنُونٌ *a waterwheel,* مَنْجَنُونَاتٌ; عُرْسٌ or عُرُسٌ *a wedding*

or marriage, عُرُسَاتٌ. From أَرْبَعِينَ *a collection of forty traditions* is

formed أَرْبَعِينَاتٌ.

   (*i*) Verbal adjectives, which are used in the plural as substantives;

as مَوْجُودٌ *entities* (from كَائِنٌ *being*); مَوْجُودَاتٌ *beings* (from كَائِنَاتٌ

found, existing); مَخْلُوقٌ *creatures* (from مَخْلُوقَاتٌ *created*); مُصَنَّفَاتٌ

literary compositions, works (from مُصَنَّفٌ *arranged, classified*);

مُجَلَّدَاتٌ *bound books, volumes* (from مُجَلَّدٌ *covered with skin,* A *bound*).

(*j*) All diminutives, except those specified in § 302, *a*; as جُبَيْلٌ *a hillock*, جُبَيْلَاتٌ; كُتَيِّبٌ *a little book*, كُتَيِّبَاتٌ.

304. The more common forms of the plur. fractus of substantives and adjectives, which are derived from triliteral roots, and in none of which (excepting أَفْعَل) does any letter precede the first radical, are B twenty-nine in number. The following is a list of these forms, with the principal corresponding singulars, and examples.

Plur. Fract.

I. فُعَلٌ.   *Sing.*

1. فُعْلَةٌ; as تُحْفَةٌ *a present,* تُحَفٌ; رُكْبَةٌ *a knee,* رُكَبٌ; غُرَّةٌ *the white spot,* or *blaze* (Germ. *Blässe*), on a horse's forehead, غُرَرٌ; أُمَّةٌ *a nation,* أُمَمٌ; قُبَّةٌ [*a leather tent,*] *a dome,* قُبَبٌ; صُورَةٌ *a form,* صُوَرٌ; كُورَةٌ *a district* (Gr. χώρα), كُوَرٌ; جُذْوَةٌ *a* C *fire-brand,* (for جُذًى or جُذُوٌ, § 213); كُلْيَةٌ *a kidney,* كُلًى (for كُلَيٌ); [بُهْمَةٌ *courageous,* بُهَمٌ].

2. فُعْلَى, fem. of أَفْعَل as a superlative (§ 234 and § 295, *b*); as أَلْعُظْمَى *the largest,* أَلْكُبْرَى *the greatest,* أَلصُّغْرَى *the smallest,* أَلصُّغَر; أَلْكُبَر; أَلْأَوَّل *the first* (fem. of أَلْأَوَّل), أَلْعُظَمُ; أَلْعُلْيَا *the highest,* أَلْعُلَى.

REM. Similarly أُخْرَى *other, another* (fem. of آخَرُ, see D § 295, rem. *b*), أُخَرُ, without tenwīn.

3. فَعْلَةٌ (especially from verba mediæ rad. و), فِعْلَةٌ, rare; as دَوْلَةٌ *a turn of fortune, a dynasty,* دُوَلٌ; نَوْبَةٌ *a turn,* نُوَبٌ; قَرْيَةٌ *a village,* قُرًى (for قُرَىٌ, § 213); لِحْيَةٌ *a beard,* لُحًى (for لُحَىٌ); حِلْيَةٌ *a trinket,* حُلًى (for حُلَىٌ).

A *Plur. Fract.*

II. فُعْل.   *Sing.*

1. أَفْعَل, not comparative and superlative (§§ 232 and 235); as أَصَمّ *deaf*, حُدْبٌ ; أَحْمَر *red*, حُمْرٌ ; أَحْدَبُ *humpbacked*, أَصَمُّ ; (سُوْدٌ for) نُودٌ *black*, أَسْوَد ; (بِيْضٌ for) بِيضٌ *white*, أَبْيَضُ ; ضُمّ ; عُمْيٌ, أَعْمَى *blind*.

2. فَعْلَاء, fem. of أَفْعَل, not comparative and superlative (§ 296); as صَفْرَاء *yellow*, صُفْر ; عَرْجَاء *lame*, عُرْج ; etc. [Accordingly بَيْدَاء a desert has بِيد.]

B
> REM. بَتْعَاء, and جَمْعَاء, كَتْعَاء, بَصْعَاء (fem. of أَجْمَع, etc., corroboratives of كُلّ *all*), make جُمَع, كُتَع, بُصَع, بُتَع, without tĕnwīn [§ 309, *a*, δ], *all together*. [Comp. § 302, *c*, and vol. ii. § 137 and rem. *c*.]

3. فُعَال, فَعَال, فُعَال, derived from verba med. rad. و; as عَوَانٌ C *a middle-aged married woman*, (عُوْنٌ for) عُون ; نَوَارٌ *timid, retiring* (of a woman), نُور ; بَوَانٌ *the pole of a tent*, بُون ; خِوَانٌ *a table, a plate*, خُون ; سِوَارٌ *a bracelet*, سُور ; أُوَارٌ *heat*, أُور. [They may be contractions from original فُعُل, as e.g. سِوَاك *a tooth-stick*, has certainly both سُوك and سُوُك. R. S.]

4. فَاعِل, derived from verba med. rad. و; as عَائِذٌ *having newly had young*, (عُوْذٌ for) عُوذ ; حَائِل *and* عَائِط [*farrow,*] *not bearing D young for some years*, عُوط [*or* عِيط, حُول]. [Also in some other cases, as فُرَّه from فَارِه and بُزَّل from بَازِل. They may, however, be contractions from فُرَّه and بُزَّل (comp. III. 5, rem.). D. G.]

> [REM. نَاقَةٌ a she-camel has نُوق.]

III. فُعُل.

1. فُعَال, فِعَال, فُعَال, not derived either from verba mediæ rad.

Plur. Fract.   A

III. فُعُلٌ continued.   *Sing.*

geminatæ or verba tertiæ rad. و et ى ; as رَدَاحٌ *a large bowl* or *dish,* رُدُحٌ ; قَذَالٌ *the neck,* قُذُلٌ ; سَيَالٌ *a mimosa tree,* سُيَلٌ ; خِمَارٌ *a veil,* خُمُرٌ ; فِرَاشٌ *a bed,* فُرُشٌ ; كِتَابٌ *a book,* كُتُبٌ ; سِوَاكٌ *a tooth-stick,* سُوُكٌ ; حِصَانٌ *a stallion,* شِيَارٌ Saturday, حُصُنٌ ; كُرَاعٌ *the shinbone of an animal,* شُيُرٌ ; قُرَادٌ كُرُعٌ *a tick,* قُرُدٌ.

                                                       B

> Rem. Exceptions are حِجَاجٌ *the bone over the eye,* حُجُجٌ ; عِنَانٌ *a rein,* عُنُنٌ. [A rare case is أُنُثٌ from أُنْثَى *female,* as though it were formed from إِنَاثٌ.]

2. فَعُولٌ, فَعِيلَةٌ, فَعِيلٌ, not derived from verba tertiæ rad. و et ى ; as قَضِيبٌ *a twig or rod,* قُضُبٌ ; كَثِيبٌ *a sandhill,* كُثُبٌ ; سَرِيرٌ *a seat, throne, bier,* سُرُرٌ ; سَفِينَةٌ *a ship,* سُفُنٌ ; مَدِينَةٌ *a city,* مُدُنٌ ; صَحِيفَةٌ *a leaf or page,* صُحُفٌ ; عَمُودٌ *a pillar,* عُمُدٌ ; رَسُولٌ *a message, a messenger,* رُسُلٌ.

3. فَعُولٌ, فَعِيلٌ, verbal adjectives not having a passive signification, and not derived from verba tertiæ rad. و et ى ; as نَذِيرٌ *one who warns,* نُذُرٌ ; صَبُورٌ *patient,* صُبُرٌ ; ذَلُولٌ *docile,* [*a dromedary,*] ذُلُلٌ ; بَيُوضٌ *laying many eggs,* بُيُضٌ ; غَيُورٌ *jealous,* غُيُرٌ.

4. فُعُلٌ, فُعَلٌ, فَعَلٌ, فَعَلَةٌ, فُعُلٌ, rare ; as سَقْفٌ *a roof,* سُقُفٌ ; سَحْلٌ *a thin, white piece of cloth,* سُحُلٌ ; أَسَدٌ *a lion,* أُسُدٌ ; فَلَكٌ *a sphere, the heavens,* فُلُكٌ ; وَثَنٌ *an idol,* وُثُنٌ ; بَدَنَةٌ *a victim for sacrifice,* بُدُنٌ ; خَشَبَةٌ *a piece of wood,* خُشُبٌ ; أَجَمَةٌ *a brake or thicket,* أُجُمٌ ; نَمِرٌ *a leopard,* نُمُرٌ ; خَشِنٌ *rough,* خُشُنٌ ; ضَبُعٌ *a hyæna,* ضُبُعٌ.

A *Plur. Fract.*

III. فُعَّل continued.   *Sing.*

5. فَاعِل, rare; as تَاجِر *a merchant,* تُجَّر; بَازِل *a full-grown camel,* بُزَّل.

REM. The form فُعُل is admissible in all these cases*, unless the word comes from a radical mediæ geminatæ; e.g. بِيض (for بُيُض, [شُيُر for] .غُدُر, بُشُر] شِير, أُسُد, رُسُل, قُضُب, كُتُب

B بُيُض, instead of which بُوض is sometimes used), نِيب *full-grown she-camels* (for نُيُب), from نَاب (for نَيَب). Forms like لَذِيذ *pleasant,* لُذّ, ذُبَاب *the common fly,* ذُبّ, are rare. Sometimes the damma of words med. rad. gemin. is changed into fètha, as جَدَد or جُدُد *new,* جَدِيد; سُرُر, سَرِير.

IV. فِعَل.

C 1. فُعْلَة; as قِطْعَة *a piece,* قِطَع; حِكْمَة *a maxim,* حِكَم; لِمَّة *a lock of hair,* لِمَم; سِيرَة *mode of walking, manner of living, character,* سِيَر; إِسْوَة *an example or pattern,* إِسًى (for إِسَى); بِنْيَة *a building,* بِنًى; [رِشْوَة *a bribe,* رِشًا or رِشَى].

2. فُعْلَة, فَعَلَة, rare; as خَيْمَة *a tent,* خِيَم; ضَيْعَة *a farm,* ضِيَع; بَدْرَة *a skin for milk,* بِدَر; هَضْبَة *a shower of rain,* هِضَب;

D تَارَة *a time,* تِيَر; قَامَة *a fathom,* قِيَم; [ثَلَّة *a flock of sheep,* ثِلَل].

V. فِعَال.

1. فُعْل (not primæ or secundæ rad. ى), فِعْل, فُعُل; as بَحْر *a sea,*

---

* [Again, شُدُف *Persian curved bows* (Ṭabarī, i. 957, l. 1) is said to be the plural of شَدْقَاءة. R. S. It may be a poetical license for شُدْف. For, as a rule, just as the form فُعُل may be changed into فُعْل (عَلَى مَذْهَب ٱلتَّعْوِيض), so فُعْل may be replaced by فُعُل.]

Plur. Fract.   A

V. فَعَالٌ continued.   *Sing.*

ظَبْيٌ a gazelle, ثِيَابٌ ; ثَوْبٌ a piece of cloth, a dress, بِحَارٌ ;

رِيحٌ a wind, ذِئَابٌ ; ذِئْبٌ a wolf, قِدَاحٌ ; قِدْحٌ an arrow, ظِبَآءٌ ;

رُمْحٌ a spear, ظِلَالٌ ; ظِلٌّ a shade, a shadow, رِمَاحٌ ; رِيَاحٌ ;

خِفَافٌ a boot, خُفٌّ.

2. فُعْلَةٌ, فَعْلَةٌ (rare), as قَصْعَةٌ a dish, قِصَاعٌ ; مَرَّةٌ an occasion,   B
a time, مِرَارٌ ; رَوْضَةٌ a garden, رِيَاضٌ ; ضَيْعَةٌ a farm, ضِيَاعٌ ;
لِقْحَةٌ a milch-camel, لِقَاحٌ ; رُقْعَةٌ a scrap of cloth or paper,
a note, رِقَاعٌ ; بُقْعَةٌ a low-lying, level district, قُبَّةٌ a
dome, قِبَابٌ.

       REM. اِمْرَأَةٌ, a woman, has a plural of this form, نِسَآءٌ.

3. فَعَلٌ, فَعْلَةٌ, not derived from verba mediæ rad. geminatæ or   C
tertiæ rad. و et ى; as جَبَلٌ a hill, جِبَالٌ ; جَمَلٌ a he-camel,
رَقَبَةٌ the neck, رِقَابٌ ; ثَمَرَةٌ a fruit, ثِمَارٌ ; حَسَنٌ, fem. جِمَالٌ
حَسَنَةٌ, handsome, حِسَانٌ.

4. فَعُلٌ; as رَجُلٌ a man, رِجَالٌ ; سَبُعٌ a beast of prey, سِبَاعٌ ; ضَبُعٌ
a hyæna, ضِبَاعٌ.

5. فَعْلٌ, fem. فَعْلَةٌ, verbal adjectives; as صَعْبٌ difficult, صِعَابٌ ;   D
صَلَابٌ, صُلْبٌ hard, عِذَابٌ ; عَذْبٌ sweet.

6. فُعْلٌ; as رُطَبٌ fresh ripe dates, رِطَابٌ ; رُبَعٌ an early born
camel's colt, رِبَاعٌ ; هُبَعٌ a late born camel's colt, هِبَاعٌ.

7. فُعْلَى, not fem. superlatives; as أُنْثَى female, إِنَاثٌ ; خُنْثَى
a hermaphrodite, خِنَاثٌ.

A *Plur. Fract.*

V. فِعَال continued.   *Sing.*

8. فُعْلَان, fem. فُعْلَانَة, verbal adjectives; as نَدْمَان *repentant,* خُمْصَان *lean, slim,* خِمَاصْ ; نِدَامْ.

9. فَعْلَان, fem. فَعْلَى, verbal adjectives; as عَطْشَان *thirsty,* غَضْبَان *angry,* غِضَابْ ; رَيَّان, f. رَيَّا, *satisfied with*
B *drink,* رِوَاءْ.

10. فَعِيل, fem. فَعِيلَة, verbal adjectives, not having a passive signification; as كَبِير *large, old,* كِبَار ; كَرِيم, شَرِيف, *noble,* [ضِعَاف, كِرَامْ ; شِرَاف ; مِرَاض] ; مَرِيض *sick,* ضَعِيف *feeble,* ; جَيِّد (for طَوِيل *long,* طِوَال (rarely طِيَال); لَئِيم *base,* لِئَامْ ; جَيِّد (for جُوَيْد) خِيَار ; جِيَاد ; خَيْر (for خُيَيْر, خِيِير) *good,* خِيَار.

C   REM. From words tertiæ rad. و et ى this form is rarely used; as نَقِى *pure,* نِقَاءْ. An example of the passive signification is فَصِيل *a weanling,* فِصَال.

11. فَاعِل, verbal adjectives; as صَاحِب *a companion,* صِحَابْ ; تَاجِر *a merchant,* تِجَار ; نَاهِل *drinking, thirsty,* نِهَال ; قَائِم *standing,* قِيَام ; نَائِم *sleeping,* نِيَامْ ; رَاع (for رَاعِى) *a shepherd,*
D رِعَاءْ ; نَاوٍ *fat,* نِوَاءْ.

[REM. *a.* Rare cases are جِيَاد from جَوَاد *a courser;* بِطَاح from بَطْحَاءْ *the channel of a torrent;* عِجَاف from أَعْجَف fem. عَجْفَاءْ *lean;* عِشَار and نِفَاس from عُشَرَاءْ and نُفَسَاءْ.]

[REM. *b.* The plural فُعَال is said to occur in a few words (see Ḥarīrī, *Dorrat,* ed. Thorb. 97 *seq.* and Ḥafāǧī's comm.

Plur. Fract. A

V. فِعَال continued. *Sing.*

141 *seq.*) as بُسَاط from بُسْط *a she-camel with her own calf,*
ثُنَاء from ثَنِىٌّ *a sheep or goat in the second year,* رِخَال from
رِخْل or رَخِل *a ewe lamb,* رُذَال from رَذْل *mean,* رُعَاء from
رَاع *a shepherd,* صُبَاء from صَابِئٌ *a Sabian* (see the Gloss. to B
Tabarī). Some say that it is another form for فِعَال, others
that it is really a collective (اسْمُ جَمْع). D. G.]

VI. فُعُول.

1. فَعْل, فِعْل, فُعْل as بَحْر *a sea,* بُحُور ; نَفْس *the soul,* نُفُوس ;
كَهْل *a middle-aged man,* كُهُول ; ضِرْس *a molar tooth or* C
grinder, ضُرُوس ; جِلْد *a skin,* جُلُود ; جُنْد *a military force,*
جُنُود ; بُرْد *a robe,* بُرُود ; جَيْش *an army,* جُيُوش ; جِيد *the neck,*
جُيُود ; ظَبْى *a gazelle,* ظُبِىٌّ (for ظُبُوىٌ) ; دَلْو *a bucket,* دُلِىٌّ (for
دُلُوىٌ) ; and, by assimilation of the vowels, ظِبِىٌّ, دِلِىٌّ (comp.
§ 215).

REM. *a.* From words med. rad. و of the forms فَعْل and
فِعْل this plural is rare ; e.g. فَوْج *a troop,* فُووج ; حَوْل *a year,* D
حُوُول (or حُووُل). قَوْس *a bow,* usually makes قُسِىٌّ or قِسِىٌّ,
as if from قَسْوٌ.

REM. *b.* In words med. rad. ى the vowel of the first
syllable is sometimes assimilated to the second radical, as
بَيْت *a house,* بُيُوت or بِيُوت ; شَيْخ *an old man, a chief, a doc-*
tor, شُيُوخ or شِيُوخ ; عَيْن *an eye,* عُيُون or عِيُون (comp. § 269,
rem. *c*).

2. فَعَل, فَعِل as أَسَد *a lion,* أُسُود ; نَدَب *a scar,* نُدُوب ; كَبِد

A *Plur. Fract.*

VI. فُعُولٌ continued. *Sing.*

the liver, كُبُودٌ ; وَعِلٌ a mountain-goat, وُعُولٌ ; مَلِكٌ a king,

مُلُوكٌ نَابٌ (for نَيَبٌ) a canine tooth, نُيُوبٌ ; عَصًا a staff,

عُصِيٌّ (for عُصُويٌ), or by assimilation عِصِيٌّ ; دَمٌ blood (for

دِمِيٌّ or دُمِيٌّ ,(دَمَوٌ ,دَمَى).

B REM. From words med. rad. و of the form فَعَلٌ this
plural is rare; as سَاقٌ (for سَوَقٌ) a stem or trunk, سُوُوقٌ (or
سُؤُوقٌ).

3. فَعَلَةٌ, فُعَلَةٌ, rare; as بَدْرَةٌ a skin for milk, a purse of money,
بُدُورٌ ; حِقْبَةٌ a period of time, حُقُوبٌ ; خُرْبَةٌ a hole, خُرُوبٌ ;
حُقَّةٌ a casket, حُقُوقٌ ; شَعَفَةٌ a top or summit, شُعُوفٌ ; دَوَاةٌ

C an inkhorn, دُوِيٌّ or دِوِيٌّ.

4. فَاعِلٌ, verbal adjectives, not mediæ rad. gemin. or med. rad. و
vel ى ; as قَاعِدٌ ,جَالِسٌ, sitting, وَاقِفٌ standing, وُقُوفٌ ; جُلُوسٌ,
قُعُودٌ ; شَاهِدٌ a witness, شُهُودٌ ; عَاتٍ proud, wicked, عُتِيٌّ (for
بِكِيٌّ or بُكِيٌّ weeping, بَاكٍ ; عِتِيٌّ or (عُتُوِيٌّ).

[REM. Rare cases are ضِلَعٌ (ضِلْعٌ) a rib; ضُلُوعٌ from
D إِرَمٌ (أَرُمٌ) a stone set up; أُرُومٌ from ظَرِيفٌ elegant; ظُرُوفٌ from أُرُومٌ.]

VII. فُعَّلٌ.

1. فَاعِلٌ, verbal adjectives, not derived from verba tertiæ rad. و et
ى (with rare exceptions); as سَاجِدٌ prostrating oneself, سُجَّدٌ ;
سَامِرٌ conversing at night, سُمَّرٌ ; نَائِمٌ sleeping, نُوَّمٌ and نُيَّمٌ ;
صَائِمٌ fasting, صُوَّمٌ and صُيَّمٌ ; شَائِلٌ pregnant, شُوَّلٌ and شُيَّلٌ ;

Plur. Fract. A

VII. فُعَّل continued. *Sing.*

غَائِضٌ [حَائِضٌ menstruating, طَالِقٌ ; حُيَّضٌ repudiated, طُلَّقٌ] ; غَائِبٌ

absent, غُيَّبٌ ; غَازٍ a soldier, غُزَّى (for غُزَّوٌ or غُزَّوٌ, § 213).

2. فَاعِلَة, fem. of the preceding ; as نَائِحَة mourning, نُوَّحٌ.

> REM. *a.* The substitution of *kesr* for *damm* is allowable
> in the first syllable of فُعَّل from verba med. و et ى. in which B
> case the و must be changed into ى ; as خِيَّفٌ for خُيَّفٌ, خُوَّفٌ,
> from خَائِفٌ *fearing ;* صِيَّمٌ, from صَائِمٌ *fasting ;* etc.

> [REM. *b.* Anomalous is عُزَّلُ from أَعْزَلُ *having no weapon.*]

VIII. فُعَّالٌ.

فَاعِل, verbal adjectives, not derived from verba tertiæ rad. و et ى
[or med. gem.] (with rare exceptions) ; as حُكَّامٌ *a judge,* حَاكِمٌ ;
تَابِعٌ *a follower,* تُبَّاعٌ ; صَانِعٌ *an artisan,* صُنَّاعٌ ; كَافِرٌ *an* C
unbeliever, كُفَّارٌ ; جَاهِلٌ *ignorant,* جُهَّالٌ ; نَائِبٌ *a deputy,*
نَوَّابٌ ; نَائِمٌ *sleeping,* نُوَّامٌ ; غَازٍ *a soldier,* غُزَّاءٌ ; جَانٍ *an offender,*
جُنَّاءٌ ; صَادٌّ *avoiding,* صُدَّادٌ]*.

IX. فَعَلَة.

1. فَاعِل, verbal adjectives, denoting rational beings, and not
derived from verba tertiæ rad. و et ى ; as فَاعِلٌ *a workman,* D
كَمَلَةٌ ; كَافِرٌ *an unbeliever,* كَفَرَةٌ ; كَامِلٌ *perfect,* فَعَلَةٌ ;
سَاحِرٌ *a conjuror,* سَحَرَةٌ ; بَارٌّ *pious, dutiful,* بَرَرَةٌ ; طَائِعٌ *obedient,*
طَاعَةٌ (for طَوَعَةٌ) ; بَائِعٌ *selling,* بَاعَةٌ (for بَيَعَةٌ).

---

* [فُلَّالٌ *defeated, fugitives,* properly pl. of فَالٌّ, is by usage pl. of
فَلٌّ. R. S.]

A *Plur. Fract.*

    IX. فَعَلَةٌ continued.   *Sing.*

        REM. فَاعِلٌ from verba med. و sometimes remains uncontracted in the plural; as جَائِرٌ *acting wrongly,* جَوَرَةٌ or جَارَةٌ; حَائِكٌ *a weaver,* حَوَكَةٌ or حَاكَةٌ; خَائِنٌ *treacherous,* خَوَنَةٌ or حَاَئِكُ حَانَةٌ.

B   [2. فَعِيلٌ rare, as خَبِيثٌ *bad,* خَبَثَةٌ; ضَعِيفٌ *feeble,* ضَعَفَةٌ; سَرِىٌّ *generous,* سَرَاةٌ; سَيِّدٌ *a chief,* سَادَةٌ.]

    X. فُعَلَةٌ.

        فَاعِلٌ, verbal adjectives, denoting rational beings, and derived from verba tertiæ rad. و et ى; as غَازٍ *a soldier,* غُزَاةٌ (for

C   غُزَوَةٌ); قَاضٍ *a judge,* قُضَاةٌ (for قُضَيَةٌ); رَاوٍ *a reciter, rehearser,* or *traditionary,* رُوَاةٌ (for رُوَيَةٌ); جَانٍ *a sinner,* جُنَاةٌ (for جُنَيَةٌ); سَاعٍ *a manager,* سُعَاةٌ. [And so in the dialect of Ḥijāz اَلصُّبَاةُ (*Sabians*) for اَلصَّابِئُونَ, a nickname given to the first Muslims. R. S.]

        [REM. An exception is بُزَاةٌ from بَازٍ *a falcon.*]

D   XI. فَعَلَةٌ.

        1. فُعْلٌ, not derived from verba tertiæ rad. و et ى; as قُرْطٌ *an earring,* قَرَطَةٌ; دُرْجٌ *a case or casket,* دَرَجَةٌ; غُصْنٌ *a branch,* غِصَنَةٌ; دُبٌّ *a bear,* دِبَبَةٌ; كُوزٌ *a jug,* كُوَزَةٌ; صُلْبٌ *a rugged place,* صَلَبَةٌ; تُرْسٌ *a shield,* تِرَسَةٌ.

        2. فَعْلٌ, فِعْلٌ, with the same restriction, rare; as ثَوْرٌ *an ox,* ثِيَرَةٌ or ثَوَرَةٌ; زَوْجٌ *a husband or wife,* زَوَجَةٌ; شَيْخٌ *an old*

Plur. Fract.　　　　　　　　　　　　　　　　　　　　　　A

XI. فَعَلَة continued.　　　　　*Sing.*

man, شِيَخَة ; غُرْد *a truffle,* غَرَدَة ; رَطْل *soft, lax, flaccid,* رِطَلَة ;
قِرْد *an ape,* قَرَدَة ; قَطّ, هِرّ *a tom-cat,* قِطَطَة, هِرَرَة ; دِيك *a cock,*
دِيَكَة ; فِيل *an elephant,* فِيَلَة.

XII. فُعْلَة.　　　　　　　　　　　　　　　　　　　　　　B

1. فَعْل ; as ثَوْر *a bull,* ثِيَرَة ; شَيْخ *an old man,* شِيَخَة.

2. فَعَل ; as وَلَد *a child,* وِلْدَة ; جَار (for جَوَر) *a neighbour,* جِيرَة ;
قَاع *level ground,* قِيعَة ; أَخ (for أَخَو) *a brother,* إِخْوَة ;
فَتًى (for فَتَى) *a youth,* فِتْيَة.

3. فُعَال, فَعَال ; as غَزَال *a gazelle,* غِزْلَة ; غُلَام *a youth, a slave,*
شُجَاع *brave,* شِجْعَة ; غِلْمَة.　　　　　　　　　　　　　C

4. فَعِيل ; as صَبِيّ (for صَبِيو) *a boy,* صِبْيَة ; جَلِيل *thick, coarse,*
big, great, جِلَّة ; خَصِيّ *a gelding, a eunuch,* خِصْيَة.

　　REM. اِمْرَأَة *a woman,* has a plural of this form, نِسْوَة.
　　[The plural فُعْلَة varies in almost all cases with فُعْلَان. R.S.]

XIII. أَفْعُل.　　　　　　　　　　　　　　　　　　　　　D

1. فَعْل, not derived from verba mediæ rad. و et ى ; as بَحْر
a sea, أَبْحُر ; نَفْس *the soul,* أَنْفُس ; فَلْس *a copper coin,* أَفْلُس ;
[سَطْر *a line of writing,* [أَسْطُر ; ضَبّ *a lizard,* أَضُبّ (for أَضْبُب) ;
وَجْه *the face,* أَوْجُه ; دَلْو *a bucket,* أَدْلٍ (for أَدْلُى or أَدْلُو) ;
ظَبْى *an antelope,* أَظْبٍ (for أَظْبُى) ; يَد (for يَدْى) *the hand,*
أَيْدٍ (for أَيْدُى).

W.　　　　　　　　　　　　　　　　　　　　　　　27

A *Plur. Fract.*

XIII. أَفْعُل continued. *Sing.*

REM. Exceptions are, for example, ثَوْب a *piece of cloth,* a *garment,* أَثْوُب or أَثْوَاب ; قَوْس a *bow,* أَقْوُس or أَقْوَاس ; سَيْف a *sword,* أَسْيُف ; عَيْن an *eye, a fountain,* أَعْيُن.

2. Feminine quadriliterals, not ending in ةٌ, which have a quiescent letter (long vowel) between the second and third radicals; as ذِرَاع *the arm,* أَذْرُع ; عَنَاق a *female kid,* أَعْنُق ;

B يَمِين *the right hand, an oath,* أَيْمُن ; شِمَال *the left hand,* أَشْمُل ; لِسَان *the tongue*,* أَلْسُن ; عُقَاب an *eagle,* أَعْقُب.

3. فَعَل, فِعْل, فُعْل, not derived from verba mediæ rad. و et ى, rare; as جَبَل a *hill,* أَجْبُل ; زَمَن *time,* أَزْمُن ; عَصًا (for عَصَو) a *staff,* أَعْصُ (for أَعْصُى or أَعْصُو) ; رِجْل a *leg or foot,* أَرْجُل ; شِبْل a *lion's cub,* أَشْبُل ; ذِئْب a *wolf,* أَذْوُب ; قُفْل a *lock,* أَقْفُل.

C REM. بِئْر, a *well,* has أَبْوُر and, by transposition, آبُر.

From radicals mediæ و et ى occur, for example, دَار a *house,* أَدْوُر, أَدُور, and, by transposition, آدُر ; سَاق *the shank,* أَسْوُق, نَاب (for نَيَب) a *canine tooth,* أَنْيُب ; نَار *fire,* أَنْوُر ; نَار, by transposition, أَسُوق, أَنْيُب.

4. فَعَلَة, rare; as أَكَمَة a *hillock,* آكُم ; رَقَبَة *the neck,* أَرْقُب ; أَمَة a *maidservant,* (for أَمَوَة), أَمِر (for أَمَى) ; نَاقَة a *she-camel,* أَنُوق, أَنْوُق, and أَنْيُق, whence, by transposition, أَيْنُق and,

D dialectically, أَوْنُق.

REM. أَفْعُل occurs now and then in a few other forms; as نَمِر a *leopard,* أَنْمُر ; سَبُع a *beast of prey,* أَسْبُع ; ضِلَع a *rib,* أَضْلُع ; نَهَار *day,* أَنْهُر ; غُرَاب a *raven,* أَغْرُب ; etc.

---

* [If fem.; for if masc. it has أَلْسِنَة (XV. 1), according to "El-Mubarrad 50, l. 5 *seq.* D. G.]

Plur. Fract.

A

XIV. أَفْعَالٌ. *Sing.*

1. Triliterals of all forms, especially فَعَلٌ, rarely فَعْلٌ (see no. 2) and فُعَلٌ; as قَدَمٌ a *footstep,* أَقْدَامٌ; طَلَلٌ a *vestige* or *trace,* أَطْلَالٌ; مَطَرٌ *rain,* أَمْطَارٌ; بَابٌ (for بَوَبٌ) a *door,* أَبْوَابٌ; نَابٌ (for نَيَبٌ) a *canine tooth, an old she-camel,* أَنْيَابٌ; اِبْنٌ (for

بَنَىٌ) a *son,* أَبْنَاءٌ; أَبٌ (for أَبَوٌ) a *father,* آبَاءٌ; بِئْرٌ a *well,* أَبْآرٌ

or, by transposition, آبَارٌ; رَأْىٌ *idea, belief, opinion,* أَرْآءٌ or آرَاءٌ; B
حِمْلٌ a *load,* أَحْمَالٌ; عِيدٌ a *festival,* أَعْيَادٌ; إِبْطٌ *the armpit,* آبَاطٌ; قُفْلٌ a *lock,* أَقْفَالٌ; حُكْمٌ a *judgment,* أَحْكَامٌ; أُذْنٌ or أُذُنٌ an *ear,* آذَانٌ; حُرٌّ *free,* أَحْرَارٌ; اِسْمٌ (for سُمْوٌ) a *name,* أَسْمَاءٌ; إِبِلٌ a *herd* of camels, آبَالٌ; نَمِرٌ a *leopard,* أَنْمَارٌ; فَخِذٌ a *thigh,* أَفْخَاذٌ; فَرْخٌ *the young of a bird,* أَفْرَاخٌ; أَلْفٌ a *thousand,* آلَافٌ; بَرٌّ *pious, dutiful,* أَبْرَارٌ; فَنٌّ a *branch,* أَفْنَانٌ; رُطَبٌ *fresh* C *ripe dates,* أَرْطَابٌ.

2. فَعْلٌ, from verba mediæ rad. و et ى, and primæ rad. و; as ثَوْبٌ a *dress,* أَثْوَابٌ; سَيْفٌ a *sword,* أَسْيَافٌ; يَوْمٌ a *day,* أَيَّامٌ; وَقْتٌ *time,* أَوْقَاتٌ; وَهْمٌ a *fancy, a notion, a mistake,* (for أَيْوَامٌ); أَوْهَامٌ.

REM. شَىْءٌ, a *thing,* makes أَشْيَاءُ, and not (as one would D naturally expect) أَشْيَاءُ.

3. فَاعِلٌ, rare; as نَاصِرٌ a *helper,* أَنْصَارٌ; شَاهِدٌ a *witness,* أَشْهَادٌ; طَاهِرٌ *pure,* أَطْهَارٌ; صَاحِبٌ a *companion, a friend,* أَصْحَابٌ; فَاتِرٌ *tepid,* أَفْتَارٌ.

4. فَعِيلٌ, verbal adjectives, not having a passive signification,

A *Plur. Fract.*

XIV. أَفْعَالٌ continued.   *Sing.*

rare ; as شَرِيفٌ *noble,* أَشْرَافٌ ; مَيِّتٌ or مَيْتٌ (for مَوِيتٌ, § 242),
dead, أَمْوَاتٌ.

REM. أَفْعَالٌ occurs now and then in a few other forms ;
as عَدُوٌّ *an enemy,* أَعْدَآءٌ ; فَلُوٌّ *a weaned foal, a colt,* أَفْلَآءٌ ;
يَمِينٌ *a right hand, an oath,* أَيْمَانٌ ; جَنَانٌ *the heart,* أَجْنَانٌ.

B XV. أَفْعِلَةٌ.

1. Quadriliterals, of which the penult letter is quiescent (a long
vowel), especially nouns of the forms فَعَالٌ, فِعَالٌ, and فُعَالٌ ;
as جَنَاحٌ *a wing,* أَجْنِحَةٌ ; طَعَامٌ *food,* أَطْعِمَةٌ ; زَمَانٌ *time,*
أَزْمِنَةٌ ; دَوَآءٌ *physic,* أَدْوِيَةٌ ; غِذَآءٌ *food,* أَغْذِيَةٌ ; لِسَانٌ *the tongue*,*
أَلْسِنَةٌ ; حِمَارٌ *an ass,* أَحْمِرَةٌ ; إِلَهٌ *a god,* آلِهَةٌ (for أَأْلِهَةٌ) ; إِمَامٌ

C *an 'imam or priest,* أَئِمَّةٌ or أَيِمَّةٌ (for أَأْمِمَةٌ) ; فِنَآءٌ *a courtyard,*
أَفْنِيَةٌ ; فُؤَادٌ *the heart,* أَفْئِدَةٌ ; غُرَابٌ *a raven,* أَغْرِبَةٌ ; غُلَامٌ *a youth,*
أَغْلِمَةٌ ; زُقَاقٌ *a lane, a strait,* أَزِقَّةٌ ; عَمُودٌ *a pillar,* أَعْمِدَةٌ ;
رَغِيفٌ *a cake of bread,* أَرْغِفَةٌ ; قَضِيبٌ *a branch, a rod,* أَقْضِبَةٌ ;
كَثِيبٌ *a sand-hill,* أَكْثِبَةٌ ; قَفِيزٌ *a certain measure,* أَقْفِزَةٌ.

2. فَعِيلٌ, verbal adjectives, derived from verba mediæ rad.
D geminatæ or ultimæ rad. و et ى ; as عَزِيزٌ *mighty, glorious,*
أَعِزَّةٌ (for أَعْزِزَةٌ) ; عَفِيفٌ *temperate, chaste,* أَعِفَّةٌ ; شَحِيحٌ
niggardly, stingy, أَشِحَّةٌ ; حَبِيبٌ *dear,* أَحِبَّةٌ ; صَبِىٌّ *a boy*
(for صَبِيوٌ), أَصْبِيَةٌ ; نَجِىٌّ *a confidant,* أَنْجِيَةٌ ; عَيِىٌّ *stammering,*
stuttering, أَعْيِيَةٌ.

---

* [If masc. ; see the footnote to XIII. 2.]

Plur. Fract.   A

XV. أَفْعِلَةٌ continued.   *Sing.*

3. فَعْلُ, فِعْلُ, فُعْلُ, rare; as فَرْخُ *the young of a bird,* أَفْرِخَةٌ;
    نَعْلُ *a shoe,* أَنْعِلَةٌ; نَجْدُ *a high land,* أَنْجِدَةٌ; زِرُّ *a button,*
    أَزِرَّةٌ (for أَزْرِرَةٌ); بُرْجُ *a tower,* أَبْرِجَةٌ; جُحْرُ *the hole of a*
    reptile, أَجْحِرَةٌ.   B

4. فَعَلُ, فُعْلُ, rare; as طَبَقُ *a cover or lid,* أَطْبِقَةٌ; زَادُ (for
    provisions, أَزْوِدَةٌ; خَالُ (for خُوَلُ) *an uncle (by the mother's*
    side), أَخْوِلَةٌ; قَفَا (for قَفَوُ or قَفَىُ) *the back of the neck,* أَقْفِيَةٌ;
    نَدًى *moisture, dew,* أَنْدِيَةٌ; خُزَزُ *a buck-*
    hare, أَخِزَّةٌ (for أَخْزِزَةٌ).

    REM. أَفْعِلَةٌ is rarely used in some other forms; as سِحَاءَةٌ   C
    or سِحَايَةٌ *a sealed strip of paper* (with which a letter is bound),
    أَسْحِيَةٌ; وَادٍ *a watercourse,* أَوْدِيَةٌ; نَادٍ *an assembly,*
    أَنْدِيَةٌ.

XVI. فَوَاعِلُ*.

1. فَاعَلُ; as خَاتَمُ *a signet-ring,* خَوَاتِمُ; طَابَعُ *a seal,* طَوَابِعُ;
    قَالَبُ *a mould,* قَوَالِبُ; طَابَقُ *a pot, a crucible,* طَوَابِقُ.

2. فَاعِلُ, substantives; بَاعِثُ *a motive or cause,* بَوَاعِثُ; حَافِرُ   D
    a hoof (of a horse or ass), حَوَافِرُ; جَانِبُ *a side,* جَوَانِبُ; كَاهِلُ
    the space between the shoulders, كَوَاهِلُ; غَارِبُ *the top of a*

---

* [By the influence of و the preceding Fètha often, in vulgar pronunciation, passes into ḍamma, as طُوَارِق Touareg, جُوَارٍ *female slaves.*
In the old language there are some instances of it in proper names,
e. g. كُوَاكِبُ, عُوَارِمُ, عُوَارِضُ, صُوَائِقُ. D. G.]

A *Plur. Fract.*

XVI. فَوَاعِلُ continued.   *Sing.*

camel's hump, of a wave, etc., غَوَارِبُ ; سَاحِلٌ *the seashore,* شَوَاحِلُ ; شَاهِدٌ *an example,* شَوَاهِدُ.

3. فَاعِلٌ, verbal adjectives, applicable to men, rare ; as فَارِسٌ *a horseman,* فَوَارِسُ ; تَابِعٌ *a follower,* تَوَابِعُ ; نَاكِسٌ *hanging* B *the head,* نَوَاكِسُ ; هَالِكٌ *perishing,* هَوَالِكُ ; خَالِفٌ *remaining behind,* خَوَالِفُ.

4. فَاعِلٌ, verbal adjectives, applicable by their signification only to females (§ 297, *d*, rem.) ; as حَامِلٌ *pregnant,* حَوَامِلُ ; نَاهِدٌ *menstruating,* حَوَائِضُ ; طَالِقٌ *divorced,* طَوَالِقُ ; *having swelling breasts,* نَوَاهِدُ.

C 5. فَاعِلَةٌ, substantives and fem. verbal adjectives ; as فَاكِهَةٌ *fruit,* فَوَاكِهُ ; صَاعِقَةٌ *a thunderbolt,* صَوَاعِقُ ; نَادِرَةٌ *a rarity, a witticism, a joke,* نَوَادِرُ ; آنِسَةٌ *cheerful, sociable,* أَوَانِسُ ; صَاحِبَةٌ *a female companion,* صَوَاحِبُ ; خَاصَّةٌ *distinguished people, the upper classes,* خَوَاصُّ (for خَوَاصِصُ) ; عَامَّةٌ *common people, the vulgar,* عَوَامُّ (for عَوَامِمُ) ; فَائِدَةٌ *gain, profit,* فَوَائِدُ ; D جَارِيَةٌ *a girl,* جَوَارٍ (for جَوَارِيُ, see no. XXIII., rem.) ; نَاحِيَةٌ *a quarter of the sky, a region, a district,* نَوَاحٍ (for نَوَاحِيُ).

REM. Initial و is changed into أ ; as وَاصِلَةٌ *joining or adding, a proximate cause,* أَوَاصِلُ (for وَوَاصِلُ) ; وَاقِيَةٌ *custody, a guard,* أَوَاقٍ (for وَوَاقِ, وَوَاقِى), which is also the plural of أُوقِيَّةٌ = وَاقِيَةٌ *an ounce.*

Plur. Fract.   A

XVI. فَوَاعِلُ continued.   *Sing.*

6. حَوَاثٍ ; as فَاعِلَاءُ، حَاثِيَاءُ، دَامَّاءُ، قَاصِعَاءُ، نَافِقَاءُ, *holes of the jerboa,* سَابِيَاءُ *a caul,* نَوَافِثُ، قَوَاصِعُ، (دَوَامِمُ) دَوَامُّ (for), (حَوَاثِيُ) (for

سَوَابٍ (for سَوَابِيُ).

XVII. فَعَائِلُ.

Fem. quadriliterals, of which the third letter is servile or quiescent B
(a long vowel), whether they have the fem. termination ـَة , or

not; as سَحَابَةٌ *a cloud,* سَحَائِبُ ; رِسَالَةٌ *an embassy, a letter,*

a treatise, رَسَائِلُ ; ذُؤَابَةٌ *a lock of hair,* ذَوَائِبُ ; جُعَالَةٌ or جَعِيلَةٌ

wages, جَعَائِلُ ; جَزِيرَةٌ *an island,* جَزَائِرُ ; صَحِيفَةٌ *a written*

leaf, a letter, a book, صَحَائِفُ ; صَفِيحَةٌ *a board or plank, a*

slab, صَفَائِحُ ; كَرِيمَةٌ *noble,* كَرَائِمُ ; ذَبِيحَةٌ *slaughtered, a*

victim, ذَبَائِحُ ; حَلُوبَةٌ *a milch-camel,* حَلَائِبُ ; شَمَالٌ *the north* C

wind, شَمَائِلُ ; شِمَالٌ *the left hand,* شَمَائِلُ ; جَزُورٌ *a she-camel*

for slaughter*,* جَزَائِرُ ; عَجُوزٌ *an old woman,* عَجَائِزُ ; ذَنُوبٌ

a large bucket, ذَنَائِبُ.

    Rem. فَعَائِلُ occurs rarely in a few other cases ; as أَفِيلٌ

a young camel, أَفَائِلُ ; [دَلِيلٌ *a proof,* ضَمِيرٌ *a pronoun,* ضَمَائِرُ ;

دَلَائِلُ ; وَصِيدٌ *a court,* [وَصَائِدُ ; حَاجَةٌ *a want or need, a thing,* D

affair or business, ضَرَائِرُ ; ضَرَّةٌ *a second wife,* حَوَائِجُ ;

a free woman, حَرَائِرُ ; [كَنَّةٌ *a daughter in law,* كَنَائِنُ ;

لَيْلٌ *the night,* [مُرَّةٌ], from مَرَائِرُ ٱلشَّجَرِ *bitter kinds of trees,*

لَيَائِلُ.

---

* [Also applied to the male, but nevertheless fem. gen. D. G.]

A *Plur. Fract.*

XVIII. فِعْلَانْ. *Sing.*

1. فُعْلْ, from radicals mediæ و ; as حُوتْ, نُونْ, *a fish*, حِيتَانْ,
سُورْ ; سِيرَانْ, عُودْ *a piece of wood, a branch*, نِينَانْ ; *a wall*,
دُودْ *a worm*, دِيدَانْ ; عِيدَانْ.

B 2. فَعَلْ ; as خَرَبْ *a male bustard*, خِرْبَانْ ; وَصَعْ *a kind of small
bird*, وِصْعَانْ ; وَرَلْ *a lizard*, وِرْلَانْ ; تَاجْ (for تَوَجْ) *a crown*,
نَارْ ; جِيرَانْ, جَارْ *a neighbour*, بِيبَانْ ; بَابْ *a door*, تِيجَانْ ;
fire, نِيرَانْ ; فَتَى (for فَتَىْ) *a youth*, فِتْيَانْ ; أَخْ (for أَخَو) *a
brother*, إِخْوَانْ.

3. فُعَلْ ; as صُرَدْ *a kind of bird*, صِرْدَانْ ; نُغَرْ *a nightingale*,
C نِغْرَانْ ; جُرَذْ *a buck-hare*, خُزَزْ *a field-rat*, جِرْذَانْ ; خِزَّانْ ;
جُعَلْ *a black beetle*, جِعْلَانْ.

4. فُعَالْ, and more rarely فِعَالْ and فَعَالْ ; as غُلَامْ *a boy, a
slave*, غِلْمَانْ ; غُرَابْ *a raven*, غِرْبَانْ ; عُقَابْ *an eagle*, عِقْبَانْ ;
a firebrand, شِهَابْ ; غَزَالْ *a gazelle*, غِزْلَانْ ; ذُبَابْ *a fly*, ذِبَّانْ ;
صِيرَانْ, صُوَارْ *a herd of wild cattle*, شِهْبَانْ ; شِهَابْ *a meteor*,

D 5. فَعْلْ and فُعْلْ, rare ; as عَبْدْ *a slave*, عِبْدَانْ ; وَغْدْ *a slave*,
فَأْرْ *a mouse*, ضَيْفْ *a guest*, ضِيفَانْ ; ثَوْرْ *a bull*, ثِيرَانْ ; وِغْدَانْ ;
رَأْلْ *a young ostrich*, رِئْلَانْ ; صِنْوْ *one of two or more
trees growing from a single root*, صِنْوَانْ ; قِنْوْ *a bunch of
dates*, نِيرَانْ ; نِيرْ *a yoke*, قِنْوَانْ.

6. فَعِيلْ, rare ; as قَضِيبْ *a branch*, قُضْبَانْ ; ظَلِيمْ *a male ostrich*,

Plur. Fract.   A

XVIII. فُعْلَانٌ continued.   *Sing.*

خَصِيٌّ ; ظِلْمَانٌ ; صَبِيٌّ (for صَبِيوٌ) *a boy* or *child,* صِبْيَانٌ ; خَصِيٌّ *a gelding, a eunuch,* خِصْيَانٌ.

[7. فَعُولٌ, rare ; as خَرُوفٌ *a lamb,* خِرْفَانٌ.]

8. فُعَيْلٌ, فُعَيْلَةٌ, not diminutives, rare ; as كُعَيْتٌ, جُمَيْلٌ *a nightingale,* جِمْلَانٌ; كُعْتَانٌ; تُمَيْلَةٌ *a sort of wild cat,* تِمْلَانٌ. B

9. فَعَلَانٌ, rare ; as شَقْذَانٌ *a male chamæleon,* كَرَوَانٌ *a bustard,* كِرْوَانٌ; وَرَشَانٌ *a wood-pigeon,* وِرْشَانٌ.

10. فَاعِلٌ, rare ; as حَائِطٌ *a wall,* حِيطَانٌ; جَانٌّ *a spiritual being of the class called* اَلْجِنُّ, جِنَّانٌ.

REM. أَمَةٌ (for أَمَوَةٌ), *a maidservant,* has إِمْوَانٌ; and C امْرَأَةٌ, *a woman,* an irregular plural نِسْوَانٌ.

XIX. فُعْلَانٌ.

1. فَعْلٌ, more rarely فِعْلٌ ; as سَقْفٌ *a roof,* سُقْفَانٌ; وَغْدٌ *a slave,* وِغْدَانٌ; عَبْدٌ *a slave,* عُبْدَانٌ; ظَهْرٌ *the back, the short side of a wing-feather,* ظُهْرَانٌ; بَطْنٌ *the belly, the long side of a wing-feather,* بُطْنَانٌ]; حَبٌّ *grain,* حُبَّانٌ; ذِئْبٌ *a wolf,* ذُوبَانٌ; D قِنْوٌ *a bunch of dates,* قُنْوَانٌ; زِقٌّ *a skin for water, etc.,* زُقَّانٌ.

2. فَعَلٌ ; as بَلَدٌ *a town,* بُلْدَانٌ; بَرَقٌ, حَمَلٌ *a lamb,* بُرْقَانٌ, ذَكَرٌ *a male,* ذُكْرَانٌ; حُمْلَانٌ.

3. فُعَالٌ, rare ; as زُقَاقٌ *a lane, a strait,* زُقَّانٌ; شُجَاعٌ *brave,* شِهَابٌ *a firebrand, a meteor,* شُهْبَانٌ; حُوَارٌ *an un-weaned foal of a camel,* حُورَانٌ.

A *Plur. Fract.*

XIX. فُعْلَانٌ continued. *Sing.*

4. فَعِيلٌ; as رَغِيفٌ *a cake of bread,* رُغْفَانٌ; قَضِيبٌ *a twig or rod,* قُضْبَانٌ; كَثِيبٌ *a sand-hill,* كُثْبَانٌ; ظَلِيمٌ *a male ostrich,* ظُلْمَانٌ; خَلِيلٌ *a friend,* خُلَّانٌ; قَرِيٌّ *a channel for irrigation,* قُرْيَانٌ; صَبِيٌّ *a boy or child,* صُبْيَانٌ.

B 5. فَاعِلٌ, verbal adjectives, used as substantives and not derived from verba mediæ rad. و et ى; as رَاكِبٌ *a rider,* رُكْبَانٌ; صَاحِبٌ *a companion,* صُحْبَانٌ; فَارِسٌ *a horseman,* فُرْسَانٌ; رَاهِبٌ *a Christian ascetic or recluse,* رُهْبَانٌ; شَابٌّ *a youth,* شُبَّانٌ; رَاعٍ *a shepherd,* رُعْيَانٌ.

6. أَفْعَلُ, fem. فَعْلَاءَ; as أَحْمَرُ *red,* حُمْرَانٌ; أَصْلَعُ *bald,* صُلْعَانٌ;
C أَصَمُّ *deaf,* صُمَّانٌ; أَعْوَرُ *blind of one eye,* عُورَانٌ; أَبْيَضُ *white,* عُمْيَانٌ; أَعْمَى *blind,* (بُيْضَانٌ for) بِيضَانٌ.

Rem. The forms فِعْلَانٌ and فُعْلَانٌ are, as some of the above examples show, used conjointly or interchangeable, even in cases where we should hardly expect it. For example, instead of عُورَانٌ, *blind of one eye,* from أَعْوَرُ, and حُورَانٌ, *unweaned foals of camels,* from حُوَارٌ, we find عِيرَانٌ and
D حِيرَانٌ. [حُشٌّ or حُشَّ *a garden* has حُشَّانٌ and حِشَّانٌ.]

XX. فُعَلَاءَ.

1. فَعِيلٌ, verbal adjectives, applicable to rational beings, which have not the passive signification, and are not derived from verba mediæ rad. geminatæ or tertiæ rad. و et ى; as فَقِيرٌ *poor,* فُقَرَاءَ; أَمِيرٌ *a commander or chief,* أُمَرَاءَ; رَئِيسٌ *a chief,* رُؤَسَاءَ; حَكِيمٌ *wise,* حُكَمَاءَ; ظَرِيفٌ *witty,* ظُرَفَاءَ; بَخِيلٌ *stingy,* بُخَلَاءَ; رُؤَسَاءَ

Plur. Fract. A

XX. فُعَلَآءُ continued. *Sing.*

a philosopher or sage, a physician, حُكَمَآءُ ; نَجِيبٌ *noble,* نُجَبَآءُ ;

بَيِّنٌ *clear, plain, eloquent,* بُيَنَآءُ.

2. فَاعِلٌ, some masc. adjectives, with the same restrictions as
above ; as عَالِمٌ *learned,* عُلَمَآءُ ; جَاهِلٌ *ignorant,* جُهَلَآءُ ; شَاعِرٌ
a poet, شُعَرَآءُ ; عَاقِلٌ *wise,* عُقَلَآءُ ; صَالِحٌ *good, right,* صُلَحَآءُ. B

REM. Examples of rarer cases are : سَمْحٌ *liberal,* سُمَحَآءُ ;
جَوَادٌ *liberal,* جُوَدَآءُ ; جَبَانٌ *cowardly,* جُبَنَآءُ (from جَبِينٌ) ;
شُجَاعٌ *brave,* شُجَعَآءُ (from شَجِيعٌ) ; قَتِيلٌ *slain,* قُتَلَآءُ ; أَسِيرٌ *a
prisoner,* أُسَرَآءُ ; [وَدُودٌ *loving,* وُدَدَآءُ].—خَلِيفَةٌ, *a successor,*
a deputy, a caliph, usually makes خُلَفَآءُ in the former senses,
and خَلَآئِفُ in the last. C

XXI. أَفْعِلَآءُ.

فَعِيلٌ, masc. adjectives of the same kind as XX. 1, but mostly
derived from verba mediæ rad. geminatæ or mediæ or tertiæ
rad. و et ى ; as صَدِيقٌ *a friend,* أَصْدِقَآءُ ; قَرِيبٌ *a relative,*
أَقْرِبَآءُ ; (أَخْلِلَآءُ, أَحْبِبَآءُ for) أَخِلَّآءُ, أَحِبَّآءُ *a friend,* خَلِيلٌ, حَبِيبٌ ;
طَبِيبٌ *a physician,* أَطِبَّآءُ ; شَدِيدٌ *strong,* أَشِدَّآءُ ; هَيِّنٌ (for هَوِينٌ) D
light, easy, أَهْوِنَآءُ ; لَيِّنٌ (for لَيِينٌ) *smooth, easy,* أَلْيِنَآءُ ; بَيِّنٌ
clear, plain, eloquent, أَبْيِنَآءُ ; غَنِىٌّ *rich,* أَغْنِيَآءُ ; عَىٌّ *stuttering,
stammering,* أَعْيِيَآءُ ; وَلِىٌّ *a friend, a welī or saint,* أَوْلِيَآءُ ;
شَقِىٌّ *wretched,* أَشْقِيَآءُ ; سَخِىٌّ *liberal,* أَسْخِيَآءُ ; تَقِىٌّ *pious,*
أَتْقِيَآءُ ; and similarly, بَرِىٌّ for بَرِىءٌ, *quit of, exempt from,*
أَبْرِيَآءُ ; نَبِىٌّ, for نَبِىءٌ, *a prophet,* أَنْبِيَآءُ.

A *Plur. Fract.*

XXII. فَعْلَى. *Sing.*

1. أَفْعَلُ, فَاعِلُ, فَعِلُ, فَعِيلُ, verbal adjectives, denoting injuries, defects, etc., of body or mind; as قَتِيلٌ *slain,* قَتْلَى; جَرِيحٌ *wounded,* جَرْحَى; لَدِيغٌ *bitten by a snake, stung by a scorpion,* لَدْغَى; أَسِيرٌ *a prisoner,* أَسْرَى; كَسِيرٌ *broken,* كَسْرَى; مَيِّتٌ

B (for مَوِيتٌ) *dead,* مَوْتَى; مَرِيضٌ *sick,* مَرْضَى; غَرِيقٌ *drowned,* غَرْقَى; هَالِكٌ *perishing,* هَلْكَى; عَائِلٌ *poor,* عَيْلَى; زَمِنٌ *paralytic,* زَمْنَى; وَجِعٌ *in pain,* وَجْعَى; هَرِمٌ *decrepit through age,* هَرْمَى; جَرِبٌ, or أَجْرَبُ, *mangy, scabby,* جَرْبَى; *حَمْقَى, or أَحْمَقُ, *silly,* حَمِقٌ or حَمْقَى; أَنْوَكُ *a fool,* نَوْكَى; جَرْبَى.

2. فَعْلَانُ, verbal adjectives; as كَسْلَانُ *lazy,* كَسْلَى;

C غَضْبَانُ *angry,* غَضْبَى; غَرْثَانُ *hungry,* غَرْثَى; سَكْرَانُ *drunken,* سَكْرَى.

REM. The plural فُعْلَى is said to occur in only two words; viz., حَجَلٌ *a partridge,* حِجْلَى, and ظَرِبَانٌ *a polecat,* ظِرْبَى.

XXIII. فَعَالٍ.

1. فَعْلَاءُ; as عَذْرَاءُ *a virgin,* عَذَارٍ; صَحْرَاءُ *a plain or desert,* صَحَارٍ; فَيْفَاءُ *a desert,* فَيَافٍ.

D 2. فُعْلَى, فَعْلَى; as فَتْوَى *a judicial opinion,* فَتَاوٍ; دَعْوَى *a claim,* دَعَاوٍ; ذِفْرَى *the prominent bone behind the ear,* ذَفَارٍ.

3. فَعْلَةٌ, فِعْلِيَةٌ; as سِعْلَاةٌ *a female ḡūl* (غُولٌ) *or goblin, an old hag,* سَعَالٍ; حِذْرِيَةٌ *rough ground,* حَذَارٍ; عِفْرِيَةٌ *the*

---

* [كَيِّسٌ *clever* has كَيْسَى in order that it may resemble (لِلِازْدِوَاجِ) its contrary حَمْقَى.]

Plur. Fract.   A

XXIII. فَعَالٍ continued.   *Sing.*

hackles of a cock, عَفَارٍ ; تَرْقُوَةٌ *the collar-bone*, تَرَاقٍ ; عَرْقُوَةٌ
the cross-handle of a bucket, عَرَاقٍ.

> REM. فَعَالٍ stands in the nom. and genit. for فَعَالِيَ and
> فَعَالِيَ (both with the art. اَلْفَعَالِي). The accus., however, is
> always فَعَالِيَ, with the art. اَلْفَعَالِيَ.—In the same way لَيْلٌ, B
> *night*, makes لَيَالٍ (acc. لَيَالِيَ) ; أَهْلٌ *one's people* or *family*,
> أَهَالٍ (acc. أَهَالِيَ) ; and أَرْضٌ, *the earth*, أَرَاضٍ (acc. أَرَاضِيَ).

XXIV. فَعَالَى.

1. فَعْلَاءَ ; as عَذْرَاءُ *a virgin*, عَذَارَى ; صَحْرَاءُ *a plain* or *desert*,
   صَحَارَى ; فَيْفَاءُ *a desert*, فَيَافَى.

2. فَعْلَى, فِعْلَى ; as فَتْوَى *a judicial opinion*, فَتَاوَى ; حَلْوَى C
   sweetmeat, حَلَاوَى ; دَعْوَى *a claim*, دَعَاوَى ; ذِفْرَى *the prominent*
   bone behind the ear, ذَفَارَى ; شَكْوَى *a complaint*, شَكَاوَى.

3. فُعْلَى, feminine adjectives, not superlatives ; as أُنْثَى *female*,
   feminine, أَنَاثَى ; حُبْلَى *pregnant*, حَبَالَى ; خُنْثَى *a hermaphro-*
   dite, خَنَاثَى.

4. فِعْلِيَةٌ ; as حِذْرِيَةٌ *rough ground*, حَذَارَى ; عِفْرِيَةٌ *the hackles* of a
   cock, عَفَارَى.

> REM. In nos. 1, 2, and 4, the forms فَعَالٍ and فَعَالَى are D
> interchangeable.

5. فَعْلَانُ, fem. فَعْلَى, and فَعِيلٌ, verbal adjectives ; as سَكْرَانُ
   drunken, سَكَارَى ; غَضْبَانُ *angry*, غَضَابَى ; غَرْثَانُ *hungry*,
   غَرَاثَى ; كَسْلَانُ *lazy*, كَسَالَى ; حَيْرَانُ *perplexed*, حَيَارَى ; غَيْرَانُ
   jealous, غَيَارَى ; أَسِيرٌ *a prisoner*, أَسَارَى ; كَسِيرٌ *broken*, كَسَارَى ;

A *Plur. Fract.*

XXIV. فَعَالَى continued.   *Sing.*

أَيِّمٌ ; نَدَامَى an orphan, يَتَامَى ; نَدِيمٌ *a boon-companion,* يَتِيمٌ

(for أَيِّمٌ) *unmarried,* أَيَامَى ; [خَزْيَانُ خَزَايَا *covered with shame,*].

6. فَعِلٌ, فَعُلٌ, verbal adjectives ; as حَبِطٌ *having a swollen belly,*

حَذَارَى ; وَجَاعَى , وَجِعٌ *in pain,* ; حَذُرٌ *cautious, wary,* حَبَاطَى ;

B حَزَانَى حَزِنٌ *sad,*.

> REM. Instead of فَعَالَى we find, in nos. 5 and 6, فُعَالَى
> and even فَعَالَى ; as سُكَارَى ,حُيَارَى ,عُجَالَى ,غُيَارَى ,أُسَارَى,
> عَاظِلٌ or رَدِيفٌ has only رُدَافَى and كُسَالَى ,وَجَاعَى ; كِسَالَى
> عُظَالَى only.

7. فَعِيلَةٌ, fem. substantives from verba tertiæ rad. و et ى ; as

C هَدِيَّةٌ *a present,* هَدَايَا ; مَنِيَّةٌ *fate,* مَنَايَا ; رَعِيَّةٌ *subjects,* رَعَايَا ;

بَلِيَّةٌ *a trial or calamity,* بَلَايَا ; مَطِيَّةٌ *an animal for riding,*

مَطَايَا ; سَجِيَّةٌ *nature, disposition,* سَجَايَا ; خَطِيَّةٌ (for خَطِيئَةٌ)

a sin, خَطَايَا ; [عَشِيَّةٌ* *evening,* عَشَايَا].

> REM. We write هَدَايَا instead of هَدَائِى, etc., to prevent
> the repetition of the letter ى (see § 179, rem. a).—Many
D grammarians regard these words as being of the form فَعَائِلُ
> (see XVII.), for هَدَائِى (هَدَآءُ), etc.

8. فَعَالَةٌ, from verba tertiæ rad. و et ى ; as جَدَايَةٌ *a young gazelle,*

جَدَايَا ; إِتَاوَةٌ *a tax,* أَتَاوَى ; إِدَاوَةٌ *a small water-skin,* أَدَاوَى ;

هَرَاوَةٌ ; عَلَاوَةٌ *the upper part, something over and above,* عَلَاوَى

---

* [In conjunction with عَشَايَا, for the sake of conformity

غَدَايَا.غُدْوَةٌ has (لِلِازْدِوَاجِ)]

Plur. Fract.

XXIV. فَعَالَى continued. *Sing.*

a stout stick, هَرَاوَى ; نُقَاوَةٌ *plants of the kind called* حَمْضٌ, *used for washing clothes,* نَقَاوَى ; نُقَايَةٌ *the pick and choice of anything,* نَقَايَا.

> REM. Here too فَعَالَى is thought to stand for فَعَائِلُ; as جَدَايَا for جَدَائِى (جَدَآءٌ), etc.

9. فَاعِلَةٌ, from verba mediæ rad. و and tertiæ rad. و et ى; as رَوَايَا ; رَاوِيَةٌ *a camel used in drawing water, a large water-skin,*; حَاوِيَةٌ *an intestine,* حَوَايَا ; زَاوِيَةٌ *a corner,* زَوَايَا.

> REM. a. Here فَعَالَى is thought to stand for فَوَاعِلُ; as رَوَايَا for رَوَائِى (رَوَآءٌ), etc.

> [REM. b. Anomalous is نَصَارَى from نَصْرَانِىٌّ *a Christian.*]

XXV. فَعِيلٌ (rare).

1. فَعَلٌ, فَعْلٌ; as عَبْدٌ *a slave,* عَبِيدٌ ; كَلْبٌ *a dog,* كَلِيبٌ ; بَقَرٌ *cattle,* بَقِيرٌ ; رَحًى *a mill,* رَحِىٌّ.

2. فِعَالٌ; as حِمَارٌ *an ass,* حَمِيرٌ.

3. فَاعِلٌ; as حَاجٌّ *a pilgrim,* حَجِيجٌ ; غَازٍ (for غَازِوٌ) *a soldier,* ضَيْشِينٌ. ضَأْنٌ *a sheep,* ضَئِينٌ ; مَاعِزٌ *a goat,* مَعِيزٌ ; غَزِىٌّ (for غَزِيوٌ).

XXVI. فُعُولَةٌ (rare).

فَعَلٌ, فَعْلٌ; as بَعْلٌ *a husband,* بُعُولَةٌ ; عَمٌّ *an uncle (by the father's side),* عُيُورَةٌ ; خَالٌ *an uncle (by the mother's side),* خُوولَةٌ (comp. § 240, rem. c); فَحْلٌ *a stallion,* صَقْرٌ ; نَمِرٌ *a panther,* نُمُورَةٌ ; خَيْطٌ [*a thread,* خُيُوطَةٌ ; فُحُولَةٌ *a hawk,* صُقُورَةٌ ; عَلَفٌ *fodder,* عُلُوفَةٌ].

A *Plur. Fract.*

XXVII. فَعَالَة (rare). *Sing.*

1. جَمَلٌ ,فَعَلٌ ; as ثَوْرٌ *a bull,* ثِيَارَةٌ ; [فَحْلٌ *a stallion,* فِحَالَةٌ ; *a camel,* جِمَالَةٌ (also جَمَالَةٌ)] ; ذَكَرٌ *male,* ذِكَارَةٌ ; حَجَرٌ *a stone,* حِجَارَةٌ.

2. فَاعِلٌ ; as صَاحِبٌ *a companion,* صِحَابَةٌ (also [the more common]

B صَحَابَةٌ).

XXVIII. فَعَلٌ (rare).

1. فَعْلَة ,فَعَلَة ; as حَلْقَةٌ *a ring, a circle,* حَلَقٌ ; بَكْرَةٌ *a pulley,* بَكَرٌ.

2. فَاعِلٌ, as نَاهِلٌ *drinking for the first time* (of camels), نَهَلٌ ; طَالِبٌ *seeking,* طَلَبٌ ; خَادِمٌ *a servant,* خَدَمٌ ; تَابِعٌ *a follower, an attendant,* تَبَعٌ ; رَاصِدٌ *lying in wait, watching,* رَصَدٌ ;

C *a guardian, a keeper,* حَرَسٌ ; جَالِبٌ *a driver, an importer,* جَلَبٌ.

XXIX. فَعْلٌ (rare).

تَاجِرٌ ; as شَارِبٌ *drinking,* شَرْبٌ ; نَاصِرٌ *a helper,* نَصْرٌ ; *a merchant,* تَجْرٌ ; صَاحِبٌ *a companion,* صَحْبٌ ; رَاكِبٌ *a rider,* رَكْبٌ ; سَافِرٌ *a traveller,* سَفْرٌ ; [زَائِرٌ *a visitor,* زَوْرٌ].

REM. *a.* The above rules regarding the correspondence of certain forms of the pluralis fractus and of the singular, are subject D to many exceptions*. The dictionaries also give various forms

---

* [Many scholars do not admit the forms XXV., XXVIII. and XXIX. as plur. fracta, but call them quasi-plurals (أَشْبَاهُ الجَمْعِ), making a distinction between them and the real collectives (أَسْمَآءُ الجَمْعِ), as قَوْمٌ etc., and the generic collectives (أَسْمَآءُ الجِنْسِ), which form a nomen unitatis, as نَحْلٌ. The forms فَعَلٌ ,فَعِيلٌ and فَعْلٌ are

which we have not thought it necessary to notice; for instance, A
عَبْدٌ, rarely مَفْعَلَةٌ and مَفْعَلَةٌ (as ضَبُعٌ *a hyæna,* مَضْبَعَةٌ;
slave, مَعْبَدَةٌ; وَعِلٌ *a mountain-goat,* مَوْعِلَةٌ; شَيْخٌ *an old man, a*
chief, a doctor, مَشْيَخَةٌ and مَشْيُخَةٌ; سَيْفٌ *a sword,* مَسْيَفَةٌ
and مَسِيفَةٌ), and مَفْعُولَاءَ, of which the principal examples in use
are: أَتَانٌ *a she-ass,* مَأْتُونَاءَ; بَغْلٌ *a mule,* مَبْغُولَاءَ; تَيْسٌ *a he-goat,*
عَبْدٌ *a he-ass,* مَشْيُوخَاءَ; شَيْخٌ *an old man,* مَحْمُورَاءَ; حِمَارٌ مَتْيُوسَاءَ; B
a slave, مَعْبُودَاءَ; عِلْجٌ *a Christian (or other not Muhammadan)*
captive or slave, مَعْلُوجَاءَ; عَيْرٌ *a wild ass,* مَعْيُورَاءَ; كَبِيرٌ *large, stout,*
مَكْبُورَاءَ.

REM. *b.* Many forms of the pluralis fractus seem to be derived,
not from the singular forms in actual use, but from others, which
are obsolete or of rare occurrence. E.g. شَاعِرٌ, فَاعِلٌ, pl. فُعَلَاءَ (as
a poet, شُعَرَاءَ,) from an obsolete فَعِيلٌ (شَعِيرٌ); and فَاعِلٌ, pl. فُعْلَى, C
(as هَالِكٌ *perishing,* هَلْكَى,) also from an obsolete فَعِيلٌ (هَلِيكٌ).

REM. *c.* From the preceding table it is obvious that one sing.
may have several forms of the pluralis fractus; e.g. بَحْرٌ *a sea,*
ثِيَارٌ, ثِيرَانٌ, ثَوَرَةٌ or ثِيرَةٌ, ثِيَرَةٌ, أَثْوَارٌ; ثَوْرٌ *a bull,* أَبْحُرٌ, بُحُورٌ, بِحَارٌ;
عِبْدَانٌ, أَعْبُدٌ, عَبِيدٌ, أَعْبِدَةٌ, أَعْبَادٌ, عُبُودٌ, عِبَادٌ, عَبْدٌ *a slave,* عَبْدٌ; ثِيَارَةٌ
(besides عَبْدٌ, عِبْدَانٌ, عِبِدَّاءَ, عَبْدَى, عِبِدَّةٌ, مَعْبَدَةٌ, مَعْبُودَاءَ, see rem. *a*);
صُحْبَانٌ, صَحَابَةٌ, أَصْحَابٌ, صِحَابٌ, صَحْبٌ *a companion,* صَاحِبٌ D
(besides صُحْبَةٌ, see rem. *a*). Or one sing. may have several plurales
fracti and a pluralis sanus besides; e.g. شَاهِدٌ *one who is present,*

---

masculine by form, feminine by signification. The forms XXVI. فُعُولَةٌ
and XXVII. فَعَالَةٌ seem to be derived respectively from فُعُولٌ and
فَعَالٌ with the termination ة to reinforce the collective meaning
[(تَآءٌ لِتَأْكِيدِ مَعْنَى ٱلْجَمْعِ).]

A an eye-witness, a witness, شَاهِدُونَ, شَهْدٌ, شُهَّدٌ, شُهُودٌ, أَشْهَادٌ; عَابِدٌ

serving, worshipping, عَابِدُونَ, عُبَّادٌ, عَبَدَةٌ. In such cases, if the sing. has several meanings, it often happens that each of them has one or more forms of the pluralis fractus which are peculiar to it, or used in preference to the rest. For example, شَاهِدٌ, in the sense of *an evidential example*, has شَوَاهِدُ. The word بَيْتٌ means:

(1) *a tent* or *house*, (2) *a verse of poetry*; in the former sense the

B plur. fract. is بُيُوتٌ or أَبْيَاتٌ, in the latter almost always أَبْيَاتٌ. Again, عَيْنٌ signifies: (1) *an eye*, (2) *a fountain*, (3) *peculiar nature or essence*, (4) *a distinguished man*; its plur. fract. in the first sense is عُيُونٌ, أَعْيُنٌ, or أَعْيَانٌ; in the second, أَعْيُنٌ or عُيُونٌ; in the third and fourth, أَعْيَانٌ. Or, to take another instance, بَطْنٌ means: (1) *the belly*, (2) *a valley*, (3) *a tribe*, (4) *the interior*, (5) *the inner* or *wider side of a wing-feather*; its plur. fract. in the first sense is بُطُونٌ, أَبْطُنٌ, or أَبْطِنَةٌ; in the second, بُطُونٌ, or

C بُطْنَانٌ; in the third, أَبْطُنٌ or بُطُونٌ; in the fourth and fifth, بُطْنَانٌ.

305. The forms of the plur. fract. of substantives and adjectives, which consist of *four* or more consonants, are exhibited, along with the corresponding singulars, in the following table.

Plur. Fract.

I. فَعَالِلُ (مَفَاعِلُ, تَفَاعِلُ, أَفَاعِلُ). *Sing.*

  1. Quadriliteral substantives and adjectives (ة not being counted as a letter), the consonants of which are all radical; as ثَعْلَبٌ

 a fox, دَرَاهِمُ; a dirham, دِرْهَمٌ; ضَفَادِعُ a frog, ضِفْدَعٌ; تَعَالِبُ;

D a claw of a lion, بَرَاثِنُ; a locust, جُنْدَبٌ; جَنَادِبُ; قَنْطَرَةٌ a bridge, قَنَاطِرُ; زِعْنِفَةٌ a fin of a fish, زَعَانِفُ; gems, جَوْهَرٌ; جَوَاهِرُ; a star, كَوْكَبٌ; كَوَاكِبُ; جَدْوَلٌ a streamlet, a column or table (in a book), جَدَاوِلُ.

  2. Quadriliterals (ة not included), formed from triliteral roots by prefixing أ, ت, or مـ; as إِصْبَعٌ, a finger, أَصَابِعُ; [أُنْمُلَةٌ *the end*

Plur. Fract.   A

I. مَفَاعِلُ, تَفَاعِلُ, أَفَاعِلُ) فَعَالِلُ) cont. *Sing.*

of a finger, أَنَامِلُ]; آدَمُ *Adam,* أَوَادِمُ; أَفْعَى *a viper,* أَفَاعٍ (for
أَفَاعِىُّ, compare § 304, no. XXIII., rem.); تَجْرِبَة *trial, ex-
perience,* تَجَارِبُ; مِخْلَبٌ *a claw* or *talon,* مَخَالِبُ; مَنْزِلَةٌ *a
halting-place, a station,* مَنَازِلُ; مَحَلَّةٌ *a place where one stops*
or *dwells, a quarter of a town,* مَحَالُّ; مَعِيشَةٌ *means of
subsistence,* مَعَايِشُ; مَعْنًى *meaning,* مَعَانٍ (for مَعَانِىُّ); مَرْثِيَةٌ B
an elegy, مَرَاثٍ (for مَرَاثِىُّ); مُرْضِعٌ *suckling,* مَرَاضِعُ].

REM. *a.* In the plur. fract. of the form مَفَاعِلُ from
verba mediæ rad. ى, the ى is not converted after the élif
productionis into hèmza (ء),—as happens, for instance, in
form XVII. of the triliterals (فَعَائِلُ), or in the nomen agentis
(فَاعِلُ, § 240),—but it remains unchanged; e.g. مَسَاحَةٌ, مَسَاحٌ,
an open space for walking (from سَاحَ for سَيَحَ), مَسَايِحُ; C
whereas مَسَائِحُ is the plural of مَسِيحَةٌ *a curl* (from مَسَحَ).
In the same form from verba mediæ rad. و, the و is usually
retained, as مِقْوَسٌ *a bowcase,* مَقَاوِسُ; مَفَازَةٌ (from فَازَ for
فَوَزَ) *a desert,* مَفَاوِزُ; مَلَامَةٌ *a reproof,* مَلَاوِمُ; مَغَاصٌ (from
غَاصَ for غَوَصَ) *a place for diving,* مَغَاوِصُ; but in one or
two instances into hèmza (ء), e.g. مُصِيبَةٌ (from صَابَ for
صَوَبَ) *a misfortune,* مَصَاوِبُ, and usually مَصَائِبُ; مَنَارَةٌ *a* D
candlestick, a lighthouse, a minaret, مَنَاوِرُ, and usually مَنَائِرُ.
The changing of the و into ى is vulgar, as مَغَايِرُ, مَنَايِرُ.

REM. *b.* Adjectives of the form أَفْعَلُ, especially with
the superlative meaning, make, when used as substantives
[and, in that case, often taking the form أَفْعَلُ, as أَجْدَلُ;
see § 309, *b,* γ], a plur. أَفَاعِلُ; e.g. أَدْهَمُ *a shackle* or *fetter,*

A *Plur. Fract.*

I. (مَفَاعِلُ, تَفَاعِلُ, أَفَاعِلُ) فَعَالِلُ) cont. *Sing.*

الْأَكَابِرُ, ; أَدَاهِمُ ; أَرْقَمُ ; أَرَاقِمُ *a mottled snake,* الْأَكْبَرُ *the greatest,* *grandees, nobles.*

II. (فَوَاعِيلُ, يَفَاعِيلُ, مَفَاعِيلُ, تَفَاعِيلُ, أَفَاعِيلُ) فَعَالِيلُ).

Quinqueliteral substantives and adjectives (ة not included), of
B which the penultimate letter is a litera productionis (١, و, ى);

as شَيْطَانٌ *a devil,* شَيَاطِينُ ; سِرْحَانٌ *a wolf,* سَرَاحِينُ ; سُلْطَانٌ
a sultan, سَلَاطِينُ ; تُبَّانٌ *short drawers,* تَبَابِينُ ; نَوَّارٌ *white
flowers,* نَوَاوِيرُ ; فُقَّاعَةٌ *a bubble,* فَقَاقِيعُ ; سِكِّينٌ *a knife,* سَكَاكِينُ ;
شَآبِيبُ ; شُؤْبُوبٌ *a heavy shower of rain,* قَنَادِيلُ ; قِنْدِيلُ *a lamp,*
مَكُّوكٌ a measure, (for كَرَاسِيُّ [*)] (for كَرَاسِيُّ كُرْسِيٌّ *a chair,*
C مَكَاكِيكُ and [مَكَاكِىُّ] بَرِّيَّةٌ *a desert,* بَرَارِيُّ (for بَرَارِيُّ);
تِمْثَالٌ *a statue,* تَمَاثِيلُ ; تَصْوِيرٌ *a picture,* تَصَاوِيرُ ; تَأْرِيخٌ *a
chronicle,* تَوَارِيخُ (compare § 303, *f,* rem.); مِفْتَاحٌ *a key,*
مَفَاتِيحُ ; مِسْكِينٌ *poor,* مَسَاكِينُ ; مَشْؤُومٌ *unlucky, inauspicious,*
مَشَائِيمُ ; مَيْمُونٌ *lucky, auspicious,* مَيَامِينُ ; مَلْعُونٌ *accursed,*
مَلَاعِينُ ; إِعْصَارٌ *a dust-storm with whirlwinds,* أَعَاصِيرُ ; إِكْلِيلٌ
a garland or crown, أَكَالِيلُ ; أُرْجُوزَةٌ *a poem in the metre*
D *rag̍ez,* أَرَاجِيزُ ; أُدْحِىٌّ or إِدْحِىٌّ (for أُدْحُوىٌّ) *an ostrich's nest,*
أَدَاحِىُّ ; آخِيَّةٌ [*a tent-rope,*] أَمَانِىُّ ; أُمْنِيَّةٌ (for أُمْنُوِيَّةٌ) *a wish,*

---

* [This may be lightened also to كَرَاسٍ, as إِنْسِىٌّ *a human being,*
has أَنَاسِىُّ and أُنَاسٍ ; بُخْتِىٌّ *a Bactrian camel,* بَخَاتِىُّ and بَخَاتٍ, مَهْرِىٌّ
a camel from Mahrah, مَهَارِىُّ and مَهَارٍ. The two latter words have
also the irregular plurals مَهَارَى and بَخَاتَى.]

Plur. Fract.	Sing.	A

II. فَعَالِيلُ (أَفَاعِيلُ, تَفَاعِيلُ, مَفَاعِيلُ, يَفَاعِيلُ, فَوَاعِيلُ) cont.

a sacred claim, يَنْبُوعٌ *a spring,* أَوَاخِىٌّ ;أَرِيَّةٌ *a stall,* [أَوَارِىٌّ];
a جَامُوسٌ ;يَعَاسِيبُ the queen-bee (rex apum), يَعْسُوبٌ ;يَنَابِيعُ
buffalo, جَوَامِيسُ; بَاسُورٌ hæmorrhoids, بَوَاسِيرُ.

REM. *a.* The plur. فَعَالِيلُ is sometimes found in cases where a quinqueliteral sing. form is either rare or does not B exist; as خَوَاتِيمُ signet-rings, from خَاتَمٌ = خَاتَامٌ (pl. خَوَاتِمُ); دَرَاهِيمُ dirhams, from دِرْهَمٌ = دِرْهَامٌ (pl. دَرَاهِمُ); قَنَاطِيرُ = قَنَاطِرُ bridges, from قَنْطَرَةٌ; مُفْطِرٌ one who breaks his fast, مَفَاطِيرُ; مُطْفِلٌ having a fawn with her, مَشَادِينُ and مَشَادٌ; مُشْدِنٌ having a young one with her, مَطَافِيلُ and مَطَافِلُ; مُنْكَرٌ clever, cunning, مَنَاكِيرُ. Conversely, فَعَالِلُ is used, chiefly by poetical license, instead of فَعَالِيلُ; as مَقَاصِرُ = مَقَاصِيرُ, C plur. of مَقْصُورَةٌ a space partitioned or railed off, a closet; أَعَاصِرُ = أَعَاصِيرُ, plur. of إِعْصَارٌ a dust-storm.

REM. *b.* دِينَارٌ a dinār, قِيرَاطٌ a carat, دِيوَانٌ a register, an account-book, a collection of poems, a public office or bureau, and إِيوَانٌ an arched or vaulted portico, vestibule or apartment, make دَنَانِيرُ, قَرَارِيطُ, دَوَاوِينُ, and أَوَاوِينُ (as if from singular forms دِنَّارٌ, قِرَّاطٌ, دِوَّانٌ and إِوَّانٌ). دِيبَاجٌ brocade, has D دَيَابِيجُ or دَبَابِيجُ; دِيمَاسٌ or دَيْمَاسٌ (δημόσιον), a dungeon, a bath, دَيَامِيسُ and دَمَامِيسُ; شِيرَازٌ or شَيْرَازٌ curds, شَوَارِيزُ, شَارِيزُ and شَرَارِيزُ; أَتُّونٌ, a furnace, أَتَانِينُ and perhaps also أَتَانِيُنُ (as if from a form أَتُّنٌ); (حُنَّاقٌ) خُنَّاقٌ quinsy, has خَوَانِيقُ and, in modern Arabic, خُنَّانِيقُ. Compare § 284, rem.

A *Plur. Fract.*

III. فَعَالِلَة. *Sing.*

1. Occasionally substantives and adjectives of five or more letters (principally foreign words), of which the penultimate letter is a litera productionis; as أُسْتَاذ (Pers. أُسْتَاذ) *a master, a teacher,*

B تِلْمِيذ (Heb. תַּלְמִיד, Syr. ܬܲܠܡܝܼܕܐ) *a* and تَلَامِذَة ; تَلَامِيذ and تَلَامِيذ ; فَيْلَسُوف (φιλόσοφος) *disciple, a pupil,* *a philosopher,* بِطْرِيق *a Grecian general* (patricius, πατρίκιος), بَطَارِيق and بَطَارِقَة ; مَطْرَان *a metropolitan bishop* (μητροπολίτης), مَطَارِين and مَطَارِنَة ; تُرْجُمَان *an interpreter,* تَرَاجِمَة and تَرَاجِم.

2. Substantives and adjectives of four or more letters, which have not a litera productionis before the last radical,—especially
C when they are words of foreign origin,—and a great many relative adjectives, consisting of more than four letters. E.g. مَلَأَك *an angel,* مَلَائِكَة ; صَيْقَل *a polisher of swords,* صَيَاقِل and صَيَاقِلَة ; تُبَّع *a king of el-Yèmèn,* تَبَابِعَة ; قُمَّس *a nobleman* (comes, κομής), قَمَامِسَة ; بَطْرَك *a patriarch or archbishop* (πατριάρχης), بَطَارِيك and بَطَارِكَة ; جَوْرَب *a stocking or sock* (Pers. كُورَب), جَوَارِب and جَوَارِبَة ; مُلْحِد *a heretic,* مَلَاحِدَة ;
D أُسْقُف (ἐπίσκοπος) *a bishop,* أَسَاقِف and أَسَاقِفَة ; قَيْصَر (*Cœsar,* Καῖσαρ) *the Byzantine emperor,* قَيَاصِرَة ; فِرْعَوْن (פַּרְעֹה) *Pharaoh,* فَرَاعِنَة ; صَيْرَف and صَيْرَفِى *a money-changer,* صَيَارِف and صَيَارِفَة ; مَغْرِبِى *a Moor,* مَغَارِبَة ; بَغْدَادِى *a native of Bagdād,* بَغَادِدَة ; مَصْمُودِى *a man of the Bèrbèr tribe of Maṣmūda,* مَصَامِدَة ; مُهَلَّبِى *a descendant of el-Muhalleb,* مَهَالِبَة.—From كِسْرَى (Pers. خُسْرَو, *Chosroes) the king of*

III. فَعَالِلَةٌ continued. *Sing.*

Persia, are formed irregularly أَكَاسِرَ ,أَكَابِرَةٌ, and كَسَابِرَةٌ ;

and سَوَآءٌ or سِىّ, *a like, an equal,* has, besides أَسْوَآءٌ, the

irregular سَوَابِوَةٌ ,سَوَاسِيَةٌ, and سَوَاسٍ (for سَوَاسِىّ).

REM. *a.* This form is also found, though rarely, in quadri-literals which have a litera productionis before the last radical; B

as جَبَّارٌ *a tyrant, a giant,* جَبَابِرَةٌ ; شَمَّاسٌ *a deacon* (Syr. ܡܫܰܡܫܳܐ),

شَمَامِسَةٌ.

REM. *b.* In forming the plur. fract. of nouns which contain five or more letters (exclusive of ة and the letters of prolongation), one of the radicals is rejected, generally the last. E.g. عَنْكَبُوتٌ *a spider,* عَنَاكِبُ ; جَحْمَرِشٌ *a fat, lazy old woman,* جَحَامِرُ ; but عَنْدَلِيبٌ *a nightingale,* عَنَادِلُ ; سَفَرْجَلٌ *a quince,* سَفَارِجُ ; فَرَزْدَقٌ *a burnt cake,* فَرَازِقُ ; قَلَنْسُوَةٌ *a sort of cap,* قَلَانِسُ ,قَلَانِسٌ (for قَلَانِسِىّ), or C

بَطَالِسَةٌ ; بَطْلَمِيُوسُ *Ptolemy,* قَلَانِسِىّ ; أُسْطُوَانَةٌ *a pillar,* أَسَاطِينُ ;

دِمَشْتَى *a Byzantine governor* (domesticus, δομεστικός). Here

may also be mentioned such plurals as عَبَادِلَةٌ from عَبْدُ ٱللّٰهِ *'Abdu 'llāh* (compare § 264, rem. *b*).

REM. *c.* The forms of the plur. fract. of quadriliterals and quinqueliterals are also used in forming plurals from other plurals

(جَمْعُ ٱلْجَمْعِ *the plur. of the plur.,* or secondary plural). In

particular, forms XIII. أَفْعُلٌ and XV. أَفْعِلَةٌ make أَفَاعِلُ, and XIV. D

أَفْعَالٌ ,أَفَاعِيلُ ; more rarely V. فِعَالٌ ,فَعَائِلُ, and XVIII. and XIX.

فُعْلَانٌ ,فَعَالِينُ. E.g. XIII. كَلْبٌ *a dog,* أَكْلُبُ ,أَكَالِبُ ; نَاقَةٌ *a she-camel,* أَنْيُقٌ ,أَيَانِقُ ; رَهْطٌ *one's people or tribe,* أَرْهُطٌ ,أَرَاهِطُ ; ضِلَعٌ *a rib,* أَضْلُعُ ,أَضَالِعُ ; يَدٌ *a hand, a benefit,* أَيْدٍ (for أَيْدُىٌ), أَيَادٍ (for أَيَادِىُ) ; مَكَانٌ *a place,* أَمْكِنَةٌ ,أَمَاكِنُ ; XV. سِوَارٌ *a bracelet,* أَسْوِرَةٌ ,أَسَاوِرُ ; (أَسَاوِرِىُ

A أَنْعَامُ, camels, نَعَمْ. XIV. أَوَانٍ, آنِيَةٌ (for أَوَانِىُ); إِنَاءٌ a vessel, أَمَاكِنُ;

قَوْلٌ a saying, a speech, أَزَاهِيرُ, أَزْهَارٌ a (yellow) flower, زَهْرٌ; أَنَاعِيمُ;

جِلَدٌ she-camels having أَظَافِيرُ, أَظْفَارٌ; ظُفْرٌ a nail, أَقَاوِيلُ, أَقْوَالٌ;

neither young ones nor milk, أَجَالِيدُ, أَجْلَادٌ; V. جَمَلٌ a he-camel,

مَصَارِينُ, مُصْرَانٌ; XVIII. XIX. مَصِيرٌ an intestine, جِمَالٌ, جَمَائِلُ;

حُشٌّ a garden (of palm trees), حُشَّانٌ, حَشَاشِينُ; عُقَابٌ an eagle,

B أَفْعِلَاتٌ; عُقْبَانٌ. عَقَابِينُ. Again, XV. أَفْعِلَةٌ forms a pluralis sanus

as شَرَابٌ a drink, دُخَانٌ; أَثْرِبَةٌ, أَثْرِبَاتٌ; دُخَانٌ smoke, أَدْخِنَةٌ, أَدْخِنَاتٌ;

بِنَاءٌ a building, أَبْنِيَةٌ, أَبْنِيَاتٌ; عَطَاءٌ a gift, pay, أَعْطِيَةٌ, أَعْطِيَاتٌ. A

pluralis sanus in ـَاتٌ may also be derived from V. فِعَالٌ, VI. فُعُولٌ,

III. فُعُلٌ, XVII. فَعَائِلُ, and a few other forms; as جَمَلٌ a he-camel,

كَلْبٌ a dog, كِلَابٌ; رِجَالٌ, رِجَالَاتٌ; رَجُلٌ a man, جِمَالٌ, جِمَالَاتٌ;

بَيْتٌ a house, بُيُوتٌ, بُيُوتَاتٌ, houses, families; كِلَابَاتٌ; طَرِيقٌ

C a road, طُرُقٌ, طُرُقَاتٌ; جَزُورٌ a she-camel for slaughter, جُزُرٌ, جُزُرَاتٌ;

حَدِيدَةٌ an iron tool, حَدَائِدُ, حَدَائِدَاتٌ; حِمَارٌ a he-ass, حُمُرٌ, حُمُرَاتٌ;

نَسِيجَةٌ anything woven or plaited, نَسَائِجُ, نَسَائِجَاتٌ; دَارٌ a house,

نَاقَةٌ [صَاحِبَةٌ a female companion, صَوَاحِبُ, صَوَاحِبَاتٌ]; دُورٌ, دُورَاتٌ

a she-camel, pl. أَيْنُقٌ, نِيَاقٌ, نِيَاقَاتٌ, أَيْنُقَاتٌ and (with the dimin.

أُيَيْنِقَاتٌ); etc. Sometimes there is even a treble formation; as

فِرْقَةٌ a band, a party or sect, فِرَقٌ, أَفْرَاقٌ, أَفَارِيقُ. Such secondary

D plurals can be properly used only when the objects denoted are at

least nine in number, or when their number is indefinite.

REM. *d.* Plurals [or rather collectives] are formed from a

great many relative adjectives,—especially those that indicate the

relations of sect, family, or clientship,—by adding the termination

ـَة; as شَافِعِىٌّ a follower of *eš-Šāfiʿī* (ٱلشَّافِعِىُّ), ٱلشَّافِعِيَّةُ the sect of

the *Šāfiʿites*; صُوفِىٌّ a *Ṣūfī*, ٱلصُّوفِيَّةُ the sect of the *Ṣūfīs*;

ٱلْمَرْوَانِيَّةُ,

اَلزُّبَيْرِيَّةُ, *the partisans of Marwān, of Ibnu 'z-Zubēir.* See § 268. A Sometimes ةـ is added with the same effect to other adjectives, especially of the forms فَاعِلٌ and فَعَّالٌ; as ثَارِبَةٌ *those who live on the bank and drink the water of (a certain stream);* [and وَارِدَةٌ وَرَّادَةٌ] *(men) drawing water or (cattle) drinking;* سَابِلَةٌ *travellers;* جَمَّالَةٌ, حَمَّارَةٌ, خَيَّالَةٌ, بَغَّالَةٌ, *persons who own or keep camels, asses, horses, mules;* سَيَّارَةٌ *a company of persons journeying together, a caravan* (Syr. ܐ̈ܪܚ); رَجَّالَةٌ *pedestrians;* نَظَّارَةٌ *spectators;* [نَهَّابَةٌ *plunderers*].

B

REM. c. The plural of some nouns is anomalous, or derived from other forms or roots than the sing. in use; as أُمٌّ *a mother,* (Syr. ܐܡ̈ܗܬܐ, ܐܡܐ), rarely أُمَّاتٌ; فَمٌ *a mouth,* أَفْوَاهٌ (from a sing. فُوهٌ or فَوْهٌ); مَآءٌ *water, a spring,* مِيَاهٌ, أَمْوَاهٌ (from a sing. مَاهٌ); شَفَةٌ *a lip,* شِفَاهٌ, شِيَاهٌ, شَآءٌ; اِسْتٌ *the anus,* أَسْتَاهٌ; شَاةٌ *a sheep or goat,* شِيَاهٌ (from the rad. شَيَه, whence اِمْرَأَةٌ *a woman,* نِسَاءٌ, نِسْوَةٌ, نِسْوَانٌ (from the rad. أَنَس, whence Heb. אִישׁ, אִשָּׁה for אֲנָשׁ, אֲנָשָׁה); خُلْدٌ *a mole,* مَنَاجِذُ (from

C

the rad. نَجَذ). إِنْسَانٌ, *a human being* (Heb. אִישׁוֹן, for אֲנָשׁוֹן), has usually نَاسٌ [especially with the article اَلنَّاسُ], instead of the older and poetic أُنَاسٌ (Heb. אֲנוֹשׁ, Aram. אֲנָשָׁא, ܐ̈ܢܫܐ).

---

306. As regards their meaning, the plurales fracti differ entirely from the sound plurals; for the latter denote several *distinct* individuals of a genus, the former a number of individuals viewed *collectively,* the idea of individuality being wholly suppressed. For D example, عَبْدُونَ are *slaves (servi),* i.e. several individuals who are slaves; عَبِيدٌ *slaves* collectively (*servitium* or *servitus*); شُبَّانٌ *young men, youth (juventus),* = شَبَابٌ; مَشْيَخَةٌ *old* men in general. The plurales fracti are consequently, strictly speaking, *singulars* with a *collective* signification, and often approach in their nature to *abstract nouns.* Hence, too, they are all of the *feminine* gender, and can be used as masc. only by a constructio ad sensum.

A   REM. We must distinguish from the plurales fracti those nouns which are called أَسْمَآءُ ٱلْجِنْسِ (*generic nouns*), as نَحْلٌ *bees*, on which see § 246 and § 292, *a*. The former may be styled *abstract*, the latter *concrete collectives*. A third class of collectives is formed by those nouns, to the meaning of which the idea of collectiveness attaches; as قَوْمٌ, رَهْطٌ, *people* or *tribe*, عَسْكَرٌ *an army* ; [إِبِلٌ] *camels*, غَنَمٌ *sheep*]. These are called أَسْمَآءُ ٱلْجَمْعِ or أَشْبَاهُ ٱلْجَمْعِ (*like the plural*), and differ from the أَسْمَآءُ ٱلْجِنْسِ in not admitting of the

B   formation of nomina unitatis (§ 246).

307. The pluralis sanus and the plurales fracti of the forms XII. فِعْلَةٌ, XIII. أَفْعُلٌ, XIV. أَفْعَالٌ, and XV. أَفْعِلَةٌ, are used only of persons and things which do not exceed *ten* in number (3 to 10), and are therefore called جُمُوعُ قِلَّةٍ, *plurals of paucity*, whilst the rest are named جُمُوعُ كَثْرَةٍ, *plurals of abundance*. This observation applies,

C   of course, only to such nouns as have also other plurals, for if one of the forms alone be used, it is necessarily employed without any limitation as to number.

4. *The Declension of Nouns.*

I. *The Declension of Undefined Nouns.*

308. (1) Undefined substantives and adjectives are, in the *singular* number, either *triptotes* or *diptotes*. Triptotes are those which have *three* terminations to indicate the different cases; viz. ـٌ

D   (Nom.), ـٍ (Gen.), and ـًا or ـً (Acc., see § 8, rem. *a*). Diptotes are those which have only *two* terminations; viz. ـُ (Nom.) and ـَ (Gen., Acc.)*.—(2) The *dual* number has only *two* case-endings, which are

---

* A noun may be مُعْرَبٌ, *declinable*, or مَبْنِىٌّ, *indeclinable*. A declinable noun may be مُنْصَرِفٌ, *declined with tenwīn*, or غَيْرُ مُنْصَرِفٍ, *declined without tenwīn*. The term مُتَمَكِّنٌ فِى ٱلِٱسْمِيَّةِ, *established in*, or *possessed of, the nominal character or nature*, or simply مُتَمَكِّنٌ, is synonymous with مُعْرَبٌ, and غَيْرُ مُتَمَكِّنٍ with مَبْنِىٌّ; whilst

common to both genders; viz. ـَانِ (Nom.) and ـَيْنِ (Gen., Acc.)*.— A
(3) The *pluralis sanus* has likewise only *two* case-endings for each

مُتَمَكِّنٌ أَمْكَنُ, *possessed of* (the nominal character) to the fullest extent,
is equivalent to مُنْصَرِفٌ, and غَيْرُ مُنْصَرِفٍ.—to مُتَمَكِّنٌ غَيْرُ أَمْكَنَ
The vowel *u* of the nominative is called اَلرَّفْعُ, *the raising* (of the voice),
and is عَلَمُ ٱلْفَاعِلِيَّةِ, *the sign of agency;* the vowel *i* is termed اَلْخَفْضُ
the depression (of the voice), or اَلْجَرُّ, *the being drawn along* or *attracted* B
(*by a governing word,* اَلْجَارُّ), and is عَلَمُ ٱلْإِضَافَةِ, *the sign of annexation;*
the vowel *a* is designated اَلنَّصْبُ, *the uplifting* or *elevation* (of the
voice), and is عَلَمُ ٱلْمَفْعُولِيَّةِ, *the sign of objectivity.*—The tenwīn may be
(*a*) اَلتَّنْوِينُ ٱلدَّالُّ عَلَى ٱلْمَكَانَةِ, *the nunation which shows that a noun is*
fully declinable, also called تَنْوِينُ ٱلتَّمْكِينِ, and found in the singular
and the pluralis fractus, as رَجُلٌ, رِجَالٌ; (*b*) تَنْوِينُ ٱلْمُقَابَلَةِ, *the*
nunation of correspondence, found in the plural feminine, as مُسْلِمَاتٌ,
because it corresponds to the ن of مُسْلِمِينَ; (*c*) تَنْوِينُ ٱلتَّنْكِيرِ, *the* C
nunation which distinguishes, in the case of an indeclinable noun,
between the definite, اَلْمَعْرِفَةِ, *and the indefinite,* اَلنَّكِرَةِ, as مَرَرْتُ بِسِيبَوَيْهِ
وَسِيبَوَيْهِ آخَرَ, *I passed by* Sībaweih *and another* (man called) Sībaweih;
and (*d*) تَنْوِينُ ٱلْعِوَضِ, *the nunation of compensation.* This last may
be of three kinds: (*a*) of compensation for the omission of an entire
proposition, as in وَأَنْتُمْ حِينَئِذٍ تَنْظُرُونَ *and ye are then looking on,*
where حِينَئِذٍ stands for حِينَ إِذْ بَلَغَتِ ٱلرُّوحُ ٱلْحُلْقُومَ, *at the time when*
the spirit has reached the throat; (*β*) of compensation for a governed D
word, as when the genitive is omitted after كُلٌّ or بَعْضٌ, as كُلٌّ قَائِمٌ
for كُلُّ إِنْسَانٍ قَائِمٌ or كُلُّهُمْ قَائِمٌ; (*γ*) of compensation for a letter, as
in جَوَارٍ, plural of جَارِيَةٌ, for جَوَارِيُ in the nominative or جَوَارِيَ in the
genitive.

* The form ـَيْنَ is used dialectically, as in the hemistich عَلَى
أَحْوَذِيَّيْنَ ٱسْتَقَلَّتْ عَشِيَّةً, *at eve it* (a bird) *rose on two nimble* (wings).

A gender; viz. for the *masculine*, ـُونَ (Nom.) and ـِينَ (Gen., Acc.)*;
for the *feminine*, ـَاتُ (Nom.) and ـَاتِ (Gen., Acc.).—(4) The *plurales
fracti* are either diptotes or triptotes, exactly like the singular (see
§ 309, *a*).—The following is the paradigm of the declension of undefined
substantives and adjectives.

TRIPTOTE OR FIRST DECLENSION.

Substantives.

B

	Masc.		Fem.	
	Proper.	Common.	Proper.	Common.
	Sing.		Sing.	
N.	زَيْدٌ *Zeïd.*	رَجُلٌ *a man.*	هِنْدُ *Hind.*	جَنَّةٌ *a garden.*
G.	زَيْدٍ	رَجُلٍ	هِنْدَ	جَنَّةٍ
Ac.	زَيْدًا	رَجُلًا	هِنْدَا	جَنَّةً
	Dual.		Dual.	
C N.	زَيْدَانِ	رَجُلَانِ	هِنْدَانِ	جَنَّتَانِ
G. Ac.	زَيْدَيْنِ	رَجُلَيْنِ	هِنْدَيْنِ	جَنَّتَيْنِ

The existence of the form ـَانِ is doubtful, despite the verse أَعْرِفُ
مِنْهَا ٱلْجِيدَ وَٱلْعَيْنَانَا وَمَنْخِرَيْنِ أَشْبَهَا ظَبْيَانَا, *I know of her the neck, and
the two eyes, and two nostrils which resemble two gazelles,* in which
D ٱلْعَيْنَانَ and ظَبْيَانَ (written in rhyme نَا) are used instead of ٱلْعَيْنَيْنِ
and ظَبْيَيْنِ.

* The form ـِينَ is said by some to be dialectical, whilst others
consider it due only to poetic license (ضَرُورَةُ ٱلشِّعْرِ); e.g. وَأَنْكَرُنَا
وَمَا ذَا تَبْتَغِى زَعَانِفَ آخَرِينَ, *and we ignore the riffraff of other (tribes);*
ٱلشُّعَرَاءُ مِنِّى وَقَدْ جَاوَزْتُ حَدَّ ٱلْأَرْبَعِينَ, *and what is it pray that the poets
want of me, since I have already passed the limit of forty (years)?*
where ٱلْأَرْبَعِينَ and آخَرِينَ are used instead of آخَرِينَ and ٱلْأَرْبَعِينَ.

Triptote or First Declension.

A

Substantives.

	Masc.		Fem.	
	Proper.	Common.	Proper.	Common.

Plur. sanus.   *Plur. sanus.*

N.	زَيْدُونَ		هِنْدَاتُ	جَنَّاتُ
G. Ac.	زَيْدِينَ	...	هِنْدَاتٍ	جَنَّاتٍ

Plur. fract.   *Plur. fract.*　　B

N.	زُيُودٌ	رِجَالٌ	هُنُودٌ	جِنَانٌ
G.	زُيُودٍ	رِجَالٍ	هُنُودٍ	جِنَانٍ
Ac.	زُيُودًا	رِجَالًا	هُنُودًا	جِنَانًا

Adjectives.

	Masc.	Fem.

Sing.　　C

N.	جَالِسٌ sitting.	نَائِحَةٌ mourning.
G.	جَالِسٍ	نَائِحَةٍ
Ac.	جَالِسًا	نَائِحَةً

Dual.

N.	جَالِسَانِ	نَائِحَتَانِ
G. Ac.	جَالِسَيْنِ	نَائِحَتَيْنِ

Plur. sanus.　　D

N.	جَالِسُونَ	نَائِحَاتٌ
G. Ac.	جَالِسِينَ	نَائِحَاتٍ

Plur. fract.

N.	جُلَّاسٌ	نُوَّحٌ
G.	جُلَّاسٍ	نُوَّحٍ
Ac.	جُلَّاسًا	نُوَّحًا

A

DIPTOTE OR SECOND DECLENSION.

Substantives.

	Masc.		Fem.	
		Sing.		
N.	عُثْمَانُ	'Othmān.	زَيْنَبُ	Zeineb.
G. Ac.	عُثْمَانَ		زَيْنَبَ	
		Dual.		
N.	عُثْمَانَانِ		زَيْنَبَانِ	
G. Ac.	عُثْمَانَيْنِ		زَيْنَبَيْنِ	

B

		Plur. sanus.		
N.	عُثْمَانُونَ		زَيْنَبَاتٌ	
G. Ac.	عُثْمَانِينَ		زَيْنَبَاتٍ	

Plur. fract.

(of دِرْهَمٌ *a dirham*)		(of جَارِيَةٌ *a young woman*)	
N.	دَرَاهِمُ	N. G.	*جَوَارٍ
G. Ac.	دَرَاهِمَ	A.	جَوَارِيَ

C

Adjectives.

	Masc.		Fem.	
		Sing.		
N.	أَسْوَدُ *black.*	أَفْضَلُ *more excellent.*	سَوْدَآءُ *black.*	
G. Ac.	أَسْوَدَ	أَفْضَلَ	سَوْدَآءَ	
		Dual.		
N.	أَسْوَدَانِ	أَفْضَلَانِ	سَوْدَاوَانِ	
G. Ac.	أَسْوَدَيْنِ	أَفْضَلَيْنِ	سَوْدَاوَيْنِ	

D

		Plur. sanus.		
N.		أَفْضَلُونَ		
G. Ac.	...	أَفْضَلِينَ		...

* جَوَارٍ stands in the Nom. for جَوَارِيُ, in the Gen. for جَوَارِيَ (identical in form with the Acc.). See p. 235, at the end of the note.

DIPTOTE OR SECOND DECLENSION. A

Adjectives.

Masc. Fem.

Plur. fract.

(of فَقِيرٌ *poor*) (of نَائِحَةٌ *mourning*)

N. فُقَرَاءُ نَوَائِحُ

G. Ac. فُقَرَاءَ نَوَائِحُ

REM. *a.* There are two words in Arabic, in which the final B flexional vowel of the singular affects the last vowel of the radical part of the substantive; viz. اِمْرُؤٌ, *a man*, and اِبْنُمٌ, *a son*, for اِمْرَأٌ and اِبْنُمٌ, which are also used (see § 19, *d*).

Sing. Nom. اِبْنُمٌ, اِمْرُؤٌ or اِمْرُو

Gen. اِبْنِمٍ, اِمْرِئٍ or اِمْرِي

Acc. اِبْنَمًا, اِمْرَأً or اِمْرَا

[According to ĕn-Naḍr ibn Šŏmĕil, as quoted by Zamaḫšarī, *Fāïḳ* C i. 524, فَمٌ *the mouth* is also doubly declined, فُمٌ, فِمٍ, فَمًا, as هٰذَا فُمُهُ and أَخْرَجَ لِسَانَهُ مِنْ فِيهِ, رَأَيْتُ فَمَهُ. Comp. Lane and Fleischer, *Kl. Schr.* i. 180. D. G.]

REM. *b.* For the comparison of the Arabic Declension with that of the other Semitic Languages see *Comp. Gr.* p. 139 *seqq.*

309. The following nouns are diptote. D

a. Several forms of the pluralis fractus; viz.

(α) Quadrisyllabic plurales fracti, the first and second syllables of which have fètḥa and the third kèsra, that is to say, the forms فَوَاعِلُ (XVI.), فَعَائِلُ (XVII.), فَعَالِلُ etc., and فَعَالِيلُ etc. (I. and II. of nouns which have more than three radical letters); as بَوَاعِثُ *causes*, عَجَائِبُ *wonders*, قَنَاطِرُ *bridges*, سَلَاطِينُ *sultans.*

(β) Plurales fracti which end in hèmza preceded by ĕlif mèmdūda

A (ﺍﹶ_ﺍﹶ), viz. ﻓَﻌَﻼَﺓ (XX.) and أَﻓْﻌَﻼَﺓ (XXI.); as ﺣُﻜَﻤَﺎﺀ *wise men,* أَوْﻟِﻴَﺎﺀ *friends* (compare *b*, *a* and *c*, *β*).

(γ) Plurales fracti which end in ـ and ﻯ_, viz. ﻓَﻌَﺎﻝ (XXIII.), ﻓَﻌْﻠَﻰ (XXII.), and ﻓَﻌَﺎﻟَﻰ (XXIV.); as ﻋَﺬَﺍﺭٍ *virgins,* ﺟَﺮْﺣَﻰ *wounded men,* أَﺳَﺎﺭَﻯ *prisoners,* ﻫَﺪَﺍﻳَﺎ *presents* (compare *b*, *β* and *c*, *β*).

(δ) أَوَّﻝ, plur. fract. of أَوَّﻝ, and of its fem. أُوﻟَﻰ, *first;* أَﺧَﺮُ, plur. fract. of آﺧَﺮُ, and of its fem. أُﺧْﺮَﻯ, *other, another;* ﺟَﻤْﻊ, B ﻛُﺘَﻊ, ﺑَﺼَﻊ, ﺑُﺘَﻊ, plur. fract. of ﺟَﻤْﻌَﺎﺀ, ﻛَﺘْﻌَﺎﺀ, ﺑَﺼْﻌَﺎﺀ, ﺑَﺘْﻌَﺎﺀ, fem. of أَﺟْﻤَﻊ, etc., *all together.*

[(ε) أَﺷْﻴَﺎﺀ, the irregular plural of ﺷَﻲﺀ (comp. XIV. 2, rem.).]

b. Various common nouns and adjectives; viz.

(*a*) Common nouns and adjectives which end in hèmza preceded by êlif mèmdûda (ﺍﹶ_ﺍﹶ); as ﻋَﺬْﺭَﺍﺀ *a virgin,* ﺑَﻴْﻀَﺎﺀ *white* (§ 296). C Compare *a*, *β* and *c*, *β*.

REM. This rule does not apply to cases in which the hèmza is *radical,* as ﻗُﺮَّﺍﺀ from ﻗَﺮَﺃ (compare § 299, rem. *c*, and § 301, rem. *e*).

(*β*) Common nouns and adjectives ending in êlif maksûra (ﻯ_); as ﺫِﻛْﺮَﻯ *memory,* ﺳَﻜْﺮَﻯ *drunken* (§ 295, *a*). Compare *a*, γ and *c*, *β*.

REM. Excepting those in which the êlif maksûra is *radical;* as D ﻫُﺪَﻯ *guidance* (for ﻫُﺪَﻱ, § 213).

(γ) Adjectives of the form أَﻓْﻌَﻞ (§§ 232, 16, and 234—5), of which the fem. is ﻓُﻌْﻠَﻰ and ﻓَﻌْﻼَﺀ (§§ 295, *b*, and 296); as أَﻋْﺠَﺐ *more wonderful;* أَﺣْﻤَﺮُ *red.*—But adjectives of the form أَﻓْﻌَﻞ, f. أَﻓْﻌَﻠَﺔ, are triptote; as أَﺭْﻣَﻞ *poor, needy, without a wife,* f. أَﺭْﻣَﻠَﺔ *poor, needy, without a husband, a widow.*—Substantives of this form are usually regarded as triptote, e.g. أَﺟْﺪَﻝ *a hawk,* أَﺧْﻴَﻞ *a green woodpecker,* أَﺭْﻧَﺐ *a hare,* أَﺯْﻣَﻞ *a humming;* but the diptote form is admissible in such as were originally adjectives, e.g. أَﺧْﻴَﻞ, أَﺟْﺪَﻝ.

Rem. *a.* Some good authorities give أَرْمَلُ as the masculine of A أَرْمَلَةٌ, which would be very irregular.

Rem. *b.* Adjectives of the form أَفْعَلُ, when used as sub-stantives, retain the diptote inflection; e.g. أَدْهَمُ *a fetter* (properly *blackish, dun*), أَسْوَدُ *a serpent* (prop. *black*), أَبْرَقُ *stony land* (prop. *mottled*), أَبْطَحُ *a wide, gravelly water-course,* أَجْرَعُ *a tract of land without herbage.*

(δ) Adjectives of the form فَعْلَانٌ, of which the fem. is فَعْلَى B (§ 295, *a*); as سَكْرَانُ, f. سَكْرَى, *drunken.*—But those of which the fem. is فَعْلَانَةٌ (§ 295, rem. *a*) are triptote; as نَدْمَانٌ, f. نَدْمَانَةٌ, *a boon companion.*—Adjectives of the form فُعْلَانٌ are all triptote, their fem. being formed by adding ةٌ‍ـ (§ 295, rem. *a*); as عُرْيَانٌ, f. عُرْيَانَةٌ, *naked.*

Rem. *a.* Adjectives of the form فَعْلَانٌ, f. فَعْلَانَةٌ, are rare. The principal examples in the language are: أَلْيَانٌ *having a large fat tail* (of a sheep); حَبْلَانٌ *angry;* دَخْنَانٌ *stiflingly hot;* سَخْنَانُ *hot;* C سَيْفَانٌ *tall and slender;* ضَحْيَانٌ *exposed to the sun, eating in the forenoon* (الضُّحَى); صَوْحَانٌ and صَوْجَانٌ *dry, withered;* عَلَّانٌ *stupid, ignorant;* قَشْوَانُ *thin, slender;* مَصَّانٌ *sucking* (sheep or cows) *out of greed, mean, vile;* مَوْتَانُ *stupid, stolid;* نَدْمَانٌ *a boon companion;* نَصْرَانٌ *Christian.* Some of these, however, have also the form فَعْلَانٌ, فَعَلَانٌ, فُعْلَانٌ, or فُعَلَانٌ; as أَلْيَانٌ and أَلَيَانٌ; سَخْنَانٌ, قَشْوَانٌ; صُوحَانٌ; سَخْنَانٌ, or سُخْنَانٌ. The word صَوْحَانٌ may perhaps be merely a mistake for صَوْحَانٌ or صُوحَانٌ.

Rem. *b.* فُلَانٌ *so and so, such and such a one,* makes irregularly D in the feminine فُلَانَةٌ, [because it takes the place of a proper name (*c, ζ*)].

(ε) The masculine numerals as mere abstract numbers; e.g. سِتَّةٌ أَكْثَرُ مِنْ خَمْسَةٍ بِوَاحِدٍ 8 *is the double of* 4; ثَمَانِيَةٌ ضِعْفُ أَرْبَعَةٍ 6 *is more than 5 by one.*

(ζ) Distributive numerals of the forms فُعَالُ and مَفْعَلُ (§ 333); as ثُنَاءُ and مَثْنَى, *two by two,* ثُلَاثُ and مَثْلَثُ, *three by three.*

A (η) The grammatical paradigms formed from the root فعل, when used without the article as a sort of definite proper names. For example : أَفْعَلُ صِفَةً لَا يَنْصَرِفُ (*the form*) *áf'al*, (*used*) *as an adjective, is declined without tènwîn* (e.g. أَفْعَلُ إِذَا كَانَ ٱسْمًا نَكِرَةً *red*) ; أَحْمَرُ فَإِنَّهُ يَنْصَرِفُ (*the form*) *áf'al, when it is an indefinite noun, is declined with tènwîn* (e.g. أَفْكَلُ *tremor,* أَجْدَلُ *a hawk*) ; وَزْنُ طَلْحَةَ وَإِصْبَعٍ فَعْلَةُ وَإِفْعَلُ *the measure of Talha and 'isba' is fa'la and 'if'al.* But if we

B say كُلُّ أَفْعَلِ يَكُونُ صِفَةً لَا يَنْصَرِفُ, *every* (*word of the form*) *'af'al, which is an adjective, is declined without tènwîn,* we must employ the nunation, because كُلّ, in the sense of *each, every*, requires an *indefinite* word after it in the genitive ; and so in other cases.

[(θ) The diminutives of all diptote nouns, as أُسَيِّدُ, with the exception of the softened diminutives (§ 283) and of those that are derived from the distributive numerals of the form فُعَالُ (§ 333), as ثُلَيِّثُ, أُحَيِّدُ.]

C *c.* Many proper names ; viz.

(a) Foreign names of men, as إِسْحَقُ *Isaac,* إِبْرَاهِيمُ *Abraham,* يُوسُفُ *Joseph,* دَاوُدُ *David;* excepting such as consist of three letters, the second of which has gèzma or is a litera productionis, as نُوحٌ *Noah,* لُوطٌ *Lot.*

(β) Proper names which end in êlif maksûra (compare *a,* γ and *b,* β) and êlif mèmdûda (compare *a,* β and *b,* a), whether Arabic or

D foreign ; as يَحْيَى *John,* عَادِيَا or عَادِيَآ *'Ādiyā,* زَكَرِيَّآ *Zachariah,* يَعْلَى *Ya'lā,* لَيْلَى *Lèilā,* سُلْمَى *Sulmā.*

(γ) Proper names in ـَانُ, whether Arabic or foreign ; as غَطَفَانُ *Ġatafān* (a tribe), عُثْمُنُ *'Othmān,* حِطَّانُ *Hiṭṭān,* سُفْيَانُ *Sufyān,* سُلَيْمُنُ *Solomon,* عِمْرَانُ *'Imrān (Amram),* [with the exception of those that were originally common nouns of the forms فَعَالُ and فِعْلَانُ, as رِضْوَانُ and سِنَانُ and سِنَانٌ.]

(δ) Proper names which resemble in form the verbal forms فَعَّلَ A and فُعِلَ, or any of the persons of the Imperfect; as شُمَّر *Šammar,* شَلَّمُ *Jerusalem,* ضُرِبُ *Dorib,* أَحْمَدُ *Aḥmĕd,* يَزِيدُ *Yĕzīd,* يَشْكُرُ *Yĕškur,* تَدْمُرُ *Tadmur* (Palmyra), تَغْلِبُ *Tağlib,* يُبْنَى *Yubnā,* تُمَاضُرُ *Tumāḍir,* يُرَامِلُ *Yurāmil.*

(ε) Common nouns of the feminine gender, consisting of more than three letters, when used as proper names; e.g. عَقْرَبُ *a scorpion,* B عَقْرَبُ *'Aḳrab* (a man's name).

(ζ) Proper names which end in ة, whether masculine or feminine; as مَكَّةُ *Mĕkka,* فَاطِمَةُ *Fāṭima* (a woman), دُغَةُ *Doğa* (a woman), طَلْحَةُ *Ṭalḥa,* قَتَادَةُ *Ḳatāda* (men). [Fem. proper names in ات keep their tĕnwīn, as عَرَفَاتٌ gen. acc. عَرَفَاتٍ; أَذْرِعَاتٌ gen. acc. أَذْرِعَاتٍ. Dialectic forms are عَرَفَاتُ gen. acc. عَرَفَاتَ and even عَرَفَاتَ.]

(η) Fem. proper names, which do not end in ة, but are either of C foreign origin, or consist of more than three letters, or, though consisting of only three letters, are trisyllabic, owing to their middle radical having a vowel; e.g. زَيْنَبُ *Egypt,* مِصْرُ *Egypt,* جُورُ *Gūr,* صُورُ *Tyre,* *Zĕinĕb,* سُعَادُ *Su'ād,* شَتَرُ *Šatar,* سَقَرُ *Hellfire* (as the name of a particular part of hell).—But fem. proper names which consist of only three letters, the second of which has gĕzma, may be either diptote or triptote (though the former is preferred); as هِنْدُ or هِنْدٌ *Hind,* دَعْدُ or دَعْدٌ *Da'd.* D

(θ) Proper names, which are actually or seemingly derived from common substantives or adjectives; especially masculine names of the form فُعَل (from فَاعِلٌ), as عُمَرُ *'Omar,* زُفَرُ *Zufar,* جُشَمُ *Gušĕm,* زُحَلُ *the planet Saturn,* قُثَمُ *the male hyœna;* and feminine names of the form فَعَالِ (from فَاعِلَةٌ), as قَطَامِ *Ḳaṭām,* رَقَاشِ *Raḳāš,* حَذَامِ *Haḍām,* بَرَاحِ *the sun,* صَلَاحِ *Ṣalāḥ* (a name of Mekka). These latter, however, have

A more usually and correctly the form فَعَالِ, and are wholly indeclinable; as ظَفَارِ Ẓafār (a city), قَثَامِ *the female hyæna,* رَقَاشِ, حَذَامِ, بَرَاحِ, صَلَاحِ, جَعَارِ *the female hyæna,* حَلَاقِ *death,* صَرَامِ *war,* أَزَامِ *a year of famine.*

Rem. *a.* Words of the form فَعَالِ, of which the last letter is *r*, as جَعَارِ *the female hyæna,* حَضَارِ Ḥaḍār (a star in the Centaur), are almost invariably indeclinable, even in the dialect of those Arabs B who in other cases use the form فَعَالُ.

Rem. *b.* Besides being used as proper names, the forms فُعَلُ and فَعَالِ are often employed as vocatives, in terms of abuse; e. g. يَا فَسَاقِ *O improbe!* f. يَا فُسَقُ *O sceleste!* f. يَا خَبَاثِ; يَا خُبَثُ; يَا لَكَاعِ *O vilis!* f. يَا لُكَعُ.

Rem. *c.* In compound proper names of the class called مُرَكَّبٌ C مَزْجِىٌّ (§ 264), the first word is usually not declined at all, and the second follows the diptote declension; nom. بَعْلَبَكُّ, حَضْرَمَوْتُ, رَامَهُرْمُزُ, gen. and acc. حَضْرَمَوْتَ, بَعْلَبَكَّ, رَامَهُرْمُزَ*. Each word may, however, be declined separately, the second being in the genitive, and the first losing the tènwīn because it is defined by the second (see § 313, foll.); nom. حَضْرَمَوْتُ, بَعْلَبَكِّ, رَامَهُرْمُزِ, gen. حَضْرَمَوْتِ, acc. حَضْرَمَوْتَ, etc. The proper name مَعْدِى كَرِب admits of three forms, for we may say مَعْدِى كَرِبُ (like حَضْرَمَوْتُ); or مَعْدِى كَرِبَ D gen. and acc. مَعْدِى كَرِبَ (like حَضْرَمَوْتَ); or مَعْدِى كَرِبِ in all three cases (like رَامَهُرْمُزِ).—Proper names of men ending in وَيْهِ are wholly indeclinable; as سِيبَوَيْهِ, نِفْطَوَيْهِ, عَمْرَوَيْهِ, بَوَيْهِ.

---

* [The kunya is sometimes considered as a single compound noun. A letter of the Prophet begins مِنْ مُحَمَّدٍ إِلَى ٱلْمُهَاجِرِ بْنِ أَبُو أُمَيَّةَ (Fāik i. 5), some Ḳor'ān readers read in Sūr. cxi., تَبَّتْ يَدَا أَبُو لَهَبٍ, and well known are مُعَاوِيَةُ بْنُ أَبُو سُفْيَانَ and عَلِىُّ بْنُ أَبُو طَالِبٍ. Compare Belādorī 60, last l. and Baiḍāwī ii. 421, l. 10. D. G.]

REM. *d.* Proper names, when used *indefinitely* [as is always A the case when they are employed in the dual or plural], are naturally declined with tenwīn; as رُبَّ إِبْرَهِيمٍ لَقِيتُهُ *many an Abraham have I met*; [فَكُلُّ دَوْرٍ مَخْصُوصٌ بِآدَمٍ وَحَوَّآءٍ] *and each period has its peculiar Adam and Eve*]; and so رُبَّ عِمْرَانٍ وَأَحْمَدَ وَفَاطِمَةَ وَسُعَادٍ وَعُمَرٍ وَقَطَامِ وَسِيبَوَيْهِ. There is, however, a doubt as to the admissibility of the *ṣarf* in the form أَفْعَلُ.

REM. *e.* The أَسْبَابُ ٱلْإِمْتِنَاعِ مِنَ ٱلصَّرْفِ, or reasons why a noun B is debarred from taking the tenwīn, are usually reckoned by the grammarians to be nine in number; viz. ٱلْعَلَمِيَّةُ *its being a proper name*; ٱلْوَصْفِيَّةُ *its being an adjective*; ٱلْعُجْمَةُ *its being a foreign word*; ٱلْمُرَكَّبُ ٱلْمَزْجِيُّ *its being a compound of the class*; ٱلتَّأْنِيثُ ٱللَّازِمُ لَفْظًا أَوْ مَعْنًى *its being necessarily feminine by form or meaning*; ٱلْأَلِفُ وَٱلنُّونُ ٱلْمُضَارِعَتَانِ لِأَلِفَيِ ٱلتَّأْنِيثِ *its ending in the termination* ـَان, *which resembles the feminine termination* ـَآءِ; C كَوْنُهُ جَمْعًا لَيْسَ عَلَى زِنَتِهِ وَاحِدٌ *its being a plural of a form which does not occur in the language as a singular* (e.g. مَسَاجِدُ *mosques*, مَصَابِيحُ *lamps*, for there is no singular noun of the form مَفَاعِلُ or مَفَاعِيلُ); ٱلْعَدْلُ عَنْ صِيغَةٍ إِلَى أُخْرَى *its being turned from one form into another* (as عُمَرُ, which is مَعْدُولٌ, or *transformed*, from عَامِرٌ, or قَطَامِ, which is مَعْدُولَةٌ from فَاطِمَةُ); and وَزْنُ ٱلْفِعْلِ *its resembling in form a part of the verb*. Any two or more of these causes in D combination prevent a noun from being declined with tenwīn; e.g. (1) ٱلْعَلَمِيَّةُ + the termination ـَان, as عُثْمَانُ. Hence we say حَسَّانُ *Ḥassān*, if we derive this name from the radical حَسَّ; but if we derive it from حَسُنَ, it is triptote, حَسَّانٌ. (2) ٱلتَّرْكِيبُ + ٱلْعَلَمِيَّةُ, as بَعْلَبَكُّ. (3) ٱلْعَلَمِيَّةُ + ٱلتَّأْنِيثُ, viz. (a) لَفْظًا وَمَعْنًى *in form and meaning*, as فَاطِمَةُ; (β) مَعْنًى لَا لَفْظًا *in meaning but not in form*,

A   as زَيْنَب ; (γ) لَفْظًا لَا مَعْنًى *in form but not in meaning,* as طَلْحَة (which, though feminine in form, yet is the name of a man).

Except feminine proper names of the form فُعَل, in *c*, *η*. (4) اَلْعَلَمِيَّة + اَلْعَلَمِيَّة + وَزْنُ اَلْفِعْلِ + (6) عُمَرُ, as اَلْعَدْلُ + اَلْعَلَمِيَّة (5) يَزِيدُ, as اَلْعُجْمَة, as بُطْرُس *Petrus.* Except the case of نُوحُ and similar names in *c*, *a*. (7) اَلْوَصْفِيَّة + اَلْعَدْلُ, as أُخَرُ, which is مَعْدُولٌ from اَلْوَصْفِيَّة + (8) جَمَعَاوَاتٌ. which is مَعْدُولٌ from جُمَعُ, or آخَرُونَ.

B   the termination اـَان, in adjectives of the form فَعْلَانُ, fem. فَعْلَى. (9) اَلْوَصْفِيَّة + وَزْنُ اَلْفِعْلِ, in adjectives of the form أَفْعَلُ.

310. Nouns ending in ـِى or اـ, for ـَوُ or ـَوُ (§§ 213 and 245), which follow the first declension, and those in ـِى and اـ, for ـِى, which follow the second (§ 309, *a*, γ; *b*, β; *c*, β), retain in the oblique cases the termination of the nominative, so that their declension is only *virtual* (تَقْدِيرِىٌّ), not expressed (لَفْظِىٌّ) or external (ظَاهِرٌ).

C E.g. عَصًا for عَصَوٌ, عَصَوٍ, and عَصَوًا ; رَحًى for رَحَىٌ, رَحَىٍ, and رَحَىًا ; بُشْرَى for بُشْرَىٌ and بُشْرَىَ.

311. Nouns ending in ـِ, for ـِى or ـُوُ (§ 167, *b*, β, and the Paradigms of the Verb, Tab. XVIII.) and ـِى or ـِى (see the same Tab. and § 218), have the same termination in the nom. and gen., but in the acc. ـِيَ (according to § 166, *a*). E.g. غَازِ for غَازِوٌ, acc. غَازِيًا ;

D رَامِ for رَامِىٌ, acc. رَامِيًا ; مُغْزِ for مُغْزِىٌّ, acc. مُغْزِيًا ; مُرْمِ for مُرْمِىٌّ, (تَمْنِىٌّ) تَمْنِ for تَمْنِىٌّ, acc. تَغْزِيًا ; (تَغْزِىٌّ) تَغْزِ for تَغْزِىٌّ, acc. مُرْمِيًا ; عَمِ (verbal adj.) شَجِ (verbal adj.) for شَجِىٌّ, acc. شَجِيًا ; عَمِ (verbal adj.) for عَمِىٌّ, acc. عَمِيًا.

312. All plurals of the second declension, which ought regularly to end in ـِى, for ـِىُ, follow in the nom. the first declension instead

of the second, and substitute ـَ (for ـِيْ). They moreover retain, A
according to § 311, the same termination in the genit., and consequently follow the first declension in that case too; but in the acc.
they remain true to the second declension, and have ـِيَ. E.g. جَارِيَة,

plur. nom. and gen. جَوَارٍ, for جَوَارِيٌ (instead of جَوَارِيُ), acc. جَوَارِيَ;

مَعْنًى, plur. nom. and gen. مَعَانٍ, for مَعَانِيٌ (instead of مَعَانِيُ), acc.

مَعَانِيَ; صَحْرَآء, plur. nom. and gen. صَحَارٍ, for صَحَارِيٌ (instead of B

صَحَارِيُ), acc. صَحَارِيَ.

II.   *The Declension of Defined Nouns.*

313. Undefined nouns become defined: 1. by prefixing the
article اَلْ; 2. (*a*) by adding a noun in the genitive, or (*b*) by adding
a pronominal suffix.

[REM.   Only proper names and words used as proper names are C
in themselves definite (§ 309, *b*, η, vol. ii. § 78); if, therefore, they
are not originally appellatives (as اَلْحَسَنُ properly *the beautiful*)
they never have the article, unless they be used as generic nouns
(as in رُبَّ إِبْرٰهِيمٍ, § 309, *c*, rem. *d*), اَلزَّيْدُ الْأَوَّلُ *the first Zèid.*—A
defined noun is called مَعْرِفَةٌ or مُعَرَّفٌ (تَعْرِيفٌ means *defining*), an
undefined noun نَكِرَةٌ or مُنَكَّرٌ (تَنْكِيرٌ means *leaving undefined*).]

314.   If an undefined noun be defined by the article, the following D
cases arise.

(*a*)   If it belongs to the first declension, it loses the tènwīn.

Nom.	اَلرَّجُلُ	اَلْحَسَنُ	اَلْمَدِينَةُ	اَلْمُحْصَنَةُ	اَلرِّجَالُ
	the man.	*El-Ḥasan.*	*the city.*	*the chaste (woman).*	*the men.*
Gen.	اَلرَّجُلِ	اَلْحَسَنِ	اَلْمَدِينَةِ	اَلْمُحْصَنَةِ	اَلرِّجَالِ
Acc.	اَلرَّجُلَ	اَلْحَسَنَ	اَلْمَدِينَةَ	اَلْمُحْصَنَةَ	اَلرِّجَالَ

REM.   The final ا of the acc. disappears along with the tènwīn.

A (*b*) If it belongs to the second declension, it assumes the terminations of the first, and becomes triptote.

Nom.	اَلْأَسْوَدُ	اَلسَّوْدَآءُ	اَلْأَكَابِرُ
	the black (m.).	*the black* (f.).	*the nobles.*
Gen.	اَلْأَسْوَدِ	اَلسَّوْدَآءِ	اَلْأَكَابِرِ
Acc.	اَلْأَسْوَدَ	اَلسَّوْدَآءَ	اَلْأَكَابِرَ

(*c*) If it be a plur. sanus fem., it loses the tènwîn.

B | | | | |
|---|---|---|---|
| Nom. | اَلظُّلُمَاتُ | اَلْمَخْلُوقَاتُ | اَلْمُؤْمِنَاتُ |
| | *the darknesses.* | *the creatures.* | *the believing (women).* |
| Gen. Acc. | اَلظُّلُمَاتِ | اَلْمَخْلُوقَاتِ | اَلْمُؤْمِنَاتِ |

REM. *a.* The plur. sanus masc. and the dual undergo no change
when the article is prefixed; as اَلضَّارِبُونَ *those who beat,* اَلرَّجُلَانِ
the two men, gen. acc. اَلرَّجُلَيْنِ, اَلضَّارِبِينَ.

REM. *b.* Nouns ending in ‗ drop the tènwîn and resume their
C original ى; as اَلتَّمَنَّى from, مَعَانٍ from اَلْمَعَانِى, رَامٍ from اَلرَّامِى
تَمَنٍّ, اَلْجَوَارِى from جَوَارٍ (see §§ 311, 312).

315. If a noun in the genitive is appended to an undefined noun,
the following changes are produced.

(*a*) The singulars and broken plurals of both declensions are
declined in the same way as if they were defined by the article
(§ 314).

D | | | | |
|---|---|---|---|
| Nom. | كِتَابُ ٱللّٰه | أَسْفَلُ ٱلْأَرْض | رِجَالُ ٱلْمَدِينَة |
| | *the book of God.* | *the lowest part of the earth.* | *the men of the city.* |
| Gen. | كِتَابِ ٱللّٰه | أَسْفَلِ ٱلْأَرْض | رِجَالِ ٱلْمَدِينَة |
| Acc. | كِتَابَ ٱللّٰه | أَسْفَلَ ٱلْأَرْض | رِجَالَ ٱلْمَدِينَة |

Nom.	عَجَائِبُ ٱلْمَخْلُوقَات	كُلُّ يَوْمٍ
	the wonders of creation.	*every day.*
Gen.	عَجَائِبِ ٱلْمَخْلُوقَات	كُلِّ يَوْمٍ
Acc.	عَجَائِبَ ٱلْمَخْلُوقَات	كُلَّ يَوْمٍ

REM. *a.* The words أَبٌ *a father,* أَخٌ *a brother,* حَمٌ *a father-* A
in-law, and less frequently هَنٌ *a thing,* after rejecting the tenwīn,
lengthen the preceding vowel.

Nom. أَبُو, أَخُو, حَمُو, هَنُو; for أَبٌ, etc.

Gen. أَبِى, أَخِى, حَمِى, هَنِى; for أَبٍ, etc.

Acc. أَبَا, أَخَا, حَمَا, هَنَا; for أَبَ, etc.*

The word ذُو, *the owner* or *possessor* of a thing, which is always
connected with a following substantive in the genitive, has in the B
gen. ذِى, in the acc. ذَا; whilst فَمٌ, *the mouth* (Aram. פֻּם), which is
used instead of فُوهٌ or فَوَهٌ, makes either:

Nom. فَمٌ, Gen. فَمِ, Acc. فَمَ;

or: فُو, فِى, فَا †.

REM. *b.* Proper names of the first declension lose their tenwīn,
when followed by the word اِبْنُ in a genealogical series; as مُحَمَّدُ

---

* The same is the case in the other Semitic languages; see *Comp.* C
Gr. p. 142 *seq.*—In Arabic the short vowels are used dialectically, as
in the verse بِأَبِه اَقْتَدَى عَدِىٌّ فِى ٱلْكَرَمِ وَمَنْ يُشَابِهْ أَبَهْ فَمَا ظَلَمْ *'Adi*
has imitated his father in generosity, and whoever tries to resemble his
father, does not do wrong; where we find بِأَبِه and أَبَهْ for بِأَبِيه and
أَبَاهُ. Some of the Arabs employ the forms أَبَا, etc., in all the three
cases [أَبٌ being, according to some lexicographers a dial. var. of أَبٌ.
Comp. vol. ii. § 39, *a,* rem. *a*], as in the verse إِنَّ أَبَاهَا وَأَبَا أَبَاهَا قَدْ بَلَغَا
فِى ٱلْمَجْدِ غَايَتَاهَا, *verily their* (the family's) *father and their father's* D
father have reached in glory their utmost limit; where the first أَبَاهَا
is the accus. after إِنَّ, and the second أَبَاهَا the genit., instead of أَبِيهَا,
whilst غَايَتَاهَا stands by poetic license (in this case اَلْإِشْبَاع) for غَايَتَهَا.
[The genuineness of this verse is not free from suspicion. Comp.
Nöldeke in *Zeitschr. D. M. G.* xlix. 321.]

† With these latter forms [which are employed only in connexion
with a following pronoun or noun in the genitive] compare in Heb.
פֶּה, constr. פִּי, with suffix פִּיךָ.

w. 32

A بْنُ جَعْفَرِ بْنِ خَالِدِ بْنِ مُحَمَّدٍ, *Muhammad, the son of Ǵaʿfar, the son of Ḫālid, the son of Muḥammad.* On the elision of the ١ in ابْنُ, see § 21, *b.*

REM. *c.* Instead of بِنْتٌ, *a daughter,* we may use, when a genitive follows, the form ابْنَةٌ. [The latter was formerly preferred, except at the beginning of a sentence. The form بنت occurs in the Ḳorʾān (Sūr. lxvi. 12) and often in old Mss.]

(*b*) The dual loses the termination نِ.

B Nom. جَاءَ عَبْدَا ٱلسُّلْطَانِ *the two slaves of the sultan came;* لَنَا مَسْجِدَا ٱللّٰهِ ٱلْحَرَامَانِ *to us belong the two holy temples of God.*

Gen. رَوَى عَنْ أَبَوَىْ بَكْرٍ ٱبْنِ طَلْحَةَ وَٱبْنِ قَسُّومٍ *he learned and transmitted (traditions, poems, etc.) from the two ʾAbū Bèkrs,* (viz. *ʾAbū Bèkr* ʾ*ibn Ṭalḥa* and (ʾ*Abū Bèkr*) ʾ*ibn Ḳassūm* (see § 299, rem. *h*).

Acc. رَأَيْتُ جَارِيَتَىْ أَبِى *I saw the two female slaves of my father.*

C REM. If an èlif conjunctionis follows the oblique cases of the dual, the final ى takes a kèsra instead of a ǵèzma; as مَرَرْتُ بِجَارِيَتَىِ ٱلْمَلِكِ *I passed by the two female slaves of the king* (see §§ 19 and 20, *c*); ٱلْمَنْسِمَانِ ظُفُرَا خُفَّىِ ٱلْبَعِيرِ *the two mansims are the extremities (nails) of the camel's hoofs.*

(*c*) The pluralis sanus loses the termination نَ.

D Nom. جَاءَ بَنُو ٱلْمَلِكِ *the sons of the king came;* مُجَرِّدُو أَسْيَافِهِمْ *drawing their swords.*

Gen. عِبْرَةٌ لِأُولِى ٱلْأَلْبَابِ *an example,* or *warning, for those who are possessed of intelligence* (see § 302, rem. *c*).

Acc. رَأَيْتُ بَنِى ٱلْمَلِكِ *I saw the king's sons;* كُنَّا مُوقِدِى ٱلنَّارِ *we were kindling the fire.*

REM. If the plur. ends in ـُوْنَ, acc. ـَيْنَ (for ـَيُونَ, ـَيِينَ), A these terminations become, before a following gen., ـُوْ, ـِيْ; and if the genit. begins with an élif conjunct., the final و takes damma, and the final ى kèsra, instead of the gèzma; as مُصْطَفُو ٱللّٰه, مُصْطَفِي ٱللّٰه (§ 20, c).—Regarding the ا otiosum which is often, though incorrectly, added to the nominal term. ـُوْ and ـَوْ, see § 7, rem. a.

316. If a pronominal suffix is added to an undefined noun, the B following changes take place.

(a) Triptotes and the plur. sanus fem. lose the tènwin, the dual and plur. sanus masc. the terminations نِ and نَ; as كِتَابٌ *a book*, كِتَابُهُ *his book*; ظُلُمَاتٌ *darkness*, ظُلُمَاتُهَا *its darkness*; كِتَابَانِ *two books*, كِتَابَاكَ *thy two books*; بَنُونَ *sons*, بَنُوكَ *thy sons*; لِبَائِعِيهِ *to its purchasers*.

(b) Before the pronominal suffix of the 1st p. sing. ـِى (see C § 185, rem. a, and § 317), the final vowels of the sing., plur. fractus, and plur. sanus fem. are elided; as كِتَابِى *my book*, from كِتَابٌ; كِلَابِى *my dogs*, from كِلَابٌ, plur. fract. of كَلْبٌ; تَوَابِعِى *my followers*, from تَوَابِعُ, plur. fract. of تَابِعٌ; جَنَّاتِى *my gardens*, from جَنَّاتٌ, plur. sanus of جَنَّةٌ.

(c) If the noun ends in ة, this letter is changed into (or rather, resumes its original form of) ت; as نِعْمَةٌ *a favour* or *benefit*, نِعْمَتِى. D

(d) If the noun ends in élif mobile or hèmza, this letter passes before the suffixes into ؤ, when it has damma (Nom.), and into ئ, when it has kèsra (Gen.); as نِسَاءٌ *women*, nom. with suffix نِسَاؤُهُ, *his women*, gen. نِسَائِهِ. But when it has fètḥa (Acc.), it remains unchanged, as acc. نِسَاءَهُ.

REM. Of the words mentioned in § 315, rem. a, أَبٌ, أَخٌ and

A حَمٌ, take the suffixes thus: nom. أَبُوكَ, أَبُوهُ; gen. أَبِيكَ, أَبِيهِ; acc. أَبَاهُ, أَبَاكَ; but حَمِى, أَخِى, أَبِى, in all the three cases.—هَنٌ makes هَنَاكَ or هَنَكَ or هَنِيكَ, هَنَكَ or هَنُوكَ; هَنِى.—فَمٌ has regularly فَمِهِ, فَمُهُ, فَمَكَ; فَمِى; but more usually, nom. فُوكَ, فُوهُ; gen. فِيكَ, فِيهِ; acc. فَاكَ, فَاهُ; and فِىّ, *my mouth*, in all the three cases.— ذُو is not used with suffixes.—On some dialectical varieties of أَبٌ

B see § 315, rem. *a*, note *.

APPENDIX.

The Pronominal Suffixes, which denote the Genitive.

317. The pronominal suffixes attached to nouns to denote the genitive, are exactly the same as those attached to verbs to denote the accusative (§ 185), with the single exception of the suffix of the
C 1st p. sing., which is ـِى, and not نِى.

REM. *a.* The suffix of the 1st p. sing. ـِ, when ى attached to a word ending in élif maksūra (ـَى), in the long vowels ـَا, ـِى, ـُو, or in the diphthongs ـَىْ and ـَوْ, becomes ـِى, the kèsra of the original form ـِى (see § 185, rem. *d*) being simply elided. Further, when the word ends in ـِى or ـَىْ, the final ى unites with the ى of the suffix into ـِّى; and when it ends in ـُو or ـَوْ, the و is changed into ى, and likewise forms ـِّى. E.g. هَوَاىَ *my love*, for هَوَائِىَ,
D from هَوًى; خَطَايَاىَ *my sins*, for خَطَايَائِىَ, from خَطَايَا, plur. fract. of خَطِيَّةٌ; غُلَامَاىَ *my two slaves*, for غُلَامَائِىَ, from غُلَامَانِ, nom. dual of غُلَامٌ; قَاضِىَّ *my judge*, for (قَاضِيِىَ), from قَاضٍ; مُسْلِمِىَّ *my Muslims*, for مُسْلِمُوىَ (مُسْلِمُوئِىَ) or غُلَامَىَّ; مُسْلِمٌ, plur. sanus of مُسْلِمُونَ, مُسْلِمِينَ (مُسْلِمِيئِىَ), my two slaves, for غُلَامَيْىَ (غُلَامَيْئِىَ), from غُلَامَيْنِ, genit. dual of مُصْطَفَىَّ *my elect*, for مُصْطَفَوْىَ (مُصْطَفَوْئِىَ) or غُلَامٌ.

A.— مُصْطَفًى sanus of plur. ,مُصْطَفَيْنَ ,مُصْطَفَوْنَ from ,(مُصْطَفَيْئَ)
From words like قَفًا, هَوًى, the form قَفَيَّ, هَوَيَّ, is used dialectically
instead of قَفَايَ, هَوَايَ.—On أَبٌ, أَخٌ, حَمٌ, هَنٌ, فَمٌ, فُو, and فُو, see
§ 316, rem.—[بُنَيٌّ a *little son* has both بُنَيَّ and بُنَيٌّ.]

REM. *b.* Just as the verbal suffix نِى is sometimes shortened
into نِ (§ 185, rem. *c*), so the nominal suffix ـِى occasionally
becomes ـِ, particularly when the noun to which it is attached is in
the vocative; as رَبِّ *my Lord!* يَا قَوْمِ *O my people!* [Comp.
vol. ii. § 38, rem. *b*.]

B.   REM. *c.* What has been said in § 185, rem. *b*, of the change of
the ḍamma in هُ, هُمَا, هُمْ, هُنَّ, into kĕsra after ـِ, ـِى, or ـَىْ,
applies to the nominal as well as the verbal suffixes. E.g. كِتَابِه
of his book, جَارِيَتَيْه *his two female slaves,* قَاتِلِيه *his murderers,*
كِتَابِهِمَا, كِتَابِهِمْ ([before waṣl and] in verse كِتَابِهِمُ, [which is the
older form] or كِتَابِهِمِ), etc.

C   [REM. *d.* If no ambiguity of meaning can arise, the dual before
a suffix in the dual is not unfrequently replaced by the singular or
the plural, as قَلْبَيْهِمَا and قُلُوبَيْهِمَا *the heart of them both.*]

B.   THE NUMERALS.

1.   *The Cardinal Numbers.*

318.   The cardinal numbers from *one* to *ten* are :—

	Masc.	Fem.		Masc.	Fem.	
1.	أَحَدٌ / وَاحِدٌ	إِحْدَى / وَاحِدَةٌ	5.	خَمْسٌ	خَمْسَةٌ	D
			6.	سِتٌّ	سِتَّةٌ	
2.	اِثْنَانِ	اِثْنَتَانِ / ثِنْتَانِ	7.	سَبْعٌ	سَبْعَةٌ	
			8.	ثَمَانٍ	ثَمَانِيَةٌ	
3.	ثَلَاثٌ	ثَلَاثَةٌ	9.	تِسْعٌ	تِسْعَةٌ	
4.	أَرْبَعٌ	أَرْبَعَةٌ	10.	عَشْرٌ	عَشَرَةٌ	

A REM. *a.* For ثَلَاثٌ, ثَلَاثَةٌ, we may also write ثَلْثٌ, ثَلْثَةٌ, and for ثَمَانِيَةٌ, ثَمْنِيَةٌ (§ 6, rem. *a*).—سِتٌّ stands, according to the Arab lexicographers, for سِدْتٌ (compare § 14, *c*), and that for سِدْسٌ. The correctness of this view is proved [as they say] by the diminutive سُدَيْسَةٌ, the fraction سُدْسٌ, *a sixth,* and the ordinal adj. سَادِسٌ, *sixth.*

REM. *b.* If we compare the above numerals with those of the cognate languages, it is easy to perceive their perfect identity; and,
B therefore, only one or two forms deserve notice here.—The Assyrian for *one* in the sing. masc. is *istin* (עֶשְׁתֵּן), apparently identical with the Heb. עַשְׁתֵּי in עַשְׁתֵּי עָשָׂר; but the fem. is *iḥit* (אֶחָת) = אַחַת (for אַחְדְּתְּ).—The Aram. תְּרֵין, f. תַּרְתֵּין, is a contraction for תִּרְין, which may be either the equivalent of the Heb. שְׁנַיִם (ת) becoming שׁ, as in תַּלְגָּא, *snow,* = שֶׁלֶג, and ן exchanging with ר,
C as in דְּנַח, *to rise,* = זְרַח); or, as others think, derived from the rad. حَدٌ, as it were the dual of وَتْر *single, sole.* The daghesh in the Heb. fem. שְׁתַּיִם (also pronounced אֶשְׁתַּיִם) indicates the loss of the *n* in ثِنْتَانِ.—The Heb. שֵׁשׁ, שִׁשָּׁה, stand for שְׁרֵשׁ, שְׁרָשָׁה (see rem. *a,* and compare the Æth. *sĕdĕstū* and *sĕssu,* for *sĕdsū*). The Jewish Aram. form שֵׁתׁ (שֵׁת), שִׁתָּה, is identical with the Arabic; whilst in the Syriac ܐܫܬܐ or ܫܬܐ the original doubling has left its trace in the hard sound of the *t* (compare שְׁתַּיִם).

D **319.** The cardinal numbers from 3 to 10 take the *fem.* form, when the objects numbered are of the *masc.* gender; and conversely, the *masc.* form, when the objects numbered are *fem.* E.g. رِجَالٌ عَشَرَةٌ, or عَشَرَةُ رِجَالٍ, *ten men* (lit., *men, a decade,* and *a decade of men*); عَشْرُ نِسَاءٍ, or نِسَاءٌ عَشْرٌ, *ten women.*

REM. *a.* The cause of this phenomenon, which also occurs in the other Semitic languages, seems to lie in the effort to give prominence to the independent substantive nature (§ 321) of the

cardinal numbers, in virtue of which they differ from the dependent A
adjectives, which follow the gender of their substantives.—That
أَرْبَعٌ، ثَلْثٌ, etc., are really *masc.*,—and consequently ثَلْثَةٌ، أَرْبَعَةٌ,
etc., *fem.*,—is evident from the construction of عَشْرُ, in the sense of
ten days, either as a singular masc. or as a broken plur. (viz. the
implied أَيَّامٌ). We may say, for example, either مِنْ اَلْعَشْرُ ٱلْأَوْسَطُ
the middle ten days of Ramaḍān, رَمَضَانَ ٱلْعَشْرُ ٱلْأَخِيرُ مِنْ رَمَضَانَ
the last ten days of R., or ٱلْعَشْرُ ٱلْأَوَاخِرُ، ٱلْعَشْرُ ٱلْأَوَاسِطُ, etc. See
also § 322, rem. *b*.   B

REM. *b*. An undefined number from 3 to 10 is expressed by
بِضْعُ ([or بَضْعٌ], literally, *a part* or *portion*); as بِضْعُ رِجَالٍ *some
men*, بِضْعُ نِسْوَةٍ *some women*, فِى بِضْعِ سِنِينَ *in a few years.* The
use of بِضْعَةُ belongs to post-classical times; as بِضْعَةَ أَشْهُرٍ *some
months.* [Comp. vol. ii. § 99, rem.]

320. The cardinal numbers from 1 to 10 are triptote, with the
exception of the duals اِثْنَانِ, and اِثْنَتَانِ or ثِنْتَانِ.—ثَمَانٍ stands for C
ثَمَانِىٌ, and has in the genit. ثَمَانٍ, acc. ثَمَانِيًا (according to § 311).

321. The cardinal numbers from 3 to 10 are always *substantives*.
They either follow the objects numbered, and are put in apposition
with them, as رِجَالٍ ثَلَاثَةُ, *of three men* (lit., *of men, a triad*); or they
precede them, in which case the numeral governs the other substantive
in the genitive of the plural, as ثَلَاثَةُ رِجَالٍ, *three men* (lit., *a triad of* D
men), except in the single instance of مِائَةٌ *a hundred* (see § 325).

REM. *a*. ثَمَانٍ has, in the construct state, nom. and gen. ثَمَانِى,
acc. ثَمَانِىَ (see § 320).

REM. *b*. If the numerals from 3 to 10 take the article, they of
course lose the tĕnwîn (§ 314, *a*).

REM. *c*. اِثْنَانِ and اِثْنَتَانِ are very rarely construed with the

A   genit. sing. of the objects numbered, and then of course drop their final ن (§ 315, *b*) ; as ثِنْتَا حَنْظَلٍ *two colocynths,* instead of اِثْنَتَانِ حَنْظَلَتَانِ. or simply مِنَ ٱلْحَنْظَلِ.

REM. *d.* بِضْعُ and بِضْعَةُ always precede the objects numbered, which are in the genitive of the plur. fractus (see § 319, rem. *b*).

322. The cardinal numbers from 11 to 19 are :—

B

	Masc.	Fem.			Masc.	Fem.
11.	عَشَرَ	أَحَدَ عَشْرَةَ إِحْدَى		15.	عَشَرَ خَمْسَةَ	عَشْرَةَ خَمْسَ
12.	عَشَرَ	اِثْنَا { عَشْرَةَ اِثْنَتَا / عَشْرَةَ ثِنْتَا }		16.	عَشَرَ سِتَّةَ	عَشْرَةَ سِتَّ
13.	عَشَرَ	ثَلَاثَةَ عَشْرَةَ ثَلَاثَ		17.	عَشَرَ سَبْعَةَ	عَشْرَةَ سَبْعَ
14.	عَشَرَ	أَرْبَعَةَ عَشْرَةَ أَرْبَعَ		18.	عَشَرَ ثَمَانِيَةَ	عَشْرَةَ ثَمَانِيَ
				19.	عَشَرَ تِسْعَةَ	عَشْرَةَ تِسْعَ

C   REM. *a.* Instead of عَشْرَةَ some of the Arabs pronounce عَشِرَةَ, and the form عَشَرَةَ is said to occur.—For ثَمَانِيَ عَشْرَةَ we also find ثَمَانِي عَشْرَةَ, [and incorrectly] ثَمَانِ عَشْرَةَ, and ثَمَانَ عَشْرَةَ. [In manuscripts we often find ثمان عشرة, which may be either of the two preceding forms, or the vulgar ثُمَانُ عشرة.]

REM. *b.* The cardinal numbers which indicate the *units* in these compounds, from 3 to 9, vary in gender according to the rule laid down in § 319 ; but the *ten* does not follow that rule, for it has

D   here the form عَشَرَ with masculine nouns, and عَشْرَةَ with feminine. The same holds with regard to the undefined number, which is in this case masc. بِضْعَةَ عَشَرَ, fem. بِضْعَ عَشْرَةَ, *some, a few* (from 11 to 19). The objects numbered are placed after them in the *acc. sing.*

REM. *c.* These numerals are usually indeclinable, even when they take the article, with the exception of اِثْنَا (ثِنْتَا) and اِثْنَا عَشَرَ عَشْرَةَ, which have in the oblique cases اِثْنَىْ (ثِنْتَىْ) and اِثْنَىْ عَشَرَ عَشْرَةَ.

Rem. *d.* The contraction of these compound numerals into *one* A
word began at a very early period, as may be seen from the
Aramaic dialects, and the Arab grammarians mention such forms
as أَحَدْعَشَرَ. In modern times they are greatly corrupted, being
pronounced, for example, in Algiers, تْلَاتَّاشْ, إِحْدَاشْ, إِتْنَاشْ,
تِسْعَتَاشْ, خَمْسْتَاشْ, سِتَّاشْ, سَبْعَتَاشْ, تَمَانْتَاشْ, أَرْبَعْتَاشْ.

323. The cardinal numbers from 20 to 90 are :—   B

20.	عِشْرُونَ	50.	خَمْسُونَ	80.	ثَمَانُونَ
30.	ثَلَاثُونَ	60.	سِتُّونَ	90.	تِسْعُونَ
40.	أَرْبَعُونَ	70.	سَبْعُونَ		

Rem. *a.* ثَلَاثُونَ and ثَمَانُونَ may also be written ثَمُنُونَ, ثَلُثُونَ.

Rem. *b.* The cardinal numbers from 20 to 90 are both masc.
and fem., and have, like the ordinary plur. sanus masc., ـُونَ in the C
nom., and ـِينَ in the oblique cases. They are *substantives*, and
take the objects numbered after them in the *acc. sing.*, so that they
do not lose the final نْ. Sometimes, however, they are construed
with the genit. of the possessor, when, of course, the نْ disappears,
leaving in the nom. ـُو, in the genit. and acc. ـِي.

Rem. *c.* The Hebrew and Aramaic dialects agree with the
Arabic as to the form of the tens ; עֶשְׂרִים, ܚܰܡܫܝܢ, etc. But the
Assyrian and Æthiopic curiously coincide in employing a form in D
ā (for *ān*) ; Assyr. *isrā, silasā, irbā, ḥansā* ; Æth. *'esrā, salasā,*
'arbeʿā, ḥamsā, etc.

324. The numerals which indicate numbers compounded of the
units and the tens, are formed by prefixing the unit to the ten, and
uniting them by the conjunction وَ, *and* ; as أَحَدٌ وَعِشْرُونَ *one and*
twenty, twenty-one. Both are declined ; as gen. أَحَدٍ وَعِشْرِينَ, acc.
أَحَدًا وَعِشْرِينَ.

w.   33

A   REM. The undefined unit is in this case نَيِّف (lit., *excess,*
surplus), as نَيِّف وَعِشْرُونَ *twenty and odd;* but بِضْعٌ and بِضْعَةٌ are
also used.

325. The numerals from 100 to 900 are :—

100. مِائَةٌ		600. سِتُّ مِائَةٍ	
200. مِائَتَانِ		700. سَبْعُ مِائَةٍ	
300. ثَلَاثُ مِائَةٍ		800. { ثَمَانِى مِائَةٍ / ثَمَانِ مِائَةٍ	
400. أَرْبَعُ مِائَةٍ			
500. خَمْسُ مِائَةٍ		900. تِسْعُ مِائَةٍ	

REM. *a.* For مِائَةٌ (Æth. �: ግዐልፕ: *me'et,* Heb. מֵאָה, Aram.
מְאָה, مِائة, Assyr. *mī*) we also find مِئَةٌ [and sometimes مِأَةٌ. For
مِئَةٌ we find often مِيَةٌ, and more recently مِيَّةٌ. The dual مِائَتَانِ is
C   written occasionally مِأَتَانِ, and hence in poetry مِاتَانِ. D. G.]
The plur. is مِئُونَ, مِئَاتٌ, or مِأًى ; the forms مِئِينَ, مُؤُونَ (like
سِنِينَ from سَنَةٌ *a year*), and مِى (with the article, الْمِئِى) are rare.
The strange spelling of مِائَةٌ seems to be due merely to a piece of
bungling on the part of the oldest writers of the Ḳorʾān. The ا was
probably meant to indicate the vowel of the second syllable, but
was inadvertently placed before, instead of after, the ى (*ĭ*).

D   REM. *b.* The numerals from 3 to 9 are often united with مِائَةٌ
into one word, as ثَلُثُمِائَةٍ. [In this case we find often in manuscripts ثَمَانِمِائَةٍ i.e. ثَمَانِمِائَةٍ, though the correct form is ثَمَانِى مِائَةٍ.]
The regular construction ثَلُثُ مِئِينَ, etc. (see § 321), is very rarely
employed [in poetry].

REM. *c.* مِائَةٌ usually takes the objects numbered after it in the
genit. sing.; as ثَلُثُمِائَةِ سَنَةٍ, مِائَةُ سَنَةٍ, مِائَتَا سَنَةٍ.

326. The numerals from 1000 upwards are :—   A

1000.	أَلْفٌ	100,000.	مِائَةُ أَلْفٍ
2000.	أَلْفَانِ	200,000.	مِائَتَا أَلْفٍ
3000.	ثَلَاثَةُ آلَافٍ	300,000.	ثَلْثُمِائَةِ أَلْفٍ
4000.	أَرْبَعَةُ آلَافٍ	400,000.	أَرْبَعُمِائَةِ أَلْفٍ
	etc.		etc. B
11,000.	أَحَدَ عَشَرَ أَلْفًا	1,000,000.	أَلْفُ أَلْفٍ
12,000.	اِثْنَا عَشَرَ أَلْفًا	2,000,000.	أَلْفَا أَلْفٍ
13,000.	ثَلَاثَةَ عَشَرَ أَلْفًا	3,000,000.	ثَلَاثَةُ آلَافٍ أَلْفٍ
	etc.		etc.

REM. The plur. of أَلْفٌ (Heb. אֶלֶף, Aram. אַלְפָּא, ܐܠܦܐ,   C
but Æth. *'elf*, 10,000) is آلَافٌ, أُلُوفٌ, and أَلْفٌ. It takes the objects
numbered after it in the *genit. sing.*, as أَلْفَا دِرْهَمٍ, أَلْفُ دِرْهَمٍ,
ثَلْثَةُ آلَافٍ دِرْهَمٍ. [The plural أَلْفٌ is only used in the combination
ثَلَاثَةُ أَلْفٍ, but آلَافٌ with all numerals from 3 to 10. In manuscripts it is often written defectively الف (أَلْف). The plurals
أُلُوفٌ and مِئُونَ, are only employed of indefinite numbers, *thousands,*
hundreds. D. G.]

327. The numerals which indicate numbers made up of thousands,   D
hundreds, tens, and units, may be compounded in two ways. Either
(*a*) the thousands are put first, and followed successively by the
hundreds, units, and tens, as ثَلَاثَةُ آلَافٍ وَسَبْعُ مِائَةٍ وَأَحَدٌ وَعِشْرُونَ,
3721 ; or (*b*) the order is reversed, and becomes units, tens, hundreds,
thousands, as أَحَدٌ وَعِشْرُونَ وَسَبْعُمِائَةٍ وَثَلْثَةُ آلَافٍ.

A

2. *The Ordinal Numbers.*

328. The ordinal adjectives from *first* to *tenth* are :—

Masc.	Fem.		Masc.	Fem.	
اَلْأَوَّلُ	اَلْأُولَى	the first.	سَادِسٌ	سَادِسَةٌ	sixth.
ثَانٍ	ثَانِيَةٌ	second.	سَابِعٌ	سَابِعَةٌ	seventh.
ثَالِثٌ	ثَالِثَةٌ	third.	ثَامِنٌ	ثَامِنَةٌ	eighth.
رَابِعٌ	رَابِعَةٌ	fourth.	تَاسِعٌ	تَاسِعَةٌ	ninth.
خَامِسٌ	خَامِسَةٌ	fifth.	عَاشِرٌ	عَاشِرَةٌ	tenth.

B

REM. *a.* اَلْأَوَّلُ stands for اَلْأَأْوَلُ or اَلْأَوْأَلُ, اَلْأُولَى for اَلْأُوْلَى or
اَلْوُوْلَى, according to the superlative form أَفْعَلُ, f. فُعْلَى, from the
rad. وأل or أول. Its plurals are : اَلْأَوَالِي, اَلْأَوَائِلُ, اَلْأَوَّلُونَ, and

C اَلْأُوَلُ for the masc.; اَلْأُوَلُ (rarely اَلْأَوَّلُ) for the fem.*

---

* [If أَوَّل is used as a noun, it takes the tenwīn, as in the verse of
the *Naḳāiḍ* (f. 182 *b*) quoted by Wright on the margin, لَهُمْ أَوَّلٌ يَعْلُو
عَلَى كُلِّ أَوَّلٍ *they have a past* (or *an ancestor*) *surpassing the past*
(or *ancestor*) *of everybody else*, and another *apud* Wright, *Opusc.* 106,

D l. 7 (where it means *ancestor*), as also in the phrase مَا تَرَكَ لَهُ أَوَّلًا وَلَا
آخِرًا *he left him neither past* (قَدِيمًا) *nor present* (حَدِيثًا). The fem.
plur. occurs in the phrase هُنَّ الْأَوَّلَاتُ دُخُولًا وَالْآخِرَاتُ خُرُوجًا *they are*
the first to enter, the last to leave, as plurals of أَوَّلَة and آخِرَةٌ. In later
times the fem. أَوَّلَةٌ is very common also as an adjective (comp.
Fleischer, *Kl. Schr.* i. 336 seq.); likewise the adverb أَوَّلًا (as in
أَوَّلًا وَآخِرًا) for the correct أَوَّلَ *formerly*. So it is interpreted in the
phrase لَقِيتُهُ عَامًا أَوَّلًا *I met him in a year before*, as some say instead of
عَامًا أَوَّلَ *last year* (comp. Lane s. v. عَام). D. G.]

Rem. *b.* ثانٍ makes, of course, in the construct state and with A the art. اَلثَّانِى ,ثَانِى; in the acc. ثَانِيًا, construct state and with the art. اَلثَّانِىَ ,ثَانِىَ. And so with the rest; اَلثَّالِثُ ,ثَالِثُ, etc.

Rem. *c.* Instead of سَادِسٌ the forms سَادٍ (acc. سَادِيًا) and سَاتٌّ (formed directly from سِتَّةٌ, سِتٌّ) are occasionally used.—ثَالٍ, acc. ثَالِيًا, also occurs for ثَالِثٌ [and خَامٍ for خَامِسٌ].

329. The ordinals from *eleventh* to *nineteenth* are:—   B

Masc.		Fem.		
حَادِىَ	عَشَرَ	حَادِيَةَ	عَشْرَةَ	*eleventh.*
ثَانِىَ	عَشَرَ	ثَانِيَةَ	عَشْرَةَ	*twelfth.*
ثَالِثَ	عَشَرَ	ثَالِثَةَ	عَشْرَةَ	*thirteenth.*
رَابِعَ	عَشَرَ	رَابِعَةَ	عَشْرَةَ	*fourteenth.*
etc.		etc.		

Rem. These numerals are not declined, when they are un- C defined; and even if defined by the article, they remain unchanged, as اَلْحَادِىَ عَشَرَ and اَلثَّانِىَ عَشَرَ ,اَلثَّالِثَ عَشَرَ. For اَلثَّالِثَةَ عَشْرَةَ we may say اَلْحَادِى عَشَرَ and اَلثَّانِى عَشَرَ. Some, however, admit the inflection of the unit, when defined, as اَلثَّالِثُ عَشَرَ ,اَلثَّالِثَةُ عَشْرَةَ; in which case اَلْحَادِى (اَلثَّانِى) عَشَرَ is the nom. and genit., اَلْحَادِىَ (اَلثَّانِىَ) عَشَرَ the accus.

330. The ordinals from *twentieth* to *ninetieth* are identical in D form with the cardinals; as عِشْرُونَ *twentieth*, اَلْعِشْرُونَ *the twentieth*. If joined to the ordinals of the units, these latter precede, and the two are united by وَ; as حَادٍ وَعِشْرُونَ *one and twentieth, twenty-first* (gen. حَادٍ وَعِشْرِينَ, acc. حَادِيًا وَعِشْرِينَ), fem. حَادِيَةٌ وَعِشْرُونَ. If a compound of this sort be defined, both its parts take the article; as

A اَلرَّابِعُ (acc. اَلْحَادِىَ وَٱلْعِشْرِينَ) the *twenty-first,* اَلْحَادِى وَٱلْعِشْرُونَ

وَٱلْعِشْرُونَ the *twenty-fourth.*

[REM. Later writers use instead of these forms حَادِى عِشْرِينَ,

رَابِعُ عِشْرِينَ and with the article, اَلْحَادِى عِشْرِينَ, اَلرَّابِعُ عِشْرِينَ, lit.

the first of the twenties, the fourth of the twenties. Comp. vol. ii.

§ 108.   D. G.]

B   **3. *The remaining Classes of Numerals.***

331. The numeral adverbs, *once, twice, thrice,* etc., are capable of
being expressed in two ways. (*a*) By the accusative of the nomen
vicis (§ 219), or, if this should be wanting, of the nomen verbi ; as
قَاتَلَ قِتَالًا وَاحِدًا أَوْ قِتَالَيْنِ, *he rose up once or twice;* قَامَ قَوْمَةً أَوْ قَوْمَتَيْنِ,
he fought once or twice. It is also permitted to use the simple
cardinal numbers, the nomen verbi being understood ; as أَمَتَّنَا ٱثْنَتَيْنِ

C وَأَحْيَيْتَنَا ٱثْنَتَيْنِ, *thou hast given us death twice, and thou hast given us*
life twice, i.e. إِحْيَاءَتَيْنِ and إِمَاتَتَيْنِ. (*b*) By the noun مَرَّةٌ, and similar
words, in the accus. ; as مَرَّةً *once,* مَرَّتَيْنِ *twice,* ثَلثَ مَرَّاتٍ, or ثَلثَ مِرَارٍ,
thrice; عِشْرِينَ كَرَّةً *twenty times;* تَارَةً وَأُخْرَى or ثَلثَ دَفَعَاتٍ *once*
and again; etc.

332. The numeral adverbs *a first, second, third time,* etc., are
D expressed either by adding the accus. of the ordinal adjective to a
finite form of a verb (in which case the corresponding nomen verbi is
understood) ; or by means of one of the words مَرَّةٌ, دَفْعَةٌ, etc., in the
accus., accompanied by an ordinal adjective agreeing with it. E.g.
جَاءَ ثَالِثًا (i.e. جَاءَ مَجِيئًا ثَالِثًا), or جَاءَ مَرَّةً ثَالِثَةً, *he came a third time;*
جَاءَ ٱلثَّالِثَ (i.e. جَاءَ ٱلْمَجِىءَ ٱلثَّالِثَ), or جَاءَ ٱلْمَرَّةَ ٱلثَّالِثَةَ, *he came the*
third time.

333. The *distributive* adjectives are expressed by repeating the
cardinal numbers once ; or by words of the forms فُعَالُ and مَفْعَلُ,

either singly or repeated. E.g. جَآءَ ٱلْقَوْمُ ٱثْنَيْنِ ٱثْنَيْنِ, or جَآءَ ٱلْقَوْمُ, or جَآءَ A

مَثْنَى, *the people came two by two*; جَآءُوا ثُلَاثَ ثُلَاثَ, or جَآءُوا مَثْلَثَ,

مَثْلَثَ, *they came three by three*; مَرَرْتُ بِقَوْمٍ مَثْنَى وَثُلَاثَ *I passed by a*

party of men, (*walking*) *by twos and threes*; فَٱنْكِحُوا مَا طَابَ لَكُمْ مِنَ

ٱلنِّسَآءِ مَثْنَى وَثُلَاثَ وَرُبَاعَ *then marry what pleaseth you of women, two*

and three and four at a time. The most common words of the forms

ثُلَاثُ, (مَثْنَى) (for) مَثْنَى, ثُنَآءَ; مَوْحَدُ, وُحَادُ, أُحَادُ are مَفْعَلُ and فُعَالُ B

مَثْلَثُ; and رُبَاعُ, مَرْبَعُ; but the formation is admitted [by some] up

to 10 [; the best authorities mentioning only عُشَارُ].

334. The *multiplicative* adjectives are expressed by nomina
patientis of the second form, derived from the cardinal numbers; e.g.

مُثَنَّى *twofold, double, dualized;* مُثَلَّثُ *threefold, triple, triangular;*

مُرَبَّعُ *fourfold, square;* مُخَمَّسُ *fivefold, pentagonal;* etc. *Single* or

simple is مُفْرَدُ (nom. patient. IV.). C

335. Numeral adjectives, expressing the number of parts of
which a whole is made up, take the form فُعَالِىُّ; as ثُنَآئِىُّ *biliteral;*

ثُلَاثِىُّ *triliteral, three cubits in length or height;* رُبَاعِىُّ *quadriliteral,*
four spans or cubits in height, a tetrastich; خُمَاسِىُّ *quinqueliteral,*
five spans in height; etc.

336. The *fractions,* from *a third* up to *a tenth,* are expressed by D
words of the forms فُعْلُ, فُعَلُ, and فَعِيلُ, pl. أَفْعَالُ; as ثُلُثُ, ثُلُثُ,

or ثَلِيثُ, pl. أَثْلَاثُ, *a third;* سُدُسُ, سُدُسُ, or سَدِيسُ, pl. أَسْدَاسُ,

a sixth; ثُمْنُ, ثُمُنُ, or ثَمِينُ, pl. أَثْمَانُ, *an eighth.*—[The form مُفْعَالُ

is exclusively employed for *a fourth* مُرْبَاعُ and *a tenth* مِعْشَارُ, together

with رُبْعُ, رُبُعُ and عُشُرُ, عُشْرُ or عَشِيرُ. According to Zamaḫšarī, *Fāik*

ii. 659 the form رَبِيعُ never occurs in this signification, nor, according

A to Abû Zèid (*Narādir* 193) ثَلِيثٌ and خَمِيسٌ. D. G.] *A half* is

نِصْفٌ, less frequently نَصْفٌ نُصْفٌ (vulg. نُصّ), or نَصِيفٌ, pl. أَنْصَافٌ.—
The fractions above *a tenth* are expressed by a circumlocution; e.g.

نِصْفٌ [; ثَلَاثَةُ أَجْزَاءٍ مِنْ عِشْرِينَ جُزْءًا, *three parts out of twenty,* 3/20 ;

نِصْفٌ وَثُلُثٌ ½ ⅓ ; نِصْفٌ وَسُدْسٌ ⅔ ; نِصْفٌ وَرُبْعٌ ¾ ; عُشُرُ الْعُشُرِ 1/100 ; الْعُشُرِ 1/10 ;

نِصْفٌ وَثُلُثٌ ⅚ ; etc.*] نِصْفٌ وَثُلُثٌ وَنِصْفُ عُشُرٍ عُشُرٍ

B   Rem. The form فُعْلٌ occurs in the same sense in Assyrian,
Heb. and Aram.; e.g. ܬܠܬܐ *a third,* "rubu," רֹבַע, *a fourth,*
חֹמֶשׁ *a fifth.*

337. The period, at the end of which an event usually recurs, is
expressed by a noun of the form فِعْلٌ, in the accus., either with or
without the article; as ثُلْثًا, or أَلثُّلْثَ, *every third* (day, month, year,
etc.); رِبْعًا, or أَلرِّبْعَ, *every fourth;* etc. Synonymous with ثِلْثٌ is غِبٌّ,

C as حُمَّى ٱلثِّلْثِ, or حُمَّى ٱلْغِبِّ, *the tertian fever.*

C. The Nomina Demonstrativa and Conjunctiva.

338. We treat of the nomina demonstrativa (including the
article), and the nomina conjunctiva (including the nomina inter-
rogativa), in one chapter, because they are both, according to our
terminology, pronouns, the former being the demonstrative pronouns,
D the latter the relative.

1. *The Demonstrative Pronouns and the Article.*

339. The demonstrative pronouns, أَسْمَآءُ ٱلْإِشَارَةِ, are either simple
or compound.

---

* [On a similar expression of whole numbers by circumlocution see
Goldziher in *Zeitschr. D. M. G.* xlix. 210 *seqq.*]

340. The simple demonstrative pronoun is ذَا, *this, that.*

	Masc.	Fem.
Sing.	ذَا	ذِى (ذِهْ ,ذِهِ ,ذِهِى) ;
		.(تِهِى ,تِهِ ,تِهْ) تِى ,تَا
Dual. Nom.	(ذَانِّ) ذَانِ	.(تَانِّ) تَانِ
Gen. Acc.	(ذَيْنِّ) ذَيْنِ	.(تَيْنِّ) تَيْنِ
Plur. comm. gen.	أُولَى ,أُلَا ,أُلَاءِ or أُولَى ; أُولَاءِ or أُولَاءِ.	

This simple form of the demonstrative pronoun is used to indicate a person or thing which is *near* to the speaker.

REM. *a.* The *u* in أُولَى and أُولَاءِ is always *short*, و being merely scriptio plena. In this way أُولَى can be distinguished in verse from أُولَى, the fem. of أَوَّلُ, *first*, in which the *u* is long. The و may have been inserted in order the more easily to distinguish أُلَى and أُلَاءِ from إِلَى and آلَاءِ.

REM. *b.* The diminutive of ذَا is ذَيَّا, f. تَيَّا ; du. ذَيَّانِ, f. تَيَّانِ ; pl. أُولَيَّاءِ, أُولَيَّا.

REM. *c.* Closely connected in its origin with ذَا is another monosyllable, viz. ذُو (= Heb. זֶה, Phœn. ז and אֵן, *this*) which is commonly used in the sense of *possessor, owner.* It is thus declined.

	Masc.	Fem.
Sing. Nom.	(זֶה) ذُو	ذَاتُ (אֵשֶׁת).
Gen.	ذِى	ذَاتِ.
Acc.	ذَا	ذَاتَ.
Du. Nom.	ذَوَا	(ذَاتَا) ذَوَاتَا.
Gen. Acc.	ذَوَىْ	(ذَاتَىْ) ذَوَاتَىْ.
Plur. Nom.	ذُوُو, أُلُو or أُولُو (אֵלֶּה)	ذَوَاتُ, أُلَاتُ or أُولَاتُ.
Gen. Acc.	ذَوِى, أُلِى or أُولِى	ذَوَاتِ, أُلَاتِ or أُولَاتِ.

A

The *u* in اُولُو and اُولَاتُ is always *short*, as in اُولَى and اُولَاءِ.—
The form اَذْوَاءُ is used as a plural of ذُو, when this word forms part
of the names or surnames of the kings or princes of el-Yèmèn, as
ذُو ٱلْكَلَاعِ, ذُو رُعَيْنٍ, ذُو نُوَاسٍ, ذُو يَزَنَ, etc. These are called اَذْوَآءُ
ٱلْيَمَنِ, formed as if from a singular ذَوًى.

[REM. *d.* كَذَا (sometimes written كَذَى) *thus, so and so, so
and so much* or *many*, is compounded of كَ *as, like* and the
B demonstrative pronoun ذَا. Comp. Vol. ii. § 44, *e,* rem. *d.*]

341. From the simple demonstrative pronoun are formed compounds :

(*a*) By adding the pronominal suffix of the second person (كَ, كِ ;
كُمَا ; كُنَّ, كُمْ, كُنَّ), either (α) alone, or (β) with the interposition of the
demonstrative syllable لِ.

(*b*) By prefixing the particle هَا.

C **342.** The gender and number of the pronominal suffix, appended
to the simple demonstrative pronoun, depend upon the sex and number
of the persons addressed. In speaking to a *single man,* ذَاكَ is used ;
to a *single woman,* ذَاكِ ; to *two persons,* ذَاكُمَا ; to *several men,* ذَاكُمْ ;
to *several women,* ذَاكُنَّ. But the form ذَاكَ may also be—and in fact
usually is—employed, whatever be the sex and number of the persons
spoken to ; and so with the rest. In regard to their signification,
these compound forms differ from the simple pronoun in indicating a
distant object.

D

	Masc.	Fem.
Sing.	ذَاكَ (*) ذَآئِكَ *that.*	تَاكَ, ذِيكَ (vulg. ذِيكَ).
Du. Nom.	ذَانِكَ	تَانِكَ.
Gen. Acc.	ذَيْنِكَ	تَيْنِكَ.
Plur. comm. gen.	أُلَاكَ or أُولَاكَ, أُولَآئِكَ or ٱلَآئِكَ, أُولَآئِكَ.	

* [Some say that ذَآئِكَ is a mispronunciation for ذَلِكَ.]

REM. *a.* The *u* is *short* in أُولَاكَ and أُولَآئِكَ, just as in أُولَى, A
أُولَآءِ, and أُولُو (§ 340, rem. *a, c*).

REM. *b.* The diminutive of ذَاكَ is ذَيَّاكَ, f. تَيَّاكَ, etc.

343. By inserting the demonstrative syllable لِ before the pronominal suffix, we get a longer form ذَالِكَ or ذٰلِكَ (often written ذلك, B
§ 6, rem. *a*).

	Masc.	Fem.
Sing.	ذٰلِكَ *that.*	تِلْكَ (تَالِكَ).
Du. Nom.	ذَانِّكَ	تَانِّكَ.
Gen. Acc.	ذَيْنِّكَ	تَيْنِّكَ.
Plur. comm. gen.	أُولَالِكَ or أُلَالِكَ.	

REM. *a.* تِلْكَ is a contraction for تَيْلِكَ. In the dual, ذَانِّكَ, C
تَانِّكَ, stand for ذَانِلِكَ, تَانِلِكَ; and تَيْنِّكَ, ذَيْنِّكَ, for ذَيْنِلِكَ, تَيْنِلِكَ.
The plur. is rare, أُولَالِكَ or أُولَآئِكَ (§ 342) being generally used instead. Some authorities regard تَانِّكَ, ذَانِّكَ, as the dual of ذَاكَ, the
second *n* being in their opinion merely corroborative.

REM. *b.* Some grammarians assert that there is a slight difference of meaning between ذَاكَ and ذٰلِكَ, the former referring in
their opinion to the nearer of two distant objects, the latter to the
more remote. D

REM. *c.* The syllable لِ must not be mistaken for the preposition لِ (which, when united with the pronominal suffixes of the
second and third persons, becomes لَ), but is to be viewed as a
demonstrative syllable, which occurs also in the article and in the
relative pronoun. See §§ 345 and 347.

REM. *d.* The diminutive of ذٰلِكَ is ذَيَّالِكَ, f. تَيَّالِكَ. [A com-

A   pound of كَ and ذٰلِكَ (comp. § 340, rem. *d*) is كَذٰلِكَ *so, in like manner**.]

344. The particle هَا (which has the same demonstrative force as the Latin *ce* in *hicce*) is called by the Arabs حَرْفُ ٱلتَّنْبِيهِ, *the particle that excites attention.* It is prefixed both to the simple demonstrative ذَا, and to the compound ذَاكَ (but not to ذٰلِكَ). Before ذَا it is usually written defectively, هٰذَا or هَذَا; before ذَاكَ in full, هَاذَاكَ.

B   Masc.   Fem.

	Masc.	Fem.
Sing.	هٰذَا *this.*	هٰذِهِ (هٰذِهْ), هٰذِى
		(هَاتِهِ, هَاتِى, هَاتَا, هٰذَاتِ).
Du. Nom.	هٰذَانِ	هَاتَانِ or هْتَانِ.
Gen. Acc.	هٰذَيْنِ	هَاتَيْنِ or هْتَيْنِ.

C   Plur. comm. gen. هٰؤُلَآءِ or هَٰاؤُلَآءِ, هُوْلَا or هَٰاؤُلَا.

In like manner, هٰذَاكَ or هَاذَاكَ, fem. هَاتَاكَ, هَاتِيكَ, etc.

REM. *a.* هَا is identical with the Aram. הָא, אןٰ‎, *this,* as an interjection, *lo!* Heb. הֵא.

REM. *b.* In the dual some say هٰذَانِّ, with double *n.*—The diminutive of هٰذَا هٰذَا is هٰذَيَّا, f. هَاتَيَّا, pl. هُوْلَيَّآءِ; of هٰذَاكَ, هٰذَيَّاكَ, pl.

D هُوْلَيَّائِكَ. [By prefixing هَا to كَذَا is formed هٰكَذَا *thus.*]

[REM. *c.* To these demonstratives belong also ذَيْتَ وَذَيْتَ and كَيْتَ وَكَيْتَ, *thus and thus, so and so, such and such things,* for which we also find (rarely ذَيْتَ وَذَيْتَ, ذَيْتِ وَكَيْتِ, كَيْتِ وَكَيْتِ) and for the former ذَيَّاءَ وَذَيَّاءَ, ذَيَّةَ وَذَيَّةَ, for the latter كَيَّةَ وَكَيَّةَ. According to some scholars there is originally a slight difference between these expressions, the former relating to what

---

* [A singular contraction (or modification) of كَذٰلِكَ is كَاكَ used by the poet ĕś-Śanfarā, as quoted in the *Ḥamāsa,* p. 244, l. 21.]

has been said, the latter to what has been done, as كَذَا refers to A quantity (comp. Harīrī, *Durrat*, ed. Thorb. p. 99). D. G.]

345. The article أَلْ—called by the Arabs أَدَاةُ ٱلتَّعْرِيفِ *the instrument of definition,* ٱلْأَلِفُ وَٱللَّامُ *the ĕlif and lām,* لَامُ [or حَرْفُ] ٱلتَّعْرِيفِ *the lām of definition,* or simply ٱللَّامُ *the lām,*—is composed of the demonstrative letter لِ (see § 343, rem. *c,* and § 347) and the prosthetic ا, which is prefixed only to lighten the pronunciation B (هَمْزَةُ ٱلْوَصْلِ, § 19 *a,* and rem. *f*). [It is always written in conjunction with the following word.] Though it has become determinative, it was originally demonstrative, as still appears in such words as ٱلْيَوْمَ *to-day,* ٱلْآنَ *now,* etc.

[Rem. *a.* The article, if employed to indicate the genus, i.e. any individual (animate or inanimate) bearing the name, is called أَهْلَكَ ٱلنَّاسَ, or simply لَامُ ٱلْجِنْسِ, as ٱللَّامُ لِتَعْرِيفِ ٱلْجِنْسِ *dinār and dirhem bring men to perdition,* ٱلرَّجُلُ ٱلدِّينَارُ وَٱلدِّرْهَمُ C خَيْرٌ مِنَ ٱلْمَرْأَةِ *man is better than woman;* if indicating a particular individual it is called ٱللَّامُ لِتَعْرِيفِ ٱلْعَهْدِ, or simply لَامُ ٱلْعَهْدِ.]

Rem. *b.* Some grammarians regard the ĕlif as an integral part of the article, and say that it was originally أَلْ (with أَلِفُ ٱلْقَطْع, of the same form as هَلْ, بَلْ), gradually weakened to أَلْ. But sometimes the Arabs suppress the ا, saying for instance لَحْمَرُ for ٱلْأَحْمَرُ (comp. Vol. ii. § 242, footnote). D

Rem. *c.* It is sometimes, though very rarely, used as a relative pronoun (=ٱلَّذِى, § 347); as مَنْ لَا يَزَالُ شَاكِرًا عَلَى ٱلْمَعَهْ *he who does not cease to be grateful for what is with him* (or *for what he has*), where ٱلْمَعَهْ = مَعَهُ ٱلَّذِى; مِنَ ٱلْقَوْمِ ٱلرَّسُولُ ٱللَّهِ مِنْهُمْ, *of the people of whom is the Apostle of God,* where ٱلَّذِينَ = ٱلرَّسُولُ ٱللَّهِ; مَا أَنْتَ بِٱلْحَكَمِ ٱلتُّرْضَى حُكُومَتُهُ; رَسُولُ ٱللَّهِ *thou art not the judge*

A *whose sentence is approved,* where ٱلتَّرْضَى = ٱلَّذِى تُرْضَى. Compare, for example, in German, *der* = *welcher,* and our *that* for *who* and *which.*

REM. *d.* اَلْ is [in all probability (see *Comp. Gr.* p. 114)] identical with the Hebrew art. .ה, for הַלְ. In South Arabia اَمْ was (and even still is) used for اَلْ, but without assimilation; as لَيْسَ مِنْ اَمْبِرّ اَمْصِيَامُ فِى اَمْسَفَرِ *fasting in journeying is not (an act) of piety;* يَرْمِى وَرَائِى بِٱلْمَسْهِمِ وَٱلْمَسْلِمَهْ *he casts (standing) behind me with arrow*

B *and stone;* for بِٱلسَّهْمِ ,ٱلسَّفَرِ ,ٱلصِّيَامُ ,ٱلْبِرِّ. and وَٱلسَّلِمَهْ.

2. The Conjunctive (Relative) and Interrogative Pronouns.

(a) The Conjunctive Pronouns.

346. The conjunctive pronouns are :—

(1) ٱلَّذِى *who, which, that;* fem. ٱلَّتِى.

(2) مَنْ *he who, she who, whoever;*

C مَا *that which, whatever.*

(3) اَىُّ *he who, whoever;* fem. اَيَّةُ *she who, whoever.*

(4) اَيْمَنْ *every one who, whosoever;*

اَيْمَا *everything which, whatsoever.*

REM. مَنْ, مَا, اَىُّ, اَيَّةُ, and their compounds, اَيْمَا, اَيْمَنْ, are also interrogatives, which indeed is their original signification (see

D § 351 and foll.). They ought therefore to be treated of first as interrogatives and then as conjunctives; but it is convenient to reverse this order, so as to connect the relatives with the demonstratives.

347. The conjunctive ٱلَّذِى is compounded of the article اَلْ, the demonstrative letter لَ (see §§ 343 and 345), and the demonstrative pronoun اِذْ, or ذُو (§ 340, rem. *c*). When used substantively, it has the same meaning as مَا, مَنْ, viz. *he who, that which, whoever,* A *whatever;* when used adjectively, it signifies *who, which, that,* and refers necessarily to a definite substantive, with which it agrees in gender, number, *and case.* It is declined as follows :—

	Masc.	Fem.
Sing.	اَلَّذِي (اَلَّذِ ;اَلَّذْ ; اَلَّذُ),	;اَلَّتِ (اَلَّتْ ;
	(لَذِي ;اَلَّذِيِّ).	(اَلَّتِي). (اَللَّاتِي).
Du. Nom.	(اَللَّذَا ; اَللَّذَانِّ) اَللَّذَانِ.	(اَللَّتَا ; اَللَّتَانِّ) اَللَّتَانِ. B
Gen. Acc.	(اَللَّذَيْنِّ) اَللَّذَيْنِ.	(اَللَّتَيْنِّ) اَللَّتَيْنِ.
Plur.	;[اَلَّلَّئِى] (اَلَّذِى) اَلَّذِينَ ;	;(اَللَّاآتِ) اَللَّاتِ ; اَللَّاتِى ;
	اَللَّآ ; [اَللَّآؤُونَ Nom.,	;(اَللَّوَا) اَللَّوَاتِ ; اَللَّوَاتِى ;
	اَللَّآئِينَ Gen. Acc.]) ;	اَللَّآئِى ; اَللَّآءِ ;
	*.اَلْأُولَى or اَلْأُلَى.	اَلْأُولَى or اَلْأُلَى. C

Rem. *a.* اَلَّذِى, اَلَّتِى, and اَلَّذِينَ, are written defectively, because of their frequent occurrence, instead of اَلَّذِى, اَلَّتِى, and اَلَّذِينَ. The other forms, which are not in such constant use, generally retain the double ل of the article and the demonstrative.—The modern, vulgar form, for all numbers and genders, is اِللِّى or اَلِّى.

Rem. *b.* The tribe of Huḏeil (هُذَيْلٌ), according to the Arab grammarians, used اَلَّذُونَ in the nom. plur. masc., اَلَّذِينَ in the gen. D and acc. This اَلَّذُونَ must, of course, at one time have been universally employed as the nom., اَلَّذِينَ being the form which belongs to the oblique cases; but gradually the latter supplanted the

---

* [According to aṣ-Ṣabbān, as quoted by Landberg (*Nylander's Specimenschrift,* p. 30) the relative pronoun is only اَلْأُلَى, the article sufficing to distinguish it from the prepos. إِلَى. Comp. § 340, rem. *a.* D. G.]

A   former, just as in modern Arabic the oblique form of the plur. sanus, ـِين, has everywhere usurped the place of the direct form ـُون. Even the sing. اَلَّذِى is an oblique form, the nom. of which ought properly to be اَلَّذُو.—The forms اَلَّاؤُونَ, gen. and acc. اَلَّاِينَ, and اَلَّاؤُو are also said to occur.

REM. *c.* اَلَّذِى was originally, as its derivation shows, a demonstrative pron., and has its precise Hebrew equivalent in הַלָּזֶה,

B   fem. הַלָּזוּ, comm. הַלָּז (= اَلَّذ). See *Comp. Gr.* p. 117.

REM. *d.* From اَلَّذِى are formed the diminutives اَللَّذَيَّا, اَللَّتَيَّا; du. اَللَّذَيَّانِ, اَللَّتَيَّانِ; pl. اَللَّذَيُّونَ, اَللَّتَيَّاتُ. The forms اَللَّذَيَّا, اَللَّتَيَّا, are vulgar and incorrect.

REM. *e.* Instead of اَلَّذِى, some of the Arabs, especially the tribe of *Ṭayyi'* (طَيِّئٌ), employ ذُو (Heb. זֶו, Aram. דִי, ד, Æth. **H** : *za*).

C   It is then either wholly *indeclinable*, which is more usual; as فَحَسْبِىَ مِنْ ذُو عِنْدَهُمْ مَا كَفَانِيَا *then enough for me of that which is with them* (of their property) *is what suffices me*, for مِنَ الَّذِى (كَفَانِى); لَاَنْتَحِيَنْ لِلْعَظْمِ ذُو أَنَا عَارِقُهُ in rhyme for كَفَانِيَا) *I will set to work in earnest on the bone which I am gnawing* (on the satire which I am meditating), for الَّذِى (عَارِقُهُ) in rhyme for (عَارِقُهُ); وَبِئْرِى ذُو حَفَرْتُ وَذُو طَوَيْتُ *and my well which I dug and which*

D   *I lined* (or *cased*), for الَّتِى and وَالَّتِى; فَلَا وَذُو بَيْتُهُ فِى السَّمَاءِ] *no! by Him whose residence is in heaven*, '*Aġānī* xi. 25, l. 18. D. G.] or else declined as follows :—

	Masc.	Fem.
Sing. Nom.	ذُو	ذَاتُ
Gen.	ذِى	(ذَاتِ) ذَاتُ
Acc.	ذَا	(ذَاتِ) ذَاتُ

A

		Masc.	Fem.
Du.	Nom.	ذَوَا	ذَوَاتَا
	Gen. Acc.	ذَوَىْ	ذَوَاتَىْ
Plur.	Nom.	ذَوُو	ذَوَاتُ
	Gen. Acc.	ذَوِى	(ذَوَاتٍ) ذَوَاتُ

An example of this use is بِٱلْفَضْلِ ذُو فَضَّلَكُمُ ٱللّٰهُ بِهِ وَٱلْكَرَامَةِ ذَاتُ أُكْرَمَكُمُ ٱللّٰهُ بِهَا *by the excellence wherewith God hath made* B *you excel, and the honour wherewith God hath honoured you,* for ٱلَّذِى and ٱلَّتِى; [a woman in Yèmèn said ('Omāra, ed. Kay, p. 147, l. 9, 11) دو بُد مِن ذِى حَكَمِ الامير for لَا بُدَّ مِنَ ٱلَّذِى حَكَمَ ٱلْأُمِيرُ *you cannot but obey the decision of the Prince.* D. G.]

348. The conjunctive pronouns مَنْ and مَا are indeclinable, and differ from ٱلَّذِى in never being used adjectively, but always sub- stantively, so that they correspond to the Latin *is qui, ea quæ, id quod,* C Gr. ὅστις, ἥτις, ὅ,τι. The former (مَنْ) is used of beings endowed with reason, the latter (مَا) of all other objects. [They are either definite (مَوْصُولٌ) as ٱلَّذِى, or indefinite (مَوْصُوفٌ), مَنْ signifying in the latter case *one who,* مَا *something that,* and may also have a collective meaning *persons who, things that,* being nevertheless construed as singulars.]

REM. For the corresponding forms in the other Semitic lan- guages see *Comp. Gr.* pp. 123—127.

349. The conjunctive pronoun أَىُّ, fem. أَيَّةُ, *he who, she who,* D *whoever,* is regularly declined in the sing. according to the triptote declension, but has commonly neither dual nor plural.

REM. The Æth. has the same word, ኦይ: ('ay) *who? of what sort?* The corresponding Heb. vocable is אֵי, used as an adverb, *where?* in interrogative phrases אֵי, which appears in Æth. in ኦይቴ: ('aytē) *where?* ኦፎ: ('ĕfō) *how?* Syr. ܐܝܟܐ *where?* ܐܝܢ *who?* ܐܡܬܝ *how long?* etc.

w.

35

A   **350.** Of أَىّ and مَنْ, مَا, are compounded أَيْمَنْ *he who, she who, whosoever,* أَيَّمَا *that which, whatsoever.* Only the first part of the compound admits of being declined; gen. أَيَّمَنْ, أَيَّمَا; acc. أَيَّمَنْ, أَيَّمَا.

(b) *The Interrogative Pronouns.*

351. It has been already stated (§ 346, rem.) that the conjunctive pronouns, with the exception of أَلَّذِى, are also interrogative, which is

B   indeed their original signification. To them may be added كَمْ [and كَأَيِّنْ or كَأَىّ], *how much* [or *many*], which are (*a*) interrogative, (*b*) according to our ideas, exclamatory, according to the Arab grammarians, enunciative (لِلْإِخْبَارِ); but never conjunctive.

> REM. The interrogative مَا may be* shortened after preposi-
> tions into مَ, and is then united in writing both with those
> prepositions with which such a union is usual, and with those with
C   > which it is not, (though, in the latter case, it is better to keep them
> apart); e.g. عَلَامَ, إِلَامَ, (عَنْ مَّ, مِنْ مَّ for عَمَّ, مِمَّ, فِيمَ, لِمَ, بِمَ,
> حَتَّامَ (حَتَّى مَ, عَلَى مَ, إِلَى مَ better). In such cases, the accent is
> transferred from مَ to the preceding syllable (as *bíma, 'ilá ma,* etc.);
> whence it happens that بِمَ and لِمَ are sometimes shortened in
> poetry into بِمْ and لِمْ. This is also the origin of كَمْ, for كَمَ or
> كَمَا (lit., *the like of what? the worth of what?*), Heb. בַּמֶּה, כַּמָּה,

D   Aram. כְּמָא, דְּכְמָא [see *Comp. Gr.* p. 125].—In pause these words are written حَتَّامَهْ, عَمَّهْ, بِمَهْ, etc. Similarly we find فَمَهْ for فَمَا *what then?* and كَيْمَهْ *that what? for what purpose?* as when one

---

* [Rather, "is usually shortened." Zamaḫšarī, *Fāiḳ,* ii. 159 calls it "the commoner" form (أَلْأَشْيَعُ). The grammarians of the school of Baṣra say that it must always be shortened in prose; in poetry the êlif may be retained. Comp. Fleischer, *Kl. Schr.* i. 364. D. G.]

says قَصَدْتُ فُلَانًا *I went to* (*the house of*) *so and so*, to which you A
rejoin كَيْمَهْ, and the answer is كَىْ أُحْسِنَ إِلَيْهِ *that I might do him*
a kindness. [The shortening of مَا takes place also in such sentences as مَجِىءٍ مَرْ جِئْتَ *in what manner did you arrive?* and
مِثْلُ مَرْ أَنْتَ *what are you like?*]

352. The interrogative pronoun مَنْ, *who?* has the distinctions
of gender, number, and case, only when it stands alone; as if one
should say *Some one is come*, or *I have seen some one*, and another B
should ask *Who? Whom?* In this case its declension is as follows:—

		Masc.		Fem.
Sing.	Nom.	مَنُو		
	Gen.	مَنِى	مَنَهْ	(مَنْتْ)
	Acc.	مَنَا		
Du.	Nom.	مَنَانْ	مَنْتَانْ	(مَنَتَانْ)
	Gen. Acc.	مَنَيْنْ	مَنْتَيْنْ	(مَنَتَيْنْ)	C
Plur.	Nom.	مَنُونْ	مَنَاتْ	
	Gen. Acc.	مَنِينْ		

REM. *a.* Only a poet could venture to say أَتَوْا نَارِى فَقُلْتُ
مَنُونَ أَنْتُمْ *they came to my fire, and I said, Who are ye?*

REM. *b.* The interrogative pronoun مَا *what?* is never declined
under any circumstances. D

[REM. *c.* From مَنْ is formed the relative adjective مَنِىُّ, with
the article ٱلْمَنِىُّ (comp. Vol. ii. § 170, rem. *b*). The dual is
ٱلْمَنِيَّانْ, the plural ٱلْمَنِيُّونْ.]

353. The interrogative pronoun أَىُّ, fem. أَيَّةٌ, *who?* is either
construed with a following noun in the genitive, or with a suffix, or
stands alone. In the first two cases, it loses the tènwin (§§ 315, *a*,
316, *a*, *c*), and, if followed by a noun, is generally masc. sing.; as

A   أَيُّ كِتَابٍ ; *which book* (lit. *quid libri*)? gen. أَيِّ كِتَابٍ, acc. أَيَّ كِتَابٍ,

أَيُّ عَيْنٍ *which eye* or *fountain?* أَيُّ ٱلْمَرْأَتَيْنِ *which of the two women?*

أَيُّ ٱلنِّسَاءِ *which of the women?* [The feminine form is of rare

occurrence, as أَيَّةُ أُكْلَةٍ *whatever morsel* (Él-Mubarrad 86, l. 17) and

أَيَّةُ أُنْثَى *which female?* (Dīw. Hudèil, n. 201, vs. 2). D. G.] In the

second case, when prefixed to a fem. pronoun, it may be masc. or fem.

أَيُّهُنَّ or أَيَّتُهُنَّ *which of them?* meaning women, the latter being the

B more common. When standing alone, or used like مَنْ in § 352, it

has all the numbers and cases, the pausal forms being :—

Sing. masc., nom. أَيُّ or أَيّْ, gen. أَيِّ or أَيّْ, acc. أَيَّا ; fem. أَيَّهْ.

Dual masc., nom. أَيَّانْ, gen. acc. أَيَّيْنْ ; fem., nom. أَيَّتَانْ, gen. acc.

أَيَّتَيْنْ.

Plur. masc., nom. أَيُّونْ, gen. acc. أَيِّينْ ; fem. أَيَّاتْ.

C   In أَيُّ and أَيِّ the final vowel is said to be obscurely sounded or

slurred (اَلرَّوْمُ).

    Rem. *a.* With the suffixes أَيُّ is sometimes shortened into أَيْ,

as أَيْهُمَا, for أَيُّهُمَا, *which of the two?* and so in [the interrogative

أَيْمَ *what?* for أَيُّ مَا, as أَيْمَ تَقُولُ *what dost thou say?* and] the

vulgar interrogative أَيْشْ *what?* for أَيُّ شَيْءٍ.

    Rem. *b.* Instead of أَيُّ with [a following noun in the genitive

or] a suffix, the more general and indefinite أَيُّمَا is sometimes used ;

D as أَيُّمَا أَحَبُّ إِلَيْكَ هُوَ أَمْ أَنَا, *which is dearer to you, he or I?* in

which example أَيُّمَا stands for أَيُّنَا, *which of us?*

    Rem. *c.* From أَيُّ are formed the relative adjective أَيِّيٌّ *from

what place?* (see Lane, art. اى, p. 134 c), and the compound كَأَيٍّ

or كَأَيِّنْ (also written كَأَيٍّ or كَأَيِّ, كَأَيِّنْ, كَىٍّ, كَىْءٍ or كَىِّنْ

and كَا (§ 351 and Vol. ii. § 34, *e*, rem. *d*).

    Rem. *d.* See *Comp. Gr.* pp. 120—122.

[3.   *The Indefinite Pronouns.*

A

353*.   1.   The interrogative pronouns مَنْ and مَا have passed into indefinites (*Comp. Gr.* p. 125)*, with the sense of *somebody*, *something*, but are never thus employed unless with a qualificative complement (صِفَة), and are therefore called مَوْصُوفَة (§ 348). This complement is very rarely an adjective or participle, but usually a preposition with following genitive, as مَا لِى *something which I have*, B or an adverb as مَنْ هُنَاكَ *somebody here*, or a qualificative clause, as مَنْ قَالَ *one who says*.   Comp. Vol. ii. § 172, rem. *a*.

2.   The indefinite pronoun مَا is used to introduce a clause equivalent to the *maṣdar* or infinitive, and is in that case called مَا ٱلْمَصْدَرِيَّة (Vol. ii. § 88, § 114, § 127, rem. *e*); hence its use in conditional clauses as مَا ٱلشَّرْطِيَّة (Vol. ii. § 6), or in reference to time as مَا ٱلزَّمَانِيَّة or مَا ٱلدَّيْمُومَة (Vol. ii. § 7); if added to certain adverbial C nouns, it gives them a conditional and general signification, as the Latin termination *cunque*, e.g. أَيْنَمَا *wherever*, حَيْثُمَا *wherever, whenever*, مَهْمَا *whatever*; if appended to كَأَنَّ, أَنَّ, إِنَّ and لَكِنَّ it hinders their regimen and is therefore called مَا ٱلْكَافَّة (Vol. ii. § 36, rem. *d*); with the same effect it is added to لَيْتَ; عَلَّ and لَعَلَّ (*ibid.* rem. *f*) and to رُبَّ (Vol. ii. § 84, rem. *a* and *b*); in apposition to an indefinite noun, it has a vague intensifying force and is called مَا ٱلْإِبْهَامِيَّة D (Vol. ii. § 136 *a*, rem. *e*); added to the affirmative لَ it serves to strengthen the affirmation مَا مَزِيدَة لِلتَّأْكِيد (see an example § 361 near the end, and Vol. ii. § 36, rem. *e*); it is often inserted after the

---

* [Prym, *Diss. de enuntiationibus relativis Semiticis*, p. 100 and Fleischer, *Kl. Schr.* i. 360 *seq.*, 706 *seq.* reject this theory, considering the indefinite meaning of مَنْ and مَا as the original, whence the interrogative has been derived.]

A prepositions مِنْ, عَنْ and بِ without affecting their regimen, and is then called مَا ٱلْمَزِيدَةُ or مَا ٱلزَّائِدَةُ (Vol. ii. § 70, rem. *f*). In like manner it is also put after رُبَّ (Vol. ii. § 84, rem. *a*) and in other cases (Vol. ii. § 90, rem.).]

3. كِنَايَاتٌ عَنْ أَسَامِى فُلَانٌ, fem. فُلَانَةُ (§ 309, *b*, δ, rem. *b*), as ٱلْأَنَاسِىّ, stand for names of persons, like ὁ, ἡ δεῖνα, *so and so*, *M.* or *N.*;

B as أَلَا قَاتَلَ ٱللّٰهُ ٱلْوُشَاةَ وَقَوْلُهُمْ فُلَانَةُ ὁ δεῖνα τοῦ δεῖνος, فُلَانٌ ٱبْنُ فُلَانٍ أَضْحَتْ خِلَّةً لِفُلَانٍ, *O may God curse all talebearers and their saying* "*So and so has become a sweetheart of so and so.*" Syr. ܦܠܢ, fem. ܦܠܢܝܬܐ, Heb. פְּלֹנִי. In speaking of animals, ٱلْفُلَانُ and ٱلْفُلَانَةُ are employed, as رَكِبْتُ ٱلْفُلَانَ *I rode on such and such a one.*—هَنْ *a thing*, and its fem. هَنَةٌ, are similarly used for substantives of the class

C أَسْمَاءُ ٱلْجِنْسِ (§ 191, rem. *b*, 3, 4).—On the use of these words in the vocative, see the Syntax.

III. THE PARTICLES.

354. There are *four* sorts of particles (حَرْفٌ, pl. حُرُوفٌ, [or أَدَاةٌ, pl, أَدَوَاتٌ]) ; viz., Prepositions, Adverbs, Conjunctions, and Inter-
D jections.

A. THE PREPOSITIONS.

355. The prepositions are called by the Arabs حُرُوفُ ٱلْجَرِّ, *the particles of attraction*, or ٱلْجِوَارُ (from the sing. ٱلْجَارَّةُ or ٱلْجَارُّ), *the attractives*, i.e. the particles which govern the genitive. They are also named حُرُوفُ ٱلْخَفْضِ, *the particles of depression*, and حُرُوفُ ٱلْإِضَافَةِ, *the particles of annexation* or *connection*, because the

distinctive vowel of the genitive (*i*), and consequently the genitive A
itself, is called اَلْخَفْضُ (see § 308, footnote), and because this case has
its peculiar place in that connection which many prepositions with
their genitives really represent (see § 358). They are divided into
separable prepositions, i.e. those which are written as separate words,
and *inseparable*, i.e. those which are always united in writing with the
following noun.

356. The *inseparable* prepositions consist of *one* consonant with B
its vowel. They are :—

(*a*) بِ *in, at, near, by, with, through* (Heb. Aram. בְּ, Æth. **በ** :
ba). [بِلَا, *without*, is a compound of بِ with the negative لَا. Comp.
Vol. ii. § 56, rem. *c*.]

(*b*) تَ *by, in swearing, as* تَاللَّهِ *by God !**

(*c*) لِ *to* (sign of the Dative), *for, on account of* (Heb. Aram. לְ,
Æth. **ለ** : *la*).

(*d*) وَ *by, in swearing, as* وَاللَّهِ *by God !*   C

REM. *a*. The damma of the suffixed pronouns of the 3d pers.
هُ, هُمَا, هُمْ, هُنَّ, is changed after بِ into kèsra ; as بِهِ, بِهِمْ. See
§ 185, rem. *b*, and § 317, rem. *c*. The ancient and poetic form
هُمُ changes either both vowels, or the first only ; بِهِمِ or بِهِمُ.

REM. *b*. The kèsra of the prep. لِ passes before the pronominal
suffixes into fètḥa ; as لَهُ *to him,* لَكُمْ *to you,* لَنَا *to us.* Except the
suffix of the 1st pers. sing., which absorbs the vowel of the prepo- D
sition ; لِي *to me.*

---

* [تَ was especially in use at Mekka. It seems to be the remnant
of some word, as it is (probably of another) in تَحِينَ (= حِينَ ?) and
تَلَانَ (= أَلْآنَ). Comp. the abbreviation of أَيْمُنُ اللَّهِ, Vol. ii. § 62,
rem. *b*. I take the و in وَاللَّهِ and the وَاوُ رُبَّ (Vol. ii. § 235) to be also
remnants of words. D. G.]

A

REM. c. كَ, *as, like* (Heb. Aram. כְּ), which is commonly reckoned a preposition, is really not so. It is a formally unde-veloped noun, which occurs only as the governing word in the genitive connection, but runs in this position through all the relations of case (*similitudo, instar*).

357. The *separable* prepositions are of *two* sorts. Those of the first class, which are all biliteral or triliteral, have different termina-tions; those of the second class are simply nouns of different forms

B in the accus. sing., determined by the following genitive, and they consequently end in fètha without tènwīn (َ).

358. The separable prepositions of the first class are :—

(a) إِلَى *to* (Heb. אֶל־, אֱלֵי).

(b) حَتَّى *till, up to, as far as* (Heb. עַד, Æth. �እስከ፡). A dialectic variety is عَتَّى.

C (c) عَلَى *over, above, upon, against, to, on account of, notwith-standing* (Heb. עַל־, עֲלֵי, Aram. עַל, ܥܠ).

(d) عَنْ *from, away from, after, for.*

(e) فِى *in, into, among, about.*

(f) لَدُنْ, or لَدَى (لَدَا), *with* (penes, apud). Rarer forms are : لَدْ, لُدْ, لَدَ, لَدُ, (لُدْنُ) لَدُنُ, (لَدُنْ) لَدُنِ, (لَدُنْ) لَدْنِ, لَدِنْ, (لَدُنْ) لَدَا لَدَّا.

D (g) مَعَ *with* (Heb. עִם, Syr. ܥܡ); dialectically مَعْ, which becomes in the waṣl مَعِ.

(h) مِنْ *of, from, on account of* (Heb. Aram. מִן, ܡܢ, Æth. ኤምነ፡ : '*ĕmna*, or ኤም፡ : *ĕm*). See § 20, *d*.

(i) مُنْذُ, or مُذْ, *from a certain time, since* (compounded of مِنْ and ذُو, *ex quo*; see § 347, rem. *e* and comp. מִן־דִּי, Ezra v. 12). Rarer

forms arc : مُنْذُ ,مُنْذَ ,مِنْذُ ,مِذْ, and مُذُ.   In the waṣl مُذُ usually becomes A
مُذْ (§ 20, *d*), rarely مُذِ or مُذَ.

Rem. *a.*   عَلَى ,إِلَى, and لَدَى, preserve before the suffixes their
original pronunciation عَلَىْ ,إِلَىْ, and لَدَىْ (compare עָלַי and אֱלַי);
as لَدَيْهَا ,إِلَيْكُمْ ,عَلَيْهِ ,إِلَيْهِ.   The ḍamma of the suffixes of the 3d pers.
passes after the diphthong into kĕsra, according to § 185, rem. *b*,
and § 317, rem. *c.*   The suffix of the 1st pers. sing., ـِيَ (orig. ـِيَ),
combines with إِلَى ,عَلَى, and لَدَى into إِلَيَّ ,عَلَيَّ ,لَدَيَّ; with فِى B
into فِيَّ.   See § 317, rem. *a.*

Rem. *b.*   The ن of عَنْ ,مِنْ, and لَدُنْ, is doubled in connection
with the suffixes of the 1st pers.; عَنِّى ,مِنِّى ,لَدُنِّى [عَنَّا, etc.].   If
عَنْ and مِنْ are prefixed to مَنْ and مَا, the ن is assimilated to the
م in pronunciation, and the two are usually written as one word;
عَمَّنْ ,عَمَّا ,مِمَّنْ ,مِمَّا, for عَنَّمْنْ or عَن مَّنْ, etc. (see § 14, *b*).

Rem. *c.*   When followed by the article, the prepositions مِنْ and C
عَلَى are occasionally abbreviated in poetry, مِنَ اَلْ being contracted
into مِلْ, and عَلَى اَلْ into عُلْ; as مِلْ مَالٍ, or مِلْمَالٍ, for مِنَ اَلْمَالِ;
عَلْمَآءِ for عَلَى اَلْمَآءِ.   [Comp. p. 24, note.]

359. Examples of prepositions of the second class are: أَمَامَ
before (of place); بَيْنَ *between, among* (בֵּין); بَعْدَ *after* (בַּעַד), dimin.
بُعَيْدَ; تَحْتَ *under, beneath* (תַּחַת), dimin. تُحَيْتَ; تُجَاهَ or تِجَاهَ, D
خَلْفَ, حِذَآءَ ,تِلْقَآءَ, *over against, opposite to*; حَوْلَ *round, about*;
behind, after; دُونَ *below, under, beneath, on this side of*, dimin. دُوَيْنَ;
عِنْدَ (also عَنْدَ, which is the modern and vulgar form, rarely عُنْدَ) *with*,
in possession of (apud, penes, Fr. chez; [עִמָּד]); قَبَلَ do.]; عِوَضَ
instead of, for; فَوْقَ *above*, dimin. فُوَيْقَ; قَبْلَ *before* (of time, קֶבֶל),

A dimin. قَبِيْل ; قُدَّام *before* (of place, קֶדֶם) ; وَرَاءَ *behind, after, beyond* ; وَسْط *in the middle, among.* These are all, as before said, the construct accusatives of nouns; such as بَيْن *interval,* حَوْل *circumference,* etc.

B. THE ADVERBS.

360. There are *three* sorts of adverbs. The first class consists of
B *particles* of various origin, partly inseparable, partly separable; the second class of *indeclinable nouns* ending in *u*; the third class of *nouns* in the *accusative.*

361. The inseparable adverbial particles are :—

(*a*) أَ, interrogative, حَرْف ٱلِٱسْتِفْهَام, *the particle of questioning* (*num? utrum? an?* Heb. הֲ) ; [comp. § 21, *d*]. The form ه occurs C dialectically, for example in هَمَا *nonne?* for أَمَا (see § 362, *h*), هَذَا ٱلَّذِى, for أَذَا ٱلَّذِى, *is this he who—?* [In alternative questions it is followed by أَمْ or أَوْ.]

[REM. When أ is followed by another êlif with hèmza, an ا is inserted between the two hèmzas, as أَاأَنْتَ, also written أَأَنْتَ, but some do not do this. If the following êlif is pronounced with kèsra, it is converted into ى with hèmza, as أَئِنَّكَ, أَئِذَا.]

D (*b*) سَ, prefixed to the Imperfect of the verb to express real futurity, as سَيَكْفِيكَهُمُ ٱللّٰه, *God will suffice thee against them.* It is an abbreviation of سَوْفَ, *in the end* (Heb. Aram. סוֹף, סוֹּם, *end*), [and is called حَرْف ٱلتَّنْفِيس *the particle of amplification*].

(*c*) لَ, affirmative, *certainly, surely.* This may be (*a*) لَامُ جَوَاب ٱلْقَسَمِ, *the* la *that corresponds to,* or *is the complement of, an oath,* as وَٱللّٰه لَأَفْعَلَنَّ *by God, I will certainly do* (*it*) ; وَٱللّٰه لَقَدْ خَرَجَ *by God,*

A *he has certainly gone out;* (β) اَللَّامُ ٱلْمُوَطِّئَةُ لِلْقَسَمِ *the* la *that smooths the way for the oath,* as the first *la* in وَٱللّٰهِ لَئِنْ أَكْرَمْتَنِى لَأُكْرِمَنَّكَ *by God, if indeed you show me honour, I will certainly show you honour;* (γ) لَامُ جَوَابِ لَوْ وَلَوْلَا *the* la *that corresponds to, or is the complement of* lau (*if*) *and* lau-lā (*if not*), as لَوْلَا فَضْلُ ٱللّٰهِ عَلَيْكُمْ وَرَحْمَتُهُ لَاتَّبَعْتُمُ ٱلشَّيْطَانَ *if it had not been for the goodness of God towards you and His mercy, verily ye would have followed Satan;*

B (δ) لَامُ ٱلْإِبْتِدَاءِ [or لَامُ ٱلتَّوْكِيدِ (ٱلتَّأْكِيدِ)] *the affirmative* la, *or the inchoative* or *inceptive* la, *prefixed to a noun or a verb in the imperfect,* as لَأَنْتُمْ أَشَدُّ رَهْبَةً فِى صُدُورِهِمْ مِنَ ٱللّٰهِ *verily ye are more feared in their breasts than God;* إِنَّ رَبَّكَ يَحْكُمُ بَيْنَهُمْ يَوْمَ ٱلْقِيٰمَةِ *verily thy Lord will judge between them on the day of the resurrection;* (ε) اَللَّامُ [or اَللَّامُ ٱلْفَاصِلَةُ ٱلْفَارِقَةُ] *the distinguishing* la, *which is prefixed to the predicate of* إِنْ, *standing for* إِنَّ (إِنِ ٱلْمُخَفَّفَةُ مِنَ ٱلثَّقِيلَةِ), [*in order to distinguish it from the negative* إِنْ], as إِنْ كُلُّ نَفْسٍ لَمَّا عَلَيْهَا حَافِظٌ

C *verily over every soul there is a guardian;* وَإِنْ كُنَّا عَنْ دِرَاسَتِهِمْ لَغَافِلِينَ *but verily we were careless of their studies.* [Comp. Vol. ii. § 36.]

362. The most common separable adverbial particles are the following.

D (a) أَجَلْ *yes, certainly;* confirming a previous statement, as مَا قَامَ زَيْدٌ قَدْ أَتَاكَ زَيْدٌ *Zèid has come to thee,* أَجَلْ *yes,* (*he has*); *Zèid did not stand up,* أَجَلْ *yes,* (*he did not*); سَوْفَ تَذْهَبُ *thou wilt go away,* أَجَلْ *yes,* (*I will*). But in reply to an interrogation, it is better to use نَعَمْ.

(b) إِذْ *and* إِذَا *in the sense of* lo! see! behold! إِذْ *is used after* بَيْنَا and بَيْنَمَا, *while,* and is followed by a verb stating a fact, as قَائِمٌ إِذْ رَأَى عَمْرًا *while Zèid was standing, behold, he saw ʿAmr;*

A فَبَيْنَمَا ٱلْعُسْرُ إِذْ دَارَتْ مَيَاسِيرُ *for while (there has been) adversity, lo, prosperity has come round.* إِذَا, called by the grammarians إِذَا ٱلْمُفَاجَأَة, or إِذَا ٱلْفُجَائِيَّة, that is to say *'iḍā indicating something unexpected,* is followed only by a nominal proposition, and refers to the same time as the preceding statement; as خَرَجْتُ فَإِذَا زَيْدٌ بِٱلْبَابِ *I went out, and lo, Zèid was at the door;* بَيْنَمَا نَحْنُ بِمَكَانِ كَذَا إِذَا زَيْدٌ قَدْ طَلَعَ عَلَيْنَا

B *while we were in such and such a place, lo, Zèid came upon us.*

[(c) إِذَّاكَ or إِذْ ذَاكَ *then.*]

(d) إِذَنْ, or إِذَا, *well then, in that case, if it be so.* See § 367, b. A rare dialectic form is ذَنْ.

(e) أَلَا *nonne?* Compounded of أَ (§ 361, a) and لَا *not* (Heb. הֲלֹא). [It is very often followed by إِنَّ or إِنَّ: أَلَا إِنَّ (وَإِنَّ) *now surely.*]

C [(f) أَلَّا *nonne?* syn. of هَلَّا.]

(g) أَمْ, interrogative, *an?* أَمْ . . . . أَ (Heb. אִם . . . . הֲ), *utrum . . . . an?*

(h) أَمَا *nonne?* Compounded of أَ and مَا *not.* Dialectic varieties are أَمَرْ, هَمَا, هَمَرْ, عَمَا, عَمَرْ, and حَمَا or حَمَى. [أَمَا إِنَّ *truly, now surely.*]

[(i) إِمَّالَى or إِمَّالَا *in that case, then at least.*]

[(k) إِنْ *not,* syn. of مَا, frequent in the Ḳor'ân and in old poems.

D In later times it is only used in combination with the negative مَا as a corroborative, مَا إِنْ *not indeed* (comp. Vol. ii. § 158 and Fleischer, *Kl. Schr.* i. 448).]

[(l) إِنْ *verily,* called *the lightened 'in* (ٱلْمُخَفَّفَةُ مِنَ ٱلثَّقِيلَةِ, § 361, c, ε), usually without government.]

(m) إِنَّ *certainly, surely, truly;* literally *lo! see! en, ecce* (Heb. הֵן, הִנֵּה, Syr. ܗܐ). It is joined to the *accus.* of a following noun or

pronominal suffix, but in the 1st pers. sing. إِنِّى is used as well as إِنَّنِى A
(Heb. הִנְנִי), [and in the 1st pers. pl. إِنَّ as well as إِنَّنَا]. The suffix ه
in this case often represents and anticipates a whole subsequent clause
(ضَمِيرُ ٱلشَّأْنِ) [or ضَمِيرُ القِصَّة] *the pronoun of the fact).*—إِنَّ introduces
the subject, and is frequently followed by لَ with the predicate; as
إِنَّ ٱللّٰهَ لَكَبِيرٌ, *verily God is great.* This the grammarians regard as an
inceptive or inchoative *la* (§ 360, *c*, δ), the example given standing for
لَإِنَّ ٱللّٰهَ كَبِيرٌ, whence it is sometimes called ٱللّٰامُ ٱلْمُزَحْلَفَة *the* la *that* B
is pushed away (from its proper place).—The form هِنّ is said to occur
in the compound لَهِنَّ for لَإِنَّ.

(*n*) إِنَّمَا, restrictive, *only (dumtaxat),* [*verily*]. Compounded of
إِنَّ and مَا.

(*o*) أَنَّى *whence?* [*where?*] *how?* [*when?* With the signification of
whencesoever, wherever, however, whenever it is a conjunction.]   C

(*p*) أَىْ, explicative, *that is,* frequently used by commentators.

(*q*) إِى *yes, yea;* always followed by an oath, as إِى وَٱللّٰه *yes, by
God!* This formula is sometimes shortened into إِى ٱللّٰهِ, إِىَ ٱللّٰهِ, and
إِ ٱللّٰهِ. The dialectic variety هِى is said to occur.—From إِى وَٱللّٰه
comes the vulgar [أَيْوَا, إِيوَهْ] أَيْوَهْ].

[(*r*) أَيَّانَ *when?* Dialectically also إِيَّانَ. It is a conjunction D
when it signifies *whenever.*]

(*s*) أَيْنَ *where?* مِنْ أَيْنَ *whence?* إِلَى أَيْنَ *whither?* أَيْنَمَا *wherever*
(Heb. אֵין in מֵאַיִן, אָן, אָנָה).

(*t*) بَلْ, *nay, nay rather, not so, on the contrary, but* (Heb.
בְּבַל, אֲבָל, Phœn. בל). [When it is followed by a single word it is a
conjunction.]

(*u*) بَلَى *yes,* used in giving an affirmative answer to a negative

A question, or in affirming a negative proposition; as أَلَسْتُ بِرَبِّكُمْ قَالُوا بَلَى *am I not your Lord? They said, Yes, (Thou art)*; لَمْ يَقُمْ زَيْدٌ *Zeid did not stand up,* بَلَى *yes, (he did).*

(v) بَيْنَ [and بَيْنَمَا] *while, whilst* (connected with the prep. بَيْنَ *between, among*).

(w) ثَمَّ [or ثَمَّه], in pause ثَمَّهْ, *there* (Heb. שָׁם, שָׁמָּה, Syr. ܬܰܡܳܢ).

B (x) جَيْرِ, sometimes جَيْرَ, *yes.*

(y) فَقَطْ *only, solely, merely* (lit. *and enough*).

(z) قَدْ, with the *Perfect, now, already, really (jam).* It expresses that something uncertain has really taken place, that something expected has been realised, that something has happened in agreement with, or in opposition to, certain symptoms or circumstances; as كُنْتُ أَرْجُو مَجِيئَهُ فَقَدْ جَاءَ, *I was hoping that he would come, and he is*

C *really come;* كَانَ سَالِمًا صَحِيحًا فَقَدْ مَاتَ, *he was hale and well, and now he is dead.* It also serves to mark the position of a past act or event as prior to the present time or to another past act or event, and consequently expresses merely our *Perf.* or *Pluperf.* With the *Imperfect* it means *sometimes, perhaps,* as إِنَّ الْكَذُوبَ قَدْ يَصْدُقُ *the (habitual) liar sometimes speaks the truth,* in which case it is said to be used لِلتَّقْلِيلِ *to express rarity* or *paucity;* [but also *frequency,* thus according with رُبَّمَا in its two acceptations*].

D (aa) قَطُّ *ever;* always with the *Perfect* or *Jussive* and a *negative,* as مَا رَأَيْتُهُ قَطُّ, or لَمْ أَرَهُ قَطُّ, *I have never seen him;* [or in an interrogative sentence هَلْ رَأَيْتَهُ قَطُّ *did you ever see him?*]†. Rarer forms are قَطُّ قَطَّ, قُطُّ, قَطِ, قَطُ and in pause قَطّْ.

---

* [In poetry قَدْ أَرَى may be used for قَدْ كُنْتُ أَرَى *videbam;* see Nöldeke, *Delectus,* 32, l. 2; 98, l. 4. R. S.]

† [On the use of قَطُّ in affirmative sentences, and its vulgar use with the Future, see Fleischer, *Kl. Schr.* i. 434 seq.]

[(*bb*) كَذَا *thus* (§ 340, rem. *d*) and كَذٰلِكَ *likewise* (§ 343, rem. *d*).]   A

(*cc*) كَلَّا *not at all, by no means,* حَرْفُ ٱلرَّدْعِ *the particle of repelling* or *averting;* as كَلَّا أَهَانَنِي رَبِّى *my Lord hath humbled* or *despised me; by no means.*

(*dd*) لَا, used (*a*) as negative of the future and indefinite present, and as representative of the other negatives after وَ (*and*), *not;* (β) as a prohibitive particle (*ne*), joined to the *Jussive*. It thus combines (like the Aram. לָא, אַל) the significations of the Heb. לֹא and אַל.   B

(*ee*) لٰكِنَّ, لٰكِنْ, often with وَ prefixed, *but, yet.* لٰكِنَّ is placed only before nouns and pronominal suffixes in the *accusative*, but in the 1st pers. لٰكِنَّا, لٰكِنِّى are used as well as لٰكِنَّنِى, لٰكِنَّنَا. [When لٰكِنْ is followed by a single word, it is a conjunction.]

(*ff*) لَمْ [in poetry also لَمَّا], negative of the *Perfect*, but always joined to the *Jussive* in the sense of the perfect, *not.*

(*gg*) لَمَّا *not yet,* joined to the *Jussive*.   C

(*hh*) لَنْ, a contraction for لَا أَنْ (i.e. لَا يَكُونُ أَنْ *it will not be that*—), *not,* joined to the *Subjunctive*.

[(*ii*) لَوْلَا and لَوْمَا *why not?* syn. of أَلَّا and هَلَّا (Vol. ii. § 169).]

(*kk*) مَا, negative of the definite or absolute present and of the perfect, *not.*

(*ll*) مَتَى *when?* Heb. מָתַי. [It is also used as a conjunction, § 367, *q.*]   D

(*mm*) نَعَمْ *yes* (abbreviated for نَعِمَ, *it is agreeable*), affirming any preceding statement or question; as أَقَامَ زَيْدٌ *has Zèid stood up?* نَعَمْ *yes,* (*he has*); لَمْ يَقُمْ *he has not stood up,* نَعَمْ *yes,* (*he has not*). Other forms are نَعِمْ, and more rarely نِعِمْ, نَعَامْ, and نَحَمْ.

[(*nn*) هٰكَذَا *thus* (§ 344, rem. *b*).]

A (*oo*) هَلْ, interrogative, *num? utrum?* The form أَلْ also occurs.

(*pp*) هَلَّا (أَلَّا) *nonne?* Compounded of هَلْ and لَ.

(*qq*) هُنَا, demonstrative, *here;* whence are derived هَاهُنَا or هُهَنَا, هُنَالِكَ, and هُنَاكَ (see §§ 342—344).

(*rr*) هَنَّا (also هِنَّا and هُنَّا), demonstrative, *there* (compare Heb. הֵנָּה); whence are derived هُهَنَّا, هَاهُنَّا or هُهُنَّا, هَنَّاكَ, and هُهَنَّاكَ.

B **363.** The same substantives of which the accusatives serve as prepositions (§ 359), can in general be used as adverbs, in which case they take the termination *u,* and are indeclinable. E.g. بَعْدُ [*yet,* mostly in negative phrases; بَعْدُ], مِنْ بَعْدُ, *afterwards;* تَحْتُ, قَبْلُ, مِنْ تَحْتُ, *beneath;* مِنْ عَلُ *above*;* فَوْقُ, مِنْ فَوْقُ, *above;* مِنْ قَبْلُ, *before;* حَيْثُ *where,* مِنْ حَيْثُ *whence,* إِلَى حَيْثُ *whither,* حَيْثُمَا *wherever;* عَوْضُ (also عَوْضَ and عَوْضٍ) *ever,* joined to the *Imperf. Indic.,* but always preceded by a *negative,* as لَ أُفَارِقُكَ عَوْضُ,

C *I will never leave you;* غَيْرُ, in غَيْرٍ لَ or لَيْسَ غَيْرُ, *nothing else, only this;* [حَسْبُ *enough, only;* also فَحَسْبُ].

364. The *accusative* is the adverbial case κατ᾽ ἐξοχήν in Arabic. A few of the most common examples of it are the following: أَبَدًا, referring to future time, *ever,* with a negative, *never;* [آنِفًا *just now, a little while ago;* أَلْبَتَّةَ *decidedly,* usually with a negative لَ أَفْعَلُهُ أَلْبَتَّةَ *I will not do it, decidedly*]; جِدًّا *very, very much, extremely,* placed

D after an adjective; جَمِيعًا *together,* of two or more; خَارِجًا *outside, without;* دَاخِلًا *inside, within;* [رُوَيْدًا *gently*]; شِمَالًا *to the left,* يَمِينًا *to the right;* كَثِيرًا *much,* قَلِيلًا *little;* لَيْلًا *by night,* نَهَارًا *by day;*

---

* [On the various forms of this phrase see ên-Naḥḥās on 'Imrulḳais *Mo'all.* p. 41. R. S.]

يَوْمًا *one day, once;* اَلْآنَ *now, at present;* اَلْيَوْمَ *today* (Æth. **ዮም፡** A
yōm), غَدًا *tomorrow;* مَجَّانًا *gratis* (Aram. مَגָּן); مَعًا *together;* etc.
To the same class belong the following adverbs:

[(a)   بَيْدَ *except, but.*]

(b)   حِينَ *when* (lit., *at the time of*—).

(c)   رُبَّمَا [*often,* but more usually] *sometimes; perhaps;* lit., *O the
quantity of that which*— (رُبَّ = Heb. רֹב); [comp. Vol. ii. § 84, rem. *c*]. B

(d)   رَيْثَ, رَيْثَمَا, *whilst, during.*

(e)   سَوْفَ, prefixed to the *Imperf.* to indicate real futurity (see
§ 361, *b*); lit., *in the end.*

(f)   لَا سِيَّمَا, and, with the omission of the negative, سِيَّمَا, *above
all, especially, particularly;* lit., *there is not the equal or like of—.*
Rarer forms are لَا سِيمَا and لَا سَيَّمَا.

(g)   كَيْفَ *how?* *   C

[(h)   لَا مَحَالَةَ *most certainly;* lit., *there is no avoiding of it,* and
therefore also construed with مِنْ like its synonym لَا بُدَّ.]†

(i)   وَحْدَ, used only in connection with pronominal suffixes, as
وَحْدَهُ *he alone,* وَحْدَهُمْ *they alone.* It is etymologically = יָחַד, but in
sense = בַּד in לְבַדָּם, לְבַדּוֹ.

[Here too may be mentioned the adverbial expressions بَيْتَ بَيْتَ
lit., *tent to tent* or *house to house* in هُوَ جَارِى بَيْتَ بَيْتَ *he is my next-* D
door neighbour; صَبَاحَ مَسَاءَ *every morning and evening;* شَتَاتَ شَتَاتَ *in*

---

* [On the derivation of كَيف see a conjecture of Fleischer's,
Kl. Schr. i. 381, footnote.]

† [لَا ذَا جَرَ (also لَا ذَا جَرَمَ and لَا ذَا جَرَمَ), *verily, truly,* seems to be
compounded of لَا *nay* and the verb جَرُمَ *it is decided* (comp. Fleischer,
Kl. Schr. i. 449 seq.)   D. G.]

A *sundry parties.* The rule is that when two nouns are made one, they lose their tènwin and become indeclinable, ending in fètḥa, as خَمْسَةَ عَشَرَ. In like manner are to be explained بَيْنَ بَيْنَ *between good and bad,* خَيْضَ بَيْضَ *straitness.* D. G.]

REM. *a.* In أَمْسِ, *yesterday,* Heb. אֶמֶשׁ, the kèsra is not the mark of the genitive, but merely a light vowel, added to render the pronunciation more easy. We may also say بِالْأَمْسِ and أَلْأَمْسَ.

B Some of the Arabs used مُذْ أَمْسَ instead of مُذْ أَمْسِ, *since yesterday.*

REM. *b.* لَيْتَ, *utinam, would that—!* and عَلَّ or لَعَلَّ, *perhaps,* seem to be, not nouns in the accusative, but *verbs.* They are construed with the accusative, and take pronominal suffixes; as لَيْتَنِي *would that I—!* (rarely لَيْتِي), لَيْتَكَ, etc.; لَعَلِّي *perhaps I—* (rarely لَعَلَّنِي), لَعَلَّكَ, etc.—Dialectically, however, لَعَلَّ governs the genitive. The word has several rarer forms, viz. لَعَنَّ, غَنَّ, أَنَّ, عَنَّ,

C لَغَنَّ, لَأَنَّ, لَوَنَّ, رَعَلَّ, and رَغَنَّ.

C. THE CONJUNCTIONS.

365. The conjunctions (which the Arab grammarians call, according to their different significations, [اَلْعَوَاطِفُ or حُرُوفُ ٱلْعَطْفِ *connective particles,* or حُرُوفُ ٱلشَّرْطِ *conditional particles,* etc.) are, D like the prepositions and adverbs, either separable or inseparable.

366. The inseparable conjunctions are :—

(*a*) وَ (حَرْفُ عَطْفٍ), which connects words and clauses as a simple co-ordinative, *and* (Æth. ⵁ: *wa,* Heb. Aram. ו, וְ).

(*b*) فَ (حَرْفُ عَطْفٍ, or more exactly حَرْفُ تَرْتِيبٍ, *particle of classification* or *gradation*), which sometimes unites single words, indicating that the objects enumerated immediately succeed or are

closely behind one another; but more usually connects two clauses, A
showing either that the latter is immediately subsequent to the former
in time, or that it is connected with it by some internal link, such as
that of cause and effect. It may be rendered *and so, and thereupon,
and consequently, for*, although in this last sense فَإِنَّ is more usually
employed. In conditional sentences, فَ is used to separate the apodosis
from the protasis, like the German *so;* and it also invariably introduces
the apodosis after the disjunctive particle أَمَّا*.

[REM. The conjunctions وَ and فَ may be preceded by the B
interrogative particle أَ; thus أَوَلَ means *nonne ?* أَفَلَا *nonne igitur ?*]

(c) لِ. This may be (a) لَامُ ٱلْأَمْرِ *the* li *of command*, which is
usually prefixed to the 3d pers. sing. of the Jussive, to give it an
imperative sense, as لِيَطِبْ قَلْبُكَ *let thy heart be at ease.* When
preceded by وَ or فَ, the kèsr is usually dropped, as فَلْيَسْتَجِيبُوا لِى
وَلْيُؤْمِنُوا بِى, *therefore let them hearken unto me, and believe in me.*
Or it may be (β) ٱللَّامُ ٱلنَّاصِبَةُ *the* li *which governs the verb in the* C
Subjunctive of the Imperfect, signifying *that, so that, in order that*, as
تُبْ لِيَغْفِرَ لَكَ ٱللّٰهُ *repent, that God may forgive thee.* This latter لِ is
identical with the preposition لِ (§ 356, *c*), used لِلتَّعْلِيلِ to indicate the
purpose for which, or the reason why, a thing is done; and hence the
Arab grammarians take it to stand in all cases for the fuller لِأَنْ
or لِكَىْ.

367. The most common separable conjunctions are :—   D

(*a*) إِذْ *when, since*, of past time, and prefixed either to a nominal
or a verbal proposition.   [Compound إِذْ مَا *whenever*.]

---

* [Sometimes in old poetry, e.g. *Ḥamāsa* 74, 1. 9, Ṭabarī i. 852,
1. 10, and very often in later prose, the apodosis is also introduced by
ف after لمّا *when.*   D. G.]

A   (*b*) إِذَا *when*, usually denoting future time and implying a condition, in which case it is always prefixed to a verbal proposition. Both of these conjunctions, as well as إِذْ (§ 362, *d*), are connected with the obsolete noun إِذْ, *time*, the genitive of which occurs, for example, in حِينَئِذٍ *at that time*, يَوْمَئِذٍ *on that day*. Compare Heb. אָז and אֱזַי, Bibl. Aram. אֱדַיִן, Æth. ኦኆ H.: *now*, ሶበ H.: *when?* [Compound إِذَامَا *whenever*.]

B   [(*c*) أَمْ *or*, as syn. of أَوْ in alternative questions.]

(*d*) أَمَّا, followed by فَ, *as for*, *as regards*; e.g. أَمَّا ٱلسَّفِينَةُ فَكَانَتْ لِمَسَاكِينَ يَعْمَلُونَ فِى ٱلْبَحْرِ *as for the ship, it belonged to poor men who worked on the sea*. The form أَيْمَا also occurs. Used twice or oftener, it corresponds to the Greek μὲν—δὲ.

(*e*) أَنْ *that, so that, in order that* (*ut*), *that* (*quod*). A dialectic

C   variety is عَنْ. Compounds: كَأَنْ *as it were, as if*; لِأَنْ *that, in order that, because*; see *g*. Further: أَلَّا *that not* (*ut non, ne, quod non*), comp. of أَنْ and لَا (see § 14, *b*); لِئَلَّا *in order that not* (*ideo ne*).—Like כִּי in Heb. and ὅτι in Gr., أَنْ also serves to introduce direct quotations (أَنِ ٱلْمُفَسِّرَة *the explicative 'an*), as وَنُودُوا أَنْ تِلْكُمُ ٱلْجَنَّةُ *and it shall be proclaimed to them, That is Paradise*; even an

D   Imperative, as أَشَارَتْ إِلَىَّ أَنْ خُذْهَا *she made a sign to me meaning Take her*.

(*f*) إِنْ [and إِمَّا, conditional particle] (حَرْفُ شَرْطٍ) *if*, dialectically وَإِنْ; هِنْ *although* (*etsi*), sometimes written وَأَنْ or وَإِنْ, to distinguish it from وَإِنْ *and if*, and hence called إِنِ ٱلْوَصْلِيَّة; compounded with لَ (§ 361, *c*), لَئِنْ *verily if, if indeed*; Aram. אִן, אֵل; Æth. ኢመ : *'ema*; Heb. אִם.—إِلَّا, compounded of إِنْ and لَا, (*a*) *if not*, in which case it stands for a whole clause; (*β*) حَرْفُ ٱسْتِثْنَاءٍ (exceptive particle), *unless*,

saving, except, but*, with a preceding negative, *only*. Heb. אִם־כִּֿי, A
Aram. אֶלָּא, [אִלּ]; Æth. አላ‎ : (*'allā*) *but.*—إِمَّا, rarely إِيمَا [or أَيْمَا],
compounded of إِنْ and مَا ; .... وَإِمَّا .... إِمَّا, or .... أَوْ .... إِمَّا,
either —— or ——.

(*g*) أَنَّ *that* (*quod*). It is followed by a noun or pronominal suffix
in the *accus.*, but in the 1st pers. أَنَّ, أَنِّى are used as well as أَنَّنِى,
أَنَّنَا. The suffix ه in this case often represents and anticipates a whole
subsequent clause (ضَمِيرُ ٱلْقِصَّةِ, or ضَمِيرُ ٱلشَّأْنِ, *the pronoun of the story* B
or *fact*). See § 362, *m.*—Compounds : كَأَنَّ *as it were, as if*; لِأَنَّ
because. See *c*.

(*h*) أَوْ *or* (*vel, sive*). Heb. אוֹ‎, Syr. ܐܘ‎.

(*i*) ثُمَّ (ثُمَّتُ, ثُمَّ, ثُمَّتَ), *then, thereupon, next;* a حَرْفُ
تَرْتِيبٍ (§ 366, *b*), connecting words and clauses, but implying succession
at an interval. [In genealogical statements ثُمَّ is often used (like the
German *und zwar*) to indicate a transition from the general to the C
more special, e.g. حُذَيْفَةُ ٱلذُّبْيَانِيُّ ثُمَّ ٱلْفَزَارِيُّ, *Hudeifa of the tribe of*
Dubyān and of the subdivision Fazāra.] Connected with it is the
adverb ثَمَّ (§ 362, *w*).

(*k*) حَتَّى *till, until, until that, so that;* identical with the preposition, § 358, *b*. [On its sense of *even*, see Vol. ii. § 52, rem. *c*.]

[(*l*) عِنْدَمَا *when* (syn. of لَمَّا).]

(*m*) كَىْ (حَرْفُ تَعْلِيلٍ, *a particle assigning the motive* or *reason*) D
in order that, with the *Subjunctive.*—Compounds : لِكَىْ *in order that*,
كَيْلَا *in order that not*.

---

* [إِلَّا أَنْ and غَيْرَ أَنْ are very often used in the sense of *but* =
لَكِنْ. D. G.]

A   (*n*) لَمَّا (also أَنْ لَمَّا) *after, when* (*postquam*), [*as, since* (*quoniam*),] with the *Perfect.* [لَمَّا is also syn. with إِلَّ *unless*, especially after the verbs that signify *to beseech.* D. G.]

     (*o*) لَوْ, hypothetical particle, *if* (Heb. לֻא).—Compounds : لَوْلَا, لَوْمَ, لَوْمَا, *if not,* [وَلَوْ *even though*].

     (*p*) مَا (مَا ٱلدَّيْمُومَةِ, *mā denoting duration*), *as long as,* with the *Perfect.*

B   [(*q*) مَتَى and مَتَى مَا (§ 362, *ll*) *when, whenever.*]

D. THE INTERJECTIONS.

368. The interjections are called by the Arabs أَصْوَاتٌ, *sounds* or *tones.* Some of those most commonly in use are : أ or آ (أَلِفُ ٱلنِّدَآءِ), يَا O! *before nouns in the nomin. or accus.* أَيْ, أَيَا (هَيَا), O! ho!
C *without the article ;* يَا أَيُّهَا, or أَيُّهَا, O! *before nouns in the nomin. with the article ;* هَا *lo! see! there!* (see § 344) ; آهِ, أَهِ, أَهْ, or آهِ, آهِ, آهِ, آهِ, ; أَوْ, آوِ, أَوِّ ; (آوَّتَاهْ) أَوَّتَاهْ (أَوَّاهُ) أَوَّاهُ ,(أَوَّهُ) أَوَّهِ, آوَّهِ, أَوَّهِ, (أَوُّهُ) أَوُّهُ ; آهَا هَاهْ (هَاهُ) ; وَا, وَاهًا, Oh! ah! alas! وَىْ woe! (Aram. וַי, سُو, Æth. **ወይ** : *vœ*) ; وَيْهَا, وَيْهَ, *come on!* هَلَّا, أَلَا, O! *up! come!* [Heb. חֵي עַל ٱلصَّلَاهْ, Aram. הֵלָךְ], حَيَّ *come!* followed by عَلَ, as حَيَّ עַל ٱلصَّلَاهْ
D *come to prayer!* in composition, حَيَّهَلَ or حَيَّهَلَ, حَيَّهَلْ or حَيَّهَلْ (حَيَّهَلَا or حَيَّهَلْ), حَيَّهَلَكَ, with إِلَى or عَلَى, and also with ب (in the sense of أَسْرِعْ *make haste*, or ٱلْزَمِ *keep to*, or ٱدْعُ *call*) ; (هِيتُ) هَيْتُ *come here!* هَلُمَّ *come here, bring here!* (Heb. הֲלֹם) as هَلُمَّ إِلَيْنَا *come here to us,* هَلُمَّ شُهَدَآءَكُمْ *bring here your witnesses ;* هَيْهَاتَ *far from it!*] ; هَيْ, هَيَّا, and هَيَّا هَيَّا *make haste ;* وَاهَ, وَاهًا, O!

excellent! bravo! بَخٍ , بَخِ , بَخّ , بَخْ بَخْ , etc., *well done! bravo!* A

capital! أَخِّ , إِخّ ; أُفِّ , أُفَّ , أُفُّ , أُفٍّ , أُفَّ , أُفّاً , أُفَّةً , ugh! faugh! fie!

صَهْ , صَهٍ , *hush! silence!* إِيهاً *be silent! give up!* مَهْ , مَهٍ , *stop! give up!*
let alone! إِيهِ , إِيهٍ , *go on! proceed! say on!*—Here too may be
mentioned: (*a*) calls to domestic animals; e.g. in driving horses, B
mules, عَدَسْ ; camels, هَيْدَ or هِيدَ , حَوْبُ , حَاءِ ; in making camels
kneel, إِيخْ or نَخّ , هِيخْ ; in calling camels to water, جَوْتِ ; in driving
sheep or goats, هُسْ ; in calling a dog, قُوس ; in driving a dog away,
هَجْ , هَجِ , هَجَا ; (*β*) words imitative of cries and sounds; e.g. مَاءِ (the
bleat of an antelope), غَاقِ (the croak of a raven), شِيبِ (the sound
made by the lips of a camel in drinking), طِيخٍ طِيخِ (laughter), أُعْ أُعْ C
or هُعْ هُعْ (vomiting), طَاقِ (a blow), قَبْ (the stroke of a sword), طَقْ
(the sound of a falling stone), طِقْ (the splash of a frog), etc.

REM. *a.* يَا is often written defectively; as يَرَسُولَ ٱللّٰه *O Apostle
of God!* يَأُخِى *O my brother!* يَٱبْنَ عَمِّى *O son of my uncle!*—
أَيُّهَا has a feminine أَيَّتُهَا , but the masc. form is often used even with
feminine nouns.

REM. *b.* The noun that follows وَا [and يَا *oh!*] not unfrequently D
takes, instead of the usual terminations, the ending ـَاهْ , in pause ـَاهْ
وَا أَمِيرَ [called أَلِفُ ٱلنُّدْبَة]; as وَا زَيْدَاهْ or وَا زَيْدَا , *Oh Zèid!*
أَلْمُومِنِينَاهْ *alas for the Commander of the Believers!* If the noun
ends in ĕlif maksūra (ـَى), the ى is changed into ا, and a simple ه
added, as وَا مُوسَاهْ , *Oh Moses!* though وَا مُوسَيَا or وَا مُوسَيَاهْ may
also be used. Instead of ـَاهْ we sometimes find ـَى, as وَا أَسَفَى , or
وَا حَرَبَى , *Oh my grief!*

A   REM. *c.* From وَى (to which suffixes may be appended, as وَيْكَ *woe to thee!*) are formed the interjectional nouns وَيْحٌ and وَيْلٌ, whence we can say, for example, وَيْحَ زَيْدٍ, وَيْحًا لِزَيْدٍ, وَيْحٌ لِزَيْدٍ, وَيْلَكَ, وَيْلِى, ٱلْوَيْلُ لَهُ, وَيْلًا لَهُ, وَيْلٌ لَهُ, وَيْحَهُ, وَيْحَكَ, etc. The expression وَيْلٌ لِأُمِّهِ or وَى لِأُمِّهِ is contracted into وَيْلُمِّهِ, usually written thus in one word.—Rarer interjectional nouns are وَيْبٌ, وَيْسٌ, and وَيْخٌ.

B   REM. *d.* [Many interjections have, by origin or use, a certain verbal force and are called therefore أَسْمَآءُ ٱلْأَفْعَالِ, that is, they are either originally Imperatives, as هَاتِ *give here* (§ 45, rem. *d*), or equivalent to Imperatives (comp. Vol. ii. § 35, *b*, δ, rem. *b*), and, in some cases, admitting its construction and inflection. Accordingly] some of the Arabs decline هَلُمَّ like an Imperative; e.g. sing. fem. هَلُمِّى, dual هَلُمَّا, plur. masc. هَلُمُّوا, fem. هَلْمُمْنَ (compare the Gothic *hiri,* du. *hirjats,* pl. *hirjith*).—هَيَّ takes the suffix of the

C   2nd pers., هَيَّكَ, or هَيْكَ, and is said to form a dual and plur., هَيَّا, هَيُّوا.—هَا may be joined with the pronominal suffixes of the second person, in which case it is equivalent to the Imperative of أَخَذَ; as هَاكَهَا *take her!* Or a hemza may be substituted for the ك, and the word declined as follows: sing. m. هَاءَ, f. هَاءِ; dual هَاؤُمَا, pl. m. هَاؤُمْ, f. هَاؤُنَّ; as هَاؤُمُ ٱقْرَؤُوا كِتَابِيَهْ, *take, read my book.* Other varieties are: هَأْ (like هَبْ), f. هَأْى, etc.; هَاءَ (like رَامِ), f. هَائِى, etc.; and هَأَكَ, f. هَأَكِ, etc.

PARADIGMS

VERBS.

38

A FIRST OR SIMPLE FORM

TABLE I. ACTIVE.

	Perfect.	Imperfect.				
		Indic.	Subj.	Jussive.	Energ. I.	Energ. II.
Sing. 3. m.	قَتَلَ	يَقْتُلُ	يَقْتُلَ	يَقْتُلْ	يَقْتُلَنَّ	يَقْتُلَنْ
B f.	قَتَلَتْ	تَقْتُلُ	تَقْتُلَ	تَقْتُلْ	تَقْتُلَنَّ	تَقْتُلَنْ
2. m.	قَتَلْتَ	تَقْتُلُ	تَقْتُلَ	تَقْتُلْ	تَقْتُلَنَّ	تَقْتُلَنْ
f.	قَتَلْتِ	تَقْتُلِينَ	تَقْتُلِى	تَقْتُلِى	تَقْتُلِنَّ	تَقْتُلِنْ
1. c.	قَتَلْتُ	أَقْتُلُ	أَقْتُلَ	أَقْتُلْ	أَقْتُلَنَّ	أَقْتُلَنْ
Dual. 3. m.	قَتَلَا	يَقْتُلَانِ	يَقْتُلَا	يَقْتُلَا	يَقْتُلَانِّ	
f.	قَتَلَتَا	تَقْتُلَانِ	تَقْتُلَا	تَقْتُلَا	تَقْتُلَانِّ	
C 2. c.	قَتَلْتُمَا	تَقْتُلَانِ	تَقْتُلَا	تَقْتُلَا	تَقْتُلَانِّ	. . .
Plur. 3. m.	قَتَلُوا	يَقْتُلُونَ	يَقْتُلُوا	يَقْتُلُوا	يَقْتُلُنَّ	يَقْتُلُنْ
f.	قَتَلْنَ	يَقْتُلْنَ	يَقْتُلْنَ	يَقْتُلْنَ	يَقْتُلْنَانِّ	. . .
2. m.	قَتَلْتُمْ	تَقْتُلُونَ	تَقْتُلُوا	تَقْتُلُوا	تَقْتُلُنَّ	تَقْتُلُنْ
f.	قَتَلْتُنَّ	تَقْتُلْنَ	تَقْتُلْنَ	تَقْتُلْنَ	تَقْتُلْنَانِّ	. . .
1. c.	قَتَلْنَا	نَقْتُلُ	نَقْتُلَ	نَقْتُلْ	نَقْتُلَنَّ	نَقْتُلَنْ

D

	N. Ag.	N. Verbi.	Imperative.			
				Simple.	En. I.	En. II.
Sing. m.	قَاتِل	قَتْل	Sing. 2. m.	اُقْتُلْ	اُقْتُلَنَّ	اُقْتُلَنْ
f.	قَاتِلَة		f.	اُقْتُلِى	اُقْتُلِنَّ	اُقْتُلِنْ
			Dual. 2. c.	اُقْتُلَا	اُقْتُلَانِّ	. . .
			Plur. 2. m.	اُقْتُلُوا	اُقْتُلُنَّ	اُقْتُلُنْ
			f.	اُقْتُلْنَ	اُقْتُلْنَانِّ	

OF THE STRONG VERB.

A

TABLE II. PASSIVE.

Perfect.	*Imperfect.*				
	Indic.	*Subj.*	*Jussive.*	*Energ.* I.	*Energ.* II.
Sing. 3. m. قُتِلَ	يُقْتَلُ	يُقْتَلَ	يُقْتَلْ	يُقْتَلَنَّ	يُقْتَلَنْ
f. قُتِلَتْ	تُقْتَلُ	تُقْتَلَ	تُقْتَلْ	تُقْتَلَنَّ	تُقْتَلَنْ
2. m. قُتِلْتَ	تُقْتَلُ	تُقْتَلَ	تُقْتَلْ	تُقْتَلَنَّ	تُقْتَلَنْ B
f. قُتِلْتِ	تُقْتَلِينَ	تُقْتَلِى	تُقْتَلِى	تُقْتَلِنَّ	تُقْتَلِنْ
1. c. قُتِلْتُ	أُقْتَلُ	أُقْتَلَ	أُقْتَلْ	أُقْتَلَنَّ	أُقْتَلَنْ
Dual. 3. m. قُتِلَا	يُقْتَلَانِ	يُقْتَلَا	يُقْتَلَا	يُقْتَلَانِّ	. . .
f. قُتِلَتَا	تُقْتَلَانِ	تُقْتَلَا	تُقْتَلَا	تُقْتَلَانِّ	. . .
2. c. قُتِلْتُمَا	تُقْتَلَانِ	تُقْتَلَا	تُقْتَلَا	تُقْتَلَانِّ	. . .
Plur. 3. m. قُتِلُوا	يُقْتَلُونَ	يُقْتَلُوا	يُقْتَلُوا	يُقْتَلُنَّ	يُقْتَلُنْ C
f. قُتِلْنَ	يُقْتَلْنَ	يُقْتَلْنَ	يُقْتَلْنَ	يُقْتَلْنَانِّ	. . .
2. m. قُتِلْتُمْ	تُقْتَلُونَ	تُقْتَلُوا	تُقْتَلُوا	تُقْتَلُنَّ	تُقْتَلُنْ
f. قُتِلْتُنَّ	تُقْتَلْنَ	تُقْتَلْنَ	تُقْتَلْنَ	تُقْتَلْنَانِّ	. . .
1. c. قُتِلْنَا	نُقْتَلُ	نُقْتَلَ	نُقْتَلْ	نُقْتَلَنَّ	نُقْتَلَنْ

Nom. Pat. Sing. m. مَقْتُولٌ   f. مَقْتُولَةٌ

Other Forms of the Perf., Impf., and Imper. Act., and the N. Verbi. D

Perf.	*Imperf.*	*Imperat.*	*N. Verbi.*
Sing. 3. m. جَلَسَ	يَجْلِسُ	اِجْلِسْ	جُلُوسٌ
رَفَعَ	يَرْفَعُ	اِرْفَعْ	رَفْعٌ
فَرِقَ (2. m. فَرِقْتَ)	يَفْرَقُ	اِفْرَقْ	فَرَقٌ
خَشُنَ (2. m. خَشُنْتَ)	يَخْشُنُ	اُخْشُنْ	خُشُونَةٌ
			خَشَانَةٌ

A   TABLE III. DERIVED FORMS

	II.	III.	IV.	V.	VI.
Active Perf.	قَتَّلَ	قَاتَلَ	أَقْتَلَ	تَقَتَّلَ	تَقَاتَلَ
Imperf.	يُقَتِّل	يُقَاتِل	يُقْتِل	يَتَقَتَّل	يَتَقَاتَل
Imperat.	قَتِّل	قَاتِل	أَقْتِل	تَقَتَّل	تَقَاتَل
B N. Ag.	مُقَتِّل	مُقَاتِل	مُقْتِل	مُتَقَتِّل	مُتَقَاتِل
N. Verbi.	تَقْتِيل	قِتَال	إِقْتَال	تَقَتُّل	تَقَاتُل
	تَقْتِلَة	مُقَاتَلَة			
Passive Perf.	قُتِّل	قُوتِل	أُقْتِل	تُقُتِّل	تُقُوتِل
Imperf.	يُقَتَّل	يُقَاتَل	يُقْتَل	يَتَقَتَّل	يَتَقَاتَل
C Nom. Pat.	مُقَتَّل	مُقَاتَل	مُقْتَل	مُتَقَتَّل	مُتَقَاتَل

TABLE IV. THE QUADRI-
ACTIVE.

	I.	II.	III.	IV.
Perf.	قَمْطَر	تَقَمْطَر	اقْمَنْطَر	اقْمَطَّر
D Imperf.	يُقَمْطِر	يَتَقَمْطَر	يَقْمَنْطِر	يَقْمَطِّر
Imperat.	قَمْطِر	تَقَمْطَر	اقْمَنْطِر	اقْمَطِرّ
N. Ag.	مُقَمْطِر	مُتَقَمْطِر	مُقْمَنْطِر	مُقْمَطِّر
N. Verbi.	قَمْطَرَة	تَقَمْطُر	اقْمِنْطَار	اقْمِطْرَار
	قِمْطَار			

OF THE STRONG VERB. A

VII.	VIII.	IX.	X.	XI.	
اِنْقَتَلَ	اِقْتَتَلَ	اِقْتَلَّ	اِسْتَقْتَلَ	اِقْتَالَّ	
يَنْقَتِل	يَقْتَتِل	يَقْتَلُّ	يَسْتَقْتِل	يَقْتَالُّ	
اِنْقَتِل	اِقْتَتِل	اِقْتَلِل	اِسْتَقْتِل	اِقْتَالِل	B
مُنْقَتَل	مُقْتَتَل	مُقْتَلٌّ	مُسْتَقْتَل	مُقْتَالٌّ	
اِنْقِتَال	اِقْتِتَال	اِقْتِلَال	اِسْتِقْتَال	اِقْتِيلَال	

اُنْقُتِلَ	اُقْتُتِلَ		اُسْتُقْتِلَ	C
يُنْقَتَل	يُقْتَتَل		يُسْتَقْتَل	
مُنْقَتَل	مُقْتَتَل		مُسْتَقْتَل	

LITERAL VERB.

PASSIVE.

	I.	II.	III.	IV.	D
Perf.	قُمْطِرَ	تُقُمْطِرَ	اُقْمُنْطِرَ	اُقْمُطِرَّ	
Imperf.	يُقَمْطَر	يُتَقَمْطَر	يُقْمَنْطَر	يُقْمَطَرُّ	
N. Pat.	مُقَمْطَر	مُتَقَمْطَر	مُقْمَنْطَر	مُقْمَطَرُّ	

A TABLE V. *a.* FIRST FORM OF THE

ACTIVE.

	Perfect.	*Imperfect.*				
		Indic.	*Subj.*	*Jussive.*	*Energ.* I.	*Energ.* II.
Sing. 3. m.	مَدَّ	يَمُدُّ	يَمُدَّ	يَمْدُدْ	يَمُدَّنْ	يَمُدَّنْ
f.	مَدَّتْ	تَمُدُّ	تَمُدَّ	تَمْدُدْ	تَمُدَّنْ	تَمُدَّنْ
B 2. m.	مَدَدْتَ	تَمُدُّ	تَمُدَّ	تَمْدُدْ	تَمُدَّنْ	تَمُدَّنْ
f.	مَدَدْتِ	تَمُدِّينَ	تَمُدِّى	تَمُدِّى	تَمُدِّنْ	تَمُدِّنْ
1. c.	مَدَدْتُ	أَمُدُّ	أَمُدَّ	أَمْدُدْ	أَمُدَّنْ	أَمُدَّنْ
Dual. 3. m.	مَدَّا	يَمُدَّانِ	يَمُدَّا	يَمُدَّا	يَمُدَّانِّ	
f.	مَدَّتَا	تَمُدَّانِ	تَمُدَّا	تَمُدَّا	تَمُدَّانِّ	. . .
2. c.	مَدَدْتُمَا	تَمُدَّانِ	تَمُدَّا	تَمُدَّا	تَمُدَّانِّ	. . .
C Plur. 3. m.	مَدُّوا	يَمُدُّونَ	يَمُدُّوا	يَمُدُّوا	يَمُدُّنْ	يَمُدُّنْ
f.	مَدَدْنَ	يَمْدُدْنَ	يَمْدُدْنَ	يَمْدُدْنَ	يَمْدُدْنَانِّ	. . .
2. m.	مَدَدْتُمْ	تَمُدُّونَ	تَمُدُّوا	تَمُدُّوا	تَمُدُّنْ	تَمُدُّنْ
f.	مَدَدْتُنَّ	تَمْدُدْنَ	تَمْدُدْنَ	تَمْدُدْنَ	تَمْدُدْنَانِّ	. . .
1. c.	مَدَدْنَا	نَمُدُّ	نَمُدَّ	نَمْدُدْ	نَمُدَّنْ	نَمُدَّنْ

D	*N. Ag.*	*N. Verbi.*	*Imperative.*		
			Simple.	*En.* I.	*En.* II.
Sing. m.	مَادٌّ	مَدٌّ	Sing. 2. m. أُمْدُدْ	أُمْدُدَنْ	أُمْدُدَنْ
f.	مَادَّةٌ		f. [أُمْدُدِى]	أُمْدُدِنْ	أُمْدُدِنْ
			Dual. 2. c. [أُمْدُدَا]	أُمْدُدَانِّ	. . .
			Plur. 2. m. [أُمْدُدُوا]	أُمْدُدُنْ	أُمْدُدُنْ
			f. أُمْدُدْنَانِّ أُمْدُدْنَ		. . .

VERBUM MEDIÆ RAD. GEMINATÆ.   A

PASSIVE.

	Perfect.	Indic.	Subj.	Jussive.	En. I.	En. II.	
Sing. 3. m.	مُدَّ	يُمَدُّ	يُمَدَّ	يُمْدَدْ	يُمَدَّنَّ	يُمَدَنْ	
f.	مُدَّتْ	تُمَدُّ	تُمَدَّ	تُمْدَدْ	تُمَدَّنَّ	تُمَدَنْ	B
2. m.	مُدِدْتَ	تُمَدُّ	تُمَدَّ	تُمْدَدْ	تُمَدَّنَّ	تُمَدَنْ	
f.	مُدِدْتِ	تُمَدِّينَ	تُمَدِّى	تُمَدِّى	تُمَدَّنَّ	تُمَدَنْ	
1. c.	مُدِدْتُ	أُمَدُّ	أُمَدَّ	أُمْدَدْ	أُمَدَّنَّ	أُمَدَنْ	
Dual. 3. m.	مُدَّا	يُمَدَّانِ	يُمَدَّا	يُمَدَّا	يُمَدَّانِّ	. . .	
f.	مُدَّتَا	تُمَدَّانِ	تُمَدَّا	تُمَدَّا	تُمَدَّانِّ	. . .	
2. c.	مُدِدْتُمَا	تُمَدَّانِ	تُمَدَّا	تُمَدَّا	تُمَدَّانِّ	. . .	C
Plur. 3. m.	مُدُّوا	يُمَدُّونَ	يُمَدُّوا	يُمَدُّوا	يُمَدَّنَّ	يُمَدُنْ	
f.	مُدِدْنَ	يُمْدَدْنَ	يُمْدَدْنَ	يُمْدَدْنَ	يُمْدَدْنَانِّ	. . .	
2. m.	مُدِدْتُمْ	تُمَدُّونَ	تُمَدُّوا	تُمَدُّوا	تُمَدَّنَّ	تُمَدُنْ	
f.	مُدِدْتُنَّ	تُمْدَدْنَ	تُمْدَدْنَ	تُمْدَدْنَ	تُمْدَدْنَانِّ	. . .	
1. c.	مُدِدْنَا	نُمَدُّ	نُمَدَّ	نُمْدَدْ	نُمَدَّنَّ	نُمَدَنْ	

Nom. Pat. Sing. m. مَمْدُودٌ, f. مَمْدُودَةٌ.   D

Other forms of the Perf., Imperf., Jussive, and Imperat. Act.

	Perf.	Imperf.	Jussive.	Imperat.
Sing. 3. m.	. . .	. . .	يَمُدُّ or يَمَدُّ	مُدُّ or مُدَّ
	فَرَّ	يَفِرُّ	يَفِرِرْ ,يَفِرَّ or يَفِرُّ	فِرِّ ,إِفْرِرْ or فِرَّ
	مَلَّ (مَلِلْتَ) (2. m.)	يَمَلُّ	يَمْلَلْ ,يَمَلَّ or يَمَلِّ	إِمْلَلْ ,مَلَّ or مَلِّ

A   TABLE V. *b.* DERIVED FORMS OF THE VERBUM
MEDIÆ RAD. GEMINATÆ.

	III.	IV.	VI.	VII.	VIII.	X.
Active Perf.	مَادَّ	أَمَدَّ	تَمَادَدَ	اِنْفَلَّ	اِمْتَدَّ	اِسْتَهَدَّ
	or مَادَّ		or تَمَادَّ			
Imperf.	يُمَادِدُ	يُمِدُّ	يَتَمَادَدُ	يَنْفَلُّ	يَمْتَدُّ	يَسْتَمِدُّ
	or يُمَادُّ		or يَتَمَادُّ			
Imperat.	مَادِدْ	أَمْدِدْ	تَمَادَدْ	اِنْفَلِلْ	اِمْتَدِدْ	اِسْتَهْدِدْ
		or أَمِدَّ			or اِمْتَدَّ	or اِسْتَمِدَّ
N. Ag.	مُمَادِدٌ	مُمِدٌّ	مُتَمَادِدٌ	مُنْفَلٌّ	مُمْتَدٌّ	مُسْتَمِدٌّ
	or مُمَادٌّ		or مُتَمَادٌّ			
N. Verbi.	مِدَادٌ	إِمْدَادٌ	تَمَادُدٌ	اِنْفِلَالٌ	اِمْتِدَادٌ	اِسْتِهْدَادٌ
C	مُمَادَّةٌ or مُمَادَدَةٌ		or تَمَادٌّ			
Passive Perf.	مُودِدَ	أُمِدَّ	تُمُودِدَ	اُنْفُلَّ	أُمْتُدَّ	أُسْتُهِدَّ
Imperf.	يُمَادَدُ	يُمَدُّ	يَتَمَادَدُ	يُنْفَلُّ	يُمْتَدُّ	يُسْتَمَدُّ
	or يُمَادُّ		or يَتَمَادُّ			
N. Pat.	مُمَادَدٌ	مُمَدٌّ	مُتَمَادَدٌ	مُنْفَلٌّ	مُمْتَدٌّ	مُسْتَمَدٌّ
	or مُمَادٌّ		or مُتَمَادٌّ			

B

D   The remaining forms present no irregularity; e.g.

	Perf.	Imperf.	Imperat.	N. Ag. et Pat.	N. Verbi.
II. Act.	مَدَّدَ	يُمَدِّدُ	مَدِّدْ	مُمَدِّدٌ	تَمْدِيدٌ
Pass.	مُدِّدَ	يُمَدَّدُ		مُمَدَّدٌ	
V. Act.	تَمَدَّدَ	يَتَمَدَّدُ	تَمَدَّدْ	مُتَمَدِّدٌ	تَمَدُّدٌ
Pass.	تُمُدِّدَ	يُتَمَدَّدُ		مُتَمَدَّدٌ	

TABLE VI. VERBUM PRIMÆ RAD. HÈMZATÆ.

A

	I.	II.	III.	IV.	V.	VI.
Active Perf.	أَسَرَ أَثَرَ	أَثَّرَ	اَثَرَ	آثَرَ	تَأَثَّرَ	تَبَائَرَ or تَوَائَرَ
Imperf.	يَأْسُرُ يَأْثُرُ	يُؤَثِّرُ	يُوَائِرُ	يُوثِرُ	يَتَأَثَّرُ	يَتَبَائَرُ or يَتَوَائَرُ
Imperat.	اِيسِرْ اُوثُرْ	أَثِّرْ	اَثِرْ	آثِرْ	تَأَثَّرْ	تَبَائَرْ or تَوَائَرْ
N. Ag.	آسِرٌ	مُؤَثِّرٌ	مُوَائِرٌ	مُوثِرٌ	مُتَأَثِّرٌ	مُتَبَائِرٌ or مُتَوَائِرٌ
N. Verbi.	أَسْرٌ	تَأْثِيرٌ إِئَارٌ	إِثَارٌ	تَأَثُّرٌ	تَبَائُرٌ or تَوَائُرٌ
		مُوَائَرَةٌ				
Passive Perf.	أُسِرَ	أُثِّرَ	اُوثِرَ	اُوثِرَ	تُوُثِّرَ	تُوُوثِرَ or تُوُوثِرَ
Imperf.	يُؤْسَرُ	يُؤَثَّرُ	يُوَائَرُ	يُوثَرُ	يَتَأَثَّرُ	يَتَبَائَرُ or يَتَوَائَرُ
N. Pat.	مَأْسُورٌ	مُؤَثَّرٌ	مُوَائَرٌ	مُوثَرٌ	مُتَأَثَّرٌ	مُتَبَائَرٌ or مُتَوَائَرٌ

B

C

	Perf.	Imperf.	Imperat.	N. Ag. et Pat.	N. Verbi.
VIII. Act.	اِيتَثَرَ	يَأْتَثِرُ	اِيتَثِرْ	مُؤْتَثِرٌ	اِيتِثَارٌ
Pass.	اُوتُثِرَ	يُوتَثَرُ		مُؤْتَثَرٌ	
X. Act.	اِسْتَأْثَرَ	يَسْتَأْثِرُ	اِسْتَأْثِرْ	مُسْتَأْثِرٌ	اِسْتِئْثَارٌ
Pass.	اُسْتُوثِرَ	يُسْتَأْثَرُ		مُسْتَأْثَرٌ	

D

The seventh form is wanting in verbs of this class, according to § 113.

A **TABLE VII. VERBUM MEDIÆ RAD. HÈMZATÆ.**

	I.			II.	III.	IV.
Active Perf.	سَأَلَ	سَئِرَ	بُؤُس	لَأَمَ	لَاَءَمَ	أَلْأَمَ
Imperf.	يَسْأَلُ	يَسْأَرُ	يَبُؤُس	يَلْئِمُ	يُلَائِمُ	يُلْئِمُ
	يَسْئَلُ	يَسْئَرُ				
Imperat.	إِسْأَلْ	إِسْأَرْ	أُبْؤُس	لَئِمْ	لَائِمْ	أَلْئِمْ
B	إِسْئَلْ	إِسْئَرْ				
N. Ag.	سَائِلٌ	سَائِرٌ	بَائِس	مُلْئِمٌ	مُلَائِمٌ	مُلْئِمٌ
N. Verbi.	سُؤَالٌ	سُور	بَأْس	تَلْئِيمٌ	مُلَاءَمَةٌ	إِلْآمٌ
Passive Perf.	سُئِلَ			لُئِمَ	لُوئِمَ	أُلْئِمَ
Imperf.	يُسْأَلُ			يُلَأَّمُ	يُلَاءَمُ	يُلْأَمُ
C	يُسْئَلُ					
N. Pat.	مَسْؤُولٌ			مُلَأَّمٌ	مُلَاءَمٌ	مُلْأَمٌ

	V.	VI.	VII.	VIII.	X.
Active Perf.	تَلَأَّمَ	تَلَاءَمَ	إِنْجَأَثَ	اِلْتَأَمَ	اِسْتَلْأَمَ
Imperf.	يَتَلَأَّمُ	يَتَلَاءَمُ	يَنْجَئِثُ	يَلْتَئِمُ	يَسْتَلْئِمُ
D Imperat.	تَلَأَّمْ	تَلَاءَمْ	اِنْجَئِثْ	اِلْتَئِمْ	اِسْتَلْئِمْ
N. Ag.	مُتَلَأَّمٌ	مُتَلَاءِمٌ	مُنْجَئِثٌ	مُلْتَئِمٌ	مُسْتَلْئِمٌ
N. Verbi.	تَلَؤُّمٌ	تَلَاؤُمٌ	اِنْجِئَاثٌ	اِلْتِئَامٌ	اِسْتِلْآمٌ
Passive Perf.	تُلُئِّمَ	تُلُوئِمَ	أُنْجِئِثَ	أُلْتِئِمَ	أُسْتُلْئِمَ
Imperf.	يُتَلَأَّمُ	يُتَلَاءَمُ	يُنْجَأَثُ	يُلْتَأَمُ	يُسْتَلْأَمُ
N. Pat.	مُتَلَأَّمٌ	مُتَلَاءَمٌ	مُنْجَأَثٌ	مُلْتَأَمٌ	مُسْتَلْأَمٌ

TABLE VIII. VERBUM TERTIÆ RAD. HÈMZATÆ.   A

	I.				II.	III.	
Active Perf. 3. s. m.	بَرَأَ	هَنَأَ	خَطِئَ	دَنُؤَ	بَرَّأَ	بَارَأَ	
f.	بَرَأَتْ	هَنَأَتْ	خَطِئَتْ	دَنُؤَتْ	بَرَّأَتْ	بَارَأَتْ	
2. s. m.	بَرَأْتَ	هَنَأْتَ	خَطِئْتَ	دَنُؤْتَ	بَرَّأْتَ	بَارَأْتَ	
Imperf.	يَبْرَأُ	يَهْنِئُ	يَخْطَأُ	يَدْنُؤُ	يُبَرِّئُ	يُبَارِئُ	
Imperat.	اِبْرَأْ	اِهْنِئْ	اِخْطَأْ	اُدْنُؤْ	بَرِّئْ	بَارِئْ	B
N. Ag.	بَارِئٌ	هَانِئٌ	خَاطِئٌ	دَانِئٌ	مُبَرِّئٌ	مُبَارِئٌ	
N. Verbi.	بَرْءٌ	هَنْءٌ	خَطَأٌ	دَنَاءَةٌ	تَبْرِئَةٌ	مُبَارَءَةٌ	
				تَجْرِىءٍ دُنُوءَةٌ			
Passive Perf.	بُرِئَ	هُنِئَ	خُطِئَ		بُرِّئَ	بُورِئَ	
Imperf.	يُبْرَأُ	يُهْنَأُ	يُخْطَأُ		يُبَرَّأُ	يُبَارَأُ	C
N. Pat.	مَبْرُوءٌ	مَهْنُوءٌ	مَخْطُوءٌ		مُبَرَّأٌ	مُبَارَأٌ	

	IV.	V.	VI.	VII.	VIII.	X.	
Active Perf.	أَبْرَأَ	تَبَرَّأَ	تَبَارَأَ	اِنْسَبَأَ	اِهْتَنَأَ	اِسْتَبْرَأَ	
Imperf.	يُبْرِئُ	يَتَبَرَّأُ	يَتَبَارَأُ	يَنْسَبِئُ	يَهْتَنِئُ	يَسْتَبْرِئُ	
Imperat.	أَبْرِئُ	تَبَرَّأْ	تَبَارَأْ	اِنْسَبِئْ	اِهْتَنِئْ	اِسْتَبْرِئْ	D
N. Ag.	مُبْرِئٌ	مُتَبَرِّئٌ	مُتَبَارِئٌ	مُنْسَبِئٌ	مُهْتَنِئٌ	مُسْتَبْرِئٌ	
N. Verbi.	إِبْرَاءٌ	تَبَرُّؤٌ	تَبَارُؤٌ	اِنْسِبَاءٌ	اِهْتَنَاءٌ	اِسْتَبْرَاءٌ	
Passive Perf.	أُبْرِئَ	تُبُرِّئَ	تُبُورِئَ	اُنْسِبِئَ	اُهْتَنِئَ	اُسْتَبْرِئَ	
Imperf.	يُبْرَأُ	يُتَبَرَّأُ	يُتَبَارَأُ	يُنْسَبَأُ	يُهْتَنَأُ	يُسْتَبْرَأُ	
N. Pat.	مُبْرَأٌ	مُتَبَرَّأٌ	مُتَبَارَأٌ	مُنْسَبَأٌ	مُهْتَنَأٌ	مُسْتَبْرَأٌ	

A TABLE IX. VERBA PRIMÆ RAD. و ET ى.

I.

Active Perf.	وَعَدَ	وَرِثَ	وَضَعَ	وَجِلَ	وَدَّ	يَسَرَ
Imperf.	يَعِدُ	يَرِثُ	يَضَعُ	يَوْجَلُ	يَوَدُّ	يَيْسِرُ
Imperat.	عِدْ	رِثْ	ضَعْ	ايجَلْ	ايدَدْ	ايسِرْ
B N. Verbi.	وَعْدٌ	وِرْثٌ	وَضْعٌ	وَجَلٌ	وُدٌّ	يَسَرٌ
	عِدَةٌ	رِثَةٌ	ضَعَةٌ			
Passive Perf.	وُعِدَ	وُرِثَ	وُضِعَ		وُدَّ	يُسَرَ
Imperf.	يُوعَدُ	يُورَثُ	يُوضَعُ		يُودُّ	يُوسَرُ
N. Pat.	مَوْعُودٌ	مَوْرُوثٌ	مَوْضُوعٌ		مَوْدُودٌ	مَيْسُورٌ

C

	IV.		VIII.		X.	
Active Perf.	أَوْجَبَ	أَيْسَرَ	اتَّعَدَ	اتَّسَرَ	اسْتَوْعَدَ	اسْتَيْسَرَ
Imperf.	يُوجِبُ	يُوسِرُ	يَتَّعِدُ	يَتَّسِرُ	يَسْتَوْعِدُ	يَسْتَيْسِرُ
Imperat.	أَوْجِبْ	أَيْسِرْ	اتَّعِدْ	اتَّسِرْ	اسْتَوْعِدْ	اسْتَيْسِرْ
N. Ag.	مُوجِبٌ	مُوسِرٌ	مُتَّعِدٌ	مُتَّسِرٌ	مُسْتَوْعِدٌ	مُسْتَيْسِرٌ
D N. Verbi.	إيجَابٌ	إيسَارٌ	اتِّعَادٌ	اتِّسَارٌ	اسْتِيعَادٌ	اسْتِيسَارٌ
Passive Perf.	أُوجِبَ	أُوسِرَ	اتُّعِدَ	اتُّسِرَ	اسْتُوعِدَ	اسْتُوسِرَ
Imperf.	يُوجَبُ	يُوسَرُ	يَتَّعَدُ	يَتَّسَرُ	يَسْتَوْعَدُ	يَسْتَيْسَرُ
N. Pat.	مُوجَبٌ	مُوسَرٌ	مُتَّعَدٌ	مُتَّسَرٌ	مُسْتَوْعَدٌ	مُسْتَيْسَرٌ

TABLE X. VERBUM MEDIÆ RAD. و.

A

Active Voice of the First Form.

	Perfect.	Imperfect. Indic.	Subj.	Jussive.	En. I.	En. II.
Sing. 3. m.	قَالَ	يَقُولُ	يَقُولَ	يَقُلْ	يَقُولَنَّ	يَقُولَنْ
f.	قَالَتْ	تَقُولُ	تَقُولَ	تَقُلْ	تَقُولَنَّ	تَقُولَنْ
2. m.	قُلْتَ	تَقُولُ	تَقُولَ	تَقُلْ	تَقُولَنَّ	تَقُولَنْ
f.	قُلْتِ	تَقُولِينَ	تَقُولِى	تَقُولِى	تَقُولِنَّ	تَقُولِنْ
1. c.	قُلْتُ	أَقُولُ	أَقُولَ	أَقُلْ	أَقُولَنَّ	أَقُولَنْ
Dual. 3. m.	قَالَا	يَقُولَانِ	يَقُولَا	يَقُولَا	يَقُولَانِّ	
f.	قَالَتَا	تَقُولَانِ	تَقُولَا	تَقُولَا	تَقُولَانِّ	
2. c.	قُلْتُمَا	تَقُولَانِ	تَقُولَا	تَقُولَا	تَقُولَانِّ	
Plur. 3. m.	قَالُوا	يَقُولُونَ	يَقُولُوا	يَقُولُوا	يَقُولُنَّ	يَقُولُنْ
f.	قُلْنَ	يَقُلْنَ	يَقُلْنَ	يَقُلْنَ	يَقُلْنَانِّ	
2. m.	قُلْتُمْ	تَقُولُونَ	تَقُولُوا	تَقُولُوا	تَقُولُنَّ	تَقُولُنْ
f.	قُلْتُنَّ	تَقُلْنَ	تَقُلْنَ	تَقُلْنَ	تَقُلْنَانِّ	
1. c.	قُلْنَا	نَقُولُ	نَقُولَ	نَقُلْ	نَقُولَنَّ	نَقُولَنْ

B (margin letter, beside the Sing. 2. m. row)

C (margin letter, beside the Plur. 3. m. row)

D

	N. Ag.	N. Verbi.
Sing. m.	قَائِلٌ	قَوْلٌ
f.	قَائِلَةٌ	

Imperative.	Simple.	En. I.	En. II.
Sing. 2. m.	قُلْ	قُولَنَّ	قُولَنْ
f.	قُولِى	قُولِنَّ	قُولِنْ
Dual. 2. c.	قُولَا	قُولَانِّ	. . .
Plur. 2. m.	قُولُوا	قُولُنَّ	قُولُنْ
f.	قُلْنَ	قُلْنَانِّ	

A   TABLE XI. VERBUM MEDIÆ RAD. ي.

ACTIVE VOICE OF THE FIRST FORM.

	Perfect.	Indic.	Subj.	Jussive.	En. I.	En. II.
Sing. 3. m.	سَارَ	يَسِيرُ	يَسِيرَ	يَسِرْ	يَسِيرَنَّ	يَسِيرَنْ
f.	سَارَتْ	تَسِيرُ	تَسِيرَ	تَسِرْ	تَسِيرَنَّ	تَسِيرَنْ
B 2. m.	سِرْتَ	تَسِيرُ	تَسِيرَ	تَسِرْ	تَسِيرَنَّ	تَسِيرَنْ
f.	سِرْتِ	تَسِيرِينَ	تَسِيرِى	تَسِيرِى	تَسِيرِنَّ	تَسِيرِنْ
1. c.	سِرْتُ	أَسِيرُ	أَسِيرَ	أَسِرْ	أَسِيرَنَّ	أَسِيرَنْ
Dual. 3. m.	سَارَا	يَسِيرَانِ	يَسِيرَا	يَسِيرَا	يَسِيرَانِّ	…
f.	سَارَتَا	تَسِيرَانِ	تَسِيرَا	تَسِيرَا	تَسِيرَانِّ	…
2. c.	سِرْتُمَا	تَسِيرَانِ	تَسِيرَا	تَسِيرَا	تَسِيرَانِّ	…
C Plur. 3. m.	سَارُوا	يَسِيرُونَ	يَسِيرُوا	يَسِيرُوا	يَسِيرُنَّ	يَسِيرُنْ
f.	سِرْنَ	يَسِرْنَ	يَسِرْنَ	يَسِرْنَ	يَسِرْنَانِّ	…
2. m.	سِرْتُمْ	تَسِيرُونَ	تَسِيرُوا	تَسِيرُوا	تَسِيرُنَّ	تَسِيرُنْ
f.	سِرْتُنَّ	تَسِرْنَ	تَسِرْنَ	تَسِرْنَ	تَسِرْنَانِّ	…
1. c.	سِرْنَا	نَسِيرُ	نَسِيرَ	نَسِرْ	نَسِيرَنَّ	نَسِيرَنْ

D

	N. Ag.	N. Verbi.	Imperative.	Simple.	En. I.	En. II.
Sing. m.	سَائِرٌ	سَيْرٌ	Sing. 2. m.	سِرْ	سِيرَنَّ	سِيرَنْ
f.	سَائِرَةٌ		f.	سِيرِى	سِيرِنَّ	سِيرِنْ
			Dual. 2. c.	سِيرَا	سِيرَانِّ	…
			Plur. 2. m.	سِيرُوا	سِيرُنَّ	سِيرُنْ
			f.	سِرْنَ	سِرْنَانِّ	

TABLE XII. VERBA MEDIÆ RAD. و ET ى.   A

Passive Voice of the First Form.

Perfect.		Imperfect.				
		Indic.	*Subj.*	*Jussive.*	*Energ.* I.	*Energ.* II.
Sing. 3. m.	قِيلَ	يُقَالُ	يُقَالَ	يُقَلْ	يُقَالَنَّ	يُقَالَنْ
f.	قِيلَتْ	تُقَالُ	تُقَالَ	تُقَلْ	تُقَالَنَّ	تُقَالَنْ B
2. m.	قِلْتَ	تُقَالُ	تُقَالَ	تُقَلْ	تُقَالَنَّ	تُقَالَنْ
f.	قِلْتِ	تُقَالِينَ	تُقَالِى	تُقَالِى	تُقَالِنَّ	تُقَالِنْ
1. c.	قِلْتُ	أُقَالُ	أُقَالَ	أُقَلْ	أُقَالَنَّ	أُقَالَنْ
Dual. 3. m.	قِيلَا	يُقَالَانِ	يُقَالَا	يُقَالَا	يُقَالَانِّ	. . .
f.	قِيلَتَا	تُقَالَانِ	تُقَالَا	تُقَالَا	تُقَالَانِّ	C
2. c.	قِلْتُمَا	تُقَالَانِ	تُقَالَا	تُقَالَا	تُقَالَانِّ	. . .
Plur. 3. m.	قِيلُوا	يُقَالُونَ	يُقَالُوا	يُقَالُوا	يُقَالَنَّ	يُقَالُنْ
f.	قِلْنَ	يُقَلْنَ	يُقَلْنَ	يُقَلْنَ	يُقَلْنَانِّ	
2. m.	قِلْتُمْ	تُقَالُونَ	تُقَالُوا	تُقَالُوا	تُقَالَنَّ	تُقَالُنْ
f.	قِلْتُنَّ	تُقَلْنَ	تُقَلْنَ	تُقَلْنَ	تُقَلْنَانِّ	D
1. c.	قِلْنَا	نُقَالُ	نُقَالَ	نُقَلْ	نُقَالَنَّ	نُقَالَنْ

Nom. Pat. Sing. m. مَقُولٌ, f. مَقُولَةٌ

مَبِيعٌ, مَبِيعَةٌ

A   TABLE XIII. VERBA MEDIÆ RAD. و ET ى.

THE DERIVED FORMS.

	IV.	VII.	VIII.	X.
Active Perf. 3. s. m.	أَقَالَ	اِنْقَالَ	اِقْتَالَ	اِسْتَقَامَ
2. s. m.	أَقَلْتَ	اِنْقَلْتَ	اِقْتَلْتَ	اِسْتَقَمْتَ
B Imperf.	يُقِيلُ	يَنْقَالُ	يَقْتَالُ	يَسْتَقِيمُ
Imperat.	أَقِلْ	اِنْقَلْ	اِقْتَلْ	اِسْتَقِمْ
N. Ag.	مُقِيلٌ	مُنْقَالٌ	مُقْتَالٌ	مُسْتَقِيمٌ
N. Verbi.	إِقَالَةٌ	اِنْقِيَالٌ	اِقْتِيَالٌ	اِسْتِقَامَةٌ
Passive Perf.	أُقِيلَ	اُنْقِيلَ	اُقْتِيلَ	اُسْتُقِيمَ
C Imperf.	يُقَالُ	يُنْقَالُ	يُقْتَالُ	يُسْتَقَامُ
N. Pat.	مُقَالٌ	مُنْقَالٌ	مُقْتَالٌ	مُسْتَقَامٌ

	II.	III.	V.	VI.
Active Perf.	قَوَّلَ سَيَّرَ	قَاوَلَ سَايَرَ	تَقَوَّلَ تَسَيَّرَ	تَقَاوَلَ تَسَايَرَ
Imperf.	يُقَوِّلُ يُسَيِّرُ	يُقَاوِلُ يُسَايِرُ	يَتَقَوَّلُ يَتَسَيَّرُ	يَتَقَاوَلُ يَتَسَايَرُ
D N. Verbi.	تَقْوِيلٌ تَسْيِيرٌ	مُقَاوَلَةٌ مُسَايَرَةٌ	تَقَوُّلٌ تَسَيُّرٌ	تَقَاوُلٌ تَسَايُرٌ
Passive Perf.	قُوِّلَ سُيِّرَ	قُوِولَ سُويِرَ	تُقُوِّلَ تُسُيِّرَ	تُقُوولَ تُسُويِرَ

IX. Perf. اِسْوَدَّ   Imperf. يَسْوَدُّ   N. Verbi. اِسْوِدَادٌ

XI.   اِسْوَادَّ   يَسْوَادُّ   اِسْوِيدَادٌ

TABLE XIV. VERBUM TERTIÆ RAD. و,
MEDIÆ RAD. FÈTHATÆ.

Active Voice of the First Form.

Perfect.	*Imperfect.*				
	Indic.	*Subj.*	*Jussive.*	*En.* I.	*En.* II.
Sing. 3. m. نَدَا	يَنْدُو	يَنْدُوَ	يَنْدُ	يَنْدُوَنَّ	يَنْدُوَنْ
f. نَدَتْ	تَنْدُو	تَنْدُوَ	تَنْدُ	تَنْدُوَنَّ	تَنْدُوَنْ
2. m. نَدَوْتَ	تَنْدُو	تَنْدُوَ	تَنْدُ	تَنْدُوَنَّ	تَنْدُوَنْ
f. نَدَوْتِ	تَنْدِينَ	تَنْدِى	تَنْدِى	تَنْدِنَّ	تَنْدِنْ
1. c. نَدَوْتُ	أَنْدُو	أَنْدُوَ	أَنْدُ	أَنْدُوَنَّ	أَنْدُوَنْ
Dual. 3. m. نَدَوَا	يَنْدُوَانِ	يَنْدُوَا	يَنْدُوَا	يَنْدُوَانِّ	
f. نَدَتَا	تَنْدُوَانِ	تَنْدُوَا	تَنْدُوَا	تَنْدُوَانِّ	
2. c. نَدَوْتُمَا	تَنْدُوَانِ	تَنْدُوَا	تَنْدُوَا	تَنْدُوَانِّ	. . .
Plur. 3. m. نَدَوْا	يَنْدُونَ	يَنْدُوا	يَنْدُوا	يَنْدُنَّ	يَنْدُنْ
f. نَدَوْنَ	يَنْدُونَ	يَنْدُونَ	يَنْدُونَ	يَنْدُونَانِّ	. . .
2. m. نَدَوْتُمْ	تَنْدُونَ	تَنْدُوا	تَنْدُوا	تَنْدُنَّ	تَنْدُنْ
f. نَدَوْتُنَّ	تَنْدُونَ	تَنْدُونَ	تَنْدُونَ	تَنْدُونَانِّ	. . .
1. c. نَدَوْنَا	نَنْدُو	نَنْدُوَ	نَنْدُ	نَنْدُوَنَّ	نَنْدُوَنْ

N. Ag.	*N. Verbi.*	*Imperative.*			
			Simple.	*En.* I.	*En.* II.
Sing. m. نَادٍ	نَدْوٌ	Sing. 2. m.	أُنْدُ	أُنْدُوَنَّ	أُنْدُوَنْ
f. نَادِيَةٌ		f.	أُنْدِى	أُنْدِنَّ	أُنْدِنْ
		Dual. 2. c.	أُنْدُوَانِّ	أُنْدُوَا	. . .
		Plur. 2. m.	أُنْدُوا	أُنْدُنَّ	أُنْدُنْ
		f.	أُنْدُونَانِّ	أُنْدُونَ	

A

B

C

D

A **TABLE XV. VERBUM TERTIÆ RAD. ى,**
MEDIÆ RAD. FÈTḤATÆ.

ACTIVE VOICE OF THE FIRST FORM.

		Perfect.	*Imperfect.*				
			Indic.	Subj.	Jussive.	En. I.	En. II.
Sing.	3. m.	رَمَى	يَرْمِى	يَرْمِىَ	يَرْمِ	يَرْمِيَنَّ	يَرْمِيَنْ
	f.	رَمَتْ	تَرْمِى	تَرْمِىَ	تَرْمِ	تَرْمِيَنَّ	تَرْمِيَنْ
B	2. m.	رَمَيْتَ	تَرْمِى	تَرْمِىَ	تَرْمِ	تَرْمِيَنَّ	تَرْمِيَنْ
	f.	رَمَيْتِ	تَرْمِينَ	تَرْمِى	تَرْمِى	تَرْمِنَّ	تَرْمِنْ
	1. c.	رَمَيْتُ	أَرْمِى	أَرْمِىَ	أَرْمِ	أَرْمِيَنَّ	أَرْمِيَنْ
Dual.	3. m.	رَمَيَا	يَرْمِيَانِ	يَرْمِيَا	يَرْمِيَا	يَرْمِيَانِّ	...
	f.	رَمَتَا	تَرْمِيَانِ	تَرْمِيَا	تَرْمِيَا	تَرْمِيَانِّ	
	2. c.	رَمَيْتُمَا	تَرْمِيَانِ	تَرْمِيَا	تَرْمِيَا	تَرْمِيَانِّ	...
C Plur.	3. m.	رَمَوْا	يَرْمُونَ	يَرْمُوا	يَرْمُوا	يَرْمُنَّ	يَرْمُنْ
	f.	رَمَيْنَ	يَرْمِينَ	يَرْمِينَ	يَرْمِينَ	يَرْمِينَانِّ	...
	2. m.	رَمَيْتُمْ	تَرْمُونَ	تَرْمُوا	تَرْمُوا	تَرْمُنَّ	تَرْمُنْ
	f.	رَمَيْتُنَّ	تَرْمِينَ	تَرْمِينَ	تَرْمِينَ	تَرْمِينَانِّ	...
	1. c.	رَمَيْنَا	نَرْمِى	نَرْمِىَ	نَرْمِ	نَرْمِيَنَّ	نَرْمِيَنْ

		N. Ag.	N. Verbi.	*Imperative.*			
					Simple.	En. I.	En. II.
D Sing.	m.	رَامٍ	رَمْىٌ	Sing. 2. m.	اِرْمِ	اِرْمِيَنَّ	اِرْمِيَنْ
	f.	رَامِيَةٌ		f.	اِرْمِى	اِرْمِنَّ	اِرْمِنْ
				Dual. 2. c.	اِرْمِيَا	اِرْمِيَانِّ	...
				Plur. 2. m.	اِرْمُوا	اِرْمُنَّ	اِرْمُنْ
				f.	اِرْمِينَ	اِرْمِينَانِّ	

TABLE XVI. VERBA TERTIÆ RAD. و ET ى, MEDIÆ RAD. KÈSRATÆ.

ACTIVE VOICE OF THE FIRST FORM.

	Perfect.	Imperfect. Indic.	Subj.	Jussive.	En. I.	En. II.
Sing. 3. m.	رَضِىَ	يَرْضَى	يَرْضَى	يَرْضَ	يَرْضَيَنَّ	يَرْضَيَنْ
f.	رَضِيَتْ	تَرْضَى	تَرْضَى	تَرْضَ	تَرْضَيَنَّ	تَرْضَيَنْ
2. m.	رَضِيتَ	تَرْضَى	تَرْضَى	تَرْضَ	تَرْضَيَنَّ	تَرْضَيَنْ
f.	رَضِيتِ	تَرْضَيْنَ	تَرْضَىْ	تَرْضَىْ	تَرْضَيِنَّ	تَرْضَيِنْ
1. c.	رَضِيتُ	أَرْضَى	أَرْضَى	أَرْضَ	أَرْضَيَنَّ	أَرْضَيَنْ
Dual. 3. m.	رَضِيَا	يَرْضَيَانِ	يَرْضَيَا	يَرْضَيَا	يَرْضَيَانِّ	
f.	رَضِيَتَا	تَرْضَيَانِ	تَرْضَيَا	تَرْضَيَا	تَرْضَيَانِّ	
2. c.	رَضِيتُمَا	تَرْضَيَانِ	تَرْضَيَا	تَرْضَيَا	تَرْضَيَانِّ	
Plur. 3. m.	رَضُوا	يَرْضَوْنَ	يَرْضَوْا	يَرْضَوْا	يَرْضَوُنَّ	يَرْضَوُنْ
f.	رَضِينَ	يَرْضَيْنَ	يَرْضَيْنَ	يَرْضَيْنَ	يَرْضَيْنَانِّ	. . .
2. m.	رَضِيتُمْ	تَرْضَوْنَ	تَرْضَوْا	تَرْضَوْا	تَرْضَوُنَّ	تَرْضَوُنْ
f.	رَضِيتُنَّ	تَرْضَيْنَ	تَرْضَيْنَ	تَرْضَيْنَ	تَرْضَيْنَانِّ	. . .
1. c.	رَضِينَا	نَرْضَى	نَرْضَى	نَرْضَ	نَرْضَيَنَّ	نَرْضَيَنْ

	N. Ag.	N. Verbi.		Imperative. Simple.	En. I.	En. II.
Sing. m.	رَاضٍ	رِضًا	Sing. 2. m.	اِرْضَ	اِرْضَيَنَّ	اِرْضَيَنْ
f.	رَاضِيَةٌ	رِضْوَانُ	f.	اِرْضَىْ	اِرْضِينَّ	اِرْضِينْ
			Dual. 2. c.	اِرْضَيَا	اِرْضَيَانِّ	. . .
			Plur. 2. m.	اِرْضَوْا	اِرْضَوُنَّ	اِرْضَوُنْ
			f.	اِرْضَيْنَ	اِرْضَيْنَانِّ	اِرْضَيْنْ

A   TABLE XVII. VERBA TERTIÆ RAD. و ET ى.

PASSIVE VOICE OF THE FIRST FORM.

	Perfect.	*Imperfect.*				
		Indic.	*Subj.*	*Jussive.*	*En.* I.	*En.* II.
Sing. 3. m.	نُدِیَ	یُنْدَی	یُنْدَی	یُنْدَ	یُنْدَیَنَّ	یُنْدَیَنْ
B f.	نُدِیَتْ	تُنْدَی	تُنْدَی	تُنْدَ	تُنْدَیَنَّ	تُنْدَیَنْ
2. m.	نُدِیتَ	تُنْدَی	تُنْدَی	تُنْدَ	تُنْدَیَنَّ	تُنْدَیَنْ
f.	نُدِیتِ	تُنْدَیْنَ	تُنْدَیْ	تُنْدَیْ	تُنْدَیِنَّ	تُنْدَیِنْ
1. c.	نُدِیتُ	أُنْدَی	أُنْدَی	أُنْدَ	أُنْدَیَنَّ	أُنْدَیَنْ
C Dual. 3. m.	نُدِیَا	یُنْدَیَانِ	یُنْدَیَا	یُنْدَیَا	یُنْدَیَانِّ	
f.	نُدِیَتَا	تُنْدَیَانِ	تُنْدَیَا	تُنْدَیَا	تُنْدَیَانِّ	
2. c.	نُدِیتُمَا	تُنْدَیَانِ	تُنْدَیَا	تُنْدَیَا	تُنْدَیَانِّ	
Plur. 3. m.	نُدُوا	یُنْدَوْنَ	یُنْدَوْا	یُنْدَوْا	یُنْدَوُنَّ	یُنْدَوْنْ
f.	نُدِینَ	یُنْدَیْنَ	یُنْدَیْنَ	یُنْدَیْنَ	یُنْدَیْنَانِّ	یُنْدَیْنْ
D 2. m.	نُدِیتُمْ	تُنْدَوْنَ	تُنْدَوْا	تُنْدَوْا	تُنْدَوُنَّ	تُنْدَوْنْ
f.	نُدِیتُنَّ	تُنْدَیْنَ	تُنْدَیْنَ	تُنْدَیْنَ	تُنْدَیْنَانِّ	تُنْدَیْنْ
1. c.	نُدِینَا	نُنْدَی	نُنْدَی	نُنْدَ	نُنْدَیَنَّ	نُنْدَیْنْ

Nom. Pat. Sing. m. مَنْدُوٌّ   f. مَنْدُوَّةٌ

مَرْمِیٌّ   مَرْمِیَّةٌ

TABLE XVIII. VERBA TERTIÆ RAD. و ET ى.   A

THE DERIVED FORMS.

	II.	III.	IV.	V.	VI.	
Active Perf.	قَضَّى	قَاضَى	أَقْضَى	تَقَضَّى	تَقَاضَى	
Imperf.	يُقَضِّى	يُقَاضِى	يُقْضِى	يَتَقَضَّى	يَتَقَاضَى	
Imperat.	قَضِّ	قَاضِ	أَقْضِ	تَقَضَّ	تَقَاضَ	B
N. Ag. m.	مُقَضٍّ	مُقَاضٍ	مُقْضٍ	مُتَقَضٍّ	مُتَقَاضٍ	
f.	مُقَضِّيَةٌ	مُقَاضِيَةٌ	مُقْضِيَةٌ	مُتَقَضِّيَةٌ	مُتَقَاضِيَةٌ	
N. Verbi.	تَقْضِيَةٌ	مُقَاضَاةٌ	إِقْضَآءٌ	تَقَضٍّ	تَقَاضٍ	
		قِضَآءٌ				
Passive Perf.	قُضِّىَ	قُوضِىَ	أُقْضِىَ	تُقُضِّىَ	تُقُوضِىَ	
Imperf.	يُقَضَّى	يُقَاضَى	يُقْضَى	يَتَقَضَّى	يُتَقَاضَى	C
N. Pat. m.	مُقَضًّى	مُقَاضًى	مُقْضًى	مُتَقَضًّى	مُتَقَاضًى	
f.	مُقَضَّاةٌ	مُقَاضَاةٌ	مُقْضَاةٌ	مُتَقَضَّاةٌ	مُتَقَاضَاةٌ	

	Perf.	Imperf.	Imperat.	N. Ag. et Pat.	N. Verbi.	
VII. Act.	اِنْقَضَى	يَنْقَضِى	اِنْقَضِ	مُنْقَضٍ	اِنْقِضَآءٌ	
Pass.	اُنْقُضِىَ	يُنْقَضَى		مُنْقَضًى		D
VIII. Act.	اِقْتَضَى	يَقْتَضِى	اِقْتَضِ	مُقْتَضٍ	اِقْتِضَآءٌ	
Pass.	اُقْتُضِىَ	يُقْتَضَى		مُقْتَضًى		
X. Act.	اِسْتَقْضَى	يَسْتَقْضِى	اِسْتَقْضِ	مُسْتَقْضٍ	اِسْتِقْضَآءٌ	
Pass.	اُسْتُقْضِىَ	يُسْتَقْضَى		مُسْتَقْضًى